POWER AND THE PURSE
ECONOMIC STATECRAFT, INTERDEPENDENCE AND NATIONAL SECURITY

CASS SERIES ON SECURITY STUDIES
ISSN 1363-2329

General Editor
Benjamin Frankel

Power and the Purse: Economic Statecraft, Interdependence, and National Security
edited by
Jean-Marc F. Blanchard, Edward D. Mansfield, and Norrin M. Ripsman

The Origins of National Interests
edited by
Glenn Chafetz, Michael Spirtas, and Benjamin Frankel

Roots of Realism
edited by Benjamin Frankel

Realism: Restatement and Renewal
edited by Benjamin Frankel

Power and the Purse
Economic Statecraft, Interdependence, and National Security

Editors

Jean-Marc F. Blanchard, Edward D. Mansfield, and Norrin M. Ripsman

FRANK CASS
LONDON • PORTLAND, OR

First published in 2000 in Great Britain by
FRANK CASS AND COMPANY, LIMITED
2 Park Square, Milton Park, Abingdon, Oxon, OX14 4RN

and in the United States of America by
FRANK CASS
270 Madison Ave, New York NY 10016

Transferred to Digital Printing 2005

British Library Cataloging-in-Publication Data:

Power and the purse : economic statecraft, interdependence,
and national security Norrin M. Ripsman, editors. –
(Cass series on security studies)
1. National security   2. International economic relations
3. Economic sanctions
I. Blanchard, Jean-Marc F.   II. Mansfield, Edward D., 1962–
III. Ripsman, Norrin M.

ISBN 0 7146 5067 6 (hardback)
ISBN 0 7146 8116 4 (paperback)

Library of Congress Cataloging-in-Publication Data:
A catalogue record for this book is available from the Library of Congress

This group of studies first appeared in a special issue, titled
"Power and the Purse: Economic Statecraft, Interdependence and National Security"
of *Security Studies*, (ISSN 0963 6412) vol. 9, nos. 1/2, Autumn 1999–Winter 2000,
published by Frank Cass & Co., Ltd.

The cover illustration depicts the arrival of the Duke of Anjou before Antwerp in
1582, from the *Nederlandsche Historieprenten* (1555-1900), edited by C. Van Rijn and
G W Kernkamp, published by S. L. Loov, 1910.

The papers in this volume were initially prepared for a conference on "Economic Power, Interdependence, and National Security." The conference was cosponsored by *Security Studies* and the Mershon Center, and held at the Mershon Center at Ohio State University on 2-5 April 1998. We are grateful to the Mershon Center for funding this conference. We are also grateful to Brian M. Pollins, João Resende-Santos, and David Rowe for serving as discussants at the conference; to Benjamin Frankel for encouraging the project and assisting in its production; to the anonymous reviewers of *Security Studies* for their helpful comments and suggestions; to Karen Weimer for coordinating the conference; and to Vaughn Shanon for preparing the bibliography for the book version of this volume.

CONTENTS

THE POLITICAL ECONOMY OF NATIONAL SECURITY:

ECONOMIC STATECRAFT, INTERDEPENDENCE, AND INTERNATIONAL CONFLICT

JEAN-MARC F. BLANCHARD, EDWARD D. MANSFIELD, AND NORRIN M. RIPSMAN

THE POLITICAL economy of national security has captured the attention of researchers and policymakers for centuries. Although scholarly interest in this topic waned during the cold war era as the fields of political economy and national security became increasingly distant,[1] such interest has been revived in recent years. Many contemporary observers have expressed the hope that the recent dramatic growth of international trade and capital flows will foster political cooperation among states. Furthermore, the particularly widespread use of economic tools of statecraft since the end of the cold war has prompted rising interest in the effectiveness of these instruments. Burgeoning literatures are emerging on the relationship between economic interdependence and international conflict and on the political economy of economic sanctions. These literatures, however, have yet to resolve various crucial questions. Does economic interdependence promote or inhibit conflict? Under what circumstances are economic sanctions and incentives most effective? How do economic inducements affect states' foreign policies?

These questions bear heavily on many core theoretical issues in the field of international relations. They also have important implications for decisionmakers weighing the merits of different strategies for achieving their foreign policy objectives. That little consensus exists on the answers to them indicates

Jean-Marc F. Blanchard is a visiting scholar in the department of Political Science at Villanova University; Edward D. Mansfield is associate professor of political science at Ohio State University; Norrin M. Ripsman is a visiting assistant professor in the Department of Political Science, and faculty fellow in the Centre for Foreign Policy Studies, at Dalhousie University.

1. Notable exceptions include Klaus Knorr, *The Power of Nations: The Political Economy of International Relations* (New York: Basic Books, 1975); Klaus Knorr and Frank N. Trager, eds., *Economic Issues and National Security* (Lawrence: Regents Press of Kansas, 1977); David A. Baldwin, *Economic Statecraft* (Princeton: Princeton University Press, 1985); Robert O. Keohane and Joseph S. Nye Jr., *Power and Interdependence: World Politics in Transition* (Boston: Little, Brown, 1977); and Nazli Choucri and Robert C. North, *Nations in Conflict: National Growth and International Violence* (San Francisco: W. H. Freeman, 1975).

the need for additional research on the relationships among power, interdependence, and national security. The purpose of this volume is to analyze these key issues.

The following articles confront a broad range of theoretical debates in the field of international relations. Some of them address controversies among realists, classical liberals, and neoliberal institutionalists about the sources of international conflict and cooperation.[2] Others bear on longstanding debates about the domestic sources of foreign policy.[3] Finally, a number of the following articles address persistent disagreements about the usefulness of economic statecraft.

These articles also have important policy implications. Economic instruments of foreign policy continue to be employed with great regularity. In the past few years alone, economic sanctions have been imposed on India, Iraq, Pakistan, and Yugoslavia; and the United States has extended economic inducements to North Korea in an effort to halt its nuclear weapons program. Observers, however, remain deeply divided over the effectiveness of economic forms of statecraft.[4] Furthermore, whereas various policymakers view the liberalization and expansion of commerce as a means to promote peace,[5] remarkably little evidence has been accumulated on whether trade actually affects international cooperation and discord. The following articles offer insights into these key issues.

The purpose of this article is to explain the central topics that are taken up in this volume. In the following section, we address the issue of economic statecraft, placing particular emphasis on how the contributions to this volume build upon the existing literature on both economic sanctions and economic

---

2. On these controversies, see Arthur A. Stein, *Why Nations Cooperate: Circumstance and Choice in International Relations* (Ithaca: Cornell University Press, 1990), chap. 1; David A. Baldwin, "Neoliberalism, Neorealism, and World Politics," in *Neorealism and Neoliberalism: The Contemporary Debate*, ed. David A. Baldwin (New York: Columbia University Press, 1993), chap. 1; and Benjamin Frankel, ed., *Realism: Restatement and Renewal* (London: Frank Cass, 1996).

3. On the domestic sources of foreign policy, see Jack Snyder, *Myths of Empire: Domestic Politics and International Ambition* (Ithaca: Cornell University Press, 1991); and Helen V. Milner, *Interests, Institutions, and Information: Domestic Politics and International Relations* (Princeton: Princeton University Press, 1997).

4. See, for example, Richard N. Haass, "Sanctioning Madness," *Foreign Affairs* 76, no. 6 (November/December 1997): 74–85; and Jesse Helms, "What Sanctions Epidemic?" *Foreign Affairs* 78, no. 1 (January/February 1999): 2–8.

5. See, for example, Remarks by the President at Conference to Support Middle East Peace and Development, 30 November, 1998, *http://www.state.gov/regions/nea/981130_clinton_mepp.html*; Statement by Winston Lord, Assistant Secretary of State for East Asian and Pacific Affairs, before the House International Relations Committee, 30 May 1996, *http://www.state.gov/www/regions/eap/960530. html*; and Dennis Swann, *The Economics of the Common Market*, 5th ed. (Harmondsworth: Penguin, 1984), 17.

inducements. Then we address the relationship between economic interdependence and international conflict. Finally, we highlight some of the themes that emerge from this project and their implications for the study and practice of international affairs.

ECONOMIC STATECRAFT

ONE SUBSTANTIVE focus of this volume is on economic statecraft, which involves the use of economic instruments by a government to influence the behavior of another state.[6] Such instruments include both economic sanctions and inducements.[7] Economic sanctions are actions taken by one state—the sender—to interfere with the economy of another state—the target—for the purpose of coercing its compliance with the sender's wishes. Economic inducements, or incentives, are rewards that a sender extends to a target to secure the target's compliance or alter its interests. In the remainder of this section, we elaborate on the distinctions between these two types of economic instruments and discuss how the articles in this volume analyze each type.

ECONOMIC SANCTIONS

Economic sanctions are designed to punish a target for failing to comply with a sender's demands. Through measures such as a reduction in financial aid or loans, restrictions on foreign trade or investment, and the seizure of assets, a sender imposing economic sanctions attempts to compel the target to change its behavior. Most of the literature on economic statecraft has focused on sanctions and the following articles address two key debates in this literature.

The first is a debate over whether sanctions "work." Various efforts have been made to resolve this controversy by analyzing whether the imposition or threat of economic punishment helps senders to meet their stated objectives.[8] Yet such efforts have been criticized on the grounds that they define the suc-

6. See Baldwin, *Economic Statecraft*, chaps. 2–3.

7. It should be noted that economic sanctions and economic inducements are sometimes referred to as negative and positive sanctions, respectively.

8. See, for example, Johan Galtung, "On the Effects of International Economic Sanctions: With Examples From the Case of Rhodesia," *World Politics* 19, no. 3 (April 1967): 378–416; Klaus Knorr, "International Economic Leverage and Its Uses," in *Economic Issues and National Security*, ed. Klaus Knorr and Frank N. Trager (Lawrence: Regents Press of Kansas, 1977), 99–126; Gary Clyde Hufbauer, Jeffrey J. Schott, and Kimberly Ann Elliott, *Economic Sanctions Reconsidered*, 2 vols., 2nd ed. (Washington, D.C.: Institute for International Economics, 1990); and Robert A. Pape, "Why Economic Sanctions Do Not Work," *International Security* 22, no. 2 (fall 1997): 90–136.

cess and failure of sanctions too narrowly. As David A. Baldwin observes, sanctions can have purposes besides those explicitly articulated by senders. These secondary and tertiary goals might include signaling displeasure with a target's behavior, deterring third parties from taking certain actions, or satisfying demands for political action abroad made by key constituents of the sender's government. Baldwin contends that sanctions achieving these subsidiary purposes are often successful, even if they fail to achieve their stated purposes.[9] Other observers, however, view these unstated objectives as relatively unimportant and conclude that sanctions can only be considered effective if they achieve their primary goals.[10]

The second debate centers on why sanctions succeed or fail. Much of the existing research on this issue addresses the factors that hinder a sender's ability to impose sufficient damage on a target's economy to prompt a change in the behavior of the target state. Among the factors on which these analyses have focused are the economic costs borne by the sender(s), the difficulties associated with organizing and maintaining multilateral sanctions, the existence of alternative sources from which the target can obtain a sanctioned good, and the existence of cheap substitutes for the sanctioned good. In addition, some authors contend that the ability of target governments to shift the costs of sanctions onto their political opposition also can undermine economic sanctions.[11]

This volume addresses both of these debates. Based on an analysis of the British oil embargo against Rhodesia in the mid-1960s, David M. Rowe contends that scholars often mistakenly classify sanctions episodes as failures because they consider only the publicly stated goals of the sender. It is commonly held that British sanctions were intended to pressure the government led by Ian Smith to establish majority rule in Rhodesia and that they failed because the Smith government did not capitulate to British demands. Rowe, however, argues that sanctions were not, in fact, imposed to achieve this end. Instead, the UK initiated the oil embargo to reduce growing pressures from Black Africa to take more forceful action against Rhodesia and to preserve the British

9. Baldwin, *Economic Statecraft*, chaps. 7–8. See also Margaret P. Doxey, *International Sanctions in Contemporary Perspective* (New York: St. Martin's, 1987).

10. See Pape, "Why Economic Sanctions Do Not Work"; T. Clifton Morgan and Valerie L. Schwebach, "Fools Suffer Gladly: The Use of Economic Sanctions in International Crises," *International Studies Quarterly* 41, no. 1 (March 1997): 29; and Kimberly Ann Elliott, "Factors Affecting the Success of Sanctions," in *Economic Sanctions: Panacea or Peacebuilding in a Post–Cold War World*, ed. David Cortright and George A. Lopez (Boulder: Westview, 1995), 52.

11. See Galtung, "On the Effects of International Economic Sanctions," 384–88; Knorr, "International Economic Leverage and Its Uses," 103; and Robin Renwick, *Economic Sanctions* (Cambridge: Center for International Affairs, Harvard University, 1981), 78–80.

Commonwealth. Consequently, the conventional wisdom faults sanctions for failing to achieve something they were never intended to accomplish. Rowe's findings, therefore, accord with Baldwin's conclusion that analysts must judge the efficacy of sanctions within a framework that accounts for the entire range of a sender's objectives, both stated and otherwise. His overall conclusion, a direct challenge to Robert A. Pape and others, is that sanctions have been more successful than is often appreciated.[12]

Like Rowe, Jean-Marc F. Blanchard and Norrin M. Ripsman argue that economic sanctions can help to achieve important political objectives. They differ from Rowe, however, by focusing on the conditions under which sanctions are most likely to achieve their primary political purposes. Blanchard and Ripsman argue that imposing economic damage on a target is insufficient to render sanctions effective; sanctions can coerce a target state to comply with a sender's demands only when the domestic and international political costs of noncompliance are sufficiently high. Moreover, if the corresponding political costs of compliance are substantial enough, or if the government of the target state is well insulated from societal groups that bear the brunt of the costs of noncompliance, even significant political costs of noncompliance may be insufficient to prompt a target to change its behavior. Blanchard and Ripsman detail the domestic and international sources of the political costs of noncompliance. They support their theoretical argument with three case studies of successful sanctions episodes: British sanctions against the Soviet Union in 1933, threatened Arab World sanctions against Canada in 1979, and Indian sanctions against Nepal from 1988 to 1990. In each case, they find that strategic and domestic political incentives caused the economic threat to resonate with the target governments.

ECONOMIC INDUCEMENTS

In contrast to the extensive body of scholarly research focusing on economic sanctions, the literature on economic inducements is surprisingly scant.[13] Inducements involve commercial concessions, technology transfers, and other economic carrots that are extended by a sender in exchange for political compliance on the part of a target.[14] The extant literature indicates that inducements can provide specific short-term returns as part of a quid pro quo and

12. Pape, "Why Economic Sanctions Do Not Work."
13. On this point, see David A. Baldwin, *Paradoxes of Power* (Oxford: Basil Blackwell, 1989), esp. chaps. 4, 7.
14. See, for example, William J. Long, "Trade and Technological Incentives and Bilateral Cooperation," *International Studies Quarterly* 40, no. 1 (March 1996): 77–106.

that they can influence the long-term behavior of a target.[15] We know little, however, about when states will prefer to employ economic incentives rather than other policy instruments; the types of incentives that tend to be most effective; and the political, economic, and strategic conditions that ease or complicate the use of economic incentives. Three articles address these shortcomings in the literature.

Paul A. Papayoanou and Scott L. Kastner argue that the effectiveness of economic inducements depends on domestic politics within the target state. Specifically, they contend that democratic states can reap the benefits of a policy of economic engagement toward a nondemocratic target only when internationally oriented coalitions—that is, those comprised of actors with an interest in expanded access to foreign markets—have considerable political clout in the target. Conversely, when economic interests which depend primarily on the domestic market are especially influential, economic engagement may actually provoke political antagonism. Papayoanou and Kastner find support for this hypothesis in analyses of Franco-Russian relations before the turn of the twentieth century and Anglo-German relations prior to the First World War. Moreover, they conclude that the contemporary U.S. strategy of economically engaging China is likely to pay strategic dividends, since the current Chinese leadership has a strong international orientation on economic matters. Papayoanou and Kastner also recognize, however, that the efficacy of an engagement strategy will depend upon whether the issues on which the U.S. attempts to gain Chinese compliance are deemed matters of vital national interest by the Chinese leadership.

While Papayoanou and Kastner examine the utility of economic inducements given the existing constellation of domestic interests and coalitions in the target state, Rawi Abdelal and Jonathan Kirshner consider how international economic ties can alter domestic interests and power relations among different segments of society in the target state. Drawing upon the seminal work of Albert O. Hirschman, they argue that international economic relations affect domestic politics and that these effects are most pronounced when large states engage in economic relations with smaller counterparts.[16] Under such conditions, domestic groups in smaller states which benefit from bilateral economic links have reason to press for maintaining and strengthening these eco-

15. The classic treatment of economic inducements is Albert O. Hirschman, *National Power and the Structure of Foreign Trade* (1945; Berkeley: University of California Press, 1980). See also Baldwin, *Paradoxes of Power*, chap. 4; Eileen Crumm, "The Value of Economic Incentives in International Relations," *Journal of Peace Research* 32, no. 3 (1995): 313–30; and David A. Cortright, ed., *The Price of Peace: Incentives and International Conflict Prevention* (New York: Rowman and Littlefield, 1997).

16. See Hirschman, *National Power and the Structure of Foreign Trade*.

nomic ties, encouraging a cooperative foreign policy. To illustrate this point, Abdelal and Kirshner analyze relations between the United States and the Hawaiian Kingdom during the nineteenth century; relations among Austria, Czechoslovakia, and the League of Nations between the First World War and the Second World War; and Ukrainian-Russian relations in the post–cold war era.

While Abdelal and Kirshner and Papayoanou and Kastner examine the longer-term effects of economic incentives and international economic relations, Daniel Drezner focuses on economic inducements designed to prompt short-term changes in a target's foreign policy. Drezner analyzes both why such carrots are seldom used and when states will prefer to use them rather than other policy instruments. He argues that unless both the sender and the target are democracies or economic incentives are tendered in the context of an international regime, the transaction costs of extending inducements are frequently too steep to render them attractive. Moreover, Drezner maintains that states will typically prefer to employ coercive strategies rather than extend carrots if political conflict is likely to erupt or if coercion appears feasible. He tests this argument by conducting a statistical analysis of economic inducements during the era since the Second World War and by examining U.S. foreign policy toward South Korea in the 1970s and toward North Korea in the 1990s.

ECONOMIC INTERDEPENDENCE AND POLITICAL CONFLICT

IN ADDITION to economic statecraft, the relationship between international economic relations and military conflict is another issue that is central to the political economy of national security. At least three competing views can be identified on the nature and strength of this relationship, and the following articles analyze each of these positions. One view, advanced most forcefully by commercial liberals, is that open international markets and heightened trade inhibit interstate hostilities. Various strands of this argument exist and the causal dynamics emphasized in each one differ.[17] Certain themes, however, have been stressed repeatedly. The first is that by increasing contact and com-

---

17. For an overview of the various strands of this argument, see Robert O. Keohane, "Economic Liberalism Reconsidered," in *The Economic Limits to Politics*, ed. John Dunn (Cambridge: Cambridge University Press, 1990), 165–94; Arthur A. Stein, "Governments, Economic Interdependence, and International Cooperation," in *Behavior, Society, and Nuclear War*, ed. Philip E. Tetlock et al., vol. 3 (New York: Oxford University Press, 1993), 241–324; and Michael W. Doyle, *Ways of War and Peace: Realism, Liberalism, and Socialism* (New York: Norton, 1997).

munication among individuals and governments, unfettered trade fosters cooperative political relations.[18] Another theme often emphasized by commercial
liberals is that commerce and conquest are substitute means of acquiring the
resources needed to promote political security and economic growth.[19] As
trade expands, the incentives to achieve these ends through territorial expansion, imperialism, and foreign aggression decline.[20] Conversely, heightened
trade barriers stimulate economic conflicts of interest that can contribute to
political-military discord.[21]

Still another variant of the argument that increased trade inhibits belligerence emphasizes the pacifying effects of economic interdependence. Commercial liberalization promotes economic integration and specialization, rendering
private traders and consumers dependent on foreign markets. Because political
antagonism threatens to disrupt economic relations among participants,
heightened commercial dependence increases the costs associated with military
conflict, thereby deterring its onset. As Montesquieu argued over two centuries
ago, "the natural effect of commerce is to lead to peace. Two nations that
trade together become mutually dependent: if one has an interest in buying,
the other has an interest in selling; and all unions are based on mutual
needs."[22]

The view that open trade promotes peace, however, has not gone unchal-
lenged. A second perspective on the relationship between commerce and conflict is offered by mercantilists and economic nationalists, who have long
maintained that, by influencing power relations among trading partners, open
commerce can undermine the national security of states.[23] Because the gains
from trade tend to be asymmetrically distributed and can be used to enhance
states' political-military capacity, those countries benefiting less from a commercial relationship may find their security jeopardized by countries benefiting
more. Similarly, if two trade partners depend on their commercial relationship
to very different degrees, trade may do little to deter belligerence on the part of
the less-dependent state. Even if states depend heavily and uniformly on trade

18. See Albert O. Hirschman, *The Passions and the Interests: Political Arguments for Capitalism
Before Its Triumph* (Princeton: Princeton University Press, 1977), 61. See also Doyle, *Ways of
War and Peace*, chap. 8; Stein, "Governments, Economic Interdependence, and International
Cooperation"; and Jacob Viner, "Peace as an Economic Problem," in *International Economics*,
ed. Jacob Viner (Glencoe, IL: Free Press, 1951), 261.
19. See, for example, Eugene Staley, *The World Economy in Transition* (New York: Council
on Foreign Relations, 1939).
20. See Richard N. Rosecrance, *The Rise of the Trading State: Commerce and Conquest in the
Modern World* (New York: Free Press, 1986).
21. Viner, "Peace as an Economic Problem," 259.
22. Quoted in Hirschman, *The Passions and the Interests*, 80.
23. See Hirschman, *National Power and the Structure of Foreign Trade*.

with each other, economic dependence could contribute to commercial disputes that, unless contained, might trigger political antagonism.[24]

More generally, realists and others have argued that the anarchic structure of the international system compels states to limit their economic dependence. As dependence rises, countries may have reason to engage in foreign expansion to manage or reduce it.[25] Consistent with such arguments, for example, Alexander Hamilton asserted in 1796 that protecting the industrial sector from foreign competition would enhance the United States' "security from external danger" and give rise to "less frequent interruption of their peace with foreign nations" than open trade policies.[26]

Finally, a wide variety of studies have concluded that international economic relations have no systematic bearing on political conflict.[27] Many of them hold that hostilities stem largely from variations in the distribution of political-military capabilities and that power relations underlie any apparent effect of economic exchange on military antagonism.

Despite enduring and heated debates about the nature and strength of the relationship between international trade and political hostilities, systematic analyses of these issues have been relatively scarce. In recent years, however, various efforts have been made to resolve these controversies and a number of the articles in this volume contribute to the growing literature on the links between commerce and conflict.[28]

Dale C. Copeland explains the resolution of enduring political rivalries by fusing liberal and realist arguments about the effects of commerce on conflict and by stressing states' expectations about future trade relations. Copeland argues that decisionmakers assessing the use of military force must consider the costs of rupturing existing commercial ties with an antagonist, as well as any forgone benefits that could otherwise accrue from future trade with the

24. See, for example, Kenneth N. Waltz, "The Myth of National Interdependence," in *The Multinational Corporation* ed., Charles P. Kindleberger (Cambridge: MIT Press, 1970), 205–23; and Stein, "Governments, Economic Interdependence, and International Cooperation."

25. See, for example, Kenneth N. Waltz, *Theory of International Politics* (New York: Random House, 1979), 104–7; and John J. Mearsheimer, "Back to the Future: Instability in Europe After the Cold War," *International Security* 15, no. 1 (summer 1990): 5–56.

26. Quoted in Edward Mead Earle, "Adam Smith, Alexander Hamilton, Frederich List: The Economic Foundations of Military Power," in *Makers of Modern Strategy from Machiavelli to the Nuclear Age*, ed. Peter Paret (Princeton: Princeton University Press, 1986), 235.

27. See, for example, Barry Buzan, "Economic Structure and International Security: The Limits of the Liberal Case," *International Organization* 38, no. 4 (autumn 1984): 597–624; Robert Gilpin, *The Political Economy of International Relations* (Princeton: Princeton University Press, 1987), 58; and Norrin M. Ripsman and Jean-Marc F. Blanchard, "Commercial Liberalism Under Fire: Evidence from 1914 and 1936," *Security Studies* 6, no. 2 (winter 1996/97): 4–50.

28. For an overview of some of this literature, see Susan M. McMillan, "Interdependence and Conflict," *Mershon International Studies Review* 41, no. 1 (May 1997): 33–58.

antagonist. If a state anticipates that the future stream of benefits from commerce with a given trading partner is likely to be substantial, then it is unlikely to engage in hostilities, which can undermine these benefits. Alternatively, if a state calculates that these benefits will be relatively small, it is more likely to pursue a belligerent foreign policy. Moreover, Copeland points out that the expected gains from trade need not be highly correlated with existing economic relations. Even if states currently conduct little commerce, diplomatic actions that signal their willingness to expand trade in the future can promote political-military cooperation.

To test this argument, Copeland analyzes U.S.-Soviet relations from 1965 until the end of the cold war. He maintains that during the early 1970s, the moderation in Soviet foreign policy was prompted partly by a desire to expand trade with the United States and the Kremlin's belief that détente would lead to a loosening of U.S. trade restrictions. Subsequent domestic political upheavals in the U.S., however, dashed these hopes and contributed to the resumption of antagonism between the superpowers. By the late 1980s, the Soviet Union had become increasingly anxious to promote trade with the United States and took actions that successfully defused U.S. opposition to greater East-West commerce. In Copeland's view, then, trade expectations played a major role in influencing the tenor of U.S.-Soviet superpower relations during the cold war and in bringing their enduring rivalry to an end.

Peter Liberman analyzes how the interaction between economic interdependence and the offense-defense balance affects the use of force. It is widely argued that when military technology renders states on the defense with an advantage against attackers, conquest is likely to be difficult and wars are likely to be drawn out and costly. Liberman, however, argues, that defense dominance also increases the desirability of conquest for states that depend on trade. If a dependent state anticipates that its ability to repel an attack by a rival could be undermined by wartime economic sanctions, this state may seek to conquer third parties that could be exploited economically in an effort to reduce its vulnerabilities.

Liberman qualifies this argument in various ways. He points out, for example, that it is unlikely to apply to states possessing nuclear weapons, since wartime sanctions will have little bearing on the ability to launch a nuclear strike. Furthermore, trade-dependent states operating in a defense dominant environment are more likely to be expansionist if they are led by individuals with a military bias who expect that conquered third parties will be economically useful in waging a war of attrition. Liberman maintains, however, that his argument helps to explain the expansionist policies of both Germany and Japan during the 1930s. In both countries, the conquest of neighbors was seen as a means to achieve the economic self-sufficiency necessary to prevail in the long wars that leaders anticipated fighting.

Finally, Edward D. Mansfield, Jon C. Pevehouse, and David H. Bearce analyze the effects of preferential trading arrangements (PTAs) on military disputes. Much of the recent empirical research on commerce and conflict centers on the effects of trade flows between states, but such research has largely ignored the institutions designed to guide commerce. PTAs are a broad class of commercial institutions which include free trade areas, common markets, and customs unions. Mansfield, Pevehouse, and Bearce argue that these arrangements tend to inhibit conflict between participants. Like Copeland, they maintain that the expectation of future commercial gains helps to dampen political tensions; and preferential arrangements provide an institutional means to promote the expectation of future economic benefits. Since political discord between members can undermine a PTA and thereby limit their ability to realize these benefits, preferential groupings help to deter the onset of hostilities. Furthermore, PTAs facilitate bargaining and negotiation between participants, reducing the specter of interstate disputes and contributing to the resolution of tensions that do arise before open hostilities break out. To test this argument, Mansfield, Pevehouse, and Bearce conduct a statistical analysis of the relationship between PTA membership and the onset of military disputes since the Second World War. They find that such disputes are much less likely to occur between PTA members than between states that do not belong to the same preferential arrangement.

POWER AND THE PURSE: RAMIFICATIONS FOR THEORY AND PRAXIS

IN RECENT years, scholars of international relations have displayed a growing interest in the political economy of national security. Particular attention has been focused on the conditions under which states impose economic sanctions, the factors influencing both the types of sanctions states impose and the effectiveness of sanctions, and the relationship between economic interdependence and military conflict. This volume sheds new light on each of these important issues. The following articles demonstrate that the relationship between international economics and national security is more complex and nuanced than conventionally acknowledged. Moreover, they have important implications for the study and practice of international relations.

Turning to the specific topics addressed in this volume, the following articles indicate that economic sanctions *can* achieve important political objectives. Rowe's analysis illustrates how sanctions can be used to signal domestic and foreign audiences. Moreover, as Blanchard and Ripsman demonstrate, sanctions can also compel a target state to comply with the sender's demands when domestic and international *political* conditions make the political cost of noncompliance prohibitive and the corresponding cost of compliance tolerable.

The contributors to this volume also indicate that domestic political conditions in the target state play a key role in determining whether economic inducements meet their objectives. A number of articles conclude, for example, that the effectiveness of such inducements often rests on the preferences and political influence of societal groups in the target state. Equally important, however, is the prospect that a reciprocal relationship exists between domestic political factors and economic inducements. As Abdelal and Kirshner suggest, inducements can help to shape the preferences and the power of domestic groups over the long run. In addition, some of the following articles caution that extending economic incentives is not without potential drawbacks. Drezner points out that since offering economic carrots may be viewed as a sign of weakness, senders may suffer damage to their international reputations; and Papayoanou and Kastner note that extending inducements may heighten the economic dependence of the sender on the target, thereby reducing the sender's ability to bear any future interruption of economic ties with the target. Thus, employing economic inducements may actually interfere with a state's ability to employ economic coercion in the future.

This volume also provides considerable evidence that international economic relations influence the onset of military conflict. This relationship, however, hinges on various factors that have not been addressed adequately to date. On the one hand, Copeland argues that the expectation of substantial future gains from trade often dampens conflict. Moreover, Mansfield, Pevehouse, and Bearce contend that preferential trading arrangements often generate such expectations and can also inhibit military disputes by facilitating bargaining and negotiations among members. On the other hand, Liberman demonstrates that when state leaders expect that wars will be drawn out affairs and neighboring countries control resources that would be valuable in wartime, then economic interdependence creates strong incentives for imperial expansion.

Beyond tackling fundamental questions about the political economy of national security, the essays in this volume speak to a number of broader themes in the field of international relations, which Michael Mastanduno addresses in greater depth in the conclusion to this volume. First, these essays suggest several challenges and refinements to realist theories of international relations. Second, they highlight how international institutions shape national security decisions. Third, they stress the influence of domestic political variables on international outcomes. Finally, they offer different perspectives on the relative weight that should be attached to political and economic factors in explanations of world politics.

Realists conventionally assume that states will balance against their adversaries. Papayoanou and Kastner, however, claim that a state may fail to do so if, in applying a strategy of economic incentives, it develops a domestic coalition with a vested interest in maintaining trade relations with an adversary. Furthermore, whereas realists often argue that economic interdependence promotes conflict, Copeland argues that this need not be the case if states anticipate substantial commercial gains. Finally, Liberman demonstrates that, contrary to the conventional realist assumption that defense dominance diminishes the incentives to use force, it may actually increase such incentives for states that are vulnerable to a wartime strategic blockade.

These essays also highlight the importance of the international institutional context within which security decisions are made. Whereas many realists, commercial liberals, and others discount the independent effects of international economic institutions on international security, some of the following articles find that these institutions often have a pronounced influence on security affairs. Drezner, for example, argues that international regimes can enhance the feasibility of economic inducements by reducing transaction costs; and Mansfield, Pevehouse, and Bearce conclude that preferential commercial institutions reduce the likelihood of military conflict between members.

The authors of these articles also contribute to the growing body of literature emphasizing the impact of domestic political variables on international security.[29] Blanchard and Ripsman and Papayoanou and Kastner, for example, argue that the efficacy of economic statecraft depends on the domestic political landscape in the target state. Drezner claims that if either the sender or the target is not a democracy, then the attractiveness of extending economic inducements is likely to decline. Liberman argues that the militaristic biases of German and Japanese military officials augmented the incentives for expansion created by each country's economic dependence and expectations of a long war of attrition. Abdelal and Kirshner posit that economic inducements can reshape domestic interests and coalitions. Thus, while many existing studies stress systemic influences on international security, this volume indicates the pitfall of ignoring domestic political factors.

---

29. On the importance of domestic politics in the security realm, see Peter B. Evans, Harold K. Jacobson, and Robert D. Putnam, eds., *Double-Edged Diplomacy* (Berkeley: University of California Press, 1993); Milner, *Interests, Institutions, and Information*; and Norrin M. Ripsman, "Democratic Institutions and the Governance of Foreign Security Policy: Peacemaking after Two World Wars" (Ph.D. diss., University of Pennsylvania, 1997).

A final theoretical controversy these articles address is the relative importance of economic factors in the realm of international security. Some authors place primacy emphasis on the political underpinnings of national security and attribute relatively little importance to economic factors. Blanchard and Ripsman, for example, argue that political costs are far more important than economic costs in determining whether states will capitulate to foreign economic coercion. Furthermore, Drezner contends that a target's status as an ally or an adversary of the sender strongly conditions whether the sender will use economic carrots or sticks. Other authors, however, give greater weight to the economic underpinnings of national security. Copeland, for example, explains the resolution of political-military rivalries largely in terms of expected future economic gains. Moreover, Abdelal and Kirshner point out that international economic exchange can bring about shifts in how economic partners define their national interests and in domestic coalitions. Still other authors emphasize both economic and political factors. Liberman, for example, argues that it is both the level of trade dependence and the offense-defense balance, together with domestic political factors, that determine the propensity for aggression. Mansfield, Pevehouse, and Bearce show that both economic and political factors influence the outbreak of military disputes. Papayoanou and Kastner argue that the ability of international economic factors to promote cooperative behavior depends on the character of the ruling domestic political coalition. Hence, while all of the following articles analyze the relative importance of political-military and economic variables in explaining security outcomes, they do not arrive at any clear consensus on this score.

The rapid and remarkable rise in international economic activity over the past decade has made it crucially important for scholars and policymakers to understand the nexus between international economic exchange and national security. To date, however, this relationship remains poorly understood. The contributors to this volume do not offer a single perspective on this issue, but they do offer a wide variety of important insights which shed new light on the political economy of national security.

TRADE EXPECTATIONS AND THE OUTBREAK OF PEACE:

DÉTENTE 1970–74 AND THE END OF THE COLD WAR 1985–91

DALE C. COPELAND

THE QUESTION of whether economic interdependence between states is a force for peace or a force for war has long puzzled international relations scholars. Liberals argue that trade ties foster peaceful relations by giving states an economic incentive to avoid war: the benefits received from trade make continued peace more advantageous than war. Realists dismiss this argument, contending that high interdependence only increases the likelihood of war, as dependent states struggle to ensure continued access to vital goods.

This paper provides an argument that helps to bridge these two perspectives. By incorporating a second causal variable in addition to a state's level of economic dependence—namely, its expectations for future trade—we can determine under what conditions interdependence will drive actors toward either peace or conflict. If trade expectations are positive, dependent states will expect to realize the positive benefits of trade into the future, and thus be more inclined toward peace. If, however, such states are pessimistic about future trade, fearing a cut-off of vital goods or the continuation of current restrictions, the negative expected value for trade will push them toward aggression (provided that they have adequate military power). Elsewhere, I show that this synthetic argument helps clear up the empirical anomalies both liberalism and realism face in dealing with the two critical major wars of this century: the First and Second World Wars.[1]

The above logic starts from the simplifying assumption that a dependent state's trade expectations are largely exogenous; that is, its expectations re-

Dale C. Copeland is assistant professor at the Department of Government and Foreign Affairs at the University of Virginia.

For their valuable comments, I wish to thank Gerard Alexander, Daniel Drezner, Steven Finkel, Allen Lynch, James Morrow, Paul Papayoanou, João Resende-Santos, Herman Schwartz, Randall Schweller, Dennis Smith, participants in the *Security Studies* Workshop on Economic Power, Interdependence, and National Security, held at the Mershon Center for International Relations, Ohio State University, 2–5 April 1998, the editors of the special issue—Jean-Marc Blanchard, Norrin Ripsman, and Edward Mansfield— and the anonymous reviewers for *Security Studies*.

1. Dale C. Copeland, "Economic Interdependence and War: A Theory of Trade Expectations," *International Security* 20, no. 4 (spring 1996): 5–41.

garding other states' willingness to trade off into the future are largely outside of its control. In some situations, however, the state may have opportunities to improve the prospects of trade by its own actions. In particular, it may be able to make commitments to moderate its foreign policy in return for commitments to higher future trade. When such opportunities to improve the trading environment are available, diplomacy may be able to turn negative expectations into positive ones, thus dampening the probability of war between the states. In the extreme, adversaries may be able to eliminate their rivalry altogether.

The paper has two main purposes. First, I build a theoretically informed argument showing how states trapped in an enduring rivalry can quell this rivalry through diplomacy which builds stronger expectations for future trade.[2] Second, I apply the causal logic to two important cases: the emergence of détente in the early 1970s (and its subsequent failure by 1975); and the end of the cold war in the late 1980s.

The paper examines how adversaries can get caught up in what might be called a "trade-security" dilemma, especially when one of the adversaries needs bilateral trade far more than the other (that is, when it is asymmetrically dependent). Since leaders cannot see into the heads of others, a dependent state must make estimates of the other's likelihood of trading over the foreseeable future based on current signals and behavior. If the other is unwilling to commit to future trade, and is currently restricting trade, this will push the dependent state toward more expansionist policies. Yet these policies in turn will reinforce the other's unwillingness to trade, producing a spiral of negative trade expectations and heightened hostility. In the 1930s, for example, Japanese leaders were driven to increasingly aggressive policies as Western and particularly American trade policies became more restrictive. Japan's behavior finally

---

2. On the growing literature on enduring rivalries, see inter alia Gary Goertz and Paul F. Diehl, "Enduring Rivalries: Theoretical Constructs and Empirical Patterns," *International Studies Quarterly* 37, no. 2 (June 1993): 147–72; Goertz and Diehl, "The Empirical Importance of Enduring Rivalries," *International Interactions* 18, no. 2 (1992): 151–63; Diehl, ed., *The Dynamics of Enduring Rivalries* (Urbana: University of Illinois Press, 1998); Paul Huth and Bruce Russett, "General Deterrence between Enduring Rivalries," *American Political Science Review* 87, no. 1 (March 1993): 61–73; Eli Lieberman, "What Makes Deterrence Work? Lessons from the Egyptian-Israel Enduring Rivalry," *Security Studies* 4, no. 4 (summer 1995): 851–910; William R. Thompson, "Principal Rivalries," *Journal of Conflict Resolution* 39, no. 2 (June 1995): 195–223. For the most part, this literature focuses on deterrence, escalation, and the causes of war within enduring rivalries, rather than on the resolution of those rivalries. For notable exceptions, see Goertz and Diehl, "The Initiation and Termination of Enduring Rivalries," *American Journal of Political Science* 39, no. 1 (February 1995): 30–52; Stephen R. Rock, *Why Peace Breaks Out: Great Power Rapprochement in Historical Perspective* (Chapel Hill: University Of North Carolina Press, 1989); Sean M. Lynn-Jones, "Rivalry and Rapprochement: Accommodation Between Adversaries in International Politics" (Ph.D. diss., Harvard University, in progress).

led to a complete embargo on Western iron and oil exports, which in turn pushed Tokyo into total war by late 1941.[3]

The trade-security spiral need not move in only one direction, however. A virtuous cycle can be established when the less dependent state is willing to commit to higher trade, in return for a moderation of the dependent state's foreign policy. In the early 1970s, and again in the late 1980s, the Soviet Union and the United States were able to moderate their cold-war rivalry through judicious diplomacy that contained a strong economic dimension. It was clear to both sides that the Soviets would gain far more from the normalization of trade relations than the Americans. Peace thus emerged as Moscow proved willing to temper its global policy, in order to convince Washington to relax its severe trade restrictions, especially trade in the high-tech goods so essential to Soviet economic revitalization. Even if the building of positive Soviet trade expectations was not the only force pushing toward an end to the enduring rivalry, the case studies below show that it was a critical dimension, and was recognized as such by both states. Indeed, the undermining of these expectations by U.S. domestic upheavals in 1973–74 was an essential cause of détente's collapse and the return to cold war in the late 1970s.

The article proceeds in three parts. I first lay out the theoretical logic for considering trade expectations as a force for peace or conflict, and the ways in which these expectations can be shaped by diplomacy. I then examine the economic underpinnings for the détente period of the 1970s and the end of the cold war in the late 1980s. Finally, in the conclusion, I consider some of the implications of the argument for current policy debates, particularly the question about whether to contain or engage China.

TRADE EXPECTATIONS AND THE RESOLUTION OF ENDURING RIVALRIES

THIS SECTION summarizes the liberal and realist perspectives on the issue of economic interdependence and international conflict.[4] It then examines an alternative approach, what I call trade expectations theory.

The core liberal argument can be expressed simply. Trade provides valuable benefits, or "gains from trade," to any particular state. A dependent state should therefore seek to avoid war, since peaceful trading gives it all the bene-

---

3. For the Japan case study, see Dale C. Copeland, "Modeling Economic Interdependence and War" (paper delivered at the annual meeting of the American Political Science Association, Chicago, 31 August–3 September 1995).

4. For more complete survey, see Copeland, "Economic Interdependence and War," 8–16; and Susan M. McMillan, "Interdependence and Conflict," *Mershon International Studies Review* 41, suppl. 1 (May 1997): 33–58.

fits of close ties without any of the costs and risks associated with military conflict. This argument can be trade to Crucé, Montesquieu, and Cobden, and was first fully developed by Norman Angell just prior to the First World War. States, Angell argued, must choose between new ways of thinking, namely, peaceful trade, and the "old method" of power politics. With modernization, war no longer pays; indeed, by destroying trade ties, it is "commercially suicidal."[5] Richard Rosecrance updates this thesis, arguing that modern conditions push states to be "trading states" rather than "territorial states" obsessed with military expansion. There is no incentive to wage war in highly interdependent systems, since "trading states recognize that they can do better through [trade]…than by trying to conquer and assimilate large tracts of land."[6]

5. Normal Angell, *The Great Illusion*, 2nd. ed. (New York: Putnam's, 1933), 59–60, 87–89. On the historical development of the liberal view, see David A. Baldwin, *Economic Statecraft* (Princeton: Princeton University Press, 1985), chap. 5; Albert O. Hirschman, *The Passions and the Interests*, (Princeton: Princeton University Press, 1977); Geoffrey Blainey, *The Causes of War*, 3rd ed. (New York: Free Press, 1988); Edmund Silberner, *The Problem of War In Nineteenth Century Economic Thought* (Princeton: Princeton University Press, 1946); Otto Mallery, *Economic Peace and Durable Union* (New York: Harper, 1943); Ramsay Muir, *The Interdependent World and its Problems* (Boston: Houghton Mifflin, 1933); Edward L. Morse, *Modernization and the Transformation of International Relations* (New York: Free Press, 1976); David Mitrany, *A Working Peace System* (Chicago: Quadrangle, 1964).

6. Richard Rosecrance, *The Rise of the Trading State* (New York: Basic Books, 1986), 13–14, 24–25. See also Rosecrance, "War, Trade, and Interdependence," in *Interdependence and Conflict in World Politics*, ed. James N. Rosenau and Hylke Tromp (Aldershot, Eng.: Averbury, 1989); Rosecrance, "A New Concert of Powers," *Foreign Affairs* 71, no. 2 (spring 1992): 64–82. For statistical tests generally upholding the liberal prediction, see Mark Gasiorowski, "Economic Interdependence and International Conflict: Some Cross-national Evidence," *International Studies Quarterly* 30, no. 1 (March 1986): 22–38; Gasiorowski and Soloman W. Polochek, "Conflict and Interdependence: East-West Trade and Linkages In the Era of Détente," *Journal of Conflict Resolution* 26, no. 4 (December 1982): 709–29; Polochek, "Conflict and Trade," *Journal of Conflict Resolution* 24, no. 1 (March 1980): 55–78; Polochek, "Conflict and Trade: An Economics Approach to Political International Interactions," in *Economics of Arms Reduction and the Peace Process*, ed. Walter Isard and Charles H. Anderton (Amsterdam: North Holland, 1992); Polochek and Judith McDonald, "Strategic Trade and the Incentive for Cooperation," in *Disarmament, Economic Conversions, and Peace Management*, ed. Manas Chatterji and Linda Rennie Forcey (New York: Praeger, 1992); John R. Oneal, Francis H. Oneal, Zeev Maoz, and Bruce Russett, "The Liberal Peace: Interdependence, Democracy, and International Conflict, 1950–1985," *Journal of Peace Research* 33, no. 1 (February 1996): 11–28; Oneal and Russett, "The Classical Liberals Were Right: Democracy, Interdependence, and Conflict, 1950–1985," *International Studies Quarterly* 41, no. 2 (June 1997): 267–94; Oneal and Russett, "Is the Liberal Peace Just an Artifact of the Cold War" (paper presented at annual meeting of International Studies Association, Minneapolis, 17–21 March 1998); William J. Domke, *War and the Changing Global System* (New Haven: Yale University Press, 1988); Edward D. Mansfield, *Power, Trade, and War* (Princeton: Princeton University Press, 1994); Mansfield and Jon Pevehouse, "Trade Blocs, Trade Flows, and International Conflict" (paper presented at annual meeting of International Studies Association, Minneapolis, 17–21 March 1998); Lois W. Sayrs, "Reconsidering Trade and Conflict: A Qualitative Response Model with Censoring," *Conflict Management and Peace Science* 10, no. 1 (spring 1988): 1–19; Sayr, "Trade and Conflict Revisited: Do Politics Matter?," *International Interactions* 15, no. 2 (1989): 155–75.

Realists turn the liberal argument on its head, arguing that economic interdependence only increases the likelihood of military conflict. Kenneth Waltz argues that while actors in domestic politics have little reason to fear specialization, the anarchic structure of international politics makes states worry about their vulnerability, compelling them "to control what they depend on or to lessen the extent of their dependency." For Waltz, this "simple thought" explains "their imperial thrusts to widen the scope of their control."[7] John Mearsheimer contends that states requiring vital goods fear cut off, and thus seek to "extend political control to the source of supply, giving rise to conflict with the source or with its other customers."[8] This argument follows mercantilist logic suggesting that states needing supplies and markets seek to reduce their dependence through colonial imperialism.[9]

The critical difference between liberals and realists comes with their emphasis on the benefits versus the costs of interdependence. Liberals focus on the benefits garnered from trade as states move away from anarchy; the opportunity costs of dependence are at most the loss of benefits if trade is ended.[10] Realists emphasize something that is downplayed in liberal arguments, namely, that after a state has restructured its economy around trade, there may be po-

7. Kenneth N. Waltz, *Theory of International Politics* (New York: Random House, 1979), 106. See also Kenneth N. Waltz, "The Myth of Interdependence," in *Globalism versus Realism* , ed. Ray Maghoori and Bennett Ramberg (Boulder: Westview, 1982).

8. John J. Mearsheimer, "Disorder Restored," in *Rethinking America's Security*, ed. Graham Allison and Gregory F. Treverton (New York: Norton, 1992): 223; Mearsheimer, "Back to the Future: Instability in Europe After the Cold War," *International Security* 15, no. 1 (Summer 1990): 45. See also Anne Uchitel, "Interdependence and Instability," in *Coping with Complexity in the International System*, ed. Jack Snyder and Robert Jervis (Boulder: Westview, 1993), 243–64; Robert Gilpin, "Economic Interdependence and National Security in Historical Perspective," in *Economic Issues and National Security*, ed. Klaus Knorr and Frank N. Trager (Lawrence, Kan.: Allen, 1977), 29; Gilpin, *U.S. Power and the Multinational Corporation* (New York: Basic Books, 1975), 259; Barry Buzan, "Economic Structure and International Security," *International Organization* 38, no. 4 (Autumn 1984): esp. 597, 609–23. Qualified statistical support for the realist thesis is provide by Katherine Barbieri, "Economic Interdependence: Path to Peace or Source of Interstate Conflict," *Journal of Peace Research* 33, no. 1 (February 1996): 29–49; Barbieri, "International Trade and Conflict: The Debatable Relationship" (paper presented at the annual meeting of the International Studies Association, Minneapolis, 17–21 March 1998).

9. See Jacob Viner, "Power Versus Plenty as Objectives of Foreign Policy in the Seventeenth and Eighteenth Centuries," *World Politics* 1, no. 1 (October 1948): 1–19; Eli F. Heckscher, *Mercantilism*, 2 vols. (London: George Allen, 1931); Philip W. Buck, *The Politics of Mercantilism* (New York: Holt, 1942); Charles Wilson, *Mercantilism* (London: Wyman, 1958); Baldwin, *Economic Statecraft*, chap. 5.

10. See David Baldwin, "Interdependence and Power: A Conceptual Analysis," *International Organization* 34, no. 4 (Autumn 1980): 478, 482–84, 489; Baldwin, "The Power of Positive Sanctions," *World Politics* 24, no. 1 (October 1971): 19–38; Albert O. Hirschman, *National Power and the Structure of Foreign Trade*, exp. ed. (Berkeley: University of California Press, 1980), chap. 2; Rosecrance, *Rise of Trading State*, 144–45; Gasiorowski, "Economic Interdependence and International Conflict."

tentially large "costs of adjustment" should trade be later severed. A state cut off after basing its economic structure around imported oil, for example, may be put in a far worse situation than if it had never moved away from autarchy in the first place.[11]

Trade expectations theory begins by fusing the liberal benefits of trade and the realist costs of severed trade into one framework. It then adds a dynamic element, namely, a state's expectations of future trade, a variable that incorporates into the theoretical logic an actor's sense of the future trends and possibilities. This variable is essential to any leader's determination not just of the immediate value of peace versus conflict at a particular moment in time, but of the overall expected value of peace and conflict over the foreseeable future.

The deductive logic of the trade expectations argument, as with liberalism and realism, centers on an individual state's efforts to manage its own situation of dependence.[12] For sake of simplicity, I focus on a two-actor scenario of asymmetrical dependence, where state A needs trade with state B more than B needs trade with A. The assumption of asymmetry means that changes in the trading environment are more likely to affect A's decision for peace or conflict than B's. This allows us to focus primarily on state A's decision calculus, since it is this actor that most determines the probability of war between the states.[13]

If state A moves away from autarchy to trade freely with state B, it will expect to receive the benefits of trade stressed by liberals, namely, the incremental increase in A's total welfare due to trade.[14] Importantly, state A can still be aware of these benefits even if present trade is nonexistent, since they represent the gains that would accrue to the state if trade levels become high in the future. As is evident in the cold war case studies, it is a state's ability to foresee future potential benefits that allows it to attach a high expected value to the peaceful trading option even when current trade levels are low (as long as it expects current restrictions to be relaxed).

When a state trades, it specializes in and exports goods where it enjoys a comparative advantage, while forgoing the production of other goods, which it then imports. As realists emphasize, this very process of specialization entails

11. On the costs of adjustment, see Ruth Arad, Seev Hirsch, and Alfred Tovias, *The Economics of Peacemaking* (New York: St. Martin's, 1983), 26–34; Robert O. Keohane and Joseph S. Nye, *Power and Interdependence* (Boston: Little, Brown, 1977), 13. For a conceptualization of "strategic goods," see Norrin M. Ripsman and Jean-Marc F. Blanchard, "Commercial Liberalism under Fire: Evidence from 1914 and 1936," *Security Studies* 6, no. 2 (winter 1996–97): 4–50.

12. See Copeland, "Economic Interdependence and War," 12–13.

13. The assumption of asymmetry can of course be later relaxed, to show the effects of symmetrical interdependence on both actors' desire for conflict versus cooperation.

14 Richard E. Caves and Ronald W. Jones, *World Trade and Payments*, 4th ed. (Boston: Little, Brown, 1985).

potentially large costs of adjustment should trade be subsequently cut off. This is especially so if the state becomes dependent on foreign oil and raw materials which are critical to the functioning of the economy. Hence, on a bilateral basis, state A's total level of dependence can be conceptualized as the sum of the benefits received from free trade (versus autarchy) and the costs of being cut off from trade after having specialized (versus autarchy).

In choosing between an aggressive or peaceful foreign policy, however, state A can not refer simply to its dependence level. Rather, it must determine the overall expected value of trade and therefore the value of continued peace into the foreseeable future. Benefits of trade and costs of severed trade on their own say nothing about this expected value. Dynamic expectations of future trade must be brought in. If the state has positive expectations that the other will maintain free and open trade over the long term, then the expected value of trade will be close to the value of the benefits of trade. On the other hand, if the state, after having specialized, comes to expect that trade will be severed by the trading partner, then the expected value of trade may be negative, that is, close to the value of the costs of severed trade. The expected value of trade may thus be anywhere between the two extremes, depending on a state's estimate of the expected probability of securing open trade, or of being cut off.

This leads to the first important hypothesis. For any given expected value of conflict,[15] we can predict that the lower the expectations of future trade, the lower the expected value of trade, and therefore the more likely it is that conflictual behavior or war will be chosen. When expectations of future trade are high and improving, however, the expected value for trade will be positive, and peaceful behavior will more likely be preferred.

It is important to note that the expected value of trade will not be based on the level of trade at a particular moment in time, but upon the stream of expected trade levels off into the future. It really does not matter if trade is high today: if state A knows that B will cut all trade tomorrow and shows no signs of restoring it later, the expected value of trade would be negative. Similarly, it does not matter if there is little or no trade at present: if state A is confident that B is committed to open trade in the future, the expected value of trade would be positive.[16]

---

15. The expected value of conflict or war, as I discuss elsewhere, will be driven by the relative power balance and the probability that certain hostile actions will lead to war through preemption or reputation-driven escalation. See Copeland, "Economic Interdependence and War," 21–23.

16. Of course, if the gain from open trade with state B is very small, due say to the low complementarity of the two countries' economies, then even highly optimistic trade expectations will produce only a small expected value of trade. In such circumstances, inter-state economic variables can have only a marginal effect on state A's foreign policies one way or

The fact that the expected value of trade can be negative even if present trade is high, due to low expectations for future trade, goes a long way toward explaining such clear anomalies for liberal theory as German aggression in the First World War. Despite high present levels of trade up to 1914, German leaders had good reason to believe that the other great powers would undermine this trade into the future; hence, a war to secure control over raw materials and markets was required for the long-term security of the German nation.[17] More importantly for our purposes here, since the expected value of trade can be positive even though present trade is low, due to strong expectations for future trade, we can understand how risky rivalries like the cold war can be ended or at least moderated. While East-West trade was still quite low during the early 1970s and again in the late 1980s, the Soviet need for Western technology combined with a growing belief that large increases in trade with the West would be forthcoming, gave the Soviets a high enough expected value of trade to convince them to be more accommodating in superpower relations.

In the above argument, state A determines its expected value for trade by estimating the likelihood that state B will trade at high or low levels into the future. Up until now, I have discussed state A's expectations of future trade as though they were largely exogenous, that is, as though they were essentially independent of any interaction between the two states. This may be a reasonable assumption in many situations. State B's reserves of a raw material that A needs, for example, might be falling dramatically, making it unlikely that B could trade extensively later on even if it wanted to. State B might also be constrained by third-party events that force a shift in trading practices. In the late 1930s, for example, Japanese leaders recognized that America would probably have to cut back on oil and iron exports to Japan as U.S. reserves were depleted or needed to supply a military buildup against Germany. There were thus exogenous reasons for the Japanese to be less optimistic about U.S. trade over the long term. Domestic factors that leaders of B cannot control will also be seen as exogenous by state A. As we will see, Richard M. Nixon's inability to control the Congress after Watergate led to the Jackson-Vanik restrictions on trade with Russia, thereby undermining his efforts to improve Soviet trade expectations within a broader détente.

Leaders often recognize, however, that by their actions they can affect the beliefs of other actors. In other words, the trade expectations which drive state

---

another. (In the cases below, the potential gains from East-West trade were seen to be significant from the Soviet perspective.)

17. For a summary of the German case up to the First World War, see Copeland, "Economic Interdependence and War," 27–33.

behavior are not wholly exogenous; they can be affected by diplomatic inter-action. State B can send certain signals that help the dependent state A form a more accurate estimate of B's likelihood of trading at high levels. This updating of beliefs, when in a positive direction, can help state A improve its expected value for trade, thus reducing its desire for conflict. Moreover, state A knows that its own behavior—the level of aggressiveness of its foreign policy—will have an effect on state B's estimate of A's type; that is, whether A is hostile or peaceful. This estimate in turn should directly affect B's willingness to send positive signals of its likelihood of trading into the future.

The fundamental problem inhibiting the easy resolution of an enduring rivalry is that of incomplete information. Neither actor can see inside the head of the other (the "problem of other minds"). State A, in evaluating the signals sent by B, must wonder whether positive signs from B really represent B's true willingness to trade at high levels in the future. State B, after all, could be promising higher trade yet end up increasing restrictions later on. Likewise, state B, in deciding whether to open up trade, has to worry about whether A is just pretending to be peaceful, but is actually planning on using the gains from trade to support a policy of future aggression. If it has reason to believe state A is inherently aggressive, it will be less likely to commit to future trade.[18]

This problem of incomplete information can lead even good, peaceful states into a situation of escalating tension and mistrust, which in turn can lead to war. This is the trade-security dilemma. When state B believes that state A is potentially aggressive, it may impose severe restrictions on trade. Yet because of these restrictions, state A, given its low trade expectations, will be pushed toward a more assertive foreign policy. In a vicious feedback loop, state A's behavior tends only to reinforce B's perceptions that A is hostile, and therefore should be cut off from the benefits of trade. The more B believes and acts upon this, by the above logic, the more negative A's trade expectations are likely to be, and thus the more aggressive A's behavior will become.[19]

Fortunately, both sides may have opportunities to escape this vicious cycle. What is required is an ability on both sides to send signals that help the other alter its beliefs. State A, the more dependent state, must be able to signal that it

18. For some of the conditions under which concern for relative gains will inhibit eco-nomic cooperation, see essays in David A. Baldwin, ed., *Neorealism and Neoliberalism: The Con-temporary Debate* (New York: Columbia University Press, 1993).

19. This logic parallels the classic security dilemma, where both states are good security-seekers but due to mistrust take actions which undermine the security of the other. Each reaction to the other's action only reinforces the negative view of the other, causing a esca-lating spiral of arms racing and crisis behavior. See esp. Robert Jervis, "Cooperation under the Security Dilemma," *World Politics* 30, no. 2 (January 1978): 167–214; Charles L. Glaser, "The Security Dilemma Revisited," *World Politics* 50, no. 1 (October 1997): 171–201.

is not as innately aggressive as state B has come to believe. State B must be willing to take steps that demonstrate that it is truly committed to providing high levels of trade off into the future.

There is an obstacle, however, which makes this process less than straight-forward. As modelers of games of incomplete information emphasize, prudent actors will dismiss signals from the other side when they have reason to believe the other is strategically misrepresenting its true nature. In short, prudent actors in anarchy have to worry that the other is actually a bad apple, and is only pretending to be a good one. They will thus be more likely to accept the other's communications as genuine if it is a "costly signal;" that is, if it is an action that bad, untrustworthy actors would find too costly to make. A signifi-cant public commitment by state B to open up trade with state A, for example, might do the trick: it would be seen by A as too costly for B to make unless B were indeed a state predisposed to trade extensively in the future. Given the domestic and international costs of reneging on this commitment, a state B which was disinclined to future trade would be unlikely to have made such a commitment. Likewise, if state A seeks to change B's belief—that is, to make B moderate its view of A's motives, and thus increase B's willingness to trade— then state A may have to make a fairly dramatic gesture of its peaceful nature.[20]

As we will see, U.S.-Soviet diplomacy of the late 1980s exhibited this pattern of costly signaling. The Soviet leadership understood that given the entrenched mistrust of the Reagan and Bush administrations, only dramatic and often unilateral gestures would convince the Americans that the Gorbachev regime was indeed "different." Only then would the Americans be willing to increase substantially their commitment to the East-West trade so essential to reversing Soviet economic decline. Fortunately, the U.S. leaders eventually reciprocated these gestures by committing to greater trade. This gave the Soviet leaders the confidence to go even further, and the cold war quickly wound down.

This does not mean more measured gestures cannot also have a positive effect in despiraling tension. By 1972–73, as I discuss, Washington was willing to offer greater future trade in exchange for Moscow's acceptance of restric-tions on strategic missiles as well as its help in ending the Vietnam war. These actions, while not as dramatic as those in the late 1980s, nevertheless played a

---

20. On costly signaling games of incomplete information, see James D. Fearon, "Threats to Use Force: Costly Signals and Bargaining in International Crisis" (Ph.D. diss., University of California Berkeley, 1992), chaps. 2–4; Fearon, "Domestic Political Audiences and the Escalation of International Disputes," *American Political Science Review* 88, no. 3 (September 1994): 577–92; Andrew Kydd, "Game Theory and the Spiral Model," *World Politics* 49, no. 3 (April 1997): 371–400; Robert Powell, "Nuclear Brinkmanship with Two-Sided Incomplete Information," *American Political Science Review* 82, no. 1 (March 1988): 155–78; Robert Gib-bons, *Game Theory for Applied Economists* (Princeton: Princeton University Press, 1992); James D. Morrow, *Game Theory for Political Scientists* (Princeton: Princeton University Press, 1994).

significant role in building trust between the superpowers and moderating their clashes in the third world.[21] The ability to go forward toward long-term peace was undermined by 1975 by an exogenous factor beyond the control of either state's executive leadership, namely, congressional opposition to the trade agreements, fueled by Nixon's domestic troubles.

To summarize, positive trade expectations can have a substantial impact on the ability of two states to move away from rivalry and conflict and toward a stable peace. Expectations will often be driven by exogenous variables, and leaders must taken these factors into account. Yet diplomacy also matters. When states are able to signal their willingness to increase future trade and to shift toward peaceful behavior, they can set in motion a cycle of greater economic exchange linked to more cooperative relations. The next section illustrates this phenomenon with two particularly important historical cases: U.S.-Soviet relations in the early 1970s, and the winding down of superpower conflict in the late 1980s.[22]

THE EMERGENCE AND BREAKDOWN OF DÉTENTE, 1965–76

THE COLD WAR from 1945 to 1990 represents the most significant enduring rivalry of the last half century. Interestingly, the influence of economic interchange on the likelihood of war and militarized conflict within this rivalry has been largely ignored by theorists within both the realist and the liberal camps. This seems to be for one simple reason. Both liberal and realist arguments about interdependence and war, as they are currently formulated, focus on the impact of actual trade (as the measure of "interdependence") on the probability of conflict.[23] Since trade levels between the superpowers remained low throughout the cold war, neither paradigm would expect interdependence

21. In the language of game theory, the diplomacy of the early 1970s and late 1980s helped both sides "update" their beliefs about the other state's character, thus making more cooperative relations possible. In the 1970s, the actions were less dramatic, but allowed for a partial updating of beliefs—the belief that the other was not quite as bad as initially thought (what game theorists would call a semi-separating equilibrium). In the late 1980s, more dramatic signals, especially from the Soviet side, helped lead to a more complete overturning of cold war perceptions. By 1990, both sides believed that the other's intentions were largely benign (a separating equilibrium had been reached, whereby both superpowers now had the confidence that they were dealing with a cooperative state). On Bayesian updating and on the various equilibria in games of incomplete information, see references in previous footnote.

22. Two cases cannot provide a full test of the argument; rather, they serve as plausibility probes of the causal logic.

23. This is especially so for quantitative studies on interdependence and war. Such studies tend to use current trade levels (usually as a percentage of GNP) as the primary economic variable, correlated against changing levels of conflict. See references in n. 6.

to explain much of the variance in system stability over time relative to other causal factors such as military power and ideology.

The argument in this paper indicates the problem with this view. State behavior is driven by expectations of future trade. Hence, even when current trade levels are low or nonexistent, expectations of high trade over the foreseeable future can lead a state to moderate its foreign policy. Moreover, a state's need for trade can change over time, due to internal changes in its economy, even if it cannot immediately satisfy this need. By the logic of this paper's theory, if a state has a strong need for trade, regardless of existing trade levels, changes in trade expectations can have a marked effect on its behavior.[24] This was the case in the cold war. Variations in the Kremlin's trade expectations after 1965, combined with the increasing Soviet need for Western goods, shaped the peacefulness of Soviet behavior, even when actual trade levels did not change significantly.

As early as the mid-1950s, the Soviets began to realize that trade with the West could have potentially large benefits, especially if it secured technology unavailable or superior to indigenous Soviet technology.[25] The first big push for greater trade came in the mid-1960s. The impetus was declining rates of economic growth. From average annual growth rates of six to ten per cent in the first decade and a half after the war, the economy was registering only five per cent growth from 1961 to 1965.[26] At the root of the decline was what Soviet analysts called the "scientific-technological revolution." The world was moving away from the emphasis on heavy industry characteristic of the industrial revolution. Growth was now seen to depend increasingly on the integration of technology—computers, scientific management techniques, information systems, and so forth—into the production process.[27] In particular, the Soviets were coming to realize that increasing GNP through "extensive" production—simply increasing the inputs of labor and capital—would be more difficult now that the economy had recovered from the war. To keep up with the Western bloc, "intensive" development was necessary, namely, growth

24. Recall that there are two independent variables in trade expectations theory: the level of dependence/need, and a state's expectation of its ability to fulfill this need over the foreseeable future.

25. See Bruce Parrott, *Politics and Technology in the Soviet Union* (Cambridge: MIT Press, 1983), chap. 4.

26. See Anders Aslund, *Gorbachev's Struggle for Economic Reform* (Ithaca: Cornell University Press, 1989), 15; Richard E. Ericson, "The Soviet Statistical Debate: Khanin vs. TsSU," in *The Impoverished Superpower*, ed. Henry S. Rowen and Charles Wolf Jr., (San Francisco: Institute for Contemporary Studies, 1990), 77.

27. See Erik P. Hoffman and Robbin F. Laird, *"The Scientific-Technological Revolution" and Soviet Foreign Policy* (New York: Pergamon, 1982), chap. 1. The scientific-technological revolution corresponds roughly to what western scholars would call the "information age" or "third wave" production.

through the more efficient use of a given level of inputs (that is, greater productivity).[28] To achieve this, changes were needed to match the West's level of technological sophistication.

The man leading the charge toward technological improvement was Premier Alexei Kosygin. The scientific-technological revolution, he began to stress by 1965–66, was now the critical dimension of the superpower competition. In this game, the Soviet Union had "essential inadequacies" that were having "serious" effects on economic growth. For the future, it was critical "to create a well-arranged system for...the most rapid...introduction of the results of scientific research into production."[29] His assessment was buttressed by analyses by Soviet economists such as Abel Aganbegyan, which showed that the U.S. economy was growing rapidly, supported by its superiority in such critical areas as computers and automation.[30]

For Kosygin, the easiest solution to the problem was greater trade with the West. In March 1965, he argued that "active international trade, [the] exchange of goods and of scientific-technological experience, is an important factor in the acceleration of economic progress." A year later, he noted that foreign technology would "permit [the] saving [of] hundreds of millions of rubles on scientific-research work."[31] Kosygin's efforts to encourage greater trade were initially resisted by the majority of Politburo members, including Leonid Brezhnev. They worried that trade dependence would leave the state vulnerable to Western political pressures and to ideological influences.[32] By 1969–70, however, Brezhnev began to see the wisdom of Kosygin's approach. Internal economic reforms begun in 1965 were not having a significant effect; growth rates remained at around five per cent, and productivity gains were minimal.[33]

28. See ibid., chap. 1.

29. Quoted in Parrott, *Politics and Technology*, 186.

30. See Martin Walker, *The Waking Giant: The Soviet Union under Gorbachev* (London: Abacus, 1987), 38–39; Georgi Arbatov, *The System: An Insider's Life in Soviet Politics* (New York: Random House, 1993), 154–55.

31. Quoted in Richard D. Anderson, *Public Policy in an Authoritarian State: Making Foreign Policy During the Brezhnev Years* (Ithaca: Cornell University Press, 1993), 127. See also the 1967 argument by two Soviet analysts that the country could use trade within the growing international division of labor to improve economic performance (Hoffman and Laird, *"Scientific-Technological Revolution"*, 80–81).

32. Indeed, Kissinger's linkage strategy after 1969 was designed precisely to exploit the fact that the Soviets would receive more from trade than the Americans. Neorealists have a hard time understanding why any great power, especially in bipolarity, would ever allow itself to become asymmetrically dependent on another great power. Once we realize that such dependence typically implies, by its very nature, *relative economic gains*, such behavior is less puzzling: the asymmetrically dependent state accepts an increase in the other's leverage, in return for economic growth.

33. Aslund, *Gorbachev's Struggle*, 15; Ed A. Hewitt, *Reforming the Soviet Economy* (Washington, D.C.: Brookings, 1988), 239.

The first signs of Brezhnev's changing views came in a Central Committee speech in December 1968. Only nine months before, he had spoken on the incurable problems of Western capitalism. Now he argued that accelerating technological innovation was "the most important of the tasks of our economic strategy." The capitalist countries were transforming quickly, and the competition for technological primary "has now become one of the main bridgeheads of the historical struggle of the two systems."[34] By 1970–71, with GNP growth rates declining still further,[35] Western trade was emerging as the panacea for Brezhnev's problems: it would revitalize the economy, allowing it to compete with West; and it would do so without requiring a fundamental restructuring of the economy.[36]

At the Twenty-fourth Party Congress in March 1971, the new orientation was formally codified in a "Peace Program" linking increased trade and the slowing of the arms race to Soviet long-term economic growth. Moscow was now willing to seek "mutually advantageous" cooperation with the West, Brezhnev announced. Further economic growth would be hampered by continued high defense expenditures.[37] Moreover, Russia must keep up with the West in technology. The economy has assumed "completely new dimensions" since the 1930s. The critical challenge was thus "organically to unite the achievements of the scientific-technological revolution with the advantages of the socialist system of economy."[38] In this regard, the expansion of foreign trade was "an important reserve for increasing the economic efficiency of the

34. Quoted in Parrott, *Politics and Technology*, 233–34.
35. Parrott, *Politics and Technology*, 291.
36. On Brezhnev's efforts to use trade to avoid large-scale internal reform, see Peter M. E. Volten, *Brezhnev's Peace Program* (Boulder: Westview, 1982), 85, 233; Robin Edmonds, *Soviet Foreign Policy: The Brezhnev Years* (Oxford: Oxford University Press, 1983), 85; Bruce W. Jentleson, *Pipeline Politics: The Complex Political Economy of East-West Energy Trade* (Ithaca: Cornell University Press, 1986), 136. This point should not be taken too far, however. As Parrott notes, Brezhnev did realize that *some* reform was necessary to secure the benefits of foreign technology. Parrott, "Soviet Foreign Policy, Internal Politics, and Trade with the West," in *Trade, Technology, and Soviet-American Relations*, ed. Bruce Parrott (Bloomington: Indiana University Press, 1985), 39–40.
37. Volten, *Brezhnev's Peace Program*, 64. On Soviet fears about being able to keep up in an extended arms race, given the West's technological superiority, see Parrott, *Politics and Technology*, 243; 197–201; Hoffman and Laird, *"Scientific-Technological Revolution"*, 119 and chap. 6; Raymond L. Garthoff, *Détente and Confrontation: American-Soviet Relations from Nixon to Reagan*, rev. ed. (Washington: Brookings, 1994), 115.
38. Quoted in Parrott, *Politics and Technology*, 249 (the phrase "organically to unite...of economy" was emphasized in the original text). See also Hoffman and Laird, *"Scientific-Technological Revolution"*, 74.

national economy." There was no doubt, he said, that greater trade would improve "all our industry."[39]

The Soviet need for Western trade, which became increasingly clear in the
talks leading up to the 1972 Moscow summit, gave Kissinger and Nixon the
opening they were looking for. Their objective was to build a "structure of
peace," a grand geopolitical deal offering the Soviets trade in return for more
accommodating Soviet behavior across the board (including an arms control
agreement, help in resolving Vietnam, and restrained Soviet policy in the third
world). For Kissinger, this linkage strategy involved both carrots and sticks.
Economic interchange would give the Soviets "incentives for...restraint,"
while U.S. strategic power and resolve would reiterate to Moscow the costs of
expansionism.[40] In short, the growing network of ties would give the Soviets a
"stake" in peace, making it "more conscious of what it would lose by a return
to confrontation."[41]

The new U.S. willingness to trade with Russia was signalled by a series of
deals and agreements in 1971 and 1972. In November 1971, a grain deal worth
$136 billion was worked out. Later that month, the secretary of commerce
facilitated the signing of $125 million in contracts between U.S. firms and the
Soviet Union. In February 1972, export licenses for truck manufacturing
equipment worth almost $400 million were approved.[42] While the Moscow
summit in May focused on the signing of the SALT treaty, the two sides also
announced that they would work actively to build their economic ties.[43] In
October 1972, a formal trade agreement was signed, promising the Soviets
Most Favored Nation status and the extension of extensive trade credits. Both
elements were very important to the Soviets: being short of hard currency,
they could not afford to buy American goods unless they could both sell Soviet products to the United States and secure the short-term credit needed to
expedite their purchases.

The impact of the new commercial spirit was felt quickly. Between October
1972 and May 1973, restrictions were removed on 477 of the 550 categories of

39. Quoted in Volten, *Brezhnev's Peace Program*, 66–67. See also Parrott, *Politics and Technology*, 248–49; Arbatov, *The System*, 206; Garthoff, *Détente and Confrontation*, 101; Jentleson, *Pipeline Politics*, 135.

40. Henry Kissinger, *White House Years* (Boston: Little, Brown, 1979), 1254–55; 152–53;
1203; 1254. See Garthoff, *Détente and Confrontation*, 33–34; 103–05; 346.

41. Kissinger's congressional testimony in 1975, cited in Garthoff, *Détente and Confrontation*, 33–34.

42. Richard W. Stevenson, *The Rise and Fall of Détente* (Urbana: University of Illinois Press,
1985), 155.

43. Jentleson, *Pipeline Politics,* 139.

products which were under export controls.[44] In March 1973, the first meeting of the Joint Commission on Scientific and Technical Cooperation was held. Also that month, a $202 million loan was extended by the Export-Import Bank to help the Soviets purchase industrial equipment. The U.S.-USSR Trade and Economic Council, made up of 300 American firms interested in doing business in the Soviet Union, opened its Moscow office. By June, Occidental Petroleum had signed a twenty-five-year deal worth $10 billion. In the eighteen months following the May 1972 summit, a plethora of contracts on energy equipment worth billions of dollars were worked out. American companies were now an integral part of Soviet plans to develop the vast Siberian oil and gas fields.[45] Overall, the trend was definitely upward: total Soviet trade with America grew from an annual average of $60–100 million in the 1960–70 period to $649 million in 1972 and then $1577 million in 1973.[46]

Even more significant for our purposes is the impact of the new relationship on Soviet expectations for the future. Kosygin had indicated in a speech in November 1971 that trade with the West had to be established on the basis of "long-term agreements" which "guarantee stable orders for [Soviet] industry," and that things were already moving in this direction.[47] The events of 1972 and the first half of 1973 solidified Soviet confidence in the U.S. Executive's commitment to stable and significant levels of future trade. Brezhnev wrote to Nixon in February 1973 expressing his confidence that their upcoming June summit in Washington would lead to even more agreements on trade and commerce, in addition to progress on arms control.[48] An internal Central Committee, report written upon Brezhnev's return, stated that the summit had provided "new prospects for the development of economic-trade relations between the Soviet Union and the United States on a long-term large-scale basis."[49] Soviet interest in such extensive long-term trade had been stressed by Brezhnev at his visits both in America and in West Germany, and was supported by analyses from Soviet academic and theoretical institutions.[50] In the April and December plenums of the Central Committee, Brezhnev secured

44. Michael Mastanduno, *Economic Containment: CoCom and the Politics of East-West Trade* (Ithaca: Cornell University Press, 1992), 147.

45. U.S. firms were essential, since they possessed the more advanced drilling and extraction technology then available. See Jentleson, *Pipeline Politics*, 139–141, 147.

46. See Mastanduno, *Economic Containment*, tables 4 and 5, pp.112 and 158.

47. Quoted in Herbert S. Levine, "Soviet Economic Development, Technological Transfer, and Foreign Policy," in *The Domestic Context of Soviet Foreign Policy*, ed. Seweryn Bialer (Boulder: Westview, 1981), 189–90. See also Volten, *Brezhnev's Peace Program*, 112.

48. Garthoff, *Détente and Confrontation*, 366–67.

49. Quoted in Garthoff from the now declassified July 1973 document, *Détente and Confrontation*, 389.

50. See ibid., 399.

general support for the promotion of East-West trade and its tie to economic revitalization.[51]

If anything, Brezhnev's expectations for future trade with the West during 1972–73 were, as Volten and Garthoff note, overly optimistic.[52] The Soviets were slow to wake up to the implications of Watergate for Nixon's ability to control domestic opposition to U.S.-Soviet trade (as I discuss below).[53] When the trade deal was signed in October, both sides committed to triple bilateral trade over next three years. Given that trade in 1972 had already reached $650 billion, this meant an anticipated jump to approximately $2 billion a year by 1975.[54] Yet the Soviet expectation—never, of course, realized—was for even more. A senior Soviet official with direct knowledge of U.S.-Soviet trade relations during this period has revealed that Soviet leaders "expected that annual trade with the United States would reach $10 billion by the end of the decade."[55]

By 1973, then, Brezhnev was staking the success of his revitalization program on the continuation of a stable U.S.-Soviet relationship. Détente had to be made "irreversible," he argued through that year; it was the key to solving outstanding Soviet domestic problems.[56] Brezhnev's minister of foreign trade noted in his annual report in December that Western trade allowed the Soviet Union to "make fuller and more rational use of its own resources" and to acquire goods "not produced in our country or whose production would cost more than it does to import them." Thus, he summarized, "foreign economic ties offer a more efficient solution to a number of problems arising in the course of economic construction."[57]

51. Ibid., 399; Volten, *Brezhnev's Peace Program*, 108–9.
52. Volten, *Brezhnev's Peace Program*, 112; Garthoff, *Détente and Confrontation*, 389.
53. The Kremlin simply couldn't understand how such an apparently minor domestic matter might bring down a president.
54. See Mastanduno, *Economic Containment*, 146, and table 5, 158. At the end of the June 1973 summit, the communiqué reiterated the gains in U.S.-Soviet economic relations, with both sides agreeing to shoot for $2–3 billion of trade over next three years. Stevenson, *Rise and Fall*, 161.
55. Garthoff's words, based on information given to him by this official, *Détente and Confrontation*, 102 n. 70.
56. Volten, *Brezhnev's Peace Program*, 108–9, 111, 234.
57. Quoted in Levine, "Soviet Economic Development," 190. A major internal study on foreign trade in 1974 concluded that trade "contributes greatly toward the development of the Soviet economy....[it] is becoming an increasingly powerful factor aiding in the successful resolution of economic and foreign economic problems facing our national economy" (quoted in Erik P. Hoffman and Robin F. Laird, *The Politics of Economic Modernization in the Soviet Union* [Ithaca: Cornell University Press, 1982], 17). This reinforced a 1972 analysis by G. M. Prokhorov that the socialist states must "use more fully the achievements of the STR [scientific-technological revolution]." "Foreign economic ties are becoming a basic factor in increasing the effectiveness of social production" (quoted in ibid., 99).

As I discuss shortly, growing domestic opposition to détente within the United States would ultimately destroy the prospects for significant future trade by January 1975. This led, as the theory would predict, to an abrupt shift toward a much more assertive Soviet foreign policy in the third world. During the period when Soviet expectations were still positive (1972–73), however, there was clear moderation in Moscow's behavior. As Kissinger had intended, the Soviets sacrificed their interests in the third world in order to secure the long-term benefits from U.S.-Soviet trade. The most obvious example of this is Soviet help in the ending of the Vietnam war. To the Americans' surprise, the Soviets went ahead with the Moscow summit in May 1972 at a time of renewed bombings against Hanoi and the American mining of the Haiphong harbor, despite the impact on the Soviet reputation throughout the southern hemisphere.[58] Moscow also pushed North Vietnam to make concessions at the bargaining table that ultimately led to the Paris accords in January 1973. Moreover, they advised Hanoi not to attempt a military attack on the south; the subsequent termination of Soviet military supplies forced North Vietnam to postpone its planned attack.[59]

The May 1972 summit had a direct effect on Soviet influence in the Middle East. In July, Anwar Sadat expelled the 20,000 Soviet military advisors and technicians stationed in Egypt, and reduced Soviet use of his military facilities. He was frustrated with the level of Soviet military and diplomatic support, and the summit only reinforced his belief that Moscow was unwilling to help him change an unacceptable status quo.[60] The Soviets also did little to counter the new U.S. push to exert more influence in the Middle East, including the aiding of Kurdish rebels in Iraq and the reestablishment of diplomatic relations with North Yemen in July 1972. Pronouncements of support for national liberation movements continued, mainly to deflect the Chinese charge that Moscow had gone soft on imperialism. Yet there was a noticeable toning down of the rhetoric and a lack of concrete action.[61]

The most dramatic example of the change in Soviet behavior due to positive trade expectations came in 1973 with regard to the brewing Israeli-Egyptian conflict. For some, the superpower crisis ignited by the Yom Kippur war in October suggests that détente had not moderated Soviet behavior (and indeed Nixon's critics used this crisis as an example of the failure of détente). Yet a

58. Indeed, many third-world nationalist and revolutionary leaders saw the Moscow summit as a sell-out of international proletarianism, a move to a superpower condominium.

59. Parrott, "Soviet Foreign Policy," 38.

60. Anwar el-Sadat, *In Search of Identity: An Autobiography* (New York: Harper and Row, 1978), 228–31; Garthoff, *Détente and Confrontation*, 355–56.

61. Garthoff, *Détente and Confrontation*, 357–58.

careful analysis of the facts leads to the opposite conclusion. The Soviets not only did not want a Middle East war and acted to prevent it; they also sought diligently to end it quickly, before too much damage to détente was done. Indeed, Kissinger admits that he sought to exploit Moscow's evident caution in order to increase U.S. influence in the region. In sum, the Middle East crisis was provoked by independent Egyptian and Syrian decisions, and despite Soviet efforts to dissuade these states from war.[62] Once underway, the economic incentives embedded in détente significantly moderated Soviet behavior—much to the delight of Kissinger and the Nixon administration.

According to the agreement on Basic Principles from May 1972, the superpowers were supposed to work together to prevent situations from arising that might lead to military confrontation. The agreement on the Prevention of Nuclear War signed at the June 1973 summit went further, emphasizing the importance of consultations should relations between the superpowers or between third parties involve the risk of nuclear conflict.[63] By the spring of 1973, it was becoming clear to Brezhnev that despite his disapproval, Egypt and Syria were gearing up for war against Israel. Brezhnev initiated a three-hour discussion of the Middle East at the June summit, and in highly emotional terms, warned Nixon that unless America and Russia worked together on a Middle East settlement, he "could not guarantee that war would not resume."[64] Throughout the summit Brezhnev made repeated pleas to Nixon to deal with the Middle East situation. Nixon would only give vague promises to give more consideration to the matter over the next year.[65] In late September, Foreign Minister Andrei Gromyko visited Nixon in the White House to warn again of the real danger of conflagration in the region. Once again the American leadership shrugged it off.

American reluctance to act had little to do with U.S. discounting of the likelihood of war given Israeli military superiority, as Kissinger implies.[66] Back in May, during Kissinger's visit to Moscow, Brezhnev had warned that he was having difficulty restraining the Arab leaders and that war was a distinct possibility. Kissinger already knew of Egypt's military maneuvers and the existence of an Egyptian war plan. On his return to Washington, he told his NSC staff to

62. Ironically, superpower détente may have inadvertently pushed Sadat into war. He was concerned that if U.S.-Soviet cooperation progressed any further, he might not be able to secure their help in getting the Israelis out of the Sinai. See ibid..

63. Ibid., 327, 376–77.

64. Richard Nixon, *RN: The Memoirs of Richard Nixon* (New York: Grosset and Dunlap, 1978), 884–86.

65. Garthoff, *Détente and Confrontation*, 408–9.

66. See Kissinger, *Years of Upheaval* (Boston: Little, Brown, 1982), 296–99, 463–64.

prepare a contingency plan for Arab-Israeli hostilities.[67] In late September and early October, Kissinger acknowledges that he learned of the concentration of Arab forces and their general attack plans, although he claims that he discounted them as bluffs.[68] It seems clear, however, that while Kissinger might have thought war was unlikely, he also believed that should it occur it would be to the evident benefit of the American side, and to the detriment of Soviet interests. In short, there was no need to work with Moscow to avoid a Middle East war, because either way—war or no war—the Americans could increase their relative influence at the Soviets' expense.

Kissinger quite candidly states that in June, as Brezhnev pleaded for joint action, the Nixon administration had little interest in a deal just to uphold the principles of détente: "We were planning a major diplomatic initiative after Israel's elections in late October and were in the meantime stalling." In short, "We were not willing to pay for détente in the coin of our geopolitical position."[69] Once the war got underway on 6 October, Kissinger saw this as a perfect opportunity to reduce Soviet influence in the Middle East as he raised America's. The Soviets' desperate need for the material benefits of détente would aid him in his task. As he puts it, he and Nixon were hardly the duped victims of a Soviet plan to use détente to expand in the Middle East via Arab proxies. Rather, "the opposite was true; our policy to reduce and where possible to eliminate Soviet influence in the Middle East was in fact making progress under the cover of détente." Without détente, Kissinger notes, the Soviets would have been far more willing to intervene forcefully in a crisis not of their making. As it was, détente operated as "a tranquilizer for Moscow as we sought to draw the Middle East into closer relations with us at the Soviets' expense."[70]

Evidence from the Soviet side supports Kissinger's view that Soviet fear of losing the benefits of détente restrained its policy in the Middle East. For the six months leading up to the war, Moscow continually advised Cairo and Damascus, by both public and private means, to solve the situation through

---

67. Garthoff, *Détente and Confrontation*, 408. This information comes from Garthoff's interview with William Quandt, a senior member of the NSC staff at the time (ibid., n. 17).

68. Kissinger, *Years of Upheaval*, 463–65.

69. Kissinger, *Years of Upheaval*, 296, 299. This phrase is subtly deceptive, since it implies that the U.S. leadership was worried about hurting America's geopolitical position vis-à-vis the status quo by working with the Soviets, when in fact it was worried about *not being able to gain* from the exploitation of Soviet caution.

70. Ibid., 594. This was not just his retrospective view. At the end of October, Kissinger received an analysis by an associate which noted that Brezhnev's conciliatory posture during the crisis was partly due to American firmness, and partly the result of "Brezhnev's own stake in his détente policy" (ibid, 600). See also Garthoff, *Détente and Confrontation*, 409–20, 434–41.

peaceful means only. Sadat has revealed that four times before the war, Brezhnev warned him to pursue peaceful not military means.[71] According to insider Victor Israelyan, who provides the most objective account of Soviet decision making during October, Brezhnev and the Politburo were very unhappy that their efforts had failed to prevent the war. The Soviet leadership was very worried that the war would undermine détente. A few hours after Syria and Egypt had launched their attack, the Politburo held its first crisis session. Brezhnev told the group that "the Arab action would whip up international tensions and complicate the Soviet Union's relations with the West, especially with the United States." Gromyko told Israelyan after the meeting that "negotiations between Brezhnev and President Nixon...had created a good foundation for a political solution to the Middle East problem" and a war there would "ruin these chances."[72]

Brezhnev's behavior reflected these concerns. In his first message to Sadat just after the war began, the Soviet leader was blunt. Arab leaders were being "imprudent" in acting against Soviet advice, he wrote; they were "interfer[ing] in the process of the development of political cooperation between the USSR and the USA."[73] Moscow asked Syria and Egypt to agree to an immediate cease-fire. While Assad in Damascus was apparently on board, Sadat rejected the idea: his forces were seeing initial success on the battlefield, and he saw little reason to stop so soon. The Soviet leadership found itself trapped between its desire to end the fighting—which would minimize the risks to détente while preserving a role for the Moscow in the subsequent negotiations—and its fear of abandoning Sadat, which would hurt its reputation in the Middle East. Brezhnev decided to supply the Arabs with arms during the war, and to support them publicly. Behind the scenes, however, the Soviets were actively pressing for a cease-fire and a negotiated settlement throughout the month of October.[74]

While the diplomatic give-and-take during October is complex, and cannot be covered here, one point must be stressed. By Kissinger's own account, the U.S. strategy was to delay a cease-fire, not only to give the Israelis time to counterattack, but to enhance America's diplomatic role in the area. "From the first," he notes, "I was convinced that we were in a good position to dominate events." Given its strength, Israel would likely win in the end, while moderate

71. Garthoff, *Détente and Confrontation*, 407.
72. Israelyan, *Inside the Kremlin During the Yom Kippur War* (University Park: Pennsylvania State University Press, 1995), 31, 2.
73. Quoted in Richard Ned Lebow and Janice Gross Stein, *We All Lost the Cold War* (Princeton: Princeton University Press, 1994), 201.
74. See Israelyan, *Inside the Kremlin*, passim; Garthoff, *Détente and Confrontation*, chap. 11.

Arab states were fearful of an Egyptian-Syrian victory achieved by Soviet arms. Moreover, Kissinger believed that he could "induce Soviet caution by threatening the end of détente while assembling the means for a confrontation should diplomacy fail." Thus, "from the outset, I was determined to use the war to start a peace process," one that Washington would control.[75]

Kissinger knew that Moscow had not colluded with the Arab states to initiated war, and that in fact the Soviets were reluctant to support Arab forces with either arms or diplomacy.[76] He thus used the crisis to bring about a solution that best suited U.S. interests. Even Kissinger's move on 25 October, placing U.S. forces on temporary nuclear alert (DEFCON 3), had little to do with fear of a superpower clash and almost everything to do with reducing the Soviet role in the final crisis settlement. With the Egyptian army on the ropes, Brezhnev had warned that he might send Soviet forces to Egypt unilaterally should Washington reject his idea of a joint U.S.-Soviet peacekeeping force to enforce a cease-fire. Kissinger makes his reasons for his subsequent actions clear. If Washington accepted a joint role with the Russians, it would "legitimize their role in the area," while reestablishing a Soviet military presence in Egypt which the Americans had "worked years to reduce." Moreover, the appearance of a U.S.-Soviet condominium would undermine four years of U.S. diplomatic effort; "the Soviet Union and its radical allies would emerge as the dominant factor in the Middle East."[77]

The above analysis shows the strong role of détente on Soviet behavior during the 1973 Middle East crisis. The Soviet leadership tried to prevent the outbreak of war, did much to warn the United States of the coming conflict, and sought to achieve a negotiated solution that would stabilize the status quo.[78] No doubt Moscow was acting solely to protect Soviet interests; given

75. Kissinger, *Years of Upheaval*, 467–68. See also Garthoff, *Détente and Confrontation*; Lebow and Stein, *We all Lost*, 210.

76. Kissinger, *Years of Upheaval*, 469.

77. Kissinger, *Years of Upheaval*, 579, 584; see also Garthoff, *Détente and Confrontation*, 422–23. A few days earlier, Nixon and Brezhnev had reached a tentative agreement to press their allies to accept a just settlement. Kissinger successfully resisted implementation of the compromise. For him, the U.S. goal was "to reduce the Soviet role in the negotiations that would follow the cease-fire." Thus a deal at that stage would allow Moscow to "receive credit with the Arabs for having forced us into a course we had heretofore avoided. Our leverage on the Arab states would disappear" (Kissinger, *Years of Upheaval*, 551; and Lebow and Stein, *We All Lost*, 210–11). Recently declassified documents support Kissinger's recollections. At the height of the crisis on 25 October, Kissinger acknowledged to the Chinese ambassador that the principle U.S. objective was "to keep the Soviet military presence out of the Middle East and to reduce Soviet political influence as much as possible" (William Burr, ed. *The Kissinger Transcripts: The Top-secret Talks with Beijing and Moscow* [New York: New Press, 1998], 155).

78. Kissinger would admit to his colleagues in a private meeting on 18 March 1974 that recent Soviet behavior had been "fairly reasonable all across the board....Even in the Middle

Arab military weakness, avoiding war or minimizing its effects was the rational strategy. The key point remains, however: the 1973 crisis reflects not the failure of détente to constrain Soviet "adventurism," but its success. Without the carrot of increased expected U.S.-Soviet trade, Moscow would have been more likely to have intervened actively in the Arab-Israeli dispute, and the probability of a dangerous superpower clash would have been that much greater. In the end, it is the U.S. leadership that must bear most of the blame for the October crisis, since it was Nixon and Kissinger who, out of a desire for geopolitical gain, did so little to avert or moderate the conflict.

While positive expectations for future trade were moderating Soviet behavior during the 1972–73 period, trouble was brewing within the United States. Liberal and conservative critics of Nixon's presidency found a common ground on which to oppose his foreign policy: they would attack it as insensitive to human rights, particularly the Jewish emigration problem. In October 1972, Senator Jackson began his campaign for an amendment linking most-favored-nation status to significant increases in Jewish emigration.[79] In March 1973 he formally introduced his amendment as part of the Trade Reform Act of 1973; a similar amendment was introduced in the House by Representative Vanik. Through 1973, the Jackson-Vanik Amendment slowly gathered momentum as the Nixon administration sank into the swamp of Watergate. In December, a month after the resolution of the Middle East crisis, the House passed a bill containing the Jackson-Vanik Amendment. This was the first significant blow to the prospects for future trade, although the domestic battle was not yet over.

During the next year, the debate was taken up in the senate. Added to the complications was a further amendment introduced by Senator Stevenson in June 1974, limiting credits offered to Russia by the federal Export-Import Bank to $300 million over four years. The Stevenson amendment was significant, since the Soviets were counting on generous U.S. credits for the billions of dollars of purchases they expected to make. In particular, Moscow needed to purchase equipment to develop the vast Siberian oil and gas reserves.[80] In the short term, MFN was not enough, since the Soviets did not have enough goods

---

East where our political strategy put them in an awful bind, they haven't really tried to screw us" (Burr, *Kissinger Transcripts*, 225).

79. On Jackson's efforts over the next three years, see esp. Garthoff, *Détente and Confrontation*; Paula Stern, *Water's Edge: Domestic Politics and the Making of American Foreign Policy* (Westport: Greenwood, 1979); Mike Bowker and Phil Williams, *Superpower Détente: A Reappraisal* (London: Royal Institute of International Affairs, 1988).

80. Once it was developed, Nixon and the Soviets had agreed that some of the oil and gas would be sold to the United States (this would ease U.S. dependence on OPEC countries). See Jentleson, *Pipeline Politics*, 136–42.

to sell. The two large consortiums established for energy exploration were thus seeking some $3 billion in credits from the Eximbank to get the projects up and running.[81]

A clear indication of the Soviet desire to save the trade agreement is their often frantic efforts to satisfy congressional critics at a price that would not greatly damage Russian global reputation. Jackson's initial efforts had been ostensibly provoked by an exit tax Brezhnev had slapped on Jewish emigrants in August 1972; the Soviets had agreed to a significant increase in emigration at the May summit, but felt that emigrants should compensate the government for their free education. In April 1973, just as Jackson was introducing his amendment, Brezhnev announced that the tax was the result of a bureaucratic foul-up and would be rescinded.

The problem, however, as it soon became clear, was that Jackson was using the emigration question for his own domestic purposes. As result of the 1972 agreements, Jewish emigration rose from 400 in 1968 to almost 35,000 in 1973.[82] Yet for Jackson this was not sufficient. In September 1974, he publicly indicated that he sought 75,000 per year, and would press for at least 60,000. The Soviets made it known through the back channels that they might indeed go as high as 55,000 to 60,000, as long as the deal was kept private.[83] Jackson, however, as Kissinger laments, "wanted an issue, not a solution."[84] On 18 October 1974, just after Jackson and Vanik signed letters at the White House apparently resolving the dispute, Jackson used the occasion to trumpet his victory, arguing that the Soviets had made a "complete turn around" to placate his demands.[85] The Soviets were outraged at this public humiliation. The trade bill with the Jackson-Vanik amendment was passed on 13 December. It included the Byrd amendment which restricted trade credits to an even greater extent than the Stevenson amendment.[86] On 3 January, President Ford reluctantly signed the Trade Reform Act into law. Ten days later, the Soviets indicated that the 1972 trade treaty was now null and void.

Thus by January 1975, as Garthoff summarizes, "the heart of the official American-Soviet trade component of détente had collapsed."[87] In terms of the

81. Jentleson, *Pipeline Politics*, 136–46.

82. Kissinger, *Years of Upheaval*, 249.

83. Gerald R. Ford, *A Time to Heal: The Autobiography of Gerald Ford* (New York: Harper and Row, 1979), 138–39; Garthoff, *Détente and Confrontation*, 506; Jentleson, *Pipeline Politics*, 143.

84. Kissinger's phrase, *Years of Upheaval*, 996.

85. Garthoff, *Détente and Confrontation*, 509.

86. It placed a $300 million ceiling on credits from all federal agencies, including the Eximbank and the Commodity Credit Corporation.

87. Garthoff, *Détente and Confrontation*, 512–13; Mastanduno, *Economic Containment*, 150.

logic of the model discussed earlier, this domestic interference in the Nixon-Kissinger plan represented an exogenous blow to Soviet trade expectations. Moscow now understood that there was little it could do, short of appearing to capitulate to ever increasing U.S. demands, to save the 1972 trade treaty. Given the evident weakness of the U.S. Executive in the wake of Watergate, by December 1974 it was clear that further negotiations would serve no purpose.[88]

What is significant is how quickly Soviet behavior on the periphery moved back toward the previous policy of "adventurism." As noted, the Soviets had restrained North Vietnam during 1972–73. In December 1974, however, Moscow reinstated weapons shipments to Hanoi. Four months later, the North launched its decisive assault on the South, undoubtedly with at least the tacit approval of Moscow. In 1973–74, the Soviets had only provided the barest of aid to leftist forces in Angola, and only after U.S. aid to antileftist groups was stepped up. This restraint vanished in 1975, when Soviet support for Angolan leftists increased dramatically.[89] By the late 1970s, Moscow had made significant inroads in Somalia and then Ethiopia and Nicaragua. Then in 1979, with the invasion of Afghanistan, Russian forces for the first time in the cold war moved into a country not formally a part of the Soviet sphere.

While the internal documents on Politburo decision making for the 1975–79 period are still sketchy,[90] it is surely no coincidence that Soviet behavior changed so suddenly after the failure of the trade treaty. As Parrott notes, "Soviet willingness to accept implicit linkages between trade and Soviet political behavior depended on how the prospective economic benefits fitted into a larger balance of political opportunities and risks....By 1975, however, the balance of benefits and costs had shifted."[91] In sum, the end of the trade treaty represents a major reason for the collapse of détente and a return to a more conflictual superpower relationship.[92] Trade expectations theory provides a

---

88. Kissinger's failure to prevent the congressional legislation, after having explicitly promised Brezhnev in late 1974 that he would do so, could only have underscored this weakness. See Burr, *Kissinger Transcripts*, 329–42, on the Kissinger-Brezhnev talks of 24 October, which focused on U.S. domestic opposition to the trade treaty.

89. Garthoff, *Détente and Confrontation*, chap. 15.

90. See *Cold War in International History Bulletin*, issues 8–9 (winter 1996–97), for some preliminary documents.

91. Parrott, "Soviet Foreign Policy," 38–39. Jackson-Vanik upset Brezhnev's fragile domestic coalition in favor of peaceful relations with the United States. After 1974, opponents to détente and economic interdependence (the "traditionalists") gained the upper hand. Parrott, *Politics and Technology*, 258–65; Volten, *Brezhnev's Peace Program*, 116–30, 238.

92. For scholars agreeing with this view, see Garthoff, *Détente and Confrontation*, 506 and passim; Jentleson, *Pipeline Politics*, chap. 5; Alexander L. George, "Détente: The Search for a Constructive Relationship," in *Managing the U.S.-Soviet Rivalry*, ed. Alexander L. George (Boulder: Westview, 1983), 22. Even Adam Ulam, an individual more inclined to blame aggressive Soviet intentions for the failure of détente, notes that with the undermining of the trade treaty, détente was not given chance, and that by 1975 Soviet behavior was more asser-

simple but powerful explanation for this. Without the anticipation of a stream of increasing trade benefits accruing from U.S.-Soviet cooperation, the Soviets no longer had the incentive to moderate their actions in the third world, as they had in 1972–73. While this explanation draws from liberal theory, note that it was less the current trade that constrained Soviet policy, and more the expectation of high future trade. This reinforces the value of taking a dynamic approach to great-power decision making within enduring rivalries.

ECONOMIC RELATIONS AND THE END OF THE COLD WAR

FOR MANY, the end of the cold war is rooted in one fundamental fact: the ascendancy of Mikhail Gorbachev and his new liberal vision for Soviet society and its place in the world. By this account, Gorbachev's belief that his country had to become an open and democratic society translated into a desire to integrate Russia into the Western liberal system, thereby ending nearly half a century of mistrust and tension. This section shows that to the extent that this interpretation emphasizes ideational epiphany over self-interested material calculation, it is inadequate.[93] Gorbachev's reforms, at least for the first two years, were not that new. They were an extension of the reform plan set down during the brief tenure of his mentor Yuri Andropov from late 1982 to early 1984. This plan in turn was based the same goal which drove the Kremlin toward reform and trade in the late 1960s, namely, the need to overcome economic and technological stagnation. Gorbachev's "new thinking" became progressively more radical only after 1986; that is, only after the failure of his initial reforms. Even here, however, his actions were largely materially driven: only by democratization within and greater peace and economic interdepend-

---

tive (*Dangerous Relations: The Soviet Union in World Politics, 1970–1982* [New York: Oxford University Press, 1983], 93–94, 134–35).

93. Putting particular stress on the former are constructivist scholars. See Alexander Wendt, "Anarchy is What States Make of It," *International Organization* 46, no. 2 (spring 1992): 391–425; Thomas Risse-Kappen, "Ideas Do not Float Freely; Transnational Coalitions, Domestic Structures, and the End of the Cold War," *International Organization* 48, no. 2 (spring 1994): 185–214; Rey Koslowski and Friedrich V. Kratochwil, "Understanding Change in International Politics: The Soviet Empire's Demise and the International System," *International Organization*, 48, no. 2 (spring 1994): 215–47. Robert G. Herman, "Identity, Norms, and National Security: The Soviet Foreign Policy Revolution and the End of the Cold War," in *The Culture of National Security*, ed. Peter J. Katzenstein (New York: Columbia University Press, 1996), 271–316. For a decisive riposte, see Stephen Brooks and William Wohlforth, "Why Identities Change: Material Forces, Identity Transformation, and the End of the Cold War" (paper delivered at the annual convention of the American Political Science Association, Boston, 3–6 September 1998). See also Robert Jervis, "Perception, Misperception, and the End of the Cold War," in *Witnesses to the End of the Cold War*, ed. William C. Wohlforth (Baltimore: Johns Hopkins University Press, 1996), 224–25.

ence without did he believe that his country could pull itself out of decline. Without radical change, the USSR could not remain a superpower into the twenty-first century. The growing expectation that America—and after U.S. approval, Europe—would offer the kind of trade and credits needed to further his reforms was an integral part of Gorbachev's larger strategy for peace.

While estimates vary, all accounts agree on one thing: by the late 1970s– early 1980s, the Soviet economy was in a deep crisis. Annual GNP growth rates which had been around ten per cent in the 1950s, and five per cent in the 1960s, were now at best zero to two per cent (and this of course meant relative decline versus the West). Productivity gains were stagnant, the quality of Soviet products far below that of the West, and inefficient factories were using up Soviet energy resources at rates many times greater than comparable Western figures.[94] Soviet leaders were not unaware of problem. Before he came to power, and when still head of the KBG, Andropov established a secret department within the KGB to study the economic problem. In the words of the senior official in charge of shaping the department, "Andropov wanted to attract the attention of the ruling circles to the coming economic catastrophe."[95] Soon after he assumed in power in late 1982, Andropov announced that economic reform was now the "highest priority;" the society must overcome the "inertia" caused by "adherence to old ways." It was therefore critical to improve "the entire area of economic management."[96]

A serious debate on the country's economic future began in April 1983. Soon after, a secret study was prepared by the economic institute of the Soviet Academy of Sciences in Novosibirsk. The "Novosibirsk Report" represented a follow-up to Aganbegyan's report in 1965 which had helped launch the previous round of reforms (and was written by a student of Aganbegyan). The existing centralized system, it argued, was "incredibly compromised and outdated," and was the primary cause of Soviet decline. Overall, it had to be made less rigid and complex, and market mechanisms were needed.[97] Andropov quickly followed up on its implications. In a speech at the June ideological ple-

94. See Aslund, *Gorbachev's Struggle*, 15; Dusko Doder, *Shadows and Whispers: Power Politics Inside the Kremlin From Brezhnev to Gorbachev* (Harsmondsworth: Penguin, 1986), 177–78; Mikhail Gorbachev, *Perestroika* (New York: Harper and Row, 1987), 18–19; Brooks and Wohlforth, "Why Identities Change;" Michael Ellman and Vladimir Kontorovich, eds., *The Disintegration of the Soviet Economic System* (London: Routledge, 1992).

95. Quoted in Robert G. Kaiser, *Why Gorbachev Happened* (New York: Simon and Schuster, 1991), 57, 59.

96. Doder, *Shadows and Whispers*, 111.

97. Doder, *Shadows and Whispers*, 186–87, 169–70; Walker, *Waking Giant*, 47–48; Michael Dobbs, *Down with Big Brother: The Fall of the Soviet Empire* (New York: Vintage, 1996), 88–89. A large number of similar studies on Soviet economic problems were undertaken during 1983—according to Gorbachev, over hundred. See Don Oberdorfer, *The Turn: From Cold War to a New Era* (New York: Poseidon, 1991), 63.

num, he argued that productivity had to be improved through greater incentives to managers and a focus on technological progress. In an August meeting of the Central Committee, he stated that the country was entering a new stage, one where increased domestic requirements "dictate the need" for reforms.[98]

Given Andropov's poor health, his protegé Gorbachev was primarily responsible for implementing the reforms. Gorbachev was fully supportive of Andropov's efforts, which at this stage were modest, focused primarily on greater "discipline" in the work place (including an end to alcoholism). Gorbachev was well of the problem of relative economic stagnation versus the rest of the world. By 1982–83, as he recounts, he understood that

> time was running out. Under the impact of achievements in science and technology, immense transformations were taking place in the world, involving production, communications, and everyday life. These processes required fundamental changes.

Yet while other states were rising to the challenge, the Soviet system "spurned innovation and moved against the general tide of progress."[99]

Gorbachev's concern with the scientific-technological revolution was as acute as Kosygin's had been in the 1960s. The leadership was aware by the early 1980s, he notes, that the country was losing "one position after another" in the technological race. Moreover, "the gap in the efficiency of production, quality of products, scientific and technological development, the production of advanced technology...began to widen, and not to our advantage."[100] That Gorbachev's primary obsession was the maintenance of the Soviet Union's position as a superpower is showed by his speech at an elite conference of economic managers, scientists, and party officials in December 1984, during the waning days of Chernenko's rule. In a speech that laid out his strategy for economic reform, he argued bluntly that

> We have to achieve a breakthrough. Only an intensive and highly developed economy can ensure the strengthening of the country's position on the world scene and enable it to enter the next millennium in a manner befitting a great and prosperous country....There is no alternative.[101]

98. Doder, *Shadows and Whispers*, 182, 185.

99. Gorbachev, *Memoirs* (New York: Doubleday, 1996), 135. According to a high-ranking Central Committee staff member, a particular worry at this time was Japan, who was seen to be in "the forefront of the Third Industrial Revolution" (quoted in Oberdorfer, *The Turn*, 215).

100. Gorbachev, *Perestroika*, 18–19. This widening gap apparently first became obvious to him as a result of his trips to the west in the early 1980s. Gorbachev, *Memoirs*, 102–3.

101. Quoted in Walker, *Waking Giant*, 58–59. See also Archie Brown, *The Gorbachev Factor* (Oxford: Oxford University Press, 1997), 79–81; Doder, *Shadows and Whispers*, 246; Aslund,

Priority, he continued, must be given to "fundamentally new, truly revolutionary scientific and technological solutions capable of increasing labor productivity many times over."[102]

Gorbachev's focus on technology by this time was not an accident. In the early summer of 1984, he had been put in charge of a taskforce to prepare a report on science and technology for a Central Committee plenum set for April 1985. Because of Chernenko's illness, and then death in March 1985, the plenum session on science and technology was never held. Gorbachev, however, used his first weeks in power to reiterate his strategy for revitalizing the Soviet economy. In his first address to his Politburo colleagues on 11 March, he spoke of the need for "more [economic] dynamism;" progress was only possible by shifting to "intensive development, rapidly achiev[ing] leading positions in science and technology, and [building] a world-class level of labor productivity."[103] Upon assuming power, he was handed a top secret KGB report detailing the bankruptcy of the old system. The report also noted that unless the country began fundamental reform, "the Soviet Union could not continue as a superpower into the twenty-first century."[104]

Gorbachev could see the geopolitical implications of Soviet decline. In an April Politburo session, Gorbachev listed the many examples of Soviet backwardness. "If we don't break this trend," he said, "then by the end of the century we will be transformed into a Third World country."[105] In late February 1986, Gorbachev told the Twenty-Seventh Party Congress that one could not rule out significant growth in the capitalist sphere. The "scientific and technical trends" would

[allow] capitalism to sustain its economic, military, political and strategic position, and in some cases, even to achieve possible social revenge, the recovery of what had been lost before.[106]

To revitalize the economy and thereby ensure Soviet long-term security, Gorbachev had three priorities. First, he had to end the arms race in order to redirect spending away from guns and toward butter. Economic reform could

---

Gorbachev's Struggle, 13; Michael MccGwire, *Perestroika and Soviet National Security* (Washington: Brookings, 1991), 175.

102. Kaiser, *Why Gorbachev Happened*, 76.

103. Fred Coleman, *The Decline and the Fall of the Soviet Empire* (New York: St. Martin's Griffin, 1996), 222 from the declassified record; and Gorbachev, *Memoirs*, 167.

104. Coleman's summary of the document, based on discussions with top Gorbachev advisor Georgi Shakhnazarov, in Coleman, *Decline and Fall*, 224. Gorbachev was handed a similar report at this time by advisor Georgi Arbatov. See Arbatov, *The System*, 322.

105. Quoted in Dobbs, *Big Brother*, 131 (this phrase was censored from the official transcript given to the Soviet press).

106. Quoted in Walker, *Waking Giant*, 51.

not succeed if the Soviet Union continued to devote 20 per cent of its GNP to the military.[107] Second, he needed to stop the American effort to build a space-based missile defense system. This system, even if not successful, would force Moscow to squander precious investment capital needed for improved economic productivity; and if it did work, it could undermine the very foundation of deterrence, and at the very least spark a new arms race.[108] Third, and increasingly important as his reforms progressed, Gorbachev had to convince the United States to relax restrictions on trade and economic credits. Like Brezhnev, Gorbachev understood that integral to overcoming the technological gap was access to superior Western products and information. Like Brezhnev, Gorbachev knew that the more Soviet economy continued to decline, the greater was the Soviet need for American goods.

In terms of domestic reforms, Gorbachev initially felt that simply extending the changes begun under Andropov and acting with more intensity would do the trick. He acknowledges that in preparing for the Twenty-seventh Party Congress of February–March 1986, "what we had in mind was not a revolution but a specific improvement of the system, which we then believed was possible." For some time, he notes, he and his associates assumed that they could rely on "the 'advantages of Socialism'," namely, better central planning in the mobilization of resources and the encouraging of a "more active attitude" from the workers. In retrospect, Gorbachev states, he should have moved quickly to total structural reform. Yet "we felt that we could fix things...by the old methods," that revitalization was possible "within the framework of the existing system." He continued in this belief until early 1988.[109] Thus contrary to those scholars who see Gorbachev as a democratic liberal held back by the old guard, Gorbachev was simply a reformist Soviet leader seeking to free socialism from existing "distortions."[110] Indeed, Gor-

---

107. See docs. nos. 19, 25, 32, 40, and 52 from *Understanding the End of the Cold War: The Reagan/Gorbachev Years*, Briefing Book prepared by the National Security Archive for an oral history conference, Brown University, May 7–10 1998 (I thank Bill Wohlforth for alerting me to these documents); Gorbachev, *Memoirs*, 215, 401; Anatoly Dobrynin, *In Confidence: Moscow's Ambassador to America's Six Cold War Presidents* (New York: Random House, 1995), 570; Jack F. Matlock, *Autopsy of an Empire* (New York: Random House, 1995), 77, 139–40; Allen Lynch, *Gorbachev's International Outlook: Intellectual Origins and Political Consequences* (New York: Institute for East-West Security Studies, 1989), chap. 4.

108. On Gorbachev's obsession with countering the U.S. Strategic Defense Initiative ("Star Wars"), see Gorbachev, *Memoirs*, 407, 417–18, 455; George P. Schultz, *Turmoil and Triumph: My Years as Secretary of State* (New York: Scribner's, 1993), 477–79, 577, 592, 768–69.

109. Gorbachev, *Memoirs*, 217–18, 250; Dobbs, *Big Brother*, 125 (quoting Gorbachev's recollection in 1993). See also Politburo notes in docs. nos. 44 and 52 in Brown University, *Understanding the End of the Cold War*, and Brooks and Wohlforth, "Why Identities Change," 28–29, on Gorbachev's initial desire to increase Soviet competitiveness in the superpower struggle through only moderate tinkering with the existing Soviet system.

110. Gorbachev, *Memoirs*, 250.

bachev candidly acknowledges that his model was not the Western system, but Lenin's New Economic Policy of the 1920s.[111] It is for these reasons that Gorbachev initially had the support of the old guard; as he kept reminding them, there was no alternative to moving beyond the Brezhnevian system.[112]

This is not to suggest that Gorbachev did not have a new vision on the means to solving his society's problems. In May 1986, three months after laying out his plans for economic reform to the Twenty-Seventh Congress, he gave a major speech to six hundred foreign aid and trade officials from the Foreign Ministry. Soviet diplomacy "must contribute to the domestic development of the country," he argued. The primary goal of foreign policy was therefore to "create the best possible external conditions" for internal growth.[113] While Gorbachev's actions indicate that ending the arms race was the key first step in this strategy, securing trade was also critical. In his first meeting with Secretary of State George Schultz and Vice-President George Bush just after assuming power, Gorbachev lamented the low level of "contacts" between the two countries. "Technology can be transferred only with the express approval of the president. Trade is not permitted."[114] Two months later, in May 1985, Gorbachev met with U.S. secretary of commerce Balridge to stress that it was "high time" to improve U.S.-Soviet cooperation. In December, one month after the Geneva summit, he met with Balridge again, and spoke on the need for increased bilateral trade.[115]

The Soviets had some reason to believe the Americans were open to greater commerce. In July 1983, Reagan had sent a personal letter to Andropov expressing hope for greater discussion on arms control and expanded trade; five months earlier, Reagan had signaled that he believed the Jackson-Vanik amendment was wrong and should be revoked.[116] Beginning in late 1984, the Commerce Department had started to relax some intra-Western export controls, an important initial sign since much of the technology desired by the Soviets was being garnered through Western European and Japanese connections. While Gorbachev's plea in December 1985 did not lead to normalized

111. Gorbachev, *Perestroika*, 25; Gorbachev, *Memoirs*, 148.
112. Coleman, *Decline and Fall*, 223; Gorbachev, *Memoirs*, 219; Kaiser, *Why Gorbachev Happened*, 83; Dobbs, *Big Brother*, 131.
113. Quoted in Oberdorfer, *The Turn*, 159–62.
114. Quoted in Schultz, *Turmoil and Triumph*, 530.
115. Raymond L. Garthoff, *The Great Transition: American-Soviet Relations and the End of the Cold War* (Washington, D.C.: Brookings, 1994), 218, 249.
116. Dobrynin, *In Confidence*, 531, 518.

trade relations, a private loan of $400 million by four American banks was al-
lowed, the first since Afghanistan.[117]

Gorbachev, however, knew that much more was needed. In a statement of
"fundamental principles" coming out of the Twenty-seventh Congress, the
first in the economic sphere was the ending of "all forms of [trade] discrimination," including the "renunciation of the [Western] policy of economic blockades and sanctions."[118] In his book *Perestroika*, released in the second half of
1987, Gorbachev offered a "message to the leadership of the Western powers": "don't be scared by perestroika [restructuring]...but rather promote it
through the mechanism of economic ties." The book chides Western states for
not always being reliable trade partners. Taking a page from Kissinger, Gorbachev argues that "boost[ing] our trade and economic relations...[will help]
build confidence between our countries." Yet "the United States has created
many obstacles in the economic field."[119]

Unlike in the early 1970s, it was clear to the Soviets that this Republican
administration was unwilling to sign a quid-pro-quo deal linking arms control
and better Soviet behavior to increased U.S. trade commitments. Reagan and
his associates were simply too mistrustful of Soviet intentions. Consequently,
the Soviets understood that they would have to make a number of dramatic
gestures that would signal that the new leadership was indeed different. That
is, they would have to offer signals that would be too costly for traditional Soviet leaders to make, were the Kremlin to change American minds and begin
to build trust. In April 1985 Gorbachev received a forty-page memorandum
from Arbatov arguing that the changing of the guard in Moscow opened up
opportunities for better relations. Yet bold new initiatives were needed quickly
to avoid the "danger of disappointment." Particularly, the analysis proposed
that "we change our negotiating style and take unilateral measures," including
the reduction of Soviet forces in Europe and a moratorium on nuclear testing.[120]

Gorbachev took this advice to heart. In January 1986, Gorbachev publicly
proposed a three-stage plan for the elimination of nuclear weapons by the turn

---

117. Mastanduno, *Economic Containment*, 300; Garthoff, *Great Transition*, 249, 198. At the
Geneva summit in November, Reagan had indicated to Gorbachev that if the Soviets made
concessions on arms control matters, then America "might be prepared to normalize relations." Still, no explicit promise of trade was proffered (ibid., Garthoff's words).

118. Quoted in Gorbachev, *Perestroika*, 231 n. 1.

119. Gorbachev, *Perestroika*, 126, 222–23.

120. Arbatov, *The System*, 321–22. Arbatov notes that Gorbachev "apparently thought [the
report] was worthwhile because he asked me to continue to advise him' (321).

of the century.[121] At Reykjavik in the fall, the Soviets were willing to agree to far-reaching reductions in strategic missiles in return for limitations on space-based weapons. While no agreement was reached, Schultz observes that the meeting was a turning point in demonstrating that the Soviets were serious about fundamental change.[122] This view was reinforced in 1987, when Moscow agreed to an INF treaty which entailed significantly disproportional cuts in intermediate-range missiles from the Soviet side. In the heady atmosphere of the December summit in Washington, Marshal Akhromeyev, the key negotiator for the Soviet side, revealed to Schultz an aspect of the Soviet strategy:

> My country is in trouble, and I am fighting alongside Mikhail Sergeyevich to save it. That is why we made such a lopsided deal on INF, and that is why we want to get along with you. We want to restructure ourselves and to be part of the modern world. We cannot continue to be isolated.[123]

These dramatic gestures were having some effect on American trade policy. In early 1987 the U.S. embargo on oil and gas drilling equipment was lifted. This was an important step, given that energy exports were the primary source of foreign currency; indeed, Gorbachev recognized early on that such exports were critical to the overall success of reform.[124] Just after the Washington summit, at a special CoCom meeting in January 1988, the United States accepted a liberalization of the list of controlled items, including computers and telecommunications. In addition, a U.S.-Soviet agreement on scientific cooperation was signed.[125]

Despite these positive developments, the U.S. Congress was once again an important hurdle. By the end of 1987, congressional legislation was being considered that would have increased, not decreased, existing restrictions. As in the early 1970s, the Kremlin knew that the U.S. Executive was more receptive to trade than the Congress; in April 1987, for example, Schultz had made a presentation to Gorbachev on the "Information Age," securing Gorbachev's agreement that technology tied to economic interdependence was the key to

---

121. Ambassador Dobyrnin reports that Secretary of State Schultz was "unmistakably impressed" by the plan. Notwithstanding its propagandistic value, it responded to Reagan's long-standing call for deep cuts in strategic nuclear weapons. Dobrynin, *In Confidence*, 597–98.

122. Schultz, *Turmoil and Triumph*, chap. 36.

123. Ibid., 1011–12.

124. See Gorbachev, *Memoirs*. Unfortunately, oil prices by 1985–86 had plunged from their high in the early 1980s, greatly complicating Gorbachev's plan and forcing more radical reforms.

125. Mastanduno, *Economic Containment*, 306; Garthoff, *Great Transition*, 342.

long-term growth.[126] Thus at the December summit, Gorbachev made sure he cultivated U.S. public opinion. He met with influential business and media opinion leaders to stress the importance of greater ties. The frustration he expressed regarding current U.S. legislation is summarized in his memoirs.

> We were isolated from each other by political decisions and restrictions aimed at preventing the transfer of new technologies. The notorious CoCom lists impeded not only the United States but also many other countries from cooperating with us on a modern technological and economic level. Linking trade to human rights caused many difficulties for those who genuinely wanted to do business with us.[127]

Soviet frustration continued into 1988. At the May summit in Moscow, Reagan asked Gorbachev to provide a detailed summary on the progress of perestroika. Gorbachev responded by reiterating that America "persisted in maintaining a discriminatory trade policy toward the Soviet Union." Reagan tried to explain that Americans still had concerns about Soviet emigration policy. Gorbachev replied that the "ideological debris" of the past must be thrown away, now that the two states had agreed in principle to foster bilateral cooperation.[128] Gorbachev pressed the issue of U.S. trade on a number of other occasions at the summit, but there were no breakthroughs.[129] Gorbachev came away from the meeting believing that even more dramatic steps were needed to break the logjam.[130] In December, in a speech to the United Nations, he took his most radical step yet. He stated that the Soviet Union would reduce its troop presence in eastern Europe over the next two years by 500,000 men—unilaterally and without relation to conventional forces talks going on in Vienna. The connection between this move and his economic goals was indirect but hard to miss. The global economy was becoming one organism, he told his audience, "and no state, whatever its social system or economic status, can normally develop outside it."[131] As Gorbachev later described it, one of the primary themes of this speech was that "perestroika...required a change in

---

126. Schultz communicated similar points to the Russians just as the December summit was beginning. See Schultz, *Turmoil and Triumph*, 892–93, 1008, 1012. See also Oberdorfer, *The Turn*, 223–24. Of course, Gorbachev hardly needed to be lectured on this point: aside from his obsession with global technological change, it was he who had stressed to Schultz in their first meeting in March 1985 that the world was experiencing a "scientific and technological revolution," and that more bilateral trade was needed. Schultz, *Turmoil and Triumph*, 530.
127. Gorbachev, *Memoirs*, 448.
128. Ibid., 456–57.
129. Oberdorfer, *The Turn*, 295.
130. Garthoff, *Great Transition*, 358.
131. Oberdorfer, *The Turn*, 316–18.

the way we conducted our foreign trade, an organic integration with the world economy."[132]

This speech, combined with the Soviet agreement to withdraw from Afghanistan, led Schultz to discuss further relaxations of controls with the Defense Department in the waning days of the Reagan administration.[133] Once George Bush assumed power, however, he decided to undertake a full review of U.S. policy toward Russia. A number of his advisors were worried that Soviet concessions were simply a ploy to give Russia the breathing space needed to restore its power.[134] Thus for many months, aside from a few vague statements applauding Soviet reforms, there was little concrete progress in normalizing relations. The Soviets were concerned. In August the Politburo approved a twenty-four-page document calling for greater Soviet participation in international organizations, including support for UN peacekeeping. Such a move was seen as furthering Soviet integration into the global economy, and thus represented "an investment in our social-economic and scientific-technological progress." Yet to implement this strategy, U.S. help was deemed essential.[135]

In September, Foreign Minister Edward Shevardnadze met with Secretary of State James Baker and stressed that Russia was going through a "very important stage." Moscow sought to "overcome the incompatibility of our economic system with those of the Western countries." Moscow did not want aid, but rather "economic cooperation" to help perestroika succeed.[136] As part of his discussions with Baker and Bush in September, Shevardnadze offered up three more important concessions: the Soviets would delink START talks from discussions on space-based weapons; they would dismantle the offending radar station at Krasnoyarsk (which the Americans saw as a violation of the SALT

132. Gorbachev, *Memoirs*, 608.

133. Mastanduno, *Economic Containment*, 308.

134. See Michael R. Beschloss and Strobe Talbott, *At the Highest Levels: The Inside Story of the End of the Cold War* (Boston: Little, Brown, 1993), 17–25. Ambassador in Moscow Matlock, however, made a push for increased trade in early 1989. Matlock, *Autopsy of an Empire*, 188.

135. Quoted in Garthoff from the document in the Central Committee archive, *Great Transition*, 400–402. This document shows that Soviet policy was hardly "other-regarding," as constructivists such as Wendt claim ("Anarchy is What States Make of It"); the analysis was purely oriented to Soviet interests, with peaceful engagement a means to self-interested ends (see Garthoff, *Great Transition*, esp. 402).

136. Quoted in James A. Baker, *The Politics of Diplomacy: Revolution, War, and Peace, 1989–1992* (New York: Putnam's, 1995), 144–45. This followed up Shevardnadze's point to Baker in July that Soviet economic and social problems were "enormous" and that the financial system was in "very grave condition." Economic cooperation with the West was needed. Ibid., 138–39.

treaty); and Moscow's insistence that the START treaty included limitations on sea-launched cruise missiles would be dropped.[137]

This additional evidence of Soviet cooperation in the foreign policy realm seemed to do the trick. By late 1989 the Bush administration made a definitive decision that Gorbachev's reforms must be supported.[138] In mid-October, Baker made a major foreign policy speech to confirm that perestroika was indeed in the U.S. interest, and that Washington was "prepared to provide technical assistance" for Soviet reforms.[139] When Bush and Gorbachev met at Malta in December 1989, the Berlin wall was down, and the Soviet position in eastern Europe was quickly unravelling. This gave new urgency to the need to help perestroika succeed, in order to keep Gorbachev in power. Bush made the promise that Gorbachev had been waiting more than four years to hear: that the White House would seek to secure most-favored-nation status for the Soviet Union and to end legislative restrictions on economic credits. In essence, this was a promise to return to the spirit of the 1972 trade agreement. Bush also offered Moscow observer status at the General Agreement on Tariffs and Trade (GATT), as a means to further integrate the Soviet Union into the world economy. Finally, Bush suggested that the two sides begin discussions on a new trade agreement, to be signed at the next summit.[140]

This was a very pleasing development for Moscow. At Malta, Gorbachev told a gathering of journalists that the summit had provided "a political impetus that had been lacking for our economic cooperation to gain momentum." He then reinforced that the Soviets would work diligently to make their economy "part and parcel of the world economic system."[141] In private discussions, he expressed his hope that Bush would apply his political will as a "signal" of the new, more open trading relationship. Among other things, this would help renew American business confidence in the Soviet Union.[142] Overall, the atmosphere at Malta was optimistic, almost jubilant. As Gorbachev announced, "The world is leaving one epoch, the 'Cold War,' and entering a new one."[143] Positive Soviet trade expectations were reinforcing the wisdom of the new

137. Garthoff, *Great Transition*, 384–85; Beschloss and Talbott, *At the Highest Levels*, 117–21.

138. See Oberdorfer, *The Turn*, 376; Matlock, *Autopsy of an Empire*, 271–72. The decision was no doubt influenced by a report earlier in the year noting that the Soviet need for western technology could be used as leverage in any negotiations. See George Bush and Brent Scowcroft, *A World Transformed* (New York: Knopf, 1998), 41.

139. Garthoff, *Great Transition*, 386–87; Baker, *Politics of Diplomacy*, 156.

140. See Garthoff, *Great Transition*, 406–7; Beschloss and Talbott, *At the Highest Levels*, 151–55; Gorbachev, *Memoirs*, 511–12; Bush and Scowcroft, *World Transformed*, 162–63, 173.

141. Quoted in Garthoff, *Great Transition*, 407.

142. Gorbachev, *Memoirs*, 512.

143. Quoted in Garthoff, *Great Transition*, 408.

peace program. A month later, Gorbachev submitted his report to the Polit-buro. He welcomed both the U.S. "readiness to give us certain practical aid in the sphere of the economy" and the "mutual understanding of the necessity for Soviet-American cooperation as a stabilizing factor" during this crucial stage of world history.[144]

Developments over the next six months were caught up in one major issue: how to deal with the apparently inevitable drive toward German unification. Soviets were adamant that a unified Germany be neutralized, and therefore that it not be a part of NATO; given their history, they were understandably reluctant to see the power of Germany joined to the Western alliance. Yet Washington and Bonn held a master card: the now almost desperate Soviet need for future trade and credits to support economic revitalization. U.S.-Soviet trade talks began in February 1990; in March, the Two-plus-Four discussions on German unification commenced. By early May, however, both sets of talks were stalled. The U.S. Senate was making MFN status contingent on an end to the Soviet embargo on Lithuania (an embargo imposed in April to deter Lithuania from carrying out its call for independence). Moreover, Moscow was still very reluctant to allow the inclusion of a unified Germany within NATO.

When Bush and Gorbachev met for the Washington summit in late May, there was still no formal agreement on either the trade issue or the German question. Following the opening ceremony on Thursday 31 May, the two lead-ers sat down for their first private meeting. Gorbachev immediately introduced his prime concern: the signing of a trade agreement to foster perestroika. The Soviet economy was in deep crisis, he said, and Western help was "really needed." He promised to find a nonviolent solution to the Lithuanian situa-tion, but Bush would not bite. The president noted certain U.S. concerns re-garding not just Lithuania but also German unification and the pace of Soviet economic reform. The meeting ended without any U.S. commitment.[145]

Meanwhile, Shevardnadze and Baker were conducting their own discus-sions. Shevardnadze and Gorbachev had indicated to Baker in mid-May that Russia needed approximately $20 billion in Western credits to keep perestroika going; Baker had tied any such promises to accelerated reform, a solution to the Lithuanian situation, and an end to Soviet subsidies to Cuba, Vietnam, and Cambodia.[146] Now Shevardnadze, more emotional than Baker had ever seen

144. Quoted in Dobrynin, *In Confidence*, 634. According to Dobyrnin, Gorbachev saw U.S. support for perestroika as the most significant result of the summit (ibid.).

145. See Oberdorfer, *The Turn*, 413–15; Beschloss and Talbott, *At the Highest Levels*, 216–19; Philip Zelikow and Condoleezza Rice, *Germany Unified and Europe Transformed* (Cambridge: Harvard University Press, 1997), 276; Bush and Scowcroft, *World Transformed*, 280–81.

146. See Baker, *Politics of Diplomacy*, 248–49; Beschloss and Talbott, *At the Highest Levels*, 210–11.

him, pressed his appeal. A bilateral trade deal was "extremely important" to Gorbachev's ability to maintain public support for internal reform. Like Bush, Baker was noncommittal.[147]

The Americans were clearly holding out for a concrete concession from the Soviet side. Later that day, they got it. In a meeting of the main players, Gorbachev suddenly let it be known that he would allow a united Germany to make up its own mind on which alliance to join. This was a significant shift in the Soviet position, since it was clear that the West Germans would control the new state and would elect to join NATO. Gorbachev's advisors present at the meeting were taken aback, and managed to get him to retreat somewhat from his position. The critical concession, however, had been made, and both sides knew it.[148]

The move by Gorbachev may seem surprising, since as Zelikow and Rice note, it is rare for a leader to change his or her mind right at the bargaining table, especially without first consulting with relevant subordinates. Yet developments over the next day suggest that Gorbachev's decision on German unification, while perhaps spontaneous, was part of a larger plan. Bush and Baker had indicated earlier that day that a trade deal would probably not be signed during the summit. Gorbachev was not going to go home empty-handed, especially during this particularly critical time for perestroika. Hence, he could make his concession on Germany on the first day, to reiterate his peaceful and cooperative intentions. He could then hint that this and other offers could be quickly withdrawn should no reciprocal concessions from the United States be forthcoming.

At a breakfast meeting with top congressional leaders the next day (1 June)—a televised meeting which he undoubtedly knew Bush would be watching—Gorbachev spent much of his time reiterating Soviet economic problems and need for a bilateral trade deal. The present trade relationship was "very primitive" he told his audience, and he appealed for a "favorable gesture from the U.S. Congress on trade." This gesture, he noted, was "very important...from a political standpoint." On the German question, however, Gorbachev's tone was subtly menacing. The West was squeezing the Soviet Union out of Europe and was trying to gain a unilateral advantage, he protested. If an

---

147. Beschloss and Talbott, *At the Highest Levels*, 218; Zelikow and Rice, *Germany Unified*, 276.

148. Zelikow and Rice, *Germany Unified*, 276–79; Beschloss and Talbott, *At the Highest Levels*, 219–21; Oberdorfer, *The Turn*, 415–18; Bush and Scowcroft, *World Transformed*, 282–83.

imbalance in Europe were to arise, the USSR would be forced to "reconsider" and "reassess" its position on arms control.[149]

Gorbachev met with Bush in the late morning. Both sides were under the clock, since a signing ceremony for summit agreements was already scheduled for 5:00 P.M. that afternoon. Bush told Gorbachev that he was still exploring whether to sign the trade agreement. Gorbachev reiterated the critical importance of such an agreement. During the day, further pressure was put on the White House through second and third-level Soviet officials, who hinted to the American side that Moscow might not agree to the new grain deal at 5:00 P.M. if Washington did not go through with broader trade agreement.[150] In the mid-afternoon, Baker phoned Bush to tell him that they should proceed with the trade deal. Shevardnadze's additional appeals that day, plus the "breakthrough" on Germany, had apparently convinced Baker that America must show its concrete support for perestroika. Bush agreed: "Let's go ahead and do it."[151]

The president kept Gorbachev hanging to the last minute. Just before entering the East Room for the signing ceremony at 6:00 P.M., Gorbachev asked "Are we going to sign the trade agreement?" Bush replied that they would. Beaming, Gorbachev told the president: "This really matters to me." Bush also agreed that he would not explicitly link the deal to Soviet behavior on Lithuania, although he managed to subtly communicate this tie in his public remarks at the signing ceremony. He made no mention of Gorbachev's compromise on Germany unification.[152] Gorbachev thus came away with the deal he wanted. The Americans were now committed to the normalization of trade relations, in return for the Soviets' quiet acquiescence to the U.S. position on Germany and private promises of moderation regarding Lithuania.[153]

It is clear that the Washington summit of May-June 1990 was a significant moment in the unwinding of the cold war. From Gorbachev's perspective, the trade agreement of 1 June represented a "turning point" in U.S.-Soviet relations,

149. Oberdorfer, *The Turn*, 418–19; Zelikow and Rice, *Germany Unified*, 279; Beschloss and Talbott, *Highest Levels*, 221–22.

150. Bush and Scowcroft, *World Transformed*, 283–84; Oberdorfer, *The Turn*, 419–20.

151. Baker, *Politics of Diplomacy*, 254; Zelikow and Rice, *Germany Unified*, 279–80; Bush and Scowcroft, *World Transformed*, 285. According to Matlock, Shevardnadze had also threatened that the spirit of confrontation would reappear if the trade agreement was not signed during the summit (*Autopsy of an Empire*, 381). Gorbachev states that during a deadlock in the negotiations on 1 June, he stood up, indicating that this was his "last word" and that Bush had to make a choice (*Memoirs*, 540). If true, these techniques reinforce that the Soviets were pulling out all the stops to secure a "trade for peace" deal.

152. Beschloss and Talbott, *Highest Levels*, 223; Zelikow and Rice, *Germany Unified*, 280–81.

153. The next day, Gorbachev would compromise on another important U.S. concern: Soviet subsidies to states like Cuba would end in the near term (Beschloss and Talbott, *Highest Levels*, 225). On the tie between the summit and subsequent Soviet moderation in the Baltics, see Matlock, *Autopsy of an Empire*, chap. 14 and 380–81.

in which the Americans went "from verbal support for our perestroika to real action."[154] On the day of the signing, he spoke of the body of agreements as a step toward a "new world." Bush's speech that day noted that while the two superpowers did not agree on everything, "we [do] believe in one great truth: the world has waited long enough; the Cold War must end."[155]

Cooperation did indeed become the norm after this point. Most surprising and immediate was the way both sides worked together during the eight-month crisis to end Iraq's occupation of Kuwait, which began less than two months after the Washington summit. At the Moscow summit in July 1991, the two sides signed the START I treaty calling for dramatic cuts in strategic weaponry. Economic matters once again reinforced this political cooperation. In June 1990, the German government promised the Kremlin $5 billion now, and $20 billion more later, to help meet Russia's growing financial need.[156] At the annual G-7 economic summit in July, the Western industrial states "agreed to task the International Monetary Fund with a serious study of the Soviet economy in order to lay the groundwork for Western assistance." Kohl reiterated that Bonn would provide massive financial aid to Moscow.[157] Negotiations to finalize the deal on German unification continued for a few more months, as the Soviets held out to ensure the maximum commitment of German credits and aid.[158] By October, however, the two Germanies were united, with the understanding that the new larger Germany would remain a part of NATO.

By the spring of 1991, East-West relations were hardly recognizable. Gorbachev was seeking an invitation to the next G-7 summit, slated for July. By this time, as Gorbachev acknowledges, "the issue of the international community's support for our reforms had taken on great urgency."

> Our ties with the Seven now had more than merely general strategic significance; they had acquired a purely practical importance, ensuring substantial economic support for the country in its most critical hour.[159]

In mid-June Gorbachev received his formal invitation to the summit. The month before, he had secured internal approval from the USSR Security Coun-

154. Gorbachev, *Memoirs*, 542.

155. Quoted in Oberdorfer, *The Turn*, 423. As Secretary of State Baker recounts, the signing of the agreements on 1 June had an immediate effect on the willingness to cooperate over third world issues. "It was almost as if Gorbachev's acceptance of Germany in NATO, and the President's decision on the trade agreement, had moved our relations to a higher, more cooperative and personal plane." Baker, *Politics of Diplomacy*, 254.

156. Baker, *Politics of Diplomacy*, 255.

157. Ibid., 259.

158. See Zelikow and Rice, *Germany Unified*, chaps. 8–9.

159. Gorbachev, *Memoirs*, 611.

cil regarding the possibility of the Soviet Union joining the IMF; by early July
the republics were on board. On 11 July, Gorbachev sent a personal letter to
the Western powers, noting that

> We feel that the time has come to take resolute steps...for a new type of
> economic interaction that would integrate the Soviet economy...into the
> world economy.

The Soviet people were seeking to "stabilize our economy." To achieve this,

> there must be reciprocal movement on the part of the Soviet Union and
> the Group of Seven, in which major measures in economic reforms and
> the opening up of the Soviet economy...would be reinforced by recip-
> rocal steps [by the Western powers].[160]

In one of the most remarkable events of the post-1945 period, the leader of
the Soviet Union—a man still dedicated to the principles of socialism—arrived
in London on 16 July 1991 to hold talks on international trade and investment
with the seven leaders of the capitalist world. At a special meeting designed to
represent the "7+1" formula—and on the same day that Bush and Gorbachev
came to a final agreement on a START treaty to reduce strategic arms (17
July)—Gorbachev spoke to the G-7 leaders. He told them bluntly that the Soviet leadership believed that

> positive processes in the world could be sustained if the political dia-
> logue we had established were to become rooted in the new economic
> cooperation.

Thus, while his people understood that economic integration stemmed from
the need for radical changes at home, integration could be achieved only by
"the lifting of legislative and other restrictions on economic and technical ties
with the Soviet Union."[161]

Gorbachev was pleased by his reception at the private meeting. Kohl of
Germany spoke of the "historic moment": "if this process we are initiating in
London goes successfully, it will have the utmost importance for Europe and
the entire world." Prime Minister John Major of Britain, host of the summit,
noted that the Western states were in a position to help Russia at the macroeconomic level. Afterwards, Major summarized publicly the points of agreement. The G-7 countries would work to build a "special association" between
the Soviet Union and the IMF and World Bank. International institutions like
the OECD, IMF, and European Bank for Reconstruction and Development

160. Ibid., 612.
161. Ibid., 613–14 (Gorbachev's paraphrases from his actual speech).

would provide practical advice on creating a market economy. The countries also expressed their resolve to reestablish full access to trade and investment. The next day Gorbachev met with Major to reiterate the list of items still controlled under CoCom. He secured Major's promise to look into the matter of eliminating these items. From his perspective, Gorbachev came away from the G-7 meeting "with a significant gain." He had achieved "a fundamental political agreement about the integration of our country [into] the world economy," thus "fulfill[ing] the national and state interests of our country."[162]

The above analysis demonstrates the profound importance of improving Soviet trade expectations on the winding down of the cold war. Gorbachev recognized the need for trade and investment early on, and worked tirelessly to secure U.S. and Western European agreement to a relaxation on existing restrictions. He understood that the probability of future trade was partly endogenous: that unless he offered dramatic concessions in arms control and geopolitics, Reagan and Bush would be unlikely to use their political capital to press for the changes in CoCom and domestic legislation. He also used the promise of better behavior—and the implicit threat of the reversal of new gains and a return to an intense cold war—as a tool to secure Western commitments to future trade. Thus a virtuous cycle of political concessions, signals of future Western trade, and further political concessions could be set in motion, leading to the ending of nearly a half century of intense cold war.

CONCLUSION: IMPLICATIONS OF THE ARGUMENT

THIS PAPER has shown that trade expectations can play a significant role in the resolution of enduring rivalries. When a dependent state in a relationship has reason to believe that large future trade benefits will be forthcoming should it moderate its foreign policy, a stable peace can emerge. The cold war cases considered above provide an important illustration of this. Yet as I have examined elsewhere, when a dependent state like Germany before 1914 and 1939 or Japan before 1941 believes that the trading environment is (or is becoming) unremittantly hostile, negative trade expectations can exacerbate fears of decline and drive the state into total war.[163] These empirical examples thus support the general hypothesis that economic interdependence can be either peace-inducing or war-inducing, depending on a state's expectations for future trade.

---

162. Ibid., 617.
163. See Copeland, "Economic Interdependence and War," 26–39.

The cold war studies also nicely illustrate the interaction between the exogenous and endogenous dimensions of a state's trade expectations. When a state sees that the other's executive will be incapable of providing the necessary trade due to factors outside its control, then the state will be more inclined to fall back on expansionist behavior. In late 1974, once it became clear that neither presidential intervention nor further Soviet concessions could stop a Congress determined to restrict trade, the Kremlin moved back to a policy of "adventurism," while continuing its arms buildup. This shift reignited an intense cold war, one that by 1983 led the Soviets to fear an impending U.S. first strike.[164] Yet when a dependent state has reason to believe that the other's leadership can both control the level of trade and is amenable to increasing that trade under certain conditions, then diplomatic agreements can be worked out that improve the dependent state's trade expectations and thus its behavior. The early 1970s initially held out this hope, until Watergate and U.S. domestic politics intervened. In the late 1980s, with the Soviets even more desperate for bilateral trade, dramatic gestures by Gorbachev were able to defuse U.S. domestic opposition. Reagan and Bush were then able to secure the trade deals needed to wind down the cold war.

The trade expectations argument has implications for the most important great power relationship in the post–cold war world: that of the United States and China. With China's rapid economic growth—a doubling of its total GNP every seven to ten years—it is becoming more and more dependent on international trade and investment. Not only has this growth been fueled by exports, but China requires increasing imports of raw materials from abroad (including oil) as it depletes resources at home. Moreover, Chinese leaders, like Soviet leaders after 1965, understand that China's ability to enhance its long-term security and prosperity depend upon access to Western technology. Given this growing dependence, Chinese trade expectations over the next two decades can be predicted to play a critical role in the shaping of global and regional stability.

In the present environment, the question of Chinese trade expectations revolves around the debate over whether to "engage" or "contain" China. This paper's logic indicates that containment would, at least at this stage, have destabilizing effects. For the last decade, China's foreign policy, while not perfect, has been relatively peaceful. Like Brezhnev in 1972–73, Chinese leaders understand that moderation in foreign policy can be expected to pay large economic

---

164. See the documents in Christopher Andrew and Oleg Gordievsky, eds., *Comrade Krychukov's Instructions: Top Secret Files on KGB Foreign Operations*, 1975–1985 (Stanford: Stanford University Press, 1993), 6, 17, 67–90. See also Oberdofer, *The Turn*, 64–66; Dobrynin, *In Confidence*, 522–24.

dividends. Containment would sever this implicit linkage, thus changing Beijing's geopolitical calculus. In particular, the renewal of CoCom-like restrictions would force Chinese leaders into a corner. Like Japan in the 1930s, China might then see the building of a regional coprosperity sphere as the only means to maintain growth in a world of hostile adversaries.[165]

In sum, the trade expectations argument offers the means to unite the insights of both the liberal and realist arguments. Liberals are correct that trade can indeed restrain leaders by providing a material incentive to stay at peace. Realists are right to stress that interdependence can have a downside: it makes states worry about being cut off from access to vital goods and markets. Yet the two paradigms remain incomplete on their own. To determine whether liberal or realist logic will predominate, we must bring in a dependent state's expectations of future trade. Only when a state has confidence that the trade benefits will be forthcoming over the foreseeable future can trade "restrain" in the way liberals expect. Thus we need to explore the conditions under which such positive expectations for future trade will arise. Yet realist pessimism that trade always predisposes states toward conflict is unwarranted. Indeed, as the empirical studies demonstrate, the building of favorable trade expectations can help defuse a rivalry even as intense as the cold war. In future research, therefore, we need to grasp the fact that at least in certain areas, liberal and realist arguments are two sides of the same coin. Only in this way can we transcend stale debates over which paradigm is more theoretically powerful and empirically sound.

---

165. For a more complete analysis of the impact of trade expectations on U.S-Chinese relations, see Dale C. Copeland, "Economic Interdependence and the Future of U.S.-Chinese Relations," paper presented to the conference on "The Emerging International Relations of the Asia-Pacific Region," Dartmouth College, 23–24 October 1998, organized by John Ikenberry and Michael Mastanduno.

THE OFFENSE-DEFENSE BALANCE, INTERDEPENDENCE, AND WAR

PETER LIBERMAN

O FFENSE-DEFENSE theory predicts that defensive military advantage, by increasing the cost of winning wars, promotes peace. Because economic interdependence also increases the cost of war, the theory of commercial liberalism claims that it too is a cause of peace. When defense dominance and economic interdependence coincide, however, the results are much less rosy than the theories separately would suggest.

This is, ironically, because conventional (that is, nonnuclear) defense dominance lengthens war and any accompanying embargoes and blockades. It thus heightens the vulnerability to economic warfare of trade-dependent states. Expecting protracted attrition warfare with severed trade links gives trade-dependent states powerful security incentives to seize resource-rich territory. Thus offense-defense theory and commercial liberalism each suffer from a common Catch-22. While defense dominance makes conquest more difficult, it also can make it more desirable as a means to economic self-sufficiency, or autarky. And while interdependence makes war more costly, it also heightens incentives to shore up economic vulnerabilities through expansion.

Several international conditions heighten the strategic economic incentives for expansion, by this logic: a state's economic dependence on trade, the vulnerability of its trade links to embargo or blockade, the expected likelihood, duration, and intensity of conventional war among great power rivals, the cumulativity of conquered economic resources, and the military weakness of smaller economic prizes. Theoretically, trade-dependent states in a nonnuclear, defense-dominant world could find war-risking expansion a rational security policy. National misperceptions exaggerating the above conditions, however, often substitute for, or exacerbate, their actual presence. Militarization—that is, the political ascendance of military organizations or actors sharing their bi-

Peter Liberman is associate professor of political science at Queens College, City University of New York

An earlier version of this paper was presented at a *Security Studies* Workshop on Economic Power, Interdependence, and National Security, held at the Mershon Center for International Relations, Ohio State University, 2–5 April 1998. The author is grateful for comments from the workshop participants, Charles Glaser, and the anonymous reviewers for *Security Studies*.

ases—leads states to exaggerate the likelihood of war and the need to bolster their strategic position. Also, leaders tend to pay too much heed to the "lessons" of the recent past, and expect coming wars to repeat what they themselves have experienced.

These hypotheses help explain why Germany and Japan's perceptions of global defense dominance failed to dampen their interwar appetite for conquest. As the empirical part of this paper will show, Germany and Japan were only moderately expansionist prior to the First World War, when conquest was thought to be relatively easy. After this long and intense attrition war, however, leaders in both states concluded that future wars with other great powers would be similar, and thus would require autarky. This might have deterred war, but militaristic leaders expecting renewed great power gained power in both nations in the 1930s. As a result, the perceived ascendance of defense, at a global if not local level, did not stop—and in fact may have stimulated—aggressive German and Japanese expansionism.

The idea that trade dependence gives states incentives to forcibly seize markets and resources, particularly when access is threatened, is an old one.[1] On the eve of the Second World War, for example, E. H. Carr observed a link between the lessons of the First World War and the autarky quests of the "have-not" powers. He wrote that the impulse that the First World War "gave to the pursuit of autarky was immediate and powerful. Blockade, and the diversion of a large part of the world's shipping to the transport of troops and munitions, imposed more or less stringent measures of autarky on both belligerents and neutrals."[2] More recently, Ann Uchitel has elaborated how economic dependence and expectations of long wars led Germany and Japan in the 1930s to adopt expansionist aims and offensive military doctrines.[3]

Yet the links between the offense-defense balance, interdependence, and war have not been fully analyzed. The literature on the offense-defense balance has completely ignored how it might affect economic incentives for conquest.[4]

1. E. H. Carr, *The Twenty Years' Crisis: 1919–1939*, 2nd ed. (1939; New York: Harper and Row, 1946), 113–24; Lionel Robbins, *The Economic Causes of War* (London: Jonathan Cape, 1939), 60–85; Jacob Viner, *International Economics* (Glencoe, Ill.: Free Press, 1951), 247–67. For earlier analyses of security and economic self-sufficiency, see Edward Mead Earle, "Adam Smith, Alexander Hamilton, Friedrich List: The Economic Foundations of Military Power," *in Makers of Modern Strategy from Machiavelli to the Nuclear Age*, ed. Peter Paret (1943; Princeton: Princeton University Press, 1986), 217–61.

2. Carr, *Twenty Years' Crisis*, 123.

3. "Interdependence and Instability," *in Coping with Complexity in the International System*, ed. Jack Snyder and Robert Jervis (Boulder: Westview, 1993), 243–64.

4. For a review, see Charles L. Glaser, "The Security Dilemma Revisited," *World Politics* 50, no. 1 (October 1997): 171–201. The classic analyses are George H. Quester, *Offense and Defense in the International System* (New York: Wiley, 1977); and Robert Jervis, "Cooperation Under the Security Dilemma," *World Politics* 30, no. 2 (January 1978): 167–214. See also Jack

The literature on interdependence and war has, for the most part, overlooked the variety of threats to economic dependence.[5] Uchitel's discussion of attrition and economic warfare is one exception, but neglects to draw implications for offense-defense theory.[6] Another exception is Dale Copeland's recent argument that pessimism about peacetime trade barriers is the root economic cause of aggression.[7] As I will argue, however, there are good theoretical and empirical reasons to believe that fears of wartime barriers are much more malignant.

While twentieth-century German and Japanese expansionism is well-trodden ground for testing international relations theory, it illuminates clearly the Catch-22's of commercial liberalism and offense-defense theory. Heightened German and Japanese expansionism after the First World War defies the conventional predictions of offense-defense theory, because offense was thought easier before that war than after. Process tracing the perceptions and calculations of German and Japanese leaders provides further evidence for my argument. Wartime autarky concerns took root in the 1920s, and dominated official policy once militarist actors gained power in the 1930s. Conquest was explicitly advocated as a means to provide for self-sufficiency in future long wars. Misperceptions played an important role, but were somewhat predictable in their sources—militarism and the lessons of the past—and consequences.

S. Levy, "The Offensive/Defensive Balance of Military Technology: A Theoretical and Historical Analysis," *International Studies Quarterly* 28, no. 2 (June 1984): 219–38; Stephen Van Evera, "The Cult of the Offensive and the Origins of the First World War," in *Military Strategy and the Origins of the First World War*, ed. Steven E. Miller (Princeton: Princeton University Press, 1985), 58–107; and Stephen Van Evera, "Offense, Defense, and the Causes of War," *International Security* 22, no. 4 (spring 1998): 5–43; Ted Hopf, "Polarity, the Offense-Defense Balance, and War," *American Political Science Review* 85, no. 2 (June 1991): 475–93; Sean M. Lynn-Jones, "Offense-Defense Theory and Its Critics," *Security Studies* 4, no. 4 (summer 1995): 660–91; and Charles L. Glaser and Chaim Kaufmann, "What is the Offense-Defense Balance and How Can We Measure It?" *International Security* 22, no. 4 (spring 1998): 44–82.

5. Most studies on interdependence and war involve quantitative correlations between these two variables, with mixed results. For an overview, see Susan M. McMillan, "Interdependence and Conflict," *Mershon International Studies Review* 41, no. 1 (May 1997): 33–58. Recent quantitative analyses include Edward D. Mansfield, *Power, Trade, and War* (Princeton: Princeton University Press, 1994), 117–50; Katherine Barbieri, "Economic Interdependence: A Path to Peace or a Source of Interstate Conflict?" *Journal of Peace Research* 33, no. 1 (February 1996): 29–49; John R. Oneal and Bruce M. Russett, "The Classical Liberals Were Right: Democracy, Interdependence, and Conflict, 1950–1985," *International Studies Quarterly* 41, no. 2 (June 1997): 267–94.

6. Thomas J. Christensen, "System Stability and the Security of the Most Vulnerable Significant Actor," in Snyder and Jervis, *Coping with Complexity*, 334.

7. Dale C. Copeland, "Economic Interdependence and War: A Theory of Trade Expectations," *International Security* 20, no. 4 (spring 1996): 5–41; "Trade Expectations and the Outbreak of Peace: Détente 1970–74 and the End of the Cold War 1985–91," *Security Studies* 9, nos. 1/2 (autumn 1999–winter 2000): 15–58.

Process tracing also helps differentiate the impact of embargo and blockade fears, on the one hand, from that of ordinary commercial pessimism, on the other. Examining only the congruence and timing of cause and effect in these cases would suggest that pessimism about peacetime trade prospects could have been an equal or greater cause of autarky-seeking in 1930s Germany and Japan. After all, both states became markedly more aggressive after the collapse of world trade following the 1929 slump. Yet while some important political actors in both states responded to the Depression by demanding various forms of empire, German and Japanese leaders were fixated on the problem of waging total war in the face of economic blockade and embargo. The Depression's main effect was to help imperialists gain power, and not by showcasing the economic merits of their empire-building plans, but by broadly delegitimizing the moderate preceding regimes.

Recent historical research also justifies reconsideration of these questions. Michael Barnhart has elaborated the importance of total war planning in Japan's quest for autarky. R. J. Overy has done the same for Germany, revising the longstanding notion that Hitler and his generals expected war to consist entirely of short, blitzkrieg battles. Yet while offense may have been easy against Germany's neighbors in central and western Europe, Hitler expected it to be difficult against Britain, Russia, and the United States. I also draw on recent studies of Wilhelmine foreign policy and Japanese business attitudes in the 1930s for evidence against the hypothesis that peacetime trade pessimism causes aggression.[8]

This article proceeds as follows. The next section analyzes the conditions that intensify the economic incentives for conquest, including the domestic biases inflating them, and explains how these ought to qualify the offense-defense and interdependence theories of war. The following section re-examines German and Japanese expansionism prior to both world wars to demonstrate the impact of economic incentives, whether leaders were impelled by fears of wartime or peacetime trade barriers, and what domestic factors biased their perceptions. The final section concludes by summarizing my findings, and discussing their implications for theory and policy.

8. Michael A. Barnhart, *Japan Prepares for Total War: The Search for Economic Security, 1919–1941* (Ithaca: Cornell University Press, 1988); R. J. Overy, *War and Economy in the Third Reich* (Oxford: Clarendon Press, 1994); William Miles Fletcher III, *The Japanese Business Community and National Trade Policy, 1920–1942* (Chapel Hill: University of North Carolina Press, 1989).

THE CAUSES OF AUTARKY-SEEKING

STATES HAVE two distinct but related reasons to seek economic self-sufficiency, or autarky. Trade disruption reduces a nation's access to resources that contribute to prosperity and growth in peacetime, and military-industrial mobilization in wartime. Theoretically, either threats of wartime blockade and threats of peacetime barriers could provoke states to seek autarky by conquering valuable territories. Only the former kind threats, however—whether real or misperceived—are frightening enough to lead a state to risk a major war in order to expand.

Thus the offense-defense balance and economic interdependence affect the likelihood of war in a way that conventional theories treating these variables separately have generally overlooked. By examining the strategic economic dictates of protracted warfare, it is possible to specify more precisely the conditions that promote aggressive autarky-seeking. In addition, it is worth considering common national misperceptions of these conditions, which have analogous effects on strategic calculations. Militarism and recent experience with long attrition wars influence national perceptions of the likelihood and nature of warfare, and foster interest in autarky and aggression.

THE OFFENSE-DEFENSE BALANCE, INTERDEPENDENCE, AND ECONOMIC WARFARE

Economic self-sufficiency can be an important asset for waging long and intense wars of attrition. Long attrition wars, like the First and Second World Wars, require a protracted and intensive mobilization of economic resources. A state's competitiveness in such conflicts depends to a great extent on its total amount of resources and a complementary balance among them; shortages of key strategic materials, parts, or equipment can cause crippling bottlenecks in a war economy. States can often rely on trade with allies and neutrals, if usually not adversaries, to maintain balance in their economic supplies.[9] Even these trade links, however, can be severed by enemy blockades.

Economic isolation is far more dangerous for trade-dependent states during long and intense wars of attrition than during short and decisive wars. If wars are short, states can import and stockpile arms, munitions, strategic materials,

---

9. Sometimes adversaries do trade during war; see Jack S. Levy, "Historical Perspectives on Interdependence and Conflict" (paper presented at the Annual Meeting of the International Studies Association, Minneapolis, Minnesota, March 1998); Katherine Barbier and Jack S. Levy, "Sleeping with the Enemy: the Impact of War on Trade," *Journal of Peace Research* 26, no. 4 (July 1999): 463–79.

and foodstuffs before military and economic warfare has commenced. Wars that drag on, however, eventually exhaust strategic stockpiles, and trade-dependent and blockaded states will be hard pressed to synthesize or replace critical supplies. Thus, whatever lengthens war puts a premium on having an autarkic economy at the outbreak of war, while factors that shorten war make trade dependence less of a security liability.

The value of autarky depends not only on the duration of war and of trade severance, but also on their likelihood and intensity. Obviously, if war and blockade are improbable, then autarky is not needed for security. The intensity of war, that is, the rate at which arms and munitions are expended, is also important. If fighting is only sporadic, and arms and supplies are expended at a low rate, war can continue for a long time without exhausting stockpiles.[10] A prolonged blockade, however, even with low levels of attrition and mobilization can still strangle a trade-dependent state.

If the likelihood and severity of military and economic warfare determine the importance of autarky, trade dependence affects the incentives to try to achieve it. Most obviously, trade dependent states are more highly motivated to expand than self-sufficient ones, as are states that are relatively vulnerable to embargo or blockade. This is the point made in the realist critique of commercial liberalism—that interdependence can have dangerous effects among autonomy- or security-seeking states.

The exploitability or "cumulativity" of conquered resources also affects the economic incentives for expansion. States will improve neither their overall economic capabilities nor their self-sufficiency by conquering ungovernable and unexploitable territories. Domestic political attributes of the conqueror matter importantly here, since dictatorial regimes are much better suited than democracies to crushing resistance and to exploiting enslaved nations.[11]

Finally, variation in the costliness of war among different countries could create opportunities for expansion. Trade-dependent states expecting long struggles with great power adversaries would have strong incentives to gobble up smaller and more vulnerable economic prizes first.

The strategic economic demands of long attrition wars suggest a paradoxical twist to the impact of the offense-defense balance on the security dilemma and war. The offense-defense balance is one of the leading systemic explanations of war. According to the theory, offense dominance—or at least the perception of it—causes war because it heightens incentives for expansion (for either defensive or opportunistic purposes), preemption, brinkmanship, and secrecy.

10. I thank Ed Mansfield for pointing this out.
11. Peter Liberman, *Does Conquest Pay? The Exploitation of Occupied Industrial Societies* (Princeton: Princeton University Press, 1996), esp. 150–51.

If the offense is dominant, wars will be short and won most often by attackers, reducing the costs and risks of aggression and increasing them for sitting on the defense. Conversely, defense dominance lengthens wars and makes the resort to conflict less appealing to all potential attackers. The belief in easy offense at the outbreak of the First World War is the paradigmatic example for the theory, even though in fact this belief was a misperception. If the belligerents had anticipated the long attrition stalemate dictated by military technology, it is argued, they would have been less willing to provoke crises and more willing and able to pull back from the brink in July 1914.[12]

Analyses of the offense-defense balance, however, have overlooked its strategic economic consequences, and how these could affect expansionism and war. Defense dominance, by making victory more difficult, lengthens war and hence increases the security value of autarky. Thus while defense dominance increases the military costs of expansion, it also increases the economic incentives to expand for states that see war and blockade as likely anyway, are dependent on trade, and expect conquered resources to be utilizable. In other words, the strategic economic effects of the offense-defense balance have precisely opposing implications for international stability from the battlefield effects. Defense dominance makes conquering foreign resources harder but more imperative, while offense dominance makes conquest easier but less imperative.

The benefits of defense dominance for international stability thus appear more complex and less promising than advertised by theorists focusing on its battlefield effects. This is not the only possible difficulty in the theory's logic. James Fearon has pointed out that by making victories more decisive without ensuring that attackers will win, offense dominance makes war a more dangerous gamble for initiators and defenders alike. Offense dominance also quickens alliance balancing, which reduces the attacker's advantage.[13] The economic consequences of the offense-defense balance, however, may provide another reason why some scholars have found a weak historical correlation between the balance and the frequency of war.[14]

This paradox does not arise for the nuclear brand of defense dominance, or "deterrence dominance." According to offense-defense theory, nuclear deter-

---

12. See the sources cited in n. 4. For opposing views on this interpretation of the First World War, see Van Evera, "Cult of the Offensive"; and Marc Trachtenberg, *History and Strategy* (Princeton: Princeton University Press, 1991), chap. 2.

13. James D. Fearon, "The Offense-Defense Balance and War Since 1648" (unpub. manuscript, University of Chicago, April 1997).

14. The most systematic study, Van Evera's "Offense, Defense, and the Causes of War," finds a strong relationship, but little correlation is found by Levy, "Offensive/Defensive Balance"; and Fearon, "Offense-Defense Balance and War."

rence strongly enhances the defense, because it is so difficult to disarm a state's nuclear retaliatory capability. Unlike conventional defense dominance, however, nuclear deterrence (or nuclear war) requires no wartime economic mobilization, and embargos or blockades cannot erode a nuclear-armed state's capability to destroy any attacker.[15] So this paradoxical consequence of the offense-defense balance is confined to relations among nonnuclear states, or where the nuclear balance is so stable that nuclear escalation is unlikely.

A mitigating factor in this offense-defense paradox stems from the fact that the value of autarky depends not only on the type of war states are likely to encounter, but also on its likelihood. If defense dominance makes war so costly as to be unthinkable, then states have less need to worry about how to wage war, militarily or economically. Conversely, the greater frequency of war caused by offense dominance may lead states to worry more about the (smaller) economic problems of fighting. If the frequency of war is not governed so dramatically by the offense-defense balance, however, then this effect does not apply, and defense dominance is more likely to generate autarky concerns.

Geographic variation in the offense-defense balance (and in the balance of power) has strong effects on the temptations of autarky and expansion. The offense-defense balance is often treated as a property of the entire international system, because it derives in large measure from the state of military technology, which in turn diffuses rapidly among competitive great powers. In fact, however, the offense-defense balance varies according to geography, force-to-space ratios, and cumulativity of resources.[16] If the offense-defense balance favors the defense globally, but not locally (or if local defensive advantages are overwhelmed by power disparities), incentives for the seizure of local economic prizes will be heightened.

In addition to creating problems for offense-defense theory, the economic exigencies of modern attrition war also throw a monkey wrench into the theory of commercial liberalism. Going back to Richard Cobden and Norman Angell, commercial liberals have argued that economic interdependence causes peace, and the greater the interdependence, the stronger

15. For a general analysis of the impact of nuclear weapons on strategy and diplomacy, see Robert Jervis, *The Meaning of the Nuclear Revolution: Statecraft and the Prospect of Armageddon* (Ithaca: Cornell University Press, 1989). Discussions of its impact on economic security are less common; for examples, see Kenneth N. Waltz, "The Emerging Structure of International Politics," *International Security* 18, no. 2 (fall 1993): 74; and Charles L. Glaser, "Realists as Optimists: Cooperation as Self-Help," *International Security* 19, no. 3 (winter 1994/95): 79.

16. Glaser and Kaufmann, "What is the Offense-Defense Balance?" 57–58, 61–68. Van Evera adds alliance diplomacy as an element of the balance; on the pros and cons of this approach see his "Offense, Defense," 21–22; and Glaser and Kaufmann, "What is the Offense-Defense Balance," 68–70.

the bulwark against war.[17] As realists are quick to point out, however, states are extremely jealous of their security and autonomy. Thus at the same time that it heightens the cost of war, economic interdependence also spurs states to take steps to reduce their vulnerability should war occur. The greater the independence, the more frightened states will become of trade severance, and the greater their incentives for autarky-seeking expansion.

EXPECTATION OF PEACETIME TRADE BARRIERS

Of course, war is not the only source of trade disruption worrisome to states. Peacetime trade barriers are an obstacle to prosperity that states could theoretically try to remove by conquest. Thus, Copeland has recently argued that expectations of reduced trade increase incentives for expansionism and war.[18] Copeland leaves open the specific conditions that cause anxieties about future trade as well as the types of reduced trade that states are likely to find most alarming. His empirical case studies and illustrations, however, refer to perceptions of increasing peacetime trade barriers. His case studies of Wilhelmine and Nazi Germany provide evidence of German economic dependence and of official worries about peacetime exclusion from essential resources and markets, leading Copeland to conclude that these were major causes of German aggressiveness leading to both world wars.[19]

Do states expand to improve their prosperity or their security? This distinction cannot be drawn too sharply, because wealth ultimately translates into power. States have reasons of security to worry about relative economic position, and hence gain. Still, states worry first about security, then prosperity.[20] Threats of prolonged wartime embargo or blockade provoke more aggressive responses than threats to ordinary trade, because only the

17. For modern formulations and tests of the theory, see Richard Rosecrance, *The Rise of the Trading State: Commerce and Conquest in the Modern World* (New York: Basic Books, 1986); and the research cited by Oneal and Russett, "Classical Liberals Were Right," 270–72.

18. Copeland, "Economic Interdependence and War." Copeland's formulation does not explain why states should find the trading status quo acceptable; if the costs of conquest become low, states may expand to increase their trading opportunities even if barriers are constant. Some prospect theory assumptions about framing could help motivate the hypothesis.

19. Copeland, "Economic Interdependence and War," 22, 27–39.

20. This is a key assumption in neorealist theory; see Waltz, *Theory of International Politics*, 126. Positing exceptions are Rosecrance, *Rise of the Trading State*; Thomas U. Berger, *Cultures of Antimilitarism: National Security in Germany and Japan* (Baltimore: Johns Hopkins University Press, 1998); Eric Heginbotham and Richard J. Samuels, "Mercantile Realism and Japanese Foreign Policy," in *Unipolar Politics: Realism and State Strategies After the Cold War*, ed. Ethan B. Kapstein and Michael Mastanduno (New York: Columbia University Press, 1999), 182–217.

former confront states with a concrete and immediate risk of military defeat.

Most kinds of peacetime trade concerns, disputes, and policies have a relatively indirect and moderate impact on security compared to military security issues. Typical peacetime trade barriers are far less severe than a blockade or embargo, and are apt to erode a state's wealth only gradually. Unless there is reason to expect that the barriers will become permanent, the damage done is usually temporary and reversible. In addition, the drag on economic growth is shared by both trading partners, and losses are likely to be mutual, with an ambiguous effects on relative power.[21] While war-risking expansion might conceivably be a cost-effective policy for coping with future wartime embargos or blockades, it is too dangerous and costly a means just to knock down ordinary trade barriers.

Domestic economic interest groups are also likely to be divided on the spoils of empire. While exporters facing high tariff barriers may see virtue in capturing secure markets for their goods, this incentive will be tempered by fears that conquest will cause other states to close their markets even more. Firms producing for the domestic market under tariff protection will also oppose expansion, when it results in the annexation of—and unprotected competition from—rival producers. And because war generally entails high costs and government controls for producers, they will often prefer more peaceful means to gain access to markets and resources. Thus even a severe closing of foreign markets will not lead to a stampede of all economic interests lobbying for conquest.

NATIONAL MISPERCEPTIONS

While actual conditions in the international system can provide powerful incentives for autarky and aggression, warped perceptions of these conditions can create or intensify beliefs about the need for expansion. Two national attributes have a predictable impact on such perceptions, the "lessons" of the past and militarization. In pointing out the role of these domestic factors, I am not attempting to provide a general unit-level theory of irrational expansion, like Jack Snyder's theory that cartellized political systems generate myths about the cumulativity of losses and gains, offensive military advantage, and the ef-

---

21. Peter Liberman, "Trading with the Enemy: Security and Relative Economic Gains," *International Security* 21, no. 1 (summer 1996): 147–75.

fectiveness of threats.[22] I am also not denying that other national factors, such as hypernationalism or raw greed, can be powerful causes of aggression. I simply want to show that common misperceptions of the nature and likelihood of future war can affect the perceived incentives for autarky-seeking expansionism.

Formative experiences, particularly the last major war, tend to have a disproportionate impact on perceptions of the present. Memory of the rapid and decisive Austro-Prussian and Franco-Prussian wars, for example, was an important cause of the illusory "cult of the offensive" in Europe prior to 1914. Memories of the protracted struggle of attrition that followed led to the exaggerated beliefs in defense dominance during the interwar period.[23]

States in which militaries have a disproportionate influence on foreign policy, or that are led by civilians with strong militaristic biases, are likely to exaggerate the advantages of autarky. Militaries' organizational interests dictate inflating the probability of war and the resources required to wage it.[24] If warfare is expected to be long and intense, this predisposition to exaggerate the likelihood of war adds a critical ingredient to the recipe for autarky seeking. Militaries tend to be less concerned about issues of peacetime trade and prosperity, issues that fall outside of their domain of professional expertise and responsibility. This makes militarized states even less likely than others to consider war as a means to protect or expand peacetime commerce.

Might not militarized states also misperceive the offense-defense balance in ways that diminish autarky seeking? One reason to expect this is that militaries also prefer offensive doctrines, which serve organizational interests in reducing uncertainty, enhancing autonomy, and justifying increased budgets.[25] This strategic preference can lead militaries to exaggerate the ease of offense, an important explanation for pre-1914 Europe's cult of the offensive, which if anything dampened Germany's prewar concerns about economic self-sufficiency and blockade.[26] Militaries, however, do not always have such a strong vested interest in exaggerating the ease of offense. Militaries in eco-

22. *Myths of Empire: Domestic Politics and International Ambition* (Ithaca: Cornell University Press, 1991). For a critique, see Charles A. Kupchan, *The Vulnerability of Empire* (Ithaca: Cornell University Press, 1994).

23. Robert Jervis, *Perception and Misperception in International Politics* (Princeton: Princeton University Press, 1976), chap. 6.

24. Samuel P. Huntington, *The Soldier and the State: The Theory and Politics of Civil-Military Relations* (Cambridge: Harvard University Press, 1957), 59–79; Stephen Van Evera, "Primed for Peace: Europe after the Cold War," in Lynn-Jones and Miller, *Cold War and After*, 204–6.

25. Barry R. Posen, *The Sources of Military Doctrine: France, Britain, and Germany Between the World Wars* (Ithaca: Cornell University Press, 1984).

26. Jack L. Snyder, *The Ideology of the Offensive: Military Decision Making and the Disasters of 1914* (Ithaca: Cornell University Press, 1984).

nomically dependent states can also justify offensive doctrines by arguing that expansion—particularly against vulnerable economic prizes—is essential for achieving autarky for later attrition wars. Because of its strong bias toward seeing a high likelihood of war, and its conditional bias about the offense-defense balance, militarization overall exacerbates the expansionist impulse.

CASE STUDIES

THE FOLLOWING case studies examine and compare the economic sources of German and Japanese expansionism prior to both world wars. Both powers were only cautiously expansionist prior to the First World War. War was believed to be short and decisive, so trade dependence did not create worrisome vulnerabilities. During and after the war, however, influential actors in Germany and Japan concluded that future wars were likely to be total and would require economic self-sufficiency. Both nations were particularly dependent on trade and vulnerable to wartime blockade and embargo. In the 1930s, moreover, their foreign policies were controlled increasingly by leaders fixated on the inevitability of major war. In Japan, this was due to the heightened influence of the Army and Navy over security policy. The German military shared these biases as well, but was under the control of Adolf Hitler, a still more fanatical believer in the inescapability of war.

Intensifying German and Japanese expansionism coincided with a deepened pessimism about peacetime trade prospects. World trade had collapsed in 1930–31, and this triggered talk about autarky and expansion. Concern about wartime trade disruptions, however, was a more important cause of expansion. The international environment did not provide clear indications of indefinitely high peacetime trade barriers. Even if it had, the economic interest groups most affected by protectionism were not particularly influential in foreign-policy making. Neither the Japanese military nor the Nazis were very concerned about peacetime trade, and neither allowed median economic interests to influence foreign policy. Ironically, the collapse of world trade and the ensuing Depression made expansionism more likely not by increasing economic incentives for expansion, but by undermining political systems that were less fatalistic about the inevitability of war.

The case studies do not attempt to provide a complete explanation for variation in German and Japanese expansionism. Naked greed and lust for power may have played a more important role than perceived insecurity, particularly in Hitler's Germany. Comparisons over time for each nation, however, at a minimum raise difficulties for standard offense-defense balance predictions that perceived offense dominance increases expansionism and defense dominance restrains it. Process tracing the perceptions and decision making in each nation also provides evidence for the hypothesized causal link between total war expectations and expansion. One need not conclude that these were the only or even the main causes of expansionism to observe the paradoxical effects of the offense-defense balance and interdependence.

WILHELMINE GERMANY

German expansionism was much more moderate in the Wilhelmine than in the Nazi periods. An historical school led by Fritz Fischer has argued that Germany was a greedy expansionist power with a premeditated plan, dating back at least to 1912, to launch a war of conquest in Europe.[27] It is doubtful that German officials had a premeditated plan of conquest, but they did recklessly risk war in July 1914 by encouraging Austria to deal harshly with Serbia.[28] Yet the case that German belligerence was motivated by greed for economic prizes on the continent and overseas is based on circumstantial evidence, and has fallen into disfavor in current German historiography. Among the motivations of German leaders, the strongest seems to be perceptions of German relative military decline. Autarky was not an important concern, because war in Europe was expected—however wrongly—to be short and decisive. Even if autarky had been desired, German leaders' doubts about the cumulativity of resources meant that it would appear hard to achieve by expansion.

Autarky for the next war? German officials' interest in autarky, and hence expansionism, was dampened by their assumption that the next European war would be short. In fact, historical memory of the quick and decisive wars of German unification, as well as a strong organizational preference for offensive doctrines, had given rise to a "cult of the offensive" throughout Europe.[29] As a result, the German civil service, War Ministry, and General Staff assumed that if war came it would last no more than nine months. Chief of Staff Helmuth Von Moltke worried to some extent about the possibility that war could last as long as two years, and conducted some studies on wartime food and raw materials requirements. He also assumed, however, that a British blockade could be circumvented by trade through the Netherlands; his decision to respect Dutch

27. Fritz Fischer, *War of Illusions: German Policies from 1911 to 1914*, trans. Marian Jackson (New York: Norton, 1975); Imanuel Geiss, *German Foreign Policy, 1871–1914* (London: Routledge and Kegan Paul, 1976).

28. Trachtenberg, *History and Strategy*, 49–57; V. R. Berghahn, *Germany and the Approach of War in 1914* (New York: St. Martin's, 1973), 193ff.

29. Van Evera, "Cult of the Offensive," esp. 67–68; Snyder, *Ideology of the Offensive*, chap. 5.

neutrality was motivated partly to preserve a commercial "windpipe."[30] The German Foreign Office did not show much concern over vulnerability to the British blockade either.[31] Reflecting these premises, as well as a preference to concentrate scarce resources on the Schlieffen Plan, Germany's economic preparations for the long war contingency were minimal.[32] Since German officials did not fear having to fight a long war under economic blockade, though this is what ultimately befell them, they did not worry about German economic vulnerability or how to overcome it. In the end, ironically, the German war economy did suffer considerably—if not catastrophically—from the Allied blockade.[33]

Recognition that governing and exploiting politically hostile foreigners would be difficult, that is, that resources were not very cumulative, also put a damper on German expansionism. Chancellor Bernhard von Bülow told the Kaiser in 1908 that "there would be nothing for us to gain in the conquest of any fresh Slav or French territory. If we annex small countries to the Empire we shall only strengthen those centrifugal elements which, alas, are never wanting in Germany."[34] His successor Theobald von Bethmann Hollweg agreed, apparently sharing the view of his trusted adviser, Kurt Riezler, that "wars between great powers [would] no longer be started because of the rewards to be gained from them, but only from necessity."[35] The Reich's experience in governing the Alsace-Lorrainers, who despite Germanic linguistic and cultural traits had complained interminably since 1871 about their lack of representation in the Reichstag, may have had a role here; even during the war, after German annexationism had grown markedly, Kaiser Wilhelm objected to Baltic annexations to avoid "a second Alsace-Lorraine."[36]

The strongest German motive for backing Austria-Hungary in the July crisis was a fear of the Central Powers' relative decline. Russia appeared to be gaining in economic strength, was building railroads in Poland, and in 1914 had

30. Snyder, *Ideology of the Offensive*, 154.

31. Norrin M. Ripsman and Jean-Marc F. Blanchard, "Commercial Liberalism Under Fire: Evidence from 1914 and 1936," *Security Studies* 6, no. 2 (winter 1996/97): 21–22.

32. Gerd Hardach, *The First World War, 1914–1918* (Berkeley: University of California Press, 1977), 55–56; Avner Offer, *The First World War: An Agrarian Interpretation* (Oxford: Clarendon Press, 1989), 321–53, esp. 344; Snyder, *Ideology of the Offensive*, 153–55.

33. The German economy suffered much more from the dislocations of war mobilization. See Hardach, *First World War*, 11–34; Offer, *First World War*, 21–78.

34. Quoted in David E. Kaiser, "Germany and the Origins of the First World War," *Journal of Modern History* 55 (September 1983): 455–56.

35. Quoted in Andreas Hillgruber, *Germany and the Two World Wars*, trans. W. Kirby (Cambridge: Harvard University Press, 1981), 23; cf. 38. See also Kaiser, "Germany and the Origins," 468.

36. Fritz Fischer, *Germany's Aims in the First World War* (New York: Norton, 1967), 603.

embarked on a "Great Program" of military expansion.[37] Germany's main ally, on the other hand, seemed besieged by Slavs from within the empire, a problem exacerbated by the Serbian victory and expansion in the Second Balkan War of 1913.[38] Belief that the offense was dominant bolstered both fears of the Russian build-up and hopes that the Schlieffen Plan could deliver a quick and cheap solution.[39] Victory by the Central Powers would stabilize Austria-Hungary by giving her complete domination over the Balkans, and would at the same time smash Russian power, perhaps permanently by carving out Poland, the Baltics, and the Ukraine as independent buffer states.

The German General Staff played a crucial role, during the summer of 1914, in convincing the Kaiser and his civilian advisers that Russia's military build-up would soon leave Germany at its mercy. Foreign Minister Gottlieb von Jagow reported von Molke's thinking in May 1914 as follows: "Russia will have completed her armaments in two or three years. The military superiority of our enemies would be so great that he did not know how we might cope with them. In his view there was no alternative to waging a preventive war in order to defeat the enemy as long as we could still more or less pass the test."[40] Jagow seems to have been convinced, for he wrote to his ambassador in London that "according to all competent observation, Russia will be prepared to fight in a few years. Then she will crush us...."[41] So was Bethmann Hollweg, as Riezler's diary shows: "The secret intelligence gives a shattering picture...Austria is becoming increasingly weaker and more and more immobile. The subversion [of the Dual Monarchy] from the north and the south-east [has] progressed very far....The military might of Russia is growing fast."[42] During the war, Bethmann Hollweg recalled that "in a sense it was a preventive war. But the war was hanging over us anyway, two years later it would have come even more dangerously and unavoidably."[43]

---

37. The perception of Russian growing strength was shared by the other great powers, despite the fact that economic trends favored Germany. William C. Wohlforth, "The Perception of Power: Russia in the Pre-1914 Balance," *World Politics* 39, no. 3 (April 1987): 353–81. Germany, however, faced tight domestic political constraints on expanding the size and budget of its army; see Niall Ferguson, "Public Finance and National Security: The Domestic Origins of the First World War Revisited," in *Past and Present*, no. 142 (February 1994): 141–68.

38. Berghahn, *Germany and the Approach of War*, 141.

39. Van Evera, "Cult of the Offensive;" Snyder, *Ideology of the Offensive*, chaps. 4–5.

40. Quoted in Berghahn, *Germany and the Approach of War*, 172; cf. 167–68, 171–72; 191–92

41. Imanuel Geiss, ed. *July 1914. The Outbreak of the First World War: Selected Documents* (London: B. T. Batsford, 1967), 123.

42. Quoted in Berghahn, *Germany and the Approach of War*, 191.

43. Quoted in Fischer, *War of Illusions*, 468.

Autarky for prosperity? This is not to argue that there were no expansionist sentiments in Wilhelmine Germany. The government was clearly interested in overseas colonies, the end purpose of a massive naval build-up and of gunboat diplomacy contesting French control over Morocco. Some industrialists, a few with official ties, worried about being shut out from foreign markets and called for an enlarged German-dominated customs zone in Europe, or a *Mitteleuropa*. Once war had broken out, moreover, and victory appeared to be at hand, a whole array of new economic and strategic ambitions swelled German war aims. On the basis of such evidence, the Fischer school contends that economic ambition drove Germany toward a premeditated war of conquest in 1914.[44] This is also the same kind of evidence used by Copeland to argue that pessimism about world trade opportunities gave German leaders a strong motive for expansion and war.[45]

The case for this interpretation is entirely circumstantial, however. If economic imperialism had been an important reason for Germany's going to war in 1914, one would expect to find evidence that the top German officials were lusting for conquest before and during the July Crisis. Economic ambitions, however, do not appear to have been among the leading concerns of German leaders in 1914, and the cabinet did not even discuss colonies during the July crisis.[46] The Fischer school has stressed Bethmann Hollweg's 29 July offer to refrain from annexing Belgian and French soil, though not their colonies, in return for British neutrality.[47] While this could be an implicit admission of expansionist ambition, it also could have been simply a clumsy ploy to dissuade British intervention. Another piece of evidence are the *Mitteleuropa* plans drawn up by Walter Rathenau, a prominent industrialist and newly appointed war economy official, during July 1914.[48] It is unclear, however, how influential or representative Rathenau's thinking was during the crisis.

The Fischer school's main evidence for economic motivations for war date from after the outbreak of war. In September 1914, as German troops advanced on the Marne, Bethmann Hollweg drew up a list of war aims that amounted to continental hegemony and overseas empire for Germany, justified on both strategic military and economic grounds. The "September Pro-

<hr/>

44. Fischer, *War of Illusions*; Geiss, *German Foreign Policy*. See also Hardach, *First World War*, 227–37; Woodruff D. Smith, *The Ideological Origins of Nazi Imperialism* (New York: Oxford University Press, 1986), chaps. 4–7.

45. Copeland, "Economic Interdependence and War," 27–30.

46. Niall Ferguson, "Germany and the Origins of the First World War: New Perspectives," *Historical Journal* 35, no. 3 (September 1992): 730.

47. Geiss, *German Foreign Policy*, 174–75.

48. Fischer, *War of Illusions*, 63; this evidence is stressed by Copeland, "Economic Interdependence and War," 32

gram" called for forcing Belgium and France into a German trading bloc, and for annexing Liège, northern French iron ore fields, and Belgian and French Africa.[49] German aims continued to grow after the conquest of western Russia, from a slight adjustment of the Prussian border with Poland, with the rest of Poland falling under Austrian control, to the attachment of the Baltics and Poland to the Reich.

The appearance of explicit economic imperialism so soon after the outbreak of the war suggests that it may have had some role in prewar thinking. There are, however, other explanations for it as well. The conduct of war itself exerts strong influence on states' war aims; states tend to form ambitious aims during war that they had not considered as *causus belli* beforehand. If leaders expect to win a war decisively, as Bethmann Hollweg did when he drew up the September Program, they view the costs of fighting as already sunk, and hence the opportunity costs of expansion as low. States also expand their war aims to justify past and coming sacrifices to national opinion.[50] In fact, the other European belligerents also dreamed of territorial gains during the war, though few historians think that these ambitions motivated their behavior in the 1914 crisis.[51]

There is also a strong case to be made against an economic explanation for German belligerence in 1914. There was considerable disagreement among German elites about the economic need for colonies. Bungled attempts to earn Germany a "place in the sun" appear to have been motivated more by considerations of international and domestic prestige.[52] After the debacle of the second Morrocan crisis in 1911, for example, Bethmann Hollweg warned against excessive nationalist propaganda "for the sake of utopian schemes of conquest."[53]

49. Fischer, *Germany's Aims*, 103–5.

50. Fred C. Iklé, *Every War Must End*, rev. ed. (New York: Columbia University Press, 1991), chaps 1 and 5; Eric J. Labs, "Beyond Victory: Offensive Realism and the Expansion of War Aims," *Security Studies* 6, no. 4 (summer 1997): 1–49.

51. David Stevenson, *The First World War and International Politics* (New York: Oxford University Press, 1988).

52. Bethmann Hollweg's understanding of *Weltpolitik* was a crude notion that Germany's world position was vaguely incommensurate with its strength and interests. David Kaiser, Jack Snyder, Charles Kupchan and others have concluded that he had fallen prey to the symbolic *Weltpolitik* propaganda purveyed by his predecessors for largely domestic political reasons. David E. Kaiser, "Germany and the Origins of the First World War," *Journal of Modern History* 55 (September 1983): 442–74; Jack Snyder, *Myths of Empire*, chap. 3; Charles A. Kupchan, *The Vulnerability of Empire* (Ithaca: Cornell University Press, 1994), chap. 6.

53. Quoted in Fischer, *War of Illusions*, 91. Paul M. Kennedy considers Bethmann Hollweg a "pragmatic imperialist", seeking *Weltpolitik* through peaceful means; *Rise of the Anglo-German Antagonism: 1860–1914* (London: Allen and Unwin, 1980), 414–15.

The lack of strong economic motives for war is unsurprising, because German trade prospects were bright during this period. German trade was booming. Between 1900 and 1913, German trade with Britain increased 105 percent, with France 137 percent, and with Russia 121 percent.[54] The Russian tariff of 1914 was a rare obstacle in Germany's overall outlook for trade access. Liberal victories in the 1906 and 1910 British elections scuttled Conservative Party campaign proposals for tariff reform and imperial preference that had worried German commercial interests at the turn of the century.[55] Britain's devotion to free trade in this period was so great, despite having to face substantial German protectionism, that its Foreign Office was not even permitted to engage in active commercial diplomacy or tariff negotiations.[56]

The lack of an economic impulse for expansion is also evident in the attitude of German business, which in general favored peaceful trade expansion and opposed war, particularly with Britain. It was professors, school teachers, and clergymen who pushed hardest for colonial gains, not businessmen.[57] While some economic sectors may have favored imperialism for economic reasons, as well as domestic political ones, they did not push for war in 1914. In fact, few businessmen were consulted during Germany's July 1914 deliberations, and among that few, shipping magnate Albert Ballin and banker Max Warburg both argued against war.[58]

Thus recent historiography has given little weight to economic ambition in explaining German policy. Neither greed nor wartime autarky were influential. "German militarists were not much concerned with economics," a recent review essay notes, and "acknowledgments that German military capability was in fact dependent on economic factors were remarkably rare."[59] Historian James Joll agrees that throughout Europe "economic considerations were not much to the fore in the minds of the politicians taking decisions in July 1914; and when they were…they underlined the disastrous effects of war."[60]

54. B. R. Mitchell, *International Historical Statistics: Europe, 1750–1988*, 3rd ed. (New York: Stockton Press, 1992), Table E2.

55. Kennedy, *Rise of the Anglo-German Antagonism*, 291–305; Aaron L. Friedberg, *The Weary Titan: Britain and the Experience of Relative Decline, 1895–1905* (Princeton: Princeton University Press, 1988), 21–88.

56. D. C. M. Platt, *Finance, Trade, and Politics in British Foreign Policy, 1815–1914* (Oxford: Clarendon Press, 1968), 147.

57. Kennedy, *Rise of the Anglo-German Antagonism*, 291–320, 410–15; Gregor Schöllgen, "Introduction: The Theme Reflected in Recent Research," in *Escape into War? The Foriegn Policy of Imperial Germany*, ed. Gregor Schöllgen (New York: Berg, 1990), 10.

58. Alfred Hugenberg was an unrepresentative exception, according to Ferguson, "Germany and the Origins," 730, 735.

59. Ferguson, "Germany and the Origins," 741–42.

60. *The Origins of the First World War*, 2nd ed. (London and New York: Longman, 1992), 165.

NAZI GERMANY

Nazi imperialism was far more aggressive than the Wilhelmine variety. The First World War had been a long drawn out struggle that had required total economic mobilization and had been won by the economically superior side. Were Germany required to wage another long war of attrition, and compelled by blockade to rely entirely on its own economic strength, size and self-sufficiency would be essential to German survival. In fact, Hitler's conquests in Europe contributed immensely to the German war economy during the Second World War.[61] Hitler's thinking, however, was hardly a model of economic or strategic rationality, and he drew mistaken lessons from the First World War. Hitler seemed to think that self-sufficiency could be attained by colonizing *Lebensraum* (living space) more than by extracting its strategic resources. Nevertheless, the expectation of future total wars, on the part of Hitler as well as the German military, gave a strong impetus to German conquest.

Autarky for the next war. German aggression resulting in the Second World War was conceived, orchestrated, and commanded by Adolf Hitler.[62] Hence, the first place to look for evidence of economic motivations is in Hitler own plans and reasons for conquest, which remained remarkably constant from the mid-1920s. Hitler believed that Germandom was pitted against other races in mortal struggles for survival. War was not only inevitable, it would also be long and demanding. To prevail, Germany needed to carve *Lebensraum* out of Soviet territory, and doing this required seizing small but economically valuable lands in central and eastern Europe, the defeat of France, and the defeat or intimidation of Britain.

Hitler's grand strategy was built upon a number of bizarre and dangerous convictions. His belief in the inevitability of war was based on a muddled concoction of Social Darwinism, Malthusianism, and racism. His obsession with *Lebensraum* stemmed from an ideological romanticization of the German peasant as the foundation of Germandom, as well as from the memory of the role of food shortages in Germany's collapse in 1918. Despite the industrialization of modern war, he believed that the power of a race depended primarily on the size of its population, the extent of its territory, and the abundance of its farmland. Only by conquering and colonizing depopulated farmland did Hitler

---

61. Liberman, *Does Conquest Pay?*, chap. 3.

62. This is not to say that Hitler started the war single handedly. His autonomy and authorship of Nazi foreign policy, however, was considerable. For a recent review of the debate on this issue, see Ian Kershaw, *The Nazi Dictatorship: Problems and Perspectives of Interpretation*, 2nd ed. (London: Edward Arnold, 1989), chaps. 4 and 6.

think that Germandom could grow enough to survive future struggles with larger nations.[63]

Despite this anachronistic agrarian focus, Hitler also had a crude understanding of geopolitics and the importance of industry and raw materials to military power. During the rearmament of the 1930s he became increasingly worried about German industry's dependence on imported raw materials. He seized Austria, the Sudetenland, and the rest of Czechoslovakia with at least one eye on their iron ore, steel, coal, engineering, arms plants, and financial reserves that would help shift the balance of power in Europe in Germany's favor.[64] In March 1939, for example, Hitler told German leaders that "German dominion over Poland is necessary, in order to guarantee the supply of agricultural products and coal for Germany."[65]

Hitler's thirst for expansion was reinforced by his belief that future wars would be long, and would have to mobilize "the whole strength of the people."[66] This is often overlooked because of the successful Blitzkrieg doctrine that devastated France in a six week campaign. Germany's initially low arms output has also been attributed to a deliberate plan to wage quick Blitzkrieg-type wars.[67] Well before the advent of the Blitzkrieg, however, in May 1939, Hitler told his generals that:

> Everybody's Armed Forces and Government must strive for a short war. But the government must, however, also prepare for a war of from ten to fifteen years' duration. History shows that wars were always expected to be short. In 1914 it was still believed that long wars could not be financed. Even today this idea buzzes in a lot of heads. Every state,

63. Norman Rich, *Hitler's War Aims*, vol. 1, *Ideology, the Nazi State, and the Course of Expansion* (New York: Norton, 1973), xxxiii–xliii, 3–10; Klaus Hildebrand, *The Foreign Policy of the Third Reich*, trans. A. Fothergill (Berkeley: University of California Press, 1973), 12–23; William Carr, *Arms, Autarky, and Aggression. A Study in German Foreign Policy, 1933–1939* (London: Edwin Arnold, 1972), 1–20; Geoffrey Stoakes, *Hitler and the Quest for World Domination* (Leamington Spa: Berg, 1986). On the historical antecedents of Hitler's ideas, see Smith, *Ideological Origins of Nazi Imperialism.*

64. R. J. Overy, *Goering: The "Iron Man"* (London: Routledge & Kegan Paul, 1984), 82; Rich, *Hitler's War Aims*, vol. 1, 97. On the actual economic results, see Williamson Murray, *The Change in the European Balance of Power, 1938–1939: The Path to Ruin* (Princeton: Princeton University Press, 1984), 149–51, 290–93; Hans-Erich Volkmann, "The National Socialist Economy in Preparation for War," in *Germany and the Second World War*, ed. Militärgeschichtliches Forschungsamt (Oxford: Clarendon Press, 1990), 323–40.

65. Quoted in Overy, *War and Economy*, 222.

66. Quoted in Overy, *War and Economy*, 1.

67. Burton H. Klein, *Germany's Economic Preparations for War* (Cambridge: 1959); Alan S. Milward, *The German Economy at War* (London: Athlone Press, 1965). Another explanation offered was that Hitler wanted to avoid domestically unpopular mobilization measures; Tim W. Mason, "The Primacy of Politics–Politics and Economics in National Socialist Germany," in *Nazism and the Third Reich*, ed. Henry A. Turner (New York, 1972), 175–200.

however, will hold out as long as it can....The idea of getting out cheaply is dangerous; there is no such possibility.[68]

Historian R. J. Overy has demonstrated persuasively that Hitler expected a long, total war and accordingly sought to mobilize the German economy earlier and more completely than has been recognized. Low output prior to 1942 was due to inefficiency and massive investment in raw material self-sufficiency projects, themselves indications of Hitler's expectation of a long war.[69] Hitler thought that Czechoslovakia and Poland would be easy pickings, and even that offense might even be easy against the French. Beyond that, however, he expected to have to wage long wars under conditions of economic blockade. "The struggle for predominance in the world will be decided in favor of Europe by the possession of the Russian space," Hitler said in September 1941. "Thus Europe will be an impregnable fortress, impregnable from all threat of blockade....The essential thing, for the moment, is to conquer."[70]

This blockade fear was due in large part to the experience of the First World War, which provided fertile ground in Germany for Hitler's emphasis on autarky and *Lebensraum*. "We Germans," Hitler said in October 1939, "have learnt much from our experiences in the First World War and are fully prepared, both militarily and economically for a long war."[71] As historian Woodruff Smith points out, "extreme autarkic versions of economic imperialism that had gained only limited currency before the war seemed more plausible under circumstances of blockade, shortages, and rationing."[72] German wartime propaganda hammered home the national need for territorial expansion, as a means of motivating popular sacrifice for the war effort. After the war was over, popular expectations of renewed conflict were sustained by the continued Allied blockade, the Ruhr occupation and reparations demands, the territorial losses imposed by Versailles, and widespread belief in German innocence of war guilt.[73]

The German military, however pleased by Hitler's emphasis on rearmament and overturning the Versailles settlement, generally lacked Hitler's fixation on inevitable struggles to the finish, and hence the same determination to conquer the necessary resources.[74] Their agreement that future wars would be total,

---

68. Quoted in Overy, *War and Economy*, 190; cf. 219.
69. Overy, *War and Economy*, chaps. 6–9.
70. *Hitler's Secret Conversations, 1941–1944*, trans. Norman Cameron and R. H. Stevens (New York: Farrar, Straus and Young, 1953), 27–28.
71. Quoted in Overy, *War and Economy*, 203.
72. Smith, *Ideological Origins*, 167.
73. Smith, *Ideological Origins*, chaps. 8–9.
74. Wilhelm Deist, *The Wehrmacht and German Rearmament* (Toronto: University of Toronto Press, 1981), 107.

however, along with Hitler's domination and manipulation of military decision making, may help explain the military's acquiescence to Nazi expansionism. General Groener, defense minister during 1928–33 and a war-economy officer during the First World War, argued in 1928 that the nature of modern war makes "it is necessary to organize the entire strength of the people for fighting and working."[75] This notion was given further authority by the publication of Erich Ludendorff's *Der Totale Krieg* (1935).[76] Colonel Georg Thomas, who headed the Army's Economics Staff and later the Military Economy Office of the High Command, agreed that "modern war is no longer a clash of armies, but a struggle for the existence of the peoples involved. All resources of the nation must be made to serve the war."[77] Hitler's Air Force chief, Hermann Göring, an ardent Nazi and advocate of *Lebensraum*, also expected that war would be protracted. He warned upon the outbreak of war in September 1939, that "today's war is a total war, whose end no one can approximately foretell."[78] Hitler appointed Göring to direct the Four Year Plan, a powerful agency established to promote the goal, in Göring's words, "of preparing the German economy for total war."[79]

Nazi racism and ruthlessness also help explain a crucial difference between Hitlerian and Wilhelmine expansionism. Bethmann and other German leaders of his era recognized that the nationalism of neighboring European peoples placed some limits on the political and economic feasibility of at least continental expansion. Wilhelmine-era *Mitteleuropa* concepts were accordingly more voluntaristic than their Nazi successors. Hitler, on the other hand, believed that resources were cumulative, though for twisted reasons. He had no qualms about expelling or exterminating the inferior races that inhabited coveted territory; he sought land for German farmers rather than dominion over non-Aryans. In the end, however, total war required the systematic mobilization of defeated European peoples, who under compulsion contributed greatly to the Nazi war effort, unlike the unsuccessful Nazi colonization schemes.[80]

Autarky for Prosperity? The onset of the Great Depression, accompanied and prolonged by the collapse of world trade and advancing protectionism, also

---

75. Quoted in Overy, *War and Economy*, 177–78; See also Deist, *The Wehrmacht and German Rearmament*, chap. 1, esp. 7–8, 17. According to Deist (p. 26), General Werner von Blomberg, Groener's successor, agreed that an effective national defense required "all its material and human resources, to meet the needs of the military…in accordance with what were generally perceived as the lessons of the First World War."

76. Berenice A. Carroll, *Design for Total War: Arms and Economics in the Third Reich* (The Hague: Morton, 1968), 41.

77. Quoted in Carroll, *Design for Total War*, 40; on Thomas's views, see chaps. 2–3.

78. Quoted in Overy, *Goering*, 78.

79. Quoted in Overy, *War and Economy*, 189.

80. Liberman, *Does Conquest Pay?*, chap. 3.

heightened German interest in autarky. This was not much of a factor in the calculations of Nazi ideologues, however, least of all Hitler, who seemed to disdain trade even more than barriers to it. Well before the collapse of world trade and the Depression, Hitler had derided "the chatter about the peaceful conquest of the world by commercial means" as being "the most completely nonsensical stuff ever raised to the dignity of a guiding principle in the policy of a state."[81] Hitler condemned the notion of Germany as a trading state in part on the grounds that German industrial exports could not compete in the long run with those from larger powers like the United States. Hitler's understanding of economics, however, was primitive and strongly colored by his Social Darwinism; he instinctively detested trade as a morally corrupting influence, one that led to "dissolute pacifism."[82] More important to Hitler's thinking was his belief that trade trade failed to provide a state with sufficient autonomy and military invulnerability, as did overseas colonies, which were vulnerable to blockade and hence an unsuitable basis for German power.[83]

Nevertheless, the steep decline in German trade in the early 1930s increased receptivity in Germany to autarkic proposals. Economic nationalists resurrected the idea of a peacefully constructed *Großraumwirtschaft*, or large-area economy, that would allow for protected and unobstructed trade in Europe, particularly between Germany and central and southeast Europe, and the Nazis soon made this a centerpiece of their economic platform.[84] Depression led industrialists to look more favorably the idea of exclusive trading zones or even conquest, partly because it offered a larger, guaranteed, and protected market, but more importantly because such policy proposals displaced social blame for unemployment away from themselves.[85]

Business, however, remained ambivalent about the need for autarky, particularly as prospects for a revival of trade improved from 1936. "Autarky cannot possibly be an ideal," argued Reichsbank head and Nazi economics minister Hjalmar Schacht in early 1937, as he unsuccessfully sought to expand trade in the face of increasing restrictions imposed by Göring.[86] Albert Vögler, the head of Germany's largest steel combine, contended that "exports should be ranked above the requirements of the armed forces."[87] Gustav Krupp remained a firm believer in trade throughout, and publicly attacked autarky poli-

81. Quoted in Volkmann, "National Socialist Economy," 175.
82. Quoted in Henry Ashby Turner Jr., *German Big Business and the Rise of Hitler* (New York: Oxford University Press, 1985), 73.
83. Carr, *Arms, Autarky, and Aggression*, 16–19.
84. Volkmann, "National Socialist Economy," 159–94.
85. Smith, *Ideological Origins*, 203–13.
86. Quoted in Overy, *War and Economy*, 95; cf. 32, 101, 216.
87. Quoted in Overy, *War and Economy*, 14.

cies in mid-1935.[88] Ruhr industrial leaders opposed Göring's expansion of domestic iron-ore production in 1937 as wasteful and threatening to increased trade.[89] Many firms, like I.G. Farben, became partisans of autarky only after Nazi policies made it politic and profitable to do so.[90]

At this point business views were moot, because by the mid-1930s they had little influence on Nazi foreign or economic policy.[91] Their opposition to Nazi autarkic schemes, however, along with evidence about Hitler's own thinking, casts doubt on the thesis that German aggression was even partly a rational response to declining opportunities for peacetime trade. If the Depression tilted Germany toward expansion, then, it was more as a result of its disastrous effect on the legitimacy of Weimar democracy and the political opportunity this created for a dictator obsessed with total war.

JAPAN

Japanese imperialism was cautious and little motivated by economic concerns before the Second World War and during the 1920s. Once the military took the reins of Japanese foreign policy in the mid-1930s, however, Japan embarked on an aggressive quest for autarky. The Japanese military had deduced from the European experience in the First World War that future wars would be long attrition struggles. Japanese policy was not a purely rational response to defense dominance and economic dependence, and rested on major blunders and miscalculations, but these factors played an important role. Concerns about peacetime trade, though increased by the Depression, had a relatively slight impact. As in Germany, its main effect on foreign policy was to enable total war fanatics to assume control of foreign policy.

Autarky for the next war. The Meiji oligarchs who governed Japan in the late nineteenth century understood the importance of industrial might to military power. With the slogan of "rich country, strong army," they embarked on a crash modernization effort that over time made the resource-poor nation increasingly dependent on imported iron, steel, oil, and other raw materials es-

---

88. Overy, *War and Economy*, chap. 4, esp. 126, 136.

89. Overy, *War and Economy*, 96.

90. Peter Hayes, *Industry and Ideology: IG Farben in the Nazi Era* (Cambridge: Cambridge University Press, 1987), chaps. 4–6; Volker R. Berghahn, "German Big Business and the Quest for a European Economic Empire in the Twentieth Century," in *Quest for Economic Empire: European Strategies of German Big Business in the Twentieth Century*, ed. Volker R. Berghahn (Providence: Berghahn Books, 1996), 1-34; and Harm G. Schröter, "Europe in the Strategies of Germany's Electrical Engineering and Chemicals Trusts, 1919–1929," in Berghahn, *Quest for Economic Empire*, 35-54.

91. Avraham Barkai, *Nazi Economics: Ideology, Theory, and Policy*, trans. Ruth Hadass-Vashitz (Oxford: Berg, 1990), 10–17; Overy, *War and Economy*, 11–18, 113.

sential for prosperity and for warfare. Before the First World War, though, little thought was given to the problem of assuring the supply of these resources. Nineteenth century wars, in Asia as well as in Europe, had been relatively short, had been readily financed and supplied with the help of neutral powers, and hence did not require full mobilization or autarky.[92]

Japanese imperialism during this period, as a consequence, lacked the economic impulse of later years.[93] Japanese designs on Taiwan and Korea, annexed in 1894 and 1910 respectively, were primarily to exclude other powers from acquiring military bases there. At the time of the Sino-Japanese War of 1894, Taiwan had little economic allure, and the Japanese prime minister thought that "we may have to spend on the lands more than we can reap from them."[94] When Japan again attacked Russia over Korea a decade later, its motives were still chiefly territorial. Japanese leaders considered Korea a "dagger pointed at the heart of Japan," and Russian troops and railways had begun to penetrate neighboring Manchuria. Japan also aimed to keep protectionist Russia from closing Korea and Manchuria to Japanese exports, but this was a secondary concern.[95]

This outlook changed once Japanese war planners had studied the military-economic lessons of the First World War. As early as 1915, responding to reports from Japanese officers posted in Europe of stalemated trench warfare and total military-economic mobilization, the Army began to examine the problem of Japanese resource vulnerability. Germany's slow strangulation by blockade and internal collapse in 1918 seemed to hold dire implications for resource-poor Japan. Unless Japan expanded, the Army concluded, it would have no chance in a prolonged war against Russia or the United States, both of whom were seen as likely enemies.[96]

A growing clique of "total war officers" in the Army, many of whom had studied or served in Germany after the First World War, proceeded to lobby for imperial expansion and economic development. As a result, subsequent

92. Barnhart, *Japan Prepares for Total War*, 22.

93. For an overview, see W. G. Beasley, *Japanese Imperialism, 1894–1945* (Oxford: Clarendon Press, 1987), 41–100.

94. Quoted in Beasley, *Japanese Imperialism*, 60. On Taiwan, see Edward I-te Chen, "Japan's Decision to Annex Taiwan: A Study of Ito-Mutsu Diplomacy," in *Journal of Asian Studies* 37, no. 1 (November 1977): 61–72.

95. James B. Crowley, "Japan's Military Foreign Policies," in *Japan's Foreign Policy 1868–1941: A Research Guide*, ed. James W. Morley (New York: Columbia University Press, 1974), 12–13; Peter Duus, "Economic Dimensions of Meiji Imperialism: The Case of Korea, 1895–1910," in *The Japanese Colonial Empire, 1895–1945*, ed. Ramon H. Myers and Mark R. Peattie (Princeton: Princeton University Press, 1984), 128–71.

96. Mark R. Peattie, *Ishiwara Kanji and Japan's Confrontation with the West* (Princeton: Princeton University Press, 1975), chaps. 1–3; Barnhart, *Japan Prepares for Total War*, 22–23.

military planning placed increasing weight on the premise that Japan needed to prepare for a protracted war and embargo.[97] The Army established a Cabinet Resources Bureau in 1927, which then embarked on a detailed study of the economic requirements for a two-year attrition war.[98] A 1936 cabinet-level assessment of grand strategy assumed that "the thing to be most feared is that future wars will be prolonged," and new major studies were pursued on how to cope with this contingency.[99] By the mid-1930s, the "majority of staff officers heading the various divisions and sections within the War Ministry and the General Staff were convinced that the events of 1914–18 had shown that the crucial element in twentieth century wars of attrition was the massive integration of military and industrial planning on a long-range basis."[100]

Paradoxically, the expectation that future wars would be intense and prolonged contests of attrition did not make war appear less likely.[101] On the contrary, the total war officers assumed that war with either the United States or the Soviet Union was inevitable, a view that was widely shared in the Japanese military. In 1927 Ishiwara predicted a final struggle against American expansionism would occur within thirty years.[102] While the Navy continued to stress the threat posed by the United States, Army officers in the mid-1930s agreed that war with the USSR was inevitable and engaged in heated debate over the exact timing of future Soviet attack.[103]

These expectations of prolonged war and its economic demands led to greater national investment in industrial expansion, centralized control over elements of the economy, and territorial expansion aimed at acquiring and developing raw materials critical to total warfare. The autarky advocates did not have their way on all issues. They still had to accommodate demands in the Army and Navy for increasing military spending, which slowed investment in industrial expansion. Other military factions, however, generally supported the total-war officers' imperialist objectives, if only to gain territorial bulwarks to protect the empire.[104] Thus when several total war officers in the Kwantung Army seized Manchuria in 1931, after having lobbied hard for "Japan-

---

97. James B. Crowley, *Japan's Quest for Autonomy: National Security and Foreign Policy 1930–1938* (Princeton: Princeton University Press, 1966), 88–89, 112, 202–4, 207; Peattie, *Ishiwara Kanji*, 67–83; Barnhart, *Japan Prepares for Total War*, chap. 1.

98. Crowley, *Japan's Quest for Autonomy*, 210; Barnhart, *Japan Prepares for Total War*, 25–26.

99. Barnhart, *Japan Prepares for Total War*, 44–45.

100. Peattie, *Ishiwara Kanji*, 186.

101. For an exception, see Akira Iriye, "The Failure of Economic Expansionism: 1918–1931," in *Japan in Crisis*, ed. Bernard Silberman and Harry Harootunian (Princeton: Princeton University Press, 1974), 245.

102. Peattie, *Ishiwara Kanji*, 63–66, 109, 111.

103. Peattie, *Ishiwara Kanji*, 186; Beasley, *Japanese Imperialism*, 182.

104. Barnhart, *Japan Prepares for Total War*, 39.

Manchuria self-sufficiency," they successfully pulled the rest of the Army along.[105]

Iron- and coal-rich north China was the next target of Japan's autarkic quest, and the Army increased its political, economic, and military penetration there quite easily between 1935 and 1937.[106] Developing its economic potential in a cooperative partnership with Chinese political leaders, however, left Japan's economic war plans vulnerable to a souring of Sino-Japanese relations. After a rebellion by north Chinese troops in July 1937, Japan resolved to crush Chiang Kai-shek, and proceeded to occupy northern and central China's principal cities and towns.[107] Prosecuting the war, however, only increased Japanese trade-dependence. Already by 1937, Japan was importing 84 percent of its iron ore and 55 percent of its scrap iron, not to mention coal, oil, tin, bauxite, and a host of ferro-alloys.[108] The war in China required more foreign iron, oil, and machinery, while Japan's trading partners, themselves engaged in rearmament and war, were reducing their exports to Japan. The China War also alienated the British and the Americans, whose concerns about Japan slamming shut the "Open Door" in China prompted them to supply Chiang via Burma and French Indochina and impose minor embargos.[109]

Japanese military leaders saw the German victories of 1940 as an opportunity to drive the Western powers out of Southeast Asia and finally create an autarkic Greater East Asia Co-Prosperity Sphere. They expected to obtain 30 million barrels of Indonesian crude oil (out of a total demand of 35 million) by 1943; the new conquests would also provide rubber, bauxite, tin, nickel, and copper.[110] With the United States threatening to cut off its oil supplies unless Japan retreated from China, and while the French and Dutch were prostrate and the British under siege from Germany, Japan launched its attack on Pearl Harbor. The chief goal was to exploit newly conquered domains to "establish the foundation for a long war."[111] Thus, as historian Michael Barnhart concludes, "the essential element that led to war was Japan's terrible economic

105. Crowley, *Japan's Quest for Autonomy*, 82–121; Peattie, *Ishiwara Kanji*, 87–181; Barnhart, *Japan Prepares for Total War*, 31–33.

106. Crowley, *Japan's Quest for Autonomy*, 187–243, 256, 280–300; Barnhart, *Japan Prepares for Total War*, 39–49; Takafusa Nakamura, "Japan's Economic Thrust into North China, 1933–1938: Formation of the North China Development Corporation," in *The Chinese and the Japanese*, ed. Akira Iriye (Princeton: Princeton University Press, 1980), 220–53.

107. Crowley, *Japan's Quest for Autonomy*, chap. 6; Peattie, *Ishiwara Kanji*, chap. 8; Barnhart, *Japan Prepares for Total War*, chap. 4.

108. Jerome B. Cohen, *Japan's Economy in War and Reconstruction* (Minneapolis: University of Minnesota Press, 1949), 114.

109. Barnhart, *Japan Prepares for Total War*, 91–114, 136–61.

110. Cohen, *Japan's Economy in War*, 135.

111. Naval Chief of Staff Admiral Nagano, October 1941, quoted in Crowley, "Military Policies," 97.

vulnerability and its decision, in light of the lessons of the First World War, to do something about it."[112]

This is not to say that Japan's strategy was rational.[113] By attacking the United States, Japan took on a much more powerful adversary in order to gain access to resources that would still be vulnerable to blockade through the interdiction of Japanese shipping. Only if war with the United States or Russia was inevitable, even if Japan withdrew from China, did this gamble make any sense. Whether organizational or psychological in origin, the Japanese military's commitments to the inevitability of total war or to avoiding defeat in China were thus necessary causes of the war. Irrational decisionmaking is evident from the fact that officials or officers who pointed out that autarky was unattainable were ignored or cashiered.[114]

A key assumption in Japanese expansionism was the assumption that resources were cumulative, that "war can maintain war," as the Army slogan put it.[115] The Japanese did not expect nationalistic resistance in any of their conquests to be strong enough to disrupt economic mobilization. This was due in part to a racist view of other Asians as so backward and impressionable that they could be gradually assimilated after many years of paternalistic Japanese domination and education. The Japanese were also willing to engage in ruthless police measures to ensure pacification and exploitation, and had a successful track record in Taiwan, Korea, and Manchuria.[116] In invading China, however, Japan bit off more than it could chew. Some recognized this, including one of the original total war officers and Manchuria conspirators, Ishiwara Kanji. Ishiwara argued that invading China would be "like what Spain was for Napoleon, an endless bog," but his warnings went unheeded.[117]

Army and Navy domination of Japanese foreign policy during the 1930s meant that their views about the inevitability of total war would carry the day. Increasing military influence in the Japanese state was due to several factors. As in Germany, the Depression delegitimized mainstream political parties and fledgling democratic institutions. At the same time, military elites—radicalized

112. Barnhart, *Japan Prepares for Total War*, 267.

113. For more detailed critiques of Japanese strategy, see Barnhart, *Japan Prepares for Total War*, Kupchan, *Vulnerability of Empire*, 324–58; Snyder, *Myths of Empire*, chap. 4. For a more sympathetic view of Japanese strategy, see Scott D. Sagan, "The Origins of the Pacific War," in *The Origin and Prevention of Major Wars*, ed. Robert I. Rotberg and Theodore K. Rabb (Cambridge: Cambridge University Press, 1989), 323–52.

114. In 1940, the head of the Planning Board, which since 1937 had been the cabinet's primary war economy agency, was fired after issuing a "defeatist" report on the impossibility of achieving self sufficiency. Barnhart, *Japan Prepares for Total War*, 171.

115. Peattie, *Ishiwara Kanji*, 68, 108, 178; cf. 167.

116. Liberman, *Does Conquest Pay?* chap. 6.

117. Quoted in Barnhart, *Japan Prepares for Total War*, 89.

by the suffering of its agrarian social base—sanctioned violent efforts to intimidate or eliminate opponents of increased military spending and imperial expansion. Radical junior officers assassinated several influential moderates, including Prime Minister Hamaguchi Yuko in 1930, Finance Minister Inoue Junnosuke and Prime Minister Inukai Tsuyoshi in 1932, and—in the course of a failed coup—former prime minister Saito Makoto and Finance Minister Takahashi Korekiyo in 1936.[118] The Army also used its constitutional authority to topple cabinets (by refusing to appoint ministers) in 1937 and 1940 to influence the selection of prime ministers, in the latter instance using a coup threat. Finally, when Prime Minister Konoe Fumimaro resigned in the face of stiff Army pressure to authorize Pearl Harbor, the emperor's representative felt compelled to appoint the hawkish Tojo out of fear of an army revolt.[119]

Autarky for prosperity? Japanese fear of being excluded from world markets and resources in peacetime, and the resulting impact on Japanese prosperity, provided a weaker incentive for Japanese imperialism. In a 1918 article Konoe, who was later to become prime minister during 1937–38, demanded "equal access to the markets and natural resources of the colonial areas" from the British and Americans, or Japan would be forced "to destroy the status quo for the sake of self-preservation, just like Germany."[120] Two developments heightened Japanese pessimism about foreign trade by the early 1930s. First, Chiang Kai-shek's consolidation of power in south and central China and rising Chinese nationalism posed a potential indigenous threat to the "Open Door" in China.[121] Second, the collapse of international trade following the 1929 Wall Street crash made Japanese access to world markets and resources seem suddenly more precarious. Trade with the colonies held up better than extraimperial trade during the ensuing depression. Foreign trade barriers and currency devaluations led many in Japan's political and economic elite to conclude that a large economic trading bloc was needed to protect their country from

---

118. Crowley, *Japan's Quest for Autonomy*, 79, 179–80; Gordon Mark Berger, *Parties out of Power in Japan, 1931–1941* (Princeton: Princeton University Press, 1977); Barnhart, *Japan Prepares for Total War*, 268–69. Barnhart (p. 67) describes the alliance between reform bureaucrats and autarky officers precipitated by the Depression, which led to greater centralized planning of the Japanese economy.

119. Barnhart, *Japan Prepares for Total War*, 250–54; Snyder, *Myths of Empire*, 141–42.

120. Quoted in Beasley, *Japanese Imperialism*, 179.

121. Beasley, *Japanese Imperialism*, 156–74; Toshiyuki Mizoguchi, "The Changing Pattern of Sino-Japanese Trade, 1884–1937," in *The Japanese Informal Empire in China, 1895–1937*, ed. Peter Duus, Ramon H. Myers, and Mark R. Peattie (Princeton: Princeton University Press, 1989), 10–30; Banno Junju, "Japanese Industrialists and Merchants and the Anti-Japanese Boycotts in China, 1919–1928," in Duus, Myers, and Peattie, *The Japanese Informal Empire in China, 1895–1937*, 314–29.

Western and Chinese "economic warfare."[122] The idea of peacetime economic security is also suggested by the Japanese propaganda slogan of "co-prosperity," which was applied to China long before Southeast Asia.[123]

Two facts suggest, however, that concerns about peacetime trade had a relatively limited effect on Japanese imperialism. First, as in Nazi Germany, in the mid-1930s Japanese business was generally unenthusiastic about the government's quest for autarky and empire. Business generally opposed increased military spending, centralized control of economy, and the material shortages resulting from empire-building. According to historian William Fletcher, "While willing to exploit opportunities in China, the business community did not display much enthusiasm toward autarky. The growth of the nation's industries mandated trade with the West. Moreover, a larger empire might lead to unwanted competition for domestic producers. The business community adjusted to the government's foreign policy rather than act forcefully to affect it."[124] The lack of enthusiasm for conquest on the part of domestic actors highly dependent upon peacetime trade demonstrates that Japan's commercial trade outlook did not provide a strong incentive for conquest.

Second, the military dominated Japanese foreign policy, as pointed out above, and was more interested in autarky for waging war than for prosperity. The Japanese military had little expertise on commercial issues and was at constant loggerheads with Japan's financial interests.[125] To the extent that military officers were sensitive to business, moreover, they were disproportionately sympathetic to the colonial banks and enterprises to which they were exposed during lengthy postings in Taiwan, Korea, or Manchuria.[126] Colonial businesses had a much greater stake in imperial trade and autarky than Japanese business as a whole, and an economic strategy based on their interests cannot be seen as a logical response to Japan's commercial opportunities.

122. Iriye, "Failure of Economic Expansionism: 1918–1931," esp. 261–69; Beasley, *Japanese Imperialism*, 188–90; cf. 118, 158; Ramon H. Myers, "Japanese Imperialism in Manchuria: The South Manchuria Railway Company, 1906–1933," in Duus, Myers, and Peattie, *Japanese Informal Empire*, 101–32; Fletcher, *Japanese Business Community*, 71–109.

123. Beasley, *Japanese Imperialism*, 118–21, 175, 190, 202.

124. Fletcher, *Japanese Business Community*, 108–9, cf. 79. See also Arthur E. Tiedemann, "Big Business and Politics in Prewar Japan," in *Dilemmas of Growth in Prewar Japan*, ed. James William Morley (Princeton: Princeton University Press, 1971), 267–318; Barnhart, *Japan Prepares for Total War*, 173–74.

125. Jonathan Kirshner, "Interwar Japan: The Defeat of Finance and the Rise of the Military" (unpub. ms, Cornell University, April 1998).

126. Beasley, *Japanese Imperialism*, 190–91.

IMPLICATIONS FOR THEORY AND POLICY

EXPANSIONIST impulses in pre–First World War Germany and Japan, in an era when wars were believed to be short and decisive, were relatively moderate. After the war, leaders in both states concluded that future wars were likely to be total, and that autarky was essential in total war. They also expected to face such wars sooner or later, leading to expansionist strategies and the Second World War. Defense dominance may not have increased the likelihood of war, but for these reasons it did not have the peace-causing effect offense-defense theory predicts.

Interdependence and defense dominance were not sufficient causes for Japanese and German expansionism, at least to the point of starting great power wars. Japan's and Germany's policies were premised on numerous misperceptions and miscalculations, many of which were due to the political ascendance of militaristic actors. Exaggerated perceptions of the inevitability of war were critical, because defense dominance and the costliness of war would otherwise have more ambiguous implications for autarky requirements. If states are predisposed to believe that war is highly likely regardless of the costs, though, defense dominance's Catch-22 arises in full force.

In the absence of this misperception, Germany and Japan probably still would have expanded in the 1930s, particularly to vulnerable nearby territories. They would have been less desperate, however, and hence less bold in risking war with other great powers. Hitler's abject craving for world dominion cannot be overemphasized as a cause of the war. Even in his warped thinking, however, and in public and bureaucratic support for his ambitions, it is possible to observe the paradoxical consequences of the offense-defense balance and economic vulnerability.

Thus, although German and Japanese reasoning in the 1930s mirrored in many respects the logic linking defense dominance to autarky-seeking, these do not represent critical case studies for testing the hypothesis. It would be useful to examine other cases as well. It is worth briefly pointing out, though, that the status quo policies of the other great powers in the 1930s are not counterexamples to the hypothesis. Despite their perception that warfare strongly favored the defense, these states still had less to fear from economic isolation in war. Russia and the United States had vast internal resources and markets. Britain and France were more dependent on trade, but their colonial empires and alliances reduced their vulnerability to embargos by hostile powers. They remained vulnerable to blockade, but naval power gave them alternative means to protect trade.[127]

What lessons can be drawn about theories of the causes of war? First, this study lends support to one version of the realist critique of the theory of commercial liberalism. Interdependence may increase the costs of war, but it also engenders vulnerability to trade severance, providing incentives to use force to control foreign resources and markets. Fears of blockade or embargo in future wars, particularly if war is expected to be protracted, are powerful reasons for risking war in the present. To the extent that defense dominance lengthens war, without a concomitant reduction in its likelihood or intensity, it represents an important intervening variable in a well-specified theory of interdependence and war. This study provides little support, however, for the other realist critique of commercial liberalism, that is, that concerns about peacetime trade cause expansionism. In the cases, the prospect of peacetime trade barriers did not have a direct an impact on German or Japanese expansionism, probably because these are rarely harmful enough to justify major war.

Offense-defense theory should also be qualified to take account of the opposing incentives arising from the economic and military consequences of the offense-defense balance. If defense dominance heightens the expectation that wars will be long, without diminishing expectations about their probability and intensity, it will increase concerns about autarky. States that expect to be involved in long wars of attrition accompanied by severe trade disruptions are more likely to expand to increase both their self-sufficiency and their aggregate economic capability. Especially where defense dominance among great powers does not shield regional territories, states will be more eager to seize economically valuable prizes. Defense dominance is thus not the unqualified boon for peace that some theorists suggest, which may help explain why some scholars have found a low historical correlation between offensive advantage and war.

This qualification of offense-defense theory, however, applies only to conventional military systems. Survivable nuclear forces render nuclear offensives futile and suicidal, and even conventional offensives breathtakingly risky. It only takes a small number of relatively inexpensive nuclear weapons, requiring neither economic mobilization nor self-sufficiency, to cause unspeakable levels of destruction. Mutual nuclear deterrence thus provides neither battlefield nor economic incentives for expansion, so nuclear "deterrence dominance" does not have the same economic Catch-22 as conventional defense dominance.

127. For a brief discussion of British interwar responses, see Uchitel, "Interdependence and Instability," 253–58.

This is relevant to the ongoing policy debate over whether a nuclear or nonnuclear world holds the safest future for mankind.[128] While much of the debate focuses on whether disarmament is verifiable, or whether new nuclear nations would be any more reckless than the present ones, any final conclusion depends on assessing how peaceful we can expect an alternative nonnuclear world to be. Conventional defense dominance, perhaps engineered though conventional arms control, would not by itself be a very reassuring guarantee of peace among economically interdependent states. While other considerations may be overriding, this one should give at least some pause to policymakers aiming to replace nuclear deterrence with a defense-only conventional world.

---

128. For an excellent sample of this debate, see Scott D. Sagan and Kenneth N. Waltz, *The Spread of Nuclear Weapons: A Debate* (New York: Norton, 1995); see also Jervis, *Meaning of the Nuclear Revolution*, chap. 1.

PREFERENTIAL TRADING ARRANGEMENTS AND MILITARY DISPUTES

EDWARD D. MANSFIELD, JON C. PEVEHOUSE, AND DAVID H. BEARCE

S
INCE THE Second World War, preferential trading arrangements (PTAs) have spread rapidly. Dozens have been formed over the past fifty years and almost every member of the World Trade Organization (WTO) is currently party to at least one.[1] The proliferation of PTAs has spurred a wide variety of studies addressing the influence of these arrangements on the economic welfare of participants and the stability of the multilateral trading system. Far less effort, however, has been made to analyze the political consequences of PTAs, especially their effects on interstate conflict.

The dearth of research on this topic is significant. Whether the contemporary growth of PTAs will yield greater good than harm is a matter of widespread and heated disagreement among both scholars and policy makers. While existing analyses of PTAs' consequences center primarily on economic considerations, any tendency for these arrangements to promote either political cooperation or discord also merits attention in such assessments. Furthermore, the impact of PTA membership on interstate hostilities bears heavily on longstanding debates about the relationship between foreign commerce and political conflict. Various statistical studies have addressed these debates by analyzing the effects of trade flows on political-military disputes. Very little quantitative evidence, however, has been accumulated on whether commercial institu-

Edward D. Mansfield is associate professor of political science at Ohio State University. Jon C. Pevehouse and David H. Bearce are Ph.D. candidates in the Department of Political Science at Ohio State University.

For comments on earlier versions of this article, we are grateful to Jean-Marc F. Blanchard, Marc L. Busch, Victor D. Cha, Joanne Gowa, Gregory D. Hess, James D. Morrow, Norrin R. Ripsman, Randall L. Schweller, two anonymous *Security Studies* referees, João Resende-Santos, and the participants at the *Security Studies* Workshop on Economic Power, Interdependence, and National Security held at the Mershon Center, Ohio State University, 2–5 April 1998. We are also grateful to John R. Oneal and Bruce M. Russett for making their data available to us. In conducting this research, Mansfield was assisted by a grant from the Mershon Center at Ohio State University and by the Hoover Institution at Stanford University, where he was a National Fellow during 1998–99.

1. See World Trade Organization, *Regionalism and the World Trading System* (Geneva: World Trade Organization, 1995).

tions influence the onset of hostilities. Our purpose is to provide some pre-liminary evidence of this sort.

Here, we argue that PTA membership tends to inhibit interstate conflict. One reason is that parties to a PTA have reason to anticipate economic gains from membership. Since political conflict among participants can damage a preferential arrangement and hence their ability to realize such gains, PTA members are less likely to become involved in military disputes than other states. Another reason is that PTAs create a forum for bargaining and negotia-tion that can dampen disputes among members and contributes to the resolu-tion of conflicts that do occur. In the same vein, PTAs can promote the con-struction of "focal points" that help coordinate states' behavior and avert the breakdown of cooperation. Our statistical results accord with these arguments. Based on an analysis of the post–Second World War era, we find that pairs of countries that belong to the same PTA are considerably less likely to become involved in military disputes than pairs that do not participate in such an arrangement.

PREFERENTIAL TRADING ARRANGEMENTS AND INTERNATIONAL CONFLICT

THE HALLMARK of a preferential trading arrangement is the stipulation that signatories impose lower trade barriers on members' goods than on those of third parties.[2] Among the different types of PTAs, free trade areas com-pletely eliminate commercial barriers on at least some goods and services, customs unions both eliminate such barriers among participants and set a common external tariff on the products of third parties, common markets permit the free flow of factors of production as well as finished goods across members' borders, and economic unions coordinate a broad range of eco-nomic policies beyond those directly pertaining to international trade.[3] Despite these institutional variations, each type of PTA grants and safeguards preferen-tial access to the markets of participants. The emphasis placed on this com-mon feature has led many economists to analyze preferential arrangements as a whole rather than focusing on variations among them, and we do likewise for

---

2. See, for example, Kym Anderson and Richard Blackhurst, "Introduction and Sum-mary," in *Regional Integration and the Global Trading System*, ed. Kym Anderson and Richard Blackhurst (New York: Harvester Wheatsheaf, 1993), 4–5; and Jaime de Melo and Arvind Panagariya, "Introduction," in *New Dimensions in Regional Integration*, ed. Jaime de Melo and Arvind Panagariya (New York: Cambridge University Press), 3–21.

3. On these distinctions, see Anderson and Blackhurst, "Introduction and Summary"; and de Melo and Panagariya, "Introduction."

the purpose of generating some initial estimates of their impact on interstate conflict.

Because many PTAs are composed of states located in the same geographic region, the rapid proliferation of these arrangements since the Second World War has prompted numerous observers to conclude that economic regionalism is becoming increasingly widespread.[4] An initial "wave" of postwar regionalism occurred during the 1950s and 1960s, spurred by the formation of the European Coal and Steel Community (ECSC), the European Economic Community (EEC), the European Free Trade Association (EFTA), the Council for Mutual Economic Assistance (CMEA), and a series of PTAs established by less developed countries. More recently, the creation of the North American Free Trade Agreement (NAFTA), the *Mercado Común del Cono Sur* (MERCOSUR), the organization for Asia-Pacific Economic Cooperation (APEC), and numerous bilateral trade agreements involving states formerly in the Soviet orbit have contributed to a second wave of regionalism.[5] Of course, regionalism is not a phenomenon limited to the period since the Second World War,[6] but both the number of countries involved in PTAs and the amount of trade they cover have risen to new heights throughout this era.[7]

Accompanying the contemporary growth of regionalism has been a surge of interest in how PTAs influence the economic welfare of states and the stability of the multilateral trading system.[8] In contrast, the links between PTAs and in-

4. Among the many recent studies of this topic, see Anderson and Blackhurst, *Regional Integration and the Global Trading System*; de Melo and Panagariya, *New Dimensions in Regional Integration*; and Jeffrey A. Frankel, ed., *The Regionalization of the World Economy* (Chicago: University of Chicago Press, 1998).

5. See Jagdish Bhagwati, "Regionalism and Multilateralism: An Overview," in de Melo and Panagariya, *New Dimensions in Regional Integration*, 22–51; and Edward D. Mansfield and Helen V. Milner, "The New Wave of Regionalism," *International Organization* 53, no. 3 (summer 1999): 589–627.

6. On earlier episodes of regionalism, see, for example, Barry Eichengreen and Douglas A. Irwin, "The Role of History in Bilateral Trade Flows," in Frankel, *The Regionalization of the World Economy*, 33–57; Albert O. Hirschman, *National Power and the Structure of Foreign Trade* (1945; Berkeley: University of California Press, 1980); Douglas A. Irwin, "Multilateral and Bilateral Trade Policies in the World Trading System: An Historical Perspective," in de Melo and Panagariya, *New Dimensions in Regional Integration*, 90–119; Mansfield and Milner, "The New Wave of Regionalism"; and Jacob Viner, *The Customs Union Issue* (New York: Carnegie Endowment for International Peace, 1950).

7. See Jaime Serra, Guillermo Aguilar, José Córdoba, Gene Grossman, Carla Hills, John Jackson, Julius Katz, Pedro Noyola, and Michael Wilson, *Reflections on Regionalism* (Washington, D.C.: Brookings, 1997); and World Trade Organization, *Regionalism and the World Trading System*.

8. See, for example, Norman D. Aitken, "The Effect of the EEC and EFTA on European Trade: A Temporal and Cross-Section Analysis," *American Economic Review* 63, no. 5 (December 1973): 881–92; Jeffrey A. Frankel, "Is Japan Creating a Yen Bloc in East Asia and the Pacific?" in *Regionalism and Rivalry: Japan and the United States in Pacific Asia*, ed. Jeffrey A. Frankel and Miles Kahler (Chicago: University of Chicago Press, 1993), 53–85; Jeffrey A.

ternational political relations have been the subject of far less research, despite the longstanding acknowledgment that such links might be important. Over a century ago, for example, Wilfred Pareto argued that "customs unions and other systems of closer commercial relations [could serve] as means to the improvement of political relations and the maintenance of peace."[9] The same view has been frequently articulated by policy makers. It is widely recognized that the founders of the European Community (EC) sought through its creation to render war between France and Germany not only "unthinkable, but also materially impossible."[10] The desire to promote both political and economic cooperation has been a central impetus to the establishment of various other PTAs as well—including the Association of Southeast Asian Nations (ASEAN), the Economic Community of West African States (ECOWAS), and MERCOSUR.

Whether parties to the same PTA actually tend to be less prone to hostilities than other states, however, is far from clear. While some preferential arrangements (like the EC) have experienced little political tension between members, it is not difficult to identify others marked by considerable antagonism (for example, the Central American Common Market and the East African Common Market). Unfortunately, systematic empirical studies of the relationship between PTAs and military conflict have been rare,[11] and the dearth of quantitative evidence bearing on this issue is especially glaring. Various statistical studies have addressed the effects of trade flows on the incidence of hostilities, but few of them directly assess the influence of international institutions designed to shape the flow of commerce.[12] We aim to fill this gap in the literature

Frankel, Ernesto Stein, and Shang-jin Wei, "Trading Blocs and the Americas: The Natural, the Unnatural, and the Super-natural," *Journal of Development Economics* 47, no. 1 (June 1995): 61–95; Edward D. Mansfield and Rachel Bronson, "Alliances, Preferential Trading Arrangements, and International Trade," *American Political Science Review* 91, no. 1 (March 1997): 97–104; and L. Alan Winters and Zhen Kun Wang, *Eastern Europe's International Trade* (Manchester: Manchester University Press, 1994).

9. Fritz Machlup, *A History of Thought on Economic Integration* (New York: Columbia University Press, 1977), 143.

10. Dennis Swann, *The Economics of the Common Market* (Harmondsworth: Penguin, 1984, 5th ed.), 17.

11. For a seminal treatment of this issue, see Joseph S. Nye, *Peace in Parts: Integration and Conflict in Regional Organization* (Boston: Little, Brown, 1971), esp. chap. 4.

12. Among the empirical studies addressing the influence of trade on interstate conflict are Katherine Barbieri, "Economic Interdependence: A Path to Peace or a Source of Interstate Conflict?" *Journal of Peace Research* 33, no. 1 (1996): 29–49; Katherine Barbieri, "Explaining Discrepant Findings in the Trade-Conflict Literature," (paper presented at the 1996 annual meeting of the International Studies Association, San Diego, 16–20 April 1996); Erik Gartzke, "Kant We All Just Get Along? Opportunity, Willingness, and the Origins of the Democratic Peace," *American Journal of Political Science* 42, no. 1 (January 1998): 1–27; Mark Gasiorowski and Solomon W. Polachek, "Conflict and Interdependence: East-West Trade and Linkages in the Era of Detente," *Journal of Conflict Resolution* 26, no. 4 (December

by conducting a preliminary quantitative analysis of the relationship between
PTA membership and the outbreak of military disputes.[13]

HOW PTAs INHIBIT MILITARY DISPUTES

There are several reasons why PTAs are likely to inhibit the onset of hostilities.[14] One reason is that parties to a preferential arrangement expect to obtain
future economic benefits from membership. Military disputes can damage
economic relations among participants, as well as the PTA itself, thereby jeopardizing the ability of states to realize these future gains. Thus, PTAs may deter
members from engaging in hostilities by raising the ex ante economic costs of
political conflict.

Preferential trading arrangements hold open the prospect of generating
various economic benefits. Central in this regard are the efficiency gains
stemming from trade creation, which are obtained if an arrangement increases
commerce among participants at the expense of inefficient producers located
in third parties.[15] Of course, many PTAs have not been trade creating. Even
trade diverting arrangements, however, can yield economic benefits by facilitating the realization of scale economies on the part of industries located in
participating states; increasing competition among firms within the bloc, leading to greater efficiency; and spurring the flow of investment both between

---

1982): 709–29; Mark Gasiorowski, "Economic Interdependence and International Conflict:
Some Cross-National Evidence," *International Studies Quarterly* 30, no. 1 (March 1986): 23–38;
Edward D. Mansfield, *Power, Trade, and War* (Princeton: Princeton University Press, 1994);
John R. Oneal and Bruce M. Russett, "The Classical Liberals Were Right: Democracy, Inter-
dependence, and Conflict, 1950–1985," *International Studies Quarterly* 41, no. 2 (June 1997):
267–94; John R. Oneal, Frances Oneal, Zeev Maoz, and Bruce Russett, "The Liberal Peace:
Interdependence, Democracy, and International Conflict, 1950–85," *Journal of Peace Research*
33, no. 1 (1996): 11–28; Solomon W. Polachek, "Conflict and Trade," *Journal of Conflict Resolution* 24, no. 1 (October 1980): 55–78; and Norrin M. Ripsman and Jean-Marc F. Blanchard,
"Commercial Liberalism Under Fire: Evidence From 1914 and 1936," *Security Studies* 6, no. 2
(winter 1996/97): 4–50. For an overview of this literature, see Susan M. McMillan,
"Interdependence and Conflict," *Mershon International Studies Review* 41, no. 1 (May 1997): 33–
58.

    13. Clearly, PTAs are not the only commercial institutions that might affect military dis-
putes. Most notably, membership in the General Agreement on Tariffs and Trade (GATT)
may also influence the likelihood of hostilities. While it is beyond the scope of this article to
address the GATT's effect on conflict, this issue is analyzed in Edward D. Mansfield and Jon
Pevehouse, "Trade Blocs, Trade Flows, and International Conflict", *International Organization*
54, no. 4 (autumn 2000), forthcoming.

    14. The remainder of this section draws on Mansfield and Pevehouse, "Trade Blocs,
Trade Flows, and International Conflict."

    15. The distinction between a "trade creating" and a "trade diverting" PTA was first
drawn by Viner in *The Customs Union Issue.*

members and from sources outside the arrangement to members.[16] Entering a preferential arrangement also can enhance the welfare of states by improving their terms of trade, since the group of states composing the arrangement will almost always have more market power than any constituent member.[17]

Certain PTAs have achieved at least some of these ends. By promoting commercial integration, investment, and economic growth, they are likely to increase economic interdependence among members, a situatuion that various observers have linked to a diminution of interstate hostilities.[18] The European Community represents the best such example. The ECSC identified as its raison d'être "substitut[ing] for age-old rivalries the merging of their essential interests; to create, by establishing an economic community, the basis for a broader and deeper community among peoples long divided by bloody conflicts."[19] The European peace since the Second World War is undoubtedly overdetermined; U.S. security guarantees and economic assistance, the cold war alliance structure, and the consolidation of democracy have all played roles in reducing conflict in the region. In addition, economic integration itself has proceeded in fits and starts. Nonetheless, many scholars agree that the economic links among members of the EC have helped to establish a Europe in which "perceptions of physical threat have disappeared."[20]

16. Ibid.; and Richard Pomfret, *The Economics of Regional Trading Arrangements* (New York: Oxford University Press, 1997).

17. See Paul Krugman, "The Move to Free Trade Zones," in *Policy Implications of Trade and Currency Zones*, ed. Federal Reserve Bank of Kansas City (Kansas City, MO: Federal Reserve Bank, 1991), 7–41; Krugman, "Regionalism versus Multilateralism: Analytical Notes," in de Melo and Panagariya, *New Dimensions in Regional Integration*, 58–79; and Viner, *The Customs Union Issue*.

18. Trade liberalization and commercial integration give rise to specialization in the production of goods and a more efficient allocation of domestic resources, developments that are likely to enhance the dependence of firms and consumers on key trading partners. Unless these partners can be replaced quickly and easily, both private actors and governments have reason to avoid hostilities with them, since political conflict often adversely affects economic relations between belligerents. On the tendency for economic interdependence to dampen political conflict, see, for example, Michael W. Doyle, *Ways of War and Peace: Realism, Liberalism, and Socialism* (New York: W.W. Norton, 1997); Robert O. Keohane, "Economic Liberalism Reconsidered," in *The Economic Limits to Modern Politics*, ed. John Dunn (Cambridge: Cambridge University Press, 1990), 165–94; Nye, *Peace in Parts*; Joseph S. Nye, "Neorealism and Neoliberalism," *World Politics* 40, no. 2 (January 1988): 235–51; and Richard Rosecrance, *The Rise of the Trading State* (New York: Basic Books, 1986).

19. Quoted in William Wallace, *Regional Integration: The Western European Experience* (Washington, D.C.: Brookings, 1994), 19.

20. Ibid., 86. See also Beverly Crawford, "The Impact of Europe's Transformation on International Relations," in *The New Europe Asserts Itself: A Changing Role in International Relations*, ed. Beverly Crawford and Peter W. Schultze (Berkeley: International and Arms Studies, 1990), 333; and Nye, *Peace in Parts*, 115.

Some preferential arrangements, however, have taken a long time to generate economic benefits and others have failed altogether.[21] We argue that even unsuccessful PTAs can inhibit military conflict between participants, as long as members expect that economic gains will be forthcoming. That participants often harbor hopes that faltering PTAs will produce future gains is suggested by the repeated attempts made to revive moribund arrangements and the rarity with which states have abandoned them without quickly establishing a replacement. Furthermore, as Dale C. Copeland has argued, the anticipation of future gains from trade tends to dampen the prospect that commercial partners will become embroiled in political disputes.[22] Membership in a PTA raises the costs of military conflict for states calculating that hostilities will undermine their ability to realize the anticipated economic benefits stemming from the commercial arrangement.

There are various ways that PTAs can foster expectations of future economic gains. Particularly important is that they reduce both trade barriers among members and the likelihood that participants will subsequently roll back trade liberalization. Absent a PTA, a state lowering trade barriers faces difficulty assuring its trade partners that these barriers will not be raised in days ahead. Entering a PTA enhances the credibility of commitments made by a state's current administration to sustain open trade with selected trade partners and helps bind subsequent administrations that might have a more protectionist orientation.[23] Similarly, PTA membership provides states with insurance against the possibility that commercial developments will arise that otherwise could have adverse economic consequences. A country, for example, can limit the prospect that its foreign trade will decline due to heightened protectionist pressures in key trading partners, the breakdown of informal commercial agreements with them, or closure of the global trading system by forming PTAs with these

21. On these issues, see Bhagwati, "Regionalism and Multilateralism"; Jagdish Bhagwati and Arvind Panagariya, "Preferential Trading Areas and Multilateralism—Strangers, Friends, or Foes?" in *The Economics of Preferential Trade Agreements*, ed. Jagdish Bhagwati and Arvind Panagariya (Washington, D.C.: AEI Press, 1996), 1–78; de Melo and Panagariya, "Introduction"; Barry Eichengreen and Jeffrey A. Frankel, "Economic Regionalism: Evidence from Two 20th Century Episodes," *North American Journal of Economics and Finance* 6, no. 2 (1995): 89–106; Robert Z. Lawrence, *Regionalism, Multilateralism, and Deeper Integration* (Washington, D.C.: Brookings, 1996); and Pomfret, *The Economics of Regional Trading Arrangements*.

22. Copeland, "Economic Interdependence and War: A Theory of Trade Expectations," *International Security* 20, no. 1 (summer 1996): 5–41; and Copeland, "Trade Expectations and the Outbreak of Peace," *Security Studies* 9, nos. 1/2 (autumn 1999–winter 2000): 15–58.

23. Furthermore, it has been argued that governments are better able to bind themselves to trade liberalization by entering a PTA, rather than by relying on either unilateral, domestic measures or multilateral institutions, like the GATT/WTO. See Raquel Fernández, "Returns to Regionalism: An Evaluation of Nontraditional Gains from Regional Trade Agreements" (typescript, World Bank, 1998), 12–13.

partners.[24] In addition, states frequently anticipate that establishing a PTA will improve their bargaining power in future negotiations with third parties, since members often can exert greater leverage in combination than individually and preferential arrangements can facilitate the coordination of members' bargaining positions.[25]

Finally, PTA membership can prompt heightened expectations about the ability of states to attract foreign investment; and many countries have joined such arrangements with this end in mind. Firms making investments in one participant gain preferential access to the markets of others as well, which may stimulate investment in PTA members. Entering a PTA can also enhance the credibility of a state's commitments not to expropriate assets, impose regulations, raise trade barriers on goods produced in member-states, or take other actions that are prohibited by the arrangement and might dampen the profitability of investments.[26] Thus, countries have reason to anticipate a rise in investment once they join a PTA.

Interstate conflict, however, can scuttle these expected gains by damaging economic relations among members and the PTA itself, thereby undermining commitments to sustain commercial liberalization and to promote integration. In the same vein, political hostilities can threaten the ability of PTA members to realize increased investment, since firms have incentives to avoid the risks attendant to investing in regions ridden with political strife. The parties to various preferential groupings have considered these issues. Participants in ECOWAS, for example, quickly recognized that, in the words of one of its former secretaries, political and military instability "retards the economic growth and development of member states and acts as a disincentive to investment."[27] The belief that integration and investment would expand within this PTA if conflict was averted led its members to adopt a nonaggression pact in 1978 and a mutual defense protocol in 1981.[28]

24. See Fernández, "Returns to Regionalism"; Edward D. Mansfield, "The Proliferation of Preferential Trading Arrangements," *Journal of Conflict Resolution* 42, no. 5 (October 1998): 523–42; and John Whalley, "Why Do Countries Seek Regional Trade Agreements?" in Frankel, *The Regionalization of the World Economy*, 63–83.

25. See Fernández, "Returns to Regionalism"; and Pomfret, *The Economics of Regional Trading Arrangements*.

26. On these issues, see Fernández, "Returns to Regionalism"; and Beth V. Yarbrough and Robert M. Yarbrough, *Cooperation and Governance in International Trade: The Strategic Organizational Approach* (Princeton: Princeton University Press, 1992).

27. Abass Bundu, "ECOWAS and the Future of Regional Integration in West Africa," in *Regional Integration and Cooperation in West Africa*, ed. Real Lavergne (Trenton, N.J.: Africa World Press, 1997), 40–41.

28. The nonaggression pact recognizes the current territorial borders of member states and commits the signatories to submit intrabloc conflicts to the ECOWAS heads of state for dispute resolution. This pact, however, was ratified by only a handful of ECOWAS member-

It is also widely understood that the parties to MERCOSUR have expected this preferential arrangement to generate substantial economic gains.[29] The realization by these states that MERCOSUR's economic goals would be difficult to meet in the face of political antagonism has contributed to the enactment of measures specifically designed to maintain peace in the southern Cone.[30] As a result, military tensions between Brazil and Argentina have been dampened and they have settled longstanding territorial disputes about the control of access to waterways. As Monica Hirst observes, "regional security cooperation has become a spill-around effect of the expansion of economic ties among Southern Cone countries."[31] Consistent with this view, President Cardoso of Brazil has stated that "The international order that has emerged in recent years, and Brazil's relations with its neighbors—maturing and consolidating at an accelerated pace with the implementation of MERCOSUR—reduce the probability that conventional external regional conflicts involving our country will manifest."[32]

The promise of economic gains has also helped to contain political-military tension among the participants in ASEAN. A central aim of this PTA has been to promote economic development and investment. Recognizing that interstate hostilities could divert "resources away from development and [render] the region unattractive to foreign investors,"[33] its members concluded the Treaty on Amity and Cooperation in 1976, establishing a code of conduct for the peaceful settlement of disputes. In addition, while ASEAN initially took few steps to promote commercial integration, certain states held out the hope that trade could be expanded within the preferential arrangement. In 1971, for example, President Marcos of the Philippines proposed that ASEAN form a common market. In 1976, an agreement designed to expand commercial integration was successfully negotiated. Soon thereafter, Marcos renounced the Phil-

---

states. See David Wippman, "Enforcing the Peace: ECOWAS and the Liberian Civil War," in *Enforcing Constraint: Collective Intervention in Internal Conflicts*, ed. Lori Fisler Damrosch (New York: Council on Foreign Relations Press, 1993), 166.

29. See, for example, Thomaz Guedes da Costa, "The Role of the Armed Forces in Brazil's Democratization," in *Civil-Military Relations: Building Democracy and Regional Security in Latin America, Southern Asia, and Central Europe*, ed. David R. Mares (Boulder: Westview, 1998), 230; and Felix Peña, "Strategies for Macroeconomic Coordination: Reflections on the Case of MERCOSUR," in *The Challenge of Integration: Europe and the Americas*, ed. Peter H. Smith (New Brunswick: Transaction Publishers, 1993), 189.

30. See Peter H. Smith, "The Politics of Integration: Concepts and Themes," in Smith, *The Challenges of Integration*, 1–14.

31. Hirst, "Security Policies, Democratization, and Regional Integration in the Southern Cone," in *International Security and Democracy*, ed. Jorge I. Dominquez (Pittsburgh: University of Pittsburgh Press, 1998), 113.

32. Quoted in da Costa, "The Role of the Armed Forces in Brazil's Democratization," 230.

33. Tim Huxley, *Insecurity in the ASEAN Region* (London: Royal Services Institute for Defence Studies, 1993), 11.

ippines' claim on the Sabah—a territory also claimed by its ASEAN partner, Malaysia. The Philippines' stated justification[34] for dropping the Sabah issue was "to eliminate one of the burdens of ASEAN" and make "a permanent contribution to the unity, the strength and prosperity of all of ASEAN."[35] M. Leann Brown argues that the "Marcos government ostensibly elected to drop the Sabah claim to facilitate cooperation within the regional economic organization."[36] Although Marcos's renunciation encountered domestic opposition due to nationalist concerns, Susan M. Feske concludes that "ASEAN contributed significantly to the prevention of a military confrontation between the Philippines and Malaysia over the Sabah issue."[37]

By increasing the ex ante costs of military conflict, PTAs are likely to discourage its onset. At the same time, it is clear that this argument requires qualification. If states anticipate that the gains from membership will be small or if they heavily discount these gains, PTAs may do little to inhibit hostilities.[38] Even in cases where the benefits of membership appear large and are not heavily discounted, a state obviously might calculate that attacking a PTA partner would yield still larger benefits. If, however, states expect that the future stream of gains from membership will outweigh the costs of membership and any potential benefits from military disputes, the prospect of antagonism between PTA members is likely to be relatively remote.

Besides fostering the expectation of future economic benefits, PTAs can inhibit political conflict among participants by providing a forum for bargaining and negotiation and by establishing procedures to resolve internal disputes before open hostilities break out.[39] Some preferential arrangements, most notably those in Europe and North America, have instituted formal dispute resolution mechanisms to adjudicate economic conflicts among parties that could otherwise contribute to political discord.[40] Others have become impor-

34. It should be noted that while Marcos renounced the Philippines' claim to the Sabah because of the future economic benefits that he anticipated a cohesive ASEAN would furnish, he also did so in the hopes that subsequently Malaysia would help squelch an Islamic insurgency in the Philippines' southern islands. On these issues, see M. Leann Brown, *Developing Countries and Regional Economic Cooperation* (Westport, Conn.: Praeger, 1994), chap. 5.

35. Quoted in ibid., 99.

36. Ibid., 100.

37. Feske, *ASEAN and Prospects for Regional Arms Control in Southeast Asia* (Berlin: Quorum Verlag, 1986), 4.

38. States might heavily discount the future gains from membership if, for example, the arrangement has been faltering for some time, members seem likely to abrogate or exit the PTA, or conflicts over the distribution of the costs and benefits from membership are likely to arise.

39. See, for example, Nye, *Peace in Parts*, 109.

40. On this issue, see Philip I. Levy and T. N. Srinivasan, "Regionalism and the (dis)advantage of Dispute-Settlement Access," *American Economic Review (Papers and Proceedings)* 86, no. 2 (May 1996): 93–98; and Beth V. Yarbrough and Robert M. Yarbrough, "Dispute

tant regional forums, helping to resolve border disputes between members and promoting political-military cooperation.

MERCOSUR, for example, has become an important forum for resolving various longstanding disputes in the Southern Cone. Luigi Manzetti maintains that, as a result, "Argentina and Brazil have been able to cooperate—successfully, and at an unprecedented level—on a number of issues. MERCOSUR has provided its member states with a forum for discussion of sensitive policy issues, such as those in relation to transport and communications, nuclear proliferation (Argentina and Brazil signed a nonproliferation treaty in 1991), environmental protection, military cooperation, illegal immigration, and the drug traffic."[41] The creation of mechanisms to facilitate the peaceful settlement of disputes also has played an important role in inhibiting conflict within ASEAN, many members of which have a border dispute or an overlapping "exclusive economic zone" claim with another participant.[42] Evaluating the arrangement's history of dispute resolution, Hans H. Indorf argues that "ASEAN has increased the likelihood that conflicts of peripheral national value would not explode into open confrontation, and those of a more serious nature would not tear the organization asunder. Personal consultations and periodic meetings have had a mitigating effect on potential bilateral hostilities."[43]

Furthermore, PTAs can help to foster reciprocity between states and ameliorate concerns over the distribution of gains from economic exchange that can forestall international cooperation.[44] These commercial institutions, as Raquel Fernández points out, "have very clear internalization of reciprocity, so that it is easier for a country to ensure that a concession on its part will elicit a coun-

Settlement in International Trade: Regionalism and Procedural Coordination," in *The Political Economy of Regionalism*, ed. Edward D. Mansfield and Helen V. Milner (New York: Columbia University Press, 1997), 134–63.

41. Manzetti, "The Political Economy of MERCOSUR," *Journal of Interamerican Studies and World Affairs* 35, no. 4 (winter 1993–94): 110.

42. It should be noted that while intra-ASEAN border disputes—such as the Singapore-Malaysia dispute over Pedra Branca Island and the Indonesia-Malaysia dispute over the Sipadan and Litigan Islands—have often been resolved by the World Court and not by the ASEAN High Council, some analysts maintain that ASEAN-reinforced norms led the states to seek dispute mediation. See Sheldon W. Simon, "Security Prospects in Southeast Asia: Collaborative Efforts and the ASEAN Regional Forum," *Pacific Review* 11, no. 2 (1998): 198–200.

43. Indorf, *Impediments to Regionalism in Southeast Asia: Bilateral Constraints Among ASEAN Member States* (Singapore: Institute of Southeast Asian Studies, 1984), 85. See also Kusuma Snitwongse, "Thirty Years of ASEAN: Achievements through Political Cooperation," *Pacific Review* 11, no. 2 (1998): 185.

44. See, for example, Joseph M. Grieco, "Anarchy and the Limits of Cooperation: A Realist Critique of the Newest Liberal Institutionalism," *International Organization* 42, no. 3 (summer 1990): 485–507; Michael Mastanduno, "Do Relative Gains Matter? America's Response to Japanese Industrial Policy," *International Security* 16, no. 1 (summer 1991): 73–113; and John J. Mearsheimer, "The False Promise of International Institutions," *International Security* 19, no. 3 (winter 1994/95): 5–49.

terpart from another country, benefiting itself."[45] They also facilitate the flow of information about the gains (and any losses) accruing to participants, thereby mitigating uncertainty about the distribution of benefits from economic exchange.[46] More generally, PTAs can help to construct focal points that guide participants' expectations as to what behavior is acceptable and aid in identifying deviations from it. As Geoffrey Garrett and Barry R. Weingast argue,

> [b]y embodying, selecting, and publicizing particular paths on which all actors are able to coordinate, institutions may provide a constructed focal point. Such institutions can also mitigate potential breakdowns in cooperation associated with ambiguity by providing the critical information about when an actor has defected and by resolving problems raised by unanticipated circumstances. Acting in this capacity, institutions not only provide individuals with critical information about defection but also help construct a shared belief system that defines for the community what actions constitute cooperation and defection.[47]

By promoting reciprocity among members, reducing uncertainty about the benefits and costs stemming from participation, and establishing focal points, PTAs can heighten economic and political cooperation, thus dampening the prospect of military hostilities.[48]

SOME ALTERNATIVE HYPOTHESES

Although the arguments advanced above suggest that PTA membership is likely to dampen conflict, some observers have suggested otherwise. Preferential trading arrangements, for example, heighten economic interaction and various scholars argue that greater economic interaction widens the range of issues over which interstate conflicts may occur.[49] In addition, since the gains from

45. Fernández, "Returns to Regionalism," 24.

46. Ibid., 17.

47. Garrett and Weingast, "Ideas, Interests, and Institutions: Constructing the European Community's Internal Market," in *Ideas and Foreign Policy: Beliefs, Institutions, and Political Change*, ed. Judith Goldstein and Robert O. Keohane (Ithaca: Cornell University Press, 1993), 176. See also Thomas C. Schelling, *The Strategy of Conflict* (Cambridge: Harvard University Press, 1960).

48. On the ability of international institutions to foster reciprocity, see Robert O. Keohane, "Reciprocity in International Relations," *International Organization* 40, no. 1 (winter 1986): 1–27.

49. See, for example, Edward Mead Earle, "Adam Smith, Alexander Hamilton, Friedrich List: The Economic Foundations of Military Power," in *Makers of Modern Strategy from Machiavelli to the Nuclear Age*, ed. Peter Paret (Princeton: Princeton University Press, 1986), 217–61; Hirschman, *National Power and the Structure of Foreign Trade*; Jacob Viner, "Power versus Plenty as Objectives of Foreign Policy in the Seventeenth and Eighteenth Centuries," *World*

trade influence states' political power and are often asymmetrically distributed, heightened commerce can prompt changes in power relations.[50] Depending on the nature of these changes, PTAs could actually promote hostilities. Furthermore, while PTAs generate expectations of future economic gains, if these expectations become sufficiently frustrated, tensions might arise. Also, while PTAs can help to ameliorate distributional conflicts among states, various arrangements have clearly failed to do so and such conflicts may foster political discord among members.

Still another possibility is that no relationship exists between PTA membership and political conflict, a position that accords with the view held by many scholars that international economic relations have little systematic bearing on the outbreak of hostilities.[51] Surveying the post–Second World War era, for example, Barry Buzan concludes that "there is a very compelling case for factors other than economic ones being prime movers in the decline in the use of force."[52]

A STATISTICAL ANALYSIS OF THE RELATIONSHIP BETWEEN PTAs AND MILITARY DISPUTES

OUR TESTS of the hypotheses advanced earlier focus on the relationship between PTA membership and the onset of militarized interstate disputes (MIDs) during the period since the Second World War. To code PTA membership, we rely primarily on the list of preferential trading arrangements notified to the General Agreement on Tariffs and Trade (GATT) under Article XXIV and the Enabling Clause.[53] Various other PTAs are included too, however, since there is no reason to expect that only those notified to the GATT have influ-

Politics 1, no. 1 (October 1948): 1–29; and Kenneth N. Waltz, "The Myth of National Interdependence," in *The International Corporation,* ed. Charles P. Kindleberger (Cambridge: MIT Press, 1970), 205–23.

50. On this point, see David A. Baldwin, *Economic Statecraft* (Princeton: Princeton University Press, 1985); Robert Gilpin, *The Political Economy of International Relations* (Princeton: Princeton University Press, 1987), 34; Joanne Gowa, *Allies, Adversaries, and International Trade* (Princeton: Princeton University Press, 1994); Hirschman, *National Power and the Structure of Foreign Trade;* and Robert O. Keohane and Joseph S. Nye, *Power and Interdependence: World Politics in Transition* (Boston: Little, Brown, 1977).

51. See, for example, Barry Buzan, "Economic Structure and International Security: The Limits of the Liberal Case," *International Organization* 38, no. 4 (autumn 1984): 597–624; and Gilpin, *The Political Economy of International Relations,* 58.

52. Buzan, "Economic Structure and International Security," 607.

53. See World Trade Organization, *Regionalism and the World Trading System,* 77–91.

enced political disputes.[54] To code MIDs—which include threats by states to use military force, the display or use of force, and wars—we rely on data compiled by the Correlates of War (COW) Project.[55] These data have been used repeatedly in prior research on the relationship between commerce and conflict, and analyzing them is appropriate in light of our interest in explaining political-military hostilities.[56]

Table 1

NUMBER OF MILITARY DISPUTES (MIDs) BEGINNING BETWEEN PTA MEMBERS AND BETWEEN OTHER STATES, 1950–85.

	MID onset	No MID onset	Total
PTA members	90	3857	3947
	(2.3)	(97.7)	(100.0)
Not PTA members	545	16498	17043
	(3.2)	(96.8)	(100.0)

Note: Numbers in parentheses are percentages.

54. To supplement the PTAs notified to the GATT, we rely on the list of preferential arrangements identified by Penelope Hartland-Thunberg and also include the CMEA, the Southern African Customs Union, ECOWAS, the Southern African Development Coordination Conference, and the Eastern and Southern African Preferential Trade Area. On these arrangements, see, for example, de Melo and Panagariya, "Introduction"; Foroutan, "Regional Integration in Sub-Saharan Africa," 246–51; Joseph Hanlon, *Beggar Your Neighbor* (London: Villiers Publications, 1986); Hartland-Thunberg, *Trading Blocs, U.S. Exports, and World Trade* (Boulder: Westview, 1980); Eliawony J. Kisanga, *Industrial and Trade Cooperation in Eastern and Southern Africa* (Hong Kong: Avebury, 1991); Adeyinka Orimalade and R. E. Ubogu, eds., *Trade and Development in Economic Community of West African States* (Delhi: Vikas Publishing, 1984); and Richard Pomfret, *Unequal Trade: The Economics of Discriminatory International Trade Policies* (Oxford: Basil Blackwell, 1988). We code states as parties to a PTA beginning in the year the arrangement enters into force. If this date is unavailable, we code states as entering a PTA in the year it was agreed upon. Note that, in some cases, the WTO and the other sources listed above date the initiation of a PTA in different years. In these cases, we rely on the earliest date provided by any of these sources. For a fuller discussion of these coding procedures, see Mansfield and Bronson, "Alliances, Preferential Trading Arrangements, and International Trade"; and Mansfield, "The Proliferation of Preferential Trading Arrangements."

55. On these data, see Charles S. Gochman and Zeev Maoz, "Militarized Interstate Disputes, 1816–1976," *Journal of Conflict Resolution* 28, no. 4 (December 1984): 585–615; and Daniel M. Jones, Stuart A. Bremer, and J. David Singer, "Militarized Interstate Disputes, 1816–1992: Rationale, Coding Rules, and Empirical Patterns," *Conflict Management and Peace Science* 15, no. 2 (fall 1996): 163–213.

56. See, for example, Oneal, Oneal, Maoz, and Russett, "The Liberal Peace"; and Oneal and Russett, "The Classical Liberals Were Right."

Our statistical analysis builds on a recent study by John R. Oneal and Bruce M. Russett, who examined the effects of democracy and commercial interdependence on military disputes during the period from 1950 to 1985. They argued that, for the purpose of explaining bilateral disputes, primary attention should be directed at contiguous dyads and those including a major power, since other pairs rarely have either a reason or the capacity to fight.[57] Based on an analysis of these dyads, Oneal and Russett found that both democracy and interdependence, as well as other factors, strongly influence the likelihood of MIDs. They did not, however, account for the effects of PTAs.[58] Extending their statistical model by doing so allows us to control for various influences on MIDs besides PTA membership and, as described further below, facilitates a direct comparison of the effects of trade flows and commercial institutions on political conflict.

Before turning to this analysis, it is useful to gain a more general sense of whether participation in a PTA affects the incidence of hostilities. We begin by identifying, for each year from 1950 to 1985, whether each pair of states included in Oneal and Russett's sample participated in the same PTA and whether a MID broke out between them. We then compare the frequency of MIDs occurring between PTA members to the frequency between other states. The results in Table 1 show that, on average, PTA members have become involved in a MID about three-quarters as frequently as other countries, thus providing preliminary support for our argument.

A MODEL OF PTAs AND MILITARY DISPUTES

The preceding results are suggestive, but clearly should be interpreted with caution, since no account was taken of various factors besides PTAs that are likely to influence the onset of MIDs. To more fully address the relationship between PTA membership and military disputes, the following model is estimated:

---

57. Oneal and Russett, "The Classical Liberals Were Right".

58. It should be noted that Russett, Oneal, and David R. Davis have recently extended this earlier study by analyzing whether participants in intergovernmental organizations (IGOs) have been less prone to military disputes than other states since the Second World War. While preferential trading arrangements seem to be one type of IGO that they examined, the purpose of their study was not to isolate the effects of commercial organizations. See Russett, Oneal, and Davis, "The Third Leg of the Kantian Tripod for Peace: International Organizations and Militarized Disputes, 1950–1985," *International Organization* 52, no. 3 (summer 1998): 441–67.

$$MID = \beta_0 + \beta_1 PTA + \beta_2 DEPEND + \beta_3 \Delta DEPEND + \beta_4 DEMOCRACY + \\ \beta_5 GROWTH + \beta_6 ALLIES + \beta_7 CONTIGUITY + \beta_8 CAPABILITY + z \quad (1)$$

The observed value of *MID* is dichotomous. It equals 1 if a militarized dispute breaks out between a pair of states, *A* and *B*, in each year, *t*, during the period from 1950 to 1985. It equals 0 otherwise.[59] To assess the effects of membership in a preferential trading arrangement, we include *PTA*, which equals 1 if states *A* and *B* are parties to the same preferential arrangement in *t*-1 and 0 otherwise.

The final seven independent variables are taken from Oneal and Russett's study.[60] One of their central purposes was to analyze the effects of commercial dependence on hostilities. Commercial liberals and others claim that heightened dependence inhibits interstate conflict, whereas mercantilists argue the opposite. Other scholars maintain that trade has no systematic influence on the outbreak of conflict.[61] To address this issue, Oneal and Russett defined two variables. First, they computed the sum of exports and imports between *A* and *B* in year *t*-1. Then they divided this sum by *A*'s gross domestic product (GDP) in *t*-1 and by *B*'s GDP in *t*-1. The smaller ratio of bilateral trade to GDP in each dyad is *DEPEND*. Second, $\Delta DEPEND$ is the change in *DEPEND* from *t*-4 to *t*-1 for the state having the higher ratio of trade to GDP in *t*-1.[62]

These variables are especially important from our standpoint. Existing statistical analyses of the relationship between commerce and conflict have placed

59. Our dependent variable indicates whether a dispute began between *A* and *B* in a given year. Note that if a dispute begins and a third state subsequently enters it on, for example, *A*'s behalf, then we code the onset of a MID between that state and *B*, which is *A*'s adversary, in the first year that state participates in the conflict. Our focus on the onset of MIDs marks a departure from Oneal and Russett's study, which centers on explaining whether a given pair of states is engaged in a dispute in a particular year. Since our purpose is to explain the onset of political disputes and much of the existing work on the relationship between trade and conflict centers on the conditions under which conflicts begin, focusing on the onset of MIDs seems appropriate. We also analyzed, however, the dependent variable used in Oneal and Russett's study and the results were very similar to those pertaining to the outbreak of military disputes.

60. The final seven variables in this model comprise Oneal and Russett's equation (4). See Oneal and Russett, "The Classical Liberals Were Right," 278.

61. On this debate, see the sources listed in nn. 18, 49, 50, and 51, above.

62. Data on bilateral imports and exports are taken from the International Monetary Fund, *Direction of Trade* (Washington, D.C.: International Monetary Fund, various years). Data on GDP are taken from Robert Summers and Alan Heston, "A New Set of International Comparisons of Real Product and Price Estimates for 130 Countries, 1950–1985," *Review of Income and Wealth* 34, no. 1 (March 1988): 1–26; and Robert Summers and Alan Heston, "The Penn World Table (Mark 5): An Expanded Set of International Comparisons," *Quarterly Journal of Economics* 106, no. 2 (May 1991): 327–68. Note that where $\Delta DEPEND$ cannot be measured over three-year intervals due to missing data, either two-year or one-year intervals are used instead.

particular emphasis on the effects of the ratio of trade flows to GDP, which is often considered a rough measure of economic interdependence.[63] Including DEPEND and ΔDEPEND in our model facilitates a direct comparison of this ratio's influence on hostilities to that of PTA membership.

Another purpose of Oneal and Russett's analysis was to test the proposition that pairs of democracies are less likely to become involved in hostilities than other pairs. They argued that claims about the "democratic peace" imply that as the least democratic state in any given pair becomes less so, the likelihood of a dispute should increase.[64] Derived using five variables in the Polity III data set and coding procedures established by Keith Jaggers and Ted Robert Gurr, DEMOCRACY measures the regime type of the least democratic state in each dyad in t.[65] It ranges from -10 to 10, taking on higher values in more democratic polities and lower values in more autocratic ones.

In addition, some of the literature on diversionary or "scapegoat" wars indicates that lagging growth may precipitate interstate conflict. Furthermore, higher rates of growth may lead to a less belligerent foreign policy if war seems likely to adversely affect a country's economy and private actors and government officials place a high priority on strong economic performance.[66] We therefore analyze the effects of GROWTH, which is the percentage change in per capita GDP over the three-year period prior to t for the state in each pair having the lowest rate of economic growth.[67] Since allies are less likely to become

63. It should be noted that using the ratio of trade to GDP as a measure of economic interdependence is subject to various well-known limitations. This measure, however, has been widely used in previous studies of the relationship between trade and military disputes, and the data needed to construct more precise measures of interdependence are unavailable for many countries included in our sample. As such, we focus on the ratio of trade to GDP in the following analysis, while recognizing that it may not furnish a very accurate indication of interdependence. On these issues, see David A. Baldwin, "Interdependence and Power: A Conceptual Analysis," *International Organization* 34, no. 4 (autumn 1980): 471–506; Gasiorowski, "Economic Interdependence and International Conflict"; Hirschman, *National Power and the Structure of Foreign Trade*; and Keohane and Nye, *Power and Interdependence*.

64. See also Bruce Bueno de Mesquita and David Lalman, *War and Reason: Domestic and International Imperatives* (New Haven: Yale University Press, 1992); and William Dixon, "Democracy and the Peaceful Settlement of International Conflict," *American Political Science Review* 88, no. 1 (March 1994): 14–32.

65. See Keith Jaggers and Ted Robert Gurr, "Tracking Democracy's Third Wave with the Polity III Data," *Journal of Peace Research* 32, no. 4 (1995): 469–82; and Ted Robert Gurr, Keith Jaggers, and Will H. Moore, "Polity II: Political Structures and Regime Change" (Inter-University Consortium for Political and Social Research no. 9263, Ann Arbor, Mich., 1989).

66. On scapegoat wars, see Geoffrey Blainey, *The Causes of War* (New York: Free Press, 1973); and Jack S. Levy and Lily Vakili, "Diversionary Action by Authoritarian Regimes," in *The Internationalization of Communal Strife*, ed. Manus Midlarsky (London: Routledge, 1992).

67. Data for this variable are taken from Summers and Heston, "The Penn World Table (Mark 5): An Expanded Set of International Comparisons." Note that in cases where GROWTH cannot be measured over a three-year period due to missing data, two-year or one-year periods are used instead.

embroiled in military disputes than other states, we include *ALLIES* as well.[68] It equals 1 if *A* and *B* are political-military allies or if both of them are allied with the United States in *t*. Otherwise, *ALLIES* equals 0.[69]

As noted earlier, Oneal and Russett's sample is comprised of all pairs of countries that are either contiguous or include at least one major power. To distinguish between these types of pairs and because it is widely recognized that contiguous dyads are especially prone to military confrontations,[70] we introduce *CONTIGUITY*. This variable equals 1 if *A* and *B* are contiguous, "including states that are indirectly contiguous through colonies."[71] It equals 0 if *A* and *B* are not contiguous and include China, France, the Soviet Union, the United Kingdom, or the United States. These are the states that, following the COW Project, Oneal and Russett define as the major powers during the period from 1950 to 1985.[72]

The distribution of capabilities is also likely to influence the onset of interstate disputes. Various studies have found that as this distribution becomes increasingly skewed, the likelihood of military conflict declines.[73] As a result, we include *CAPABILITY*, which is the ratio of the larger state's power capabilities in each dyad to the smaller state's capabilities and is measured in *t*.[74] Finally, z is a stochastic error term.

Not only are the seven independent variables drawn from Oneal and Russett's study likely to affect the onset of military disputes, many of them

68. See Oneal and Russett, "The Classical Liberals Were Right"; and Russett, Oneal, and Davis, "The Third Leg of the Kantian Tripod for Peace."

69. Data on alliances compiled by the COW Project are used to code this variable. See Melvin Small and J. David Singer, "Formal Alliances, 1816–1965: An Extension of the Basic Data," *Journal of Peace Research* 6, no. 3 (1969): 257–82; and subsequent updates of these data made by the COW Project.

70. See, for example, Stuart A. Bremer, "Dangerous Dyads: Conditions Affecting the Likelihood of Interstate War," *Journal of Conflict Resolution* 36, no. 2 (June 1992): 309–41.

71. Oneal and Russett, "The Classical Liberals Were Right," 276.

72. See Melvin Small and J. David Singer, *Resort to Arms: International and Civil Wars, 1816–1980* (Beverly Hills: Sage, 1982); and J. David Singer and Melvin Small, "Correlates of War Project: International and Civil War Data, 1816–1992" (Inter-University Consortium for Political and Social Research no. 9905, Ann Arbor, Mich., 1994).

73. On the relationship between the distribution of capabilities and the onset of conflict, see Blainey, *The Causes of War*; Jack S. Levy, "The Causes of War: A Review of Theories and Evidence," in *Behavior, Society, and Nuclear War*, ed. Philip E. Tetlock et al. (New York: Oxford University Press, 1989), 209–313; and Hans Morgenthau and Kenneth Thompson, *Politics Among Nations* (New York: Alfred Knopf, 1985, 6th ed.).

74. The capabilities used to measure this variable are a country's total population, urban population, military expenditures, military personnel, iron and steel production, and energy consumption. These variables are equally weighted in arriving at the value of *CAPABILITY*. For more on this procedure, see J. David Singer, Stuart Bremer, and John Stuckey, "Capability Distribution, Uncertainty, and Major Power War, 1820–1965," in *Peace, War, and Numbers*, ed. Bruce Russett (Beverly Hills: Sage, 1972), 19–48. These data are taken from the COW Project, "National Material Capabilities Dataset" (Ann Arbor, Mich., 1991).

may help to determine whether a pair of states participates in the same PTA as well. Earlier studies of regional integration, for example, concluded that heightened economic flows between states increase the prospects that they will form such an arrangement.[75] Some recent research also indicates that deteriorating macroeconomic conditions can spur states to form PTAs, that pairs of democracies and political-military allies are especially likely to establish one, and that PTA members tend to be located in close geographical proximity.[76] We therefore need to include these factors in our model to ensure that they do not account for any observed relationship between PTA membership and political disputes.

Equation (1) includes variables describing political and economic conditions within A and B, as well as variables pertaining to political and economic relations between them. It omits, however, systemic influences—like shifts in the global distribution of power, the number of nation-states that exist, and international economic conditions—that also might affect both the likelihood of military disputes and the propensity for states to participate in PTAs in a given year. In a preliminary effort to address the effects of these systemic factors, we include in equation (1) a dummy variable for each year in the sample except one (which is 1985). The results of a likelihood ratio test allow us to reject the null hypothesis that these year-specific fixed effects should be excluded ($\chi^2 = 91.10$; $p < .0001$). Logistic regression is then used to estimate the coefficients in equation (1). These estimates are reported in the first column of Table 2.

In addition to year-specific effects, we also would like to account for any factors that are specific to a given dyad and that might affect the likelihood of military conflict between the constituent states. We could do so by including a dummy variable for all but one pair of states in the sample. Those dyads that did not engage in a dispute during the period analyzed here, however, would then be excluded when estimating equation (1). Since, based on our sample, such dyads are roughly twice as likely to be composed of PTA members than dyads that did experience a dispute, this procedure threatens to introduce an important source of bias in our results. Including a dummy variable for each state rather than each pair of states would do little to ameliorate this problem. Consequently, we use an alternative procedure. By treating the dyad-specific

75. See, for example, Ernst Haas, *The Uniting of Europe: Political, Social, and Economic Forces, 1950–1957* (Stanford: Stanford University Press, 1958); and Philippe Schmitter, "Three Neo-Functionalist Hypotheses about International Integration," *International Organization* 23, no. 2 (winter 1969): 161–66.

76. See Edward D. Mansfield, Helen V. Milner, and B. Peter Rosendorff, "Why Democracies Cooperate More: Electoral Control and International Trade Agreements" (paper presented at the 1998 annual meeting of the American Political Science Association, Boston, Mass., 3–6 September 1998).

Table 2

LOGIT ESTIMATES OF THE EFFECTS OF PTA MEMBERSHIP, TRADE,
DEMOCRACY, ECONOMIC GROWTH, ALLIANCES, CONTIGUITY, AND POWER
CAPABILITIES ON THE ONSET OF MILITARY DISPUTES, 1950–85.

Variable	1	2	3	4
INTERCEPT	-1.234***	-1.253***	-2.432***	-2.447***
	(.312)	(.310)	(.251)	(.248)
PTA	-.397***	-.424***	-.383***	-.400***
	(.141)	(.141)	(.152)	(.150)
DEPEND	-13.103		-7.446	
	(11.957)		(12.419)	
ΔDEPEND	-3.876	-3.949		
	(3.741)	(3.444)		
DEMOCRACY	-.026*	-.029**	-.030**	-.032**
	(.013)	(.012)	(.014)	(.012)
GROWTH	-.004	-.004	-.002	-.001
	(.012)	(.012)	(.012)	(.012)
ALLIES	-.302*	-.300*	-.347*	-.347*
	(.166)	(.166)	(.175)	(.176)
CONTIGUITY	1.042***	1.023***	1.070***	1.059***
	(.178)	(.174)	(.189)	(.184)
CAPABILITY	-.0023***	-.0023***	-.0030***	-.0030***
	(.0009)	(.0009)	(.0011)	(.0011)
N	19772	19772	20990	20990
χ^2	891.22***	868.05***	738.85***	730.59***

Note: Entries are estimates derived using a logit model, with Huber standard errors in parentheses. Each model is estimated after including a cubic spline function that includes three knots and year-specific dummy variables. Statistical significance is indicated as follows: *** $p \le .01$; ** $p \le .05$; * $p \le .10$. Two-tailed tests are conducted for each estimate.

Table 3

PROBIT ESTIMATES OF THE EFFECTS OF PTA MEMBERSHIP, TRADE, DEMOCRACY, ECONOMIC GROWTH, ALLIANCES, CONTIGUITY, AND POWER CAPABILITIES ON THE ONSET OF MILITARY DISPUTES, 1950–85.

Variable	1	2	3	4
INTERCEPT	-1.555***	-1.563***	-1.622***	-1.626***
	(.120)	(.120)	(.102)	(.102)
PTA	-.137**	-.145**	-.124*	-.127*
	(.061)	(.060)	(.063)	(.061)
DEPEND	-3.794		-1.330	
	(3.766)		(3.655)	
ΔDEPEND	-2.061	-2.072		
	(1.593)	(1.491)		
DEMOCRACY	-.012***	-.013***	-.015***	-.015***
	(.005)	(.005)	(.005)	(.005)
GROWTH	-.016***	-.017***	-.013**	-.015**
	(.006)	(.006)	(.005)	(.005)
ALLIES	-.297***	-.297***	-.287***	-.288***
	(.088)	(.088)	(.086)	(.086)
CONTIGUITY	.613***	.607***	.597***	.596***
	(.090)	(.088)	(.088)	(.087)
CAPABILITY	-.0009***	-.0009***	-.0012***	-.0012***
	(.0003)	(.0003)	(.0004)	(.0004)
N	19772	19772	20990	20990
χ^2	194.40***	191.33***	218.90***	217.52***

Note: Entries are estimates derived using a random-effects probit model, with Huber standard errors in parentheses. Each model is estimated after including a cubic spline function that includes three knots. Statistical significance is indicated as follows: *** $p \leq$ .01; ** $p \leq$ .05; * $p \leq$ .10. Two-tailed tests are conducted for each estimate.

effects as randomly distributed rather than fixed across pairs, we can account for factors that are not included in our model and that might affect the incidence of conflict without dropping any observations from our sample.[77] Because it has been suggested that a probit model is better suited to random-effects treatments than a logit model, we also estimate equation (1) using a random-effects probit model.[78] The results are presented in the first column of Table 3.

As noted earlier, our data set includes annual observations for various pairs of countries during the period from 1950 to 1985. It is widely recognized that logit and probit analyses of such data will yield biased results if the observations for each pair are temporally dependent. A recent set of studies has suggested a solution to this problem.[79] For present purposes, it involves including in equation (1) a natural spline function (with three knots) of the number of years since states A and B last initiated a military dispute. Moreover, controlling for the length of time since a dispute last began between a given pair of countries is especially useful from our standpoint because it helps to guard against the possibility that any observed effect of PTAs on disputes stems from some tendency for military conflict to influence whether states are involved in a preferential arrangement. We therefore derive all of the estimates shown in Tables 2 and 3 after including this spline function in equation (1). In addition, all of the following tests of statistical significance are based on Huber standard errors, which previous studies have recommended when estimating time-series cross-section models like ours.[80]

77. On these issues, see William H. Greene, *Econometric Analysis* (New York: Macmillan, 1993, 2d ed.), chap. 16.

78. Ibid., 655–57.

79. See Nathaniel Beck and Richard Tucker, "Conflict in Space and Time: Time-Series-Cross-Section Analysis with Binary Dependent Variable," (paper presented at the 1996 annual meeting of the American Political Science Association, San Francisco, Calif., 29 August–1 September 1996); Nathaniel Beck and Jonathan N. Katz, "The Analysis of Binary Time-Series-Cross-Sectional Data and/or the Democratic Peace," (paper presented at the 1997 annual meeting of the Political Methodology Group, Columbus, Ohio, 23–27 July 1997); and Nathaniel Beck, Jonathan N. Katz, and Richard Tucker, "Beyond Ordinary Logit: Taking Time Seriously in Binary Time-Series Cross-Section Models," *American Journal of Political Science*, 42, no. 4 (October 1998): 1260–88. Note that the base of this spline function and each knot are statistically significant ($p < .01$).

80. See Beck and Tucker, "Conflict in Space and Time;" and Beck and Katz, "The Analysis of Binary Time-Series-Cross-Sectional Data and/or the Democratic Peace."

ESTIMATES OF THE MODEL

CONSISTENT WITH our argument, there is evidence that states participating in the same PTA are less likely to become involved in hostilities than other countries. The estimate of PTA is negative and statistically significant, based on both the logit model (in Table 2) and the probit model (in Table 3). Moreover, PTA membership's effect on political conflict is relatively large. Table 4 reports the predicted probability of a military dispute occurring between states that belong to the same preferential arrangement and between those that do not, holding constant ΔDEPEND, DEMOCRACY, CAPABILITY, GROWTH, and the terms of the spline function at their respective means, and DEPEND at its median (because it is highly skewed).[81] Since CONTIGUITY and ALLIES are dummy variables, the probability of a dispute is computed for both contiguous and noncontiguous pairs, as well as for allies and nonallies. The entries in Table 4 are clearly small, which is not surprising given the relative rarity of military disputes.[82] On average, however, states that do not belong to the same PTA are roughly 30 to 45 percent more likely to become involved in a dispute than PTA members.

Table 4

PREDICTED PROBABILITY OF A MID'S ONSET.

	Logit Model (1)	Probit Model (1)
Noncontiguous/no alliance/no PTA	.0159	.0127
Noncontiguous/no alliance/PTA	.0107	.0089
Noncontiguous/alliance/no PTA	.0118	.0057
Noncontiguous/alliance/PTA	.0179	.0038
Contiguous/no alliance/no PTA	.0437	.0526
Contiguous/no alliance/PTA	.0298	.0395
Contiguous/alliance/no PTA	.0327	.0274
Contiguous/alliance/PTA	.0222	.0200

81. These mean values are as follows: GROWTH = .772, CAPABILITY = 163.3, ΔDEPEND = .00012, and DEMOCRACY = -3.5. The median value of DEPEND is .0002.

82. It is important to note that, on average, the probability of a MID's onset between a given pair of states based on our data set is .030.

Besides PTA membership, most of the remaining variables in equation (1) are also strongly related to the onset of MIDs. The estimate of CONTIGUITY is positive, while the estimates of DEMOCRACY, ALLIES, CAPABILITY, and GROWTH are negative. All of them are statistically significant based on the probit model and all but GROWTH are significant based on the logit model. Conforming to earlier findings, our results indicate that noncontiguous pairs of states (involving a major power), dyads in which both states are relatively democratic, and those composed of political-military allies are less likely to engage in military conflicts than other pairs. They also indicate that the probability of a dispute rises as capabilities become more uniformly distributed between states and for pairs including countries experiencing lagging economic growth.[83]

The negative estimates of both DEPEND and ΔDEPEND suggest that higher levels of and increases in commercial dependence inhibit the outbreak of political conflict. Neither estimate is statistically significant, however, which accords with the findings of some recent studies.[84] Furthermore, if DEPEND and ΔDEPEND are omitted from equation (1), the estimate of PTA is relatively unaffected (see columns 2, 3, and 4 in Tables 2 and 3). The ratio of trade to GDP therefore seems to be a less salient influence on conflict than the institutions designed to guide commerce. This finding is especially noteworthy in light of the widespread attention that studies of the relationship between commerce and conflict have placed on trade flows, and the lack of attention they have focused on commercial institutions.[85]

ADDITIONAL STATISTICAL ANALYSES

IN THE PRECEDING analysis, we considered PTAs as a group. While it is beyond the scope of this article to address the effects of variations across preferential arrangements, it is important to ensure that our results do not stem from the influence of any single arrangement. We therefore define a separate dummy variable for each preferential arrangement included in the sample and then estimate both a logit and a probit model after introducing each variable, one at a time, in equation (1).[86] Based on our findings, there is no case in

---

83. See, for example, Oneal and Russett, "The Classical Liberals Were Right."

84. Beck and Tucker, "Conflict in Space and Time"; Beck and Katz, "The Analysis of Binary Time-Series-Cross-Sectional Data and/or the Democratic Peace"; and Beck, Katz, and Tucker, "Beyond Ordinary Logit."

85. This issue is addressed at greater length in Mansfield and Pevehouse, "Trade Blocs, Trade Flows, and International Conflict."

86. Various pairs of countries that belong to the same PTA in our sample involve a member of the EC and a state outside the EC having an association agreement with this institution

which controlling for the effect of a particular arrangement has much bearing on the estimate of *PTA*, which is always negative and statistically significant. Hence, the influence of PTAs on conflict is not due to any single arrangement.

Although our analysis centers on whether participants in the same PTA are less likely to become involved in military disputes than other states, we also need to address the possibility that a reciprocal relationship exists between PTA membership and conflict. Hostile political relations between states, for example, may limit their willingness to join the same PTA, since each country faces the prospect that the economic gains from such an arrangement will augment its adversary's political-military capacity, thus undermining its own security. Conversely, antagonists may choose to enter a preferential arrangement to help improve their political relations.

To avoid any potential problems of simultaneity between *PTA* and *MID*, we have lagged the effects of preferential arrangements and included variables pertaining to the length of time since a dispute last broke out between each pair of states (the spline function) in equation (1). To further address this issue, we estimate two logit models. In the first, *PTA* is measured in year *t* and regressed on *MID* in *t*. Next, we estimate the same model after measuring *MID* in year *t*-1. Both models also include the remaining variables in equation (1), as well as some additional variables that have been united to the the onset of PTAs.[87] In both analyses, the estimate of *MID* is negative, indicating that the onset of a MID reduces the likelihood that a pair of states participates in the same PTA, but it is not statistically significant. These results continue to provide no indication that military disputes affect PTA membership. Based on our analyses and other related research,[88] there is no reason to suspect that the preceding results are undermined by problems of endogeneity.

Finally, it is useful to assess whether PTAs influence the escalation of military tensions. Since much of the existing empirical literature on the links between commerce and conflict focuses on explaining the incidence of militarized interstate disputes, we have done likewise. MIDs, however, include a variety of conflicts, ranging from incidents involving the threat of armed force to full-blown wars.[89] We have found that PTA members are less likely to become involved in military disputes than other states. Are disputes also less likely to escalate between parties to the same PTA?

(for example, parties to the Lomé Convention). For the purpose of conducting these tests, we consider all association agreements to comprise a single PTA.

87. See Mansfield, Milner, and Rosendorff, "Why Democracies Cooperate More."
88. Ibid.
89. See the sources listed in n. 55, above.

The data on MIDs indicate how violent each dispute became. The most violent conflicts are wars. In an initial effort to answer the aforementioned question, we compute the percentage of MIDs beginning between members of the same preferential arrangement that escalate to wars. We then compute the corresponding percentage for states that do not belong to the same PTA. Our results indicate that roughly 11 percent of the MIDs between non-PTA members escalated to war and that only about 2 percent of the MIDs between PTA members escalated to such heights. While the preliminary nature of this analysis is obvious, PTA members seem to stand a better chance of resolving military disputes short of war than other states. This issue merits a more comprehensive treatment in future research.

THE SECURITY GAINS FROM COMMERCIAL REGIONALISM

PREFERENTIAL trading arrangements have proliferated rapidly in recent decades, a trend that shows no signs of abating. The United States and various other countries have placed a high priority on forming and expanding such arrangements in the hopes that they will promote greater commercial openness throughout the world. Whether these hopes will be realized is the subject of heated debate, but even the most outspoken critics of policies intended to promote the spread of PTAs concede that they are likely to remain important features of the international economic landscape for the foreseeable future.[90]

Despite the widespread interest that has been expressed in the growth of PTAs, systematic analyses of their political implications have been scarce; and virtually no quantitative evidence has been accumulated on the links between preferential arrangements and the incidence of military conflict. In this article, we have argued that PTAs can inhibit the onset of interstate hostilities. Parties to a preferential arrangement have reason to anticipate economic gains from membership. Since military antagonism can undermine a PTA and economic relations among members, the outbreak of disputes jeopardizes the ability of states to realize these gains. Preferential trading agreements therefore increase the ex ante economic costs of political conflict, which is likely to deter its outbreak. Furthermore, PTAs create a forum for bargaining and negotiation that reduces tensions among participants, helps resolve conflicts that do occur, and fosters the establishment of focal points, shaping members' expectations and facilitating the identification of deviations from accepted norms.

90. See, for example, Bhagwati, "Regionalism and Multilateralism."

Our statistical results accord with this argument. During the period since the Second World War, parties to the same PTA have been less prone to engage in military disputes than other states. Indeed, our initial estimates indicate that PTA membership reduces the likelihood of hostilities by as much as one-third.

These findings have both theoretical and policy implications. The relationship between commerce and political conflict has long been of interest to scholars of international relations. Most of the empirical work on this topic focuses on whether the flow of trade (as a percentage of national income) affects interstate hostilities. While useful, this focus is also limited, since it neglects how the institutions designed to guide trade influence political disputes. Our results indicate that, on average, preferential commercial institutions have played a key role in dampening interstate tensions.

Of course, we are not suggesting that conflict has been absent among PTA members or that all PTAs have faired equally well in reducing the incidence of military disputes. Nor are we suggesting that PTAs are more important influences on the onset of hostilities than various other factors that also have been linked to interstate conflict, such as regime type, power relations, and alliances. Holding constant these other factors, however, PTA membership helps to explain the outbreak of conflict and it had a statistically stronger influence than trade flows on the incidence of interstate disputes during the cold war.

Analyses of commercial regionalism have focused largely on the welfare implications of preferential economic arrangements. While these implications are obviously important, it is equally clear that any overall assessment of regionalism's consequences requires an evaluation of the political effects of PTAs. Although preliminary, our results strongly suggest that the current wave of economic regionalism may give rise to international political benefits that have been underappreciated to date.

STRATEGY, ECONOMIC RELATIONS, AND THE DEFINITION OF NATIONAL INTERESTS

RAWI ABDELAL AND JONATHAN KIRSHNER

T HIS ARTICLE addresses the ways that economic incentives shape national interests and foreign policies, applying arguments that are derived from Albert Hirschman's *National Power and the Structure of Foreign Trade*.[1] Hirschman's focus was on the political consequences of asymmetric economic relationships, and he illustrated these with a study of German trade strategy in the interwar period. *National Power* also illustrated how the pattern of economic relations can profoundly affect international politics by shaping the way governments define their interests. Although states must always provide for their own security, different domestic political actors typically have competing visions of their country's best interests. Basic foreign policy choices often result from domestic political struggles, and the foreign economic policies of other states affect the outcomes of those internal political contests.

National Power, unfailingly cited as a classic, has not generated a substantial body of applied literature.[2] We argue that this is a serious omission by international relations scholars and that an understanding of "Hirschmanesque effects" is likely to be even more important in the coming years.[3] This paper therefore accomplishes two goals: first, we revisit *National Power* and offer a

Rawi Abdelal is assistant professor at the Graduate School of Business Administration, Harvard University; Jonathan Kirshner is associate professor of government, Cornell University.

For comments that have improved this paper we thank Richard Bensel, Valerie Bunce, Daniel Drezner, Peter Katzenstein, Brian Pollins; participants in and organizers of the *Security Studies* workshop on Economic Power, Interdependence, and National Security, held at the Mershon Center, Ohio State University, 2–5 April 1998; members of Cornell University's Political Economy Research Colloquium, and the anonymous reviewers for *Security Studies*.

1. Albert O. Hirschman *National Power and the Structure of Foreign Trade* (1945; Berkeley: University of California Press, 1980).
2. For an application of Hirschman to international monetary relations, see Jonathan Kirshner, *Currency and Coercion: The Political Economy of International Monetary Power* (Princeton: Princeton University Press, 1995), chapter 4. Several studies have looked at the same case as *National Power*. See Robert Mark Spaulding, *Osthandel and Ostpolitik: German Foreign Trade Policies in Eastern Europe from Bismarck to Adenauer* (Providence: Berghahn Books, 1997); Antonín Basch, *The Danube Basin and the German Economic Sphere* (New York: Columbia University Press, 1943); Allan G. B. Fisher, "The German Trade Drive in South-Eastern Europe," *International Affairs* 18, no. 2 (March 1939): 143–70.
3. Jonathan Kirshner, "Political Economy in Security Studies After the Cold War," *Review of International Political Economy* 5, no. 1 (spring 1998): 64–91.

richer interpretation of its conceptual contributions; and, second, we provide three illustrations of the empirical relevance of our interpretation.

There are three principal reasons why *National Power* has not inspired a more practical legacy, and these relate to the way its argument has been interpreted. First, IR scholarship has incorporated only some of the political effects that the book addresses. Hirschman clearly illustrates how asymmetric trade relations accrue political benefits to the larger state. If large country A trades with small country B, commerce between them might account for only two or three percent of country A's exports and imports, but might well represent over half of country B's. Such a relationship gives the larger country coercive power over the smaller, because an interruption of the relationship would cause much greater distress in B than in A. Threats of interruption, then, both explicit and implicit, give A power. This coercive aspect of Hirschman's theory has attracted the most attention of international relations scholars, and is central to its most celebrated theoretical application.[4]

There is, however, much more to Hirschman's story than coercion; there is also an argument about influence.[5] While Hirschman develops more fully and systematically the mechanics of the former, he also illustrates the important role of the latter,[6] and we argue that this is the more profound of the two. Simply put, *National Power* shows that the pattern of international economic relations affects domestic politics, which in turn shapes national interests. This is always true but is most vivid in asymmetric relations, where the effects are typically large, visible, and almost wholly found within the smaller economy. Consider, for example, a free trade agreement between a large and a small state. The likely result is a change in the smaller state's perception of its own interest: it will converge toward that of the larger. Why? Because the simple act of participation in the arrangement strengthens those who benefit from it relative to those who do not (by definition). This strength should translate into political power.[7] Further, because firms and sectors engage in patterns of activity based on economic incentives, and since this constellation of incentives

4. Stephen Krasner, "State Power and the Structure of International Trade," *World Politics* 28, no. 3 (April 1976): 320.

5. Those familiar with Hirschman's terminology will note a slightly different usage here. Hirschman referred to "supply" and "influence" effects from trade (14–16). "Supply effects" (of secondary importance to Hirschman and not addressed here) refer to the ways that gains from trade "enhance the potential military force" of a country. Hirschman considers "influence effects" to include both power that accrues to one state from asymmetric costs of exit *and* changes in domestic politics that result from international economic relations. We call the former "coercion" and the latter "influence." In other words, coercion refers to changes in policy, influence refers to changes in the definition of interests.

6. See Hirschman, *National Power*, 18, 28, 29, 34, 37.

7. Gary S. Becker, "A Theory of Competition Among Pressure Groups for Political Influence," *Quarterly Journal of Economics* 98, no. 3 (August 1983): 373–400.

will be transformed by the trade agreement, the subsequent reshuffling of behavior will lead to new interests and the formation of political coalitions to
advance those interests.[8] Most importantly, decisions based on these new incentives give firms a stake in their country's continued participation, and they
will direct their political energies to that end. In Hirschman's words, "...these
regions or industries will exert a powerful influence in favor of a 'friendly' attitude toward the state to the imports of which they owe their interests."[9] Finally, the central government can find its own interests reshaped, above and
beyond that which results from domestic political pressures.[10]

In practice, Hirschmanesque effects are more profoundly felt with regard to
influence than coercion. They are about the fact that, to paraphrase one report,
"a salesman of [country A's] exports in his own market" becomes "a spokes-
man of [country A's] interests with his own government."[11] Resulting changes
in international political behavior do not occur because of pressure, but because new incentives alter perceptions of interest. This is akin to what Joseph
S. Nye has called "soft power." Rather than forcing others to do what you
want them to do, soft power, or influence, is about "getting others to want
what you want."[12]

The second reason that *National Power*'s framework has been underapplied is
that the emphasis on the coercive part of the story has given the illusion that
few states have employed Hirschmanesque strategies. In fact, the opposite is
true. There are indeed very few instances of large states' cutting off intimate
relations with small states. Tellingly, when this occurs, it is most often as a

8. Charles P. Kindleberger, "Group Behavior and International Trade," *Journal of Political Economy* 59, no. 1 (February 1959): 30–47; Peter Gourevitch, *Politics in Hard Times* (Ithaca: Cornell University Press, 1986); Jeffry A. Frieden and Ronald Rogowski, "The Impact of the International Economy on National Policies," in *Internationalization and Domestic Politics*, ed. Robert O. Keohane and Helen V. Milner (Cambridge: Cambridge University Press, 1996). Kindleberger emphasizes sectors, Gourevitch coalitions, Frieden and Rogowski factors and price incentives. Hirschman demonstrates the consequences for power politics of economic incentives and group conflict.

9. Hirschman, *National Power*, 29.

10. This can result from concerns regarding the overall balance of trade, revenue from tariffs, or trade undertaken or controlled by the government. In monetary relations central governments are particularly likely to be affected, given their role in supervising monetary stability, and the likely composition of their own reserves. See Kirshner, *Currency and Coercion*, chap. 4. Trade and financial flows can have a direct effect on elites' foreign policy prefer-ences, as illustrated in Valerie Bunce, "The Empire Strikes Back: The Evolution of the East-ern Bloc from a Soviet Asset to a Soviet Liability," *International Organization* 39, no. 1 (winter 1985): 1–46.

11. "The Aski Mark," *Economist*, 12 August 1939, 322 (referring to Latin American im-porters of German products).

12. Joseph S. Nye Jr., *Bound to Lead: The Changing Nature of American Power* (New York: Basic Books, 1990), 188. Nye argues that "trends today are making...soft power resources more important" (see also 189–201).

measure of last resort, more a punishment designed to hurt a state with which relations have been irreparably breached, than an instrument of diplomacy designed to change the behavior of the target. States are loath to exercise Hirschmanesque coercion because it means that they are forgoing more valuable Hirschmanesque influence. The dearth of examples of such coercion underscores the fact that large states are routinely and continuously attempting to cultivate influence with others.

Finally, *National Power* has not been more broadly utilized because of some confusion (exacerbated by Hirschman in the preface to the second edition[13]) about the concept of "dependence." Fostering dependence, as used by Hirschman and in this paper, is undertaken by states using economic means to advance political goals. This is distinct, and in essence the converse of "dependency," in which large states use their political power to enforce economic extraction. From the dependency perspective, then, power is a means to achieve an economic end. In Hirschman's story of dependence, wealth is used to advance a political goal. Small states in this version typically gain in an economic sense, often handsomely.

In the cases that follow, we contribute to what we hope will become an expanding data base designed to study the political economy of influence. These cases do not test a theory; they are chosen to demonstrate the broad applicability of the concept of influence and to illustrate distinct and variable aspects of Hirschmanesque statecraft. The first case, of relations between the United States and Kingdom of Hawaii, offers a classic Hirschmanesque story of asymmetric relations and interest transformation. The latter two cases, which focus on interwar Austria and Czechoslovakia and post–cold war Ukraine and Russia, also illustrate states pursuing Hirschmanesque strategies. These cases, however, extend the analysis further. They demonstrate how the pattern of economic activity can have significant political effects long after the power that shaped them has faded from view. These cases also address the broader and most profound point raised by *National Power*, that there are a range of plausible directions "National Interests" can take. The pattern of economic relations, especially during periods of political transition when national interests are most malleable, will have a formative influence on their trajectories.[14]

---

13. *National Power*, v–xii, esp. vi, where Hirschman claims to be a "founding grandfather" of dependency theory.

14. We therefore engage the international relations literature that describes the influence of domestic political and economic bargaining on foreign policies. See, for example, Jack Snyder, *Myths of Empire* (Ithaca: Cornell University Press, 1991); and Helen Milner, *Resisting Protectionism* (Princeton: Princeton University Press, 1988). For elaborations of the influence of the economic preferences of domestic actors on security policies, see also Paul A. Papayoanou, "Interdependence, Institutions, and the Balance of Power," *International Security*

THE UNITED STATES AND THE HAWAIIAN KINGDOM

THE CASE of the United States and the Hawaiian Kingdom in the second half of the nineteenth century offers an excellent illustration of Hirschmanesque forces at work.[15] Trade relations between the two states, and in particular the establishment of a reciprocity treaty in 1875 and its political consequences, can only be understood in this context. At all times, the United States was motivated by political goals in its economic relations with Hawaii, and, from an economic standpoint, was almost certainly worse off as a consequence of reciprocity. Hawaii, on the other hand, reaped great economic benefits from greater access to the American market. At the same time, however, its domestic politics were transformed by the agreement, which led to greater political concessions when the treaty was renewed and contributed to the revolution of 1893.

THE ROAD TO RECIPROCITY

The treaty of trade reciprocity with the United States that Hawaii ultimately secured represented the culmination of over twenty-five years of diplomatic efforts during which the Kingdom repeatedly sought such a treaty with the United States but was continually rebuffed. Hawaii's desire to expand its agricultural exports to the United States resulted from the decline of the whaling industry, which was the mainstay of the Hawaiian economy during the first half of the nineteenth century. Whaling had brought good times to Hawaii, with Honolulu serving as the hub for the majority of the world's whaling fleet. Whale oil was at one time a profoundly important source of energy, especially for artificial light, but a growing scarcity of the mammals, the emergence of alternative fuel sources, and the diversion of ships during the American Civil War signaled the industry's secular decline.[16] At the same time, increased de-

---

20, no. 4 (spring 1996): 42–76; and Brian Pollins, "Conflict, Cooperation, and Commerce," *American Journal of Political Science* 33, no. 3 (August 1989): 737–61.

15. Two recent articles brought this case to our attention: Sumner J. La Croix and Christopher Grandy, "The Political Instability of Reciprocal Trade and the Overthrow of the Hawaiian Kingdom," *Journal of Economic History* 57, no. 1 (March 1997): 161–89; and John McClaren, "Size, Sunk Costs, and Judge Bowker's Objection to Free Trade," *American Economic Review* 87, no. 3 (June 1997): 400–420. La Croix and Grandy offer an excellent analysis of the transformation of Hawaii's domestic political economy. McClaren makes a more general argument regarding how "sunk costs" (new investments following a trade agreement that alter the structure of the domestic economy) can place small states at a bargaining disadvantage vis-à-vis large states. On U.S. policy, see United States Department of State, *Foreign Relations of the United States: 1894*, app. 2, *Affairs in Hawaii* (Washington: Government Printing Office, 1895), hereafter *FRUS*.

16. Ralph S. Kuykendall and A. Grove Day, *Hawaii: A History* (Englewood Cliffs: Prentice Hall, 1961), 89–90.

mand in California for agricultural products, stimulated by its acquisition by the United States and by the gold rush, presented new economic opportunities. Hawaii's sugar industry in particular, which had just started organized production in 1837 but was already exporting by 1841, was in a position to expand its sales to the U.S. market. American tariffs and foreign competitors, however, placed limits on the ability of Hawaii to fully exploit the opportunities offered by the American market.[17]

A treaty of trade reciprocity would solve both of these problems, allowing Hawaiian sugar into the United States duty free and giving it a price advantage over competitors. The Monarchy first proposed such a pact in 1848 and did so again in 1852. An agreement was actually reached in 1855, but it could not secure ratification in the U.S. Senate, where a coalition led by domestic sugar and wool producers successfully derailed its progress.[18] Even without the treaty, however, Hawaii was able to increase both its sugar production and its sugar exports to the United States The U.S. tariff act of 1857 included a twenty percent reduction on the sugar tariff, and the American Civil War resulted in a huge increase in the demand of the North for imported sugar. The price of sugar rose from just under seven cents per pound in the 1850s to over seventeen cents in 1864. It was at this time that sugar emerged as a force in the Hawaiian economy. The island, which had exported just over half-a-million pounds in 1856, exported five times that amount in 1861. Exports surged throughout the 1860s, reaching ten million pounds in 1864 and over seventeen million in 1866.[19]

The end of the American Civil War was associated with an expansion in the global supply of sugar and a reduction in its price, contributing to a serious economic downturn in Hawaii. Once again the Kingdom attempted to secure a reciprocity treaty with the United States, and an agreement was reached in May 1867, but for a second time it failed to secure passage in the U.S. Senate, in this case after three years of intermittent debate.[20]

Although it rejected successive treaties of reciprocity, the United States maintained a keen interest in the affairs of Hawaii. As early as 1842, Daniel

17. Sylvester K. Stevens, *American Expansion in Hawaii: 1842–1898* (Harrisburg: Archives Publishing, 1945), 34; Merze Tate, *Hawaii: Reciprocity or Annexation* (East Lansing: Michigan State University Press: 1968), 26.

18. Ralph S. Kuykendall, *The Hawaiian Kingdom 1854–1874: Twenty Critical Years* (Honolulu: University of Hawaii Press, 1953), 45; Tate, *Reciprocity or Annexation*, 26, 28, 35–39.

19 Tate, *Reciprocity or Annexation*, 39–41; Kuykendall, *Hawaiian Kingdom*, 141 (export figures), 143; Noel J. Kent, *Hawaii: Islands Under the Influence* (New York: Monthly Review Press, 1983), 38 (sugar prices).

20. Tate, *Annexation or Reciprocity*, 41–42, 47, 53, 67; Kuykendall, *Hawaiian Kingdom*, 209, 212, 218. In this instance, unrelated domestic political issues associated with the impeachment of President Johnson played an important role in distracting attention from the issue.

Webster, then secretary of state in the Tyler administration, pronounced what was in essence a "Monroe Doctrine" for Hawaii. Webster asserted that the United States was "more interested in the fate of the islands, and their Government, than any other nation can be." Not only did the United States oppose the colonization of the islands by any foreign power, but it also insisted that "no power ought to seek for any undue control over the existing Government."[21] While Hawaii's interest in the United States was principally economic, America's interest in the Pacific Islands was almost solely political. There was continuous concern that the Kingdom might be conquered by Britain or France, or possibly even by Germany or Japan. Concerns regarding British dominance were particularly acute in the first half of the nineteenth century. The great Hawaiian King Kamehameha I, who unified the islands under his rule, had essentially placed the islands under British protection, and his son continued that policy when he ascended the throne in 1819. British influence in Hawaii waned steadily over the years, but there was considerable concern in the United States over a perceived pro-British tilt in Hawaiian foreign policy in the 1850s.[22]

The executive branch of the United States government continuously sought to achieve a reciprocity treaty with Hawaii in order to assure U.S. political dominance, but it was consistently resisted by narrow domestic economic interests. Presidents Franklin Pierce, Andrew Johnson, and Ulysses S. Grant all supported reciprocity, even though they recognized that there would be little, if any, economic benefit to the United States and that the treaty would hurt the interests of the U.S. sugar producers. Johnson's treasury secretary Hugh McCulloch stated explicitly that the treaty did not have much economic value, "but political considerations...appear to be of such importance as to entirely overwhelm the comparatively trifling interests involved in the commerce of these islands." Nevertheless, national security arguments could not carry the day in the face of the organized opposition of economic interests, at least in the middle third of the century.[23]

21. *FRUS*, 40. See also Webster's related comments, 60–62, and President Tyler's message to congress, 39–41.

22. Kuykendall and Day, *Hawaii*, 47; Merze Tate, *The United States and the Hawaiian Kingdom: A Political History* (New Haven: Yale University Press, 1965), 20; Kuykendall, *Hawaiian Kingdom*, 35–36, 196–97. For examples of U.S. concerns regarding France, Britain, and Japan, see *FRUS*, 97–102, 134, 142.

23. John Patterson, "The United States and Hawaiian Reciprocity, 1867–1870," *Pacific Historical Review* 7, no. 1 (March 1938): 17; Stevens, *American Expansion in Hawaii*, 78.

RECIPROCITY ACHIEVED

The demise of the 1867 treaty, which lingered in congressional purgatory until 1870, did not put an end to the desire of actors both in the United States and on Hawaii to reach a reciprocal trade agreement. A fall in the price of sugar in the early 1870s again threw the Hawaiian economy into depression and political distress and raised new demands for a trade agreement. Having failed repeatedly in the past, proreciprocity forces within Hawaii searched for a way to sweeten the pot. On 8 February 1873, the *Pacific Commercial Advertiser* urged the government to offer the U.S. "a position of harbor and coaling station"; namely, Pearl Harbor. Four days later the Hawaiian Chamber of Commerce also called for the government consider whether "any measure can be devised to induce the Government of the United States to enter into a Treaty of Reciprocity." King Lunalilo, who had only recently succeeded the last holder of the Kamehameha line, followed the advice of his cabinet and reluctantly authorized his representatives to make such an offer to the United States. When the offer became known to the Hawaiian public, however, there was overwhelming popular and political opposition, and the King was forced to withdraw the proposal.[24]

Still, pressure to do something remained, and the withdrawal of the Pearl harbor offer did not affect Hawaii's broader policy goals. With the ascension to the throne of the relatively pro-American David Kalakaua in February 1874 (following the death of King Lunalilo), efforts to secure a reciprocity treaty intensified even further. In November Hawaiian representatives arrived in the United States and were quickly able to achieve a reciprocity agreement, even though it did not include the cession of Pearl Harbor. President Grant submitted the treaty to the U.S. Senate on 1 February 1875.[25] In the Senate the third time was the charm. Despite opposition from the same economic interests that had opposed previous reciprocity agreements, the treaty passed the U.S. Senate on 18 March by a vote of 51-12.

Why were the United States and Hawaii able to implement a reciprocity treaty in 1875 when they had repeatedly failed to do so in the past? Hawaii consistently favored such a treaty; it is U.S. policy that demands an explanation. Simply put, U.S. policy changed because its broad international political concerns dominated narrow economic interests. In the last quarter of the nineteenth century, the fading politics of sectionalism, increasing U.S. power, and,

---

24. Kuykendall, *The Hawaiian Kingdom*, 247, 250 (quotes), 251–57; Michael Dougherty, *To Steal a Kingdom: Probing Hawaiian History* (Waimanalo, Hawaii: Island Style Press, 1992), 127–28.

25. Stevens, *American Expansion in Hawaii*, 93, 118, 120.

importantly, heightened concern within the U.S. about foreign political influence in Hawaii, caused the shift in policy.

After the failure of the 1867 treaty Hawaii began to explore the possibility that other export markets might substitute for the United States. In 1873, the kingdom had achieved some success in seeking out other markets. While the United States was still its largest customer, taking 14.8 million pounds of Hawaiian sugar, Australia and New Zealand took 7 million pounds, and British Columbia purchased an additional 1.2 million. This raised fears of resurgent British influence in the islands. At the same time the United States harbored increasing suspicions about the interests of France, Germany, Japan, and even Russia in the Hawaiian Islands, states the United States recognized as potential rivals in the Pacific.[26]

U.S. concerns escalated with reports that the Hawaiian sugar producers were desperate to improve their economic situation. Reports that New Zealand was to offer Hawaii a loan did little to allay fears that Britain was hoping to increase its influence there. The U.S. minister in Hawaii reported to Secretary of State Hamilton Fish that in the absence of a reciprocity treaty with the United States, Hawaii would increasingly turn to Canada and the British colonies in the Pacific. He reported that the entire 1876–77 sugar crop might be sold to British possessions.[27]

It was these heightened international political concerns that caused the change in U.S. policy.[28] In the words of one of the leading historians of Hawaii, if trade patterns did shift, "Hawaii might soon drift into the British sphere. To forestall such a turn of events off its pacific shores, the United States was willing to try reciprocity." The political motives of the treaty from the U.S. per-

26. Jean Ingram Brooks, *International Rivalry in the Pacific Islands 1800–1875* (Berkeley: University of California Press, 1941), 345, 359, 361; Tate, *Reciprocity or Annexation*, 100.

27. Tate, *Reciprocity or Annexation*, 101. Tate argues that these concerns were overstated, and that a significant permanent shift in the pattern of Hawaii's trade relations was unlikely. He also concedes, however, that "the spectre of an economic swing by the Hawaiian Kingdom toward the British Empire, with its resultant political consequences, was frequently and effectively raised in Honolulu to excite fears and to produce action in Washington" (104). Indeed, James Garfield, at that time a representative from Ohio, argued on the House floor that if the U.S. failed to act, Hawaii would seek an alliance with Great Britain or France (115). See also Merze Tate, "Canada's Interest in the Trade and the Sovereignty of Hawaii," *The Canadian Historical Review* 44, no. 1 (March 1963): 20–42; and Tate, "Australasian Interest in the Commerce and the Sovereignty of Hawaii," *Historical Studies Australia and New Zealand* 11, no. 44 (April 1965): 499–512.

28. Walter LaFeber, who would stress the importance of economic interests (Hawaii as a bridge to Asia) in influencing the U.S. decision for annexation in 1898, wrote of the 1875 agreement: "Both Fish and Congress said nothing about direct commercial benefits, because none existed" (*The New Empire: An Interpretation of American Expansion, 1860–1898* [Ithaca: Cornell University Press, 1963], 35). Also, personal communication with authors, 4 August 1998.

spective are clearly seen with the Senate's amendment to Article IV. This revision of the treaty, a novel extension not addressed by its drafters, prevented Hawaii from reaching similar reciprocity treaties with other states. Further, regarding its ports, harbors, and territory in general, Hawaii was prohibited from granting "any special privilege or rights or use therein, to any other power, state, or government." Secretary of State James G. Blaine would later instruct U.S. representatives on the island to emphasize the fact that "the government of the United States considers this stipulation as the very essence of the treaty." Without this clause, one leading scholar has argued, "the treaty probably would have been rejected." Newspapers at the time reported what a Senate Foreign Relations Committee report of 1894 concluded, "the treaty was negotiated for the purpose of securing political control of those islands," and "preventing any other great power from acquiring a foothold there."[29]

THE CONSEQUENCES OF RECIPROCITY

The positive economic effects of reciprocity in Hawaii exceeded even the most optimistic forecasts. Sluggish economic activity in 1875 was followed by an unprecedented expansion that lasted seven years. Sugar led the way, but few aspects of the island economy were left untouched, especially activities that were associated with the sugar economy, such as construction, merchandising, banking, and transportation. Sugar production doubled within four years from 26 million pounds in 1876 to 63.5 million in 1880. Within five years production tripled again, reaching 171 million pounds—ten times the level associated with the civil war boom. The crop's value increased over this period from $1.27 million to $8.35 million.[30]

The reciprocity bonanza brought with it fundamental changes in Hawaii's domestic political economy and its international relations. On the home front, the sugar industry, and especially "big sugar," came to dominate all economic activity on the islands. Land under sugar cultivation increased from 8,500 acres in 1870 to 26,019 in 1880 to 87,016 in 1890, while capital investments in the sugar industry increased from $1.4 million to $4.5 million to $14.7 million over the same period. The increasing cost of land and greater use of expensive machinery privileged large operations and contributed to the concentration of

29. Kuykendall and Day, Hawaii, 151–52 (first quote); Stevens, American Expansion, 125 (quotes from Article 4), 130 (New York Times commentary); FRUS, 1153 (Blaine instructions); Tate, The United States and the Hawaiian Kingdom, 41 (quote, San Francisco Morning Call commentary); Patterson, "The United States and Hawaiian Reciprocity," 14 (quotes from senate report).

30. Stevens, American Expansion, 141; Tate, Reciprocity or Annexation, 118.

production.[31] Internationally, the Hawaiian economy became fundamentally intertwined with that of the United States. Almost all of the new sugar grown was exported to the United States. In 1885 trade with America accounted for 92 per cent of Hawaii's total trade; trade with Britain had fallen to only 3.75 percent. Magnifying the political consequence of these effects was the fact that the United States took an even greater proportion of Hawaiian exports than it provided Hawaiian imports, and this also yielded for the Kingdom a surplus on its American trade account. Continued Hawaiian prosperity, and the interests of the dominant commercial interests there, depended on sustained privileged access to the U.S. market.[32]

The United States, on the other hand, received no economic benefits from the reciprocity treaty. Because Hawaii's exports of sugar accounted for a relatively small proportion of total U.S. consumption (and because other foreign suppliers still faced U.S. protectionism) the price of sugar paid by U.S. consumers did not fall. Hawaiian producers thus gained the full benefits of the treaty, at the expense of the U.S. government, which lost tariff revenue.[33]

The lack of tangible economic benefits at home contrasted sharply with the visible economic and export boom in Hawaii. Rutherford B. Hayes administration treasury secretary John Sherman stated plainly in 1878 that "the advantages thus far have not been reciprocal...and it is probable that the benefits in Favor of Hawaii will increase largely." Not surprisingly, opponents of reciprocity in the United States, principally sugar interests (southern producers and eastern refiners) redoubled their efforts. The attempt initiated by Louisiana congressmen to secure a vote to abrogate the treaty failed. Once again, treaty proponents stressed the political benefits of the treaty. The House Committee on Foreign Affairs, for example, opposed abrogation because "the effect of the treaty has already been to give to this government the benefit of a satisfactory political influence with the Government of the Hawaiian Islands."[34]

Opposition to the treaty, however, became more consequential as the date when it was terminable, 9 September 1883, approached. The United States

31. La Croix and Grandy, "The Political Instability of Reciprocal Trade," 172; Stevens, *American Expansion*, 142. The increased production of sugar also required the increased use of foreign labor, mostly from China and Japan, and this affected racial politics. While not emphasized here, the tensions between Asians, natives, and whites (mostly Americans and American-Hawaiians) were a central aspect of Hawaiian domestic politics.

32. Tate, *Reciprocity or Annexation*, 118–19, 130; Dougherty, *Stolen Kingdom*, 130–31; Kent, *Islands Under the Influence*, 46–67, 58.

33. See J. Laurence Laughlin and H. Parker Willis, *Reciprocity* (New York: Baker and Taylor, 1903), 78–80; F. W. Taussig, *The Tariff History of the United States* (6th ed.) (New York: Putnam, 1914), 279. This result is illustrated more formally in La Croix and Grandy, "The Political Instability of Reciprocal Trade," 170–71.

34. Donald Marquand Dozer, "The Opposition to Hawaiian Reciprocity, 1876–1888," *Pacific Historical Review* 14, no. 2 (June 1945), 158, 169.

executive branch continued to support reciprocity regardless of who was in power: Presidents Grant, Hayes, James A. Garfield, and Chester A. Arthur all supported reciprocity and its extension. President Grover Cleveland's support of the Hawaiian treaty, explicitly for reasons of national security and as an exception to his general opposition to reciprocal trade treaties, supports the view that the treaty was seen as serving the broad national interest.[35]

Parochial interests did not simply disappear, however. While efforts by Louisiana Senators J. B. Eustis and Randall L. Gibson to formally terminate the agreement failed, neither was the treaty extended. In fact, if anything, momentum was building against the seven-year extension of the treaty desperately sought by Hawaii and supported by President Arthur in 1883. Opponents of the treaty pointed out that it had cost the United States $22,808,085 in tariff revenue, while during the same period total U.S. exports to Hawaii amounted to $22,872,371. Why not, critics sarcastically suggested, just restore sugar duty and send all of our exports to Hawaii free of charge? At the same time, the bulging profits and monopolistic practices of newly emergent west-coast sugar refiners lent credibility to the complaints of southern and eastern sugar interests that the treaty was unfairly hurting them. Citing the west-coast monopolists, the San Francisco Chronicle began a campaign against the treaty.[36]

With no prompt and definitive resolution, the task of selling an extension of the treaty fell to the Cleveland administration, and Secretary of State Thomas Bayard. Opponents of the treaty, like Illinois Senator William Morrison, continued to stress its apparent one-sidedness, arguing that "much is given and nothing received." Bayard responded that "I trust that you will not allow a commercial question to outweigh political considerations so important as I believe the control of these contiguous Islands...to be," but supporters of the treaty realized that they had to show a more tangible benefit for the United States.[37]

The cessation of Pearl Harbor to the United States could fill that role. The Senate Foreign Relations Committee, searching for a salient political counterweight, proposed that the treaty be amended to grant the United States exclusive rights to create "a coaling and repair station" at Pearl River.[38] The United States was clearly interested in the port, and it had been discussed during the original reciprocity negotiations. As early as 1872 the secretary of war ordered an on-site investigation and a confidential report to evaluate the potential

35. On Cleveland, Laughlin and Willis, *Reciprocity*, 94–95.
36. Dozer, "Opposition to Hawaiian Reciprocity," 160, 173–74.
37. Charles Tansill, *The Foreign Policy of Thomas F. Bayard* (New York: Fordham University Press, 1940), 373–74.
38. Dozer, "Opposition to Hawaiian Reciprocity," 176.

military utility of Hawaiian ports. Pearl Harbor was found to be the only location that "can be made to satisfy all the conditions necessary for a harbor of refuge in time of war."[39]

More than just a selling point, senators on the Committee recognized that acquiring Pearl Harbor would end once and for all the question of political influence in Hawaii: keeping the Americans in and the Europeans out, thus achieving a long-standing U.S. policy goal. Opposition in Hawaii to any cessation of sovereign territory remained high, however, and this was the position of both King Kalakaua and Premier Walter M. Gibson. The European powers would also strongly protest such a move. Given these foreign complications, Bayard was initially opposed to the amendment, and hoped to secure an extension of the treaty without it.[40] International concerns, however, would change his mind. The specter of British influence resurfaced, as rumors of a British loan to Hawaii coincided with the completion of the Canadian-Pacific Railroad, and a report published in the London Times that, should the U.S. treaty fail to be extended, Great Britain, through the colonial office, would pursue a reciprocity treaty between Hawaii and Canada. Even more alarming to Bayard was the erratic behavior of Hawaiian foreign policy. The secretary was especially concerned that Hawaiian pretensions to form a confederation with Samoa would bring the Island Kingdom into conflict with Germany. Bayard thus decided that rapid ratification of the treaty (with the Pearl Harbor clause) was the best course of action. With the amendment in place, a seven year extension of the trade reciprocity treaty was passed by the U.S. Senate on 20 January 1887.[41]

The treaty still needed to be ratified in Hawaii, where there remained strong opposition to the Pearl Harbor clause. Debate was ended, however, by the "bloodless revolution" in June 1887. Members of the Hawaiian League, a secret organization of the captains of industry in sugar and related support sectors such as banking, commerce, and transportation, were able to capitalize on general dissatisfaction with the behavior of the Royal government. Their challenge resulted in the removal of Premier Gibson and the introduction of a new constitution that significantly circumscribed the power of the monarchy. The Hawaiian League was strongly in favor of the reciprocity treaty, even with the cessation of Pearl Harbor, and although the King remained personally op-

---

39. "Confidential report of General John Schofield and Lieutenant Colonel Burton Alexander, May 8, 1873," reprinted in *American Historical Review* 30, no. 4 (July 1925): 561–65, quote on 562.

40. Tansill, *Foreign Policy of Bayard*, 377, 381; Tate, *Reciprocity or Annexation*, 188–89.

41. Tansill, *Foreign Policy of Bayard*, 386–87; Kuykendall and Day, *Hawaii*, 168–69; Tate, *Reciprocity or Annexation*, 184; Dozer, "Opposition to Hawaiian Reciprocity," 178–79.

posed, he recognized the new political realities on the Island and acceded to the treaty.[42]

It would be an oversimplification to assert that the revolutionaries were motivated solely to assure ratification of the new reciprocity treaty. Although the Hawaiian League itself was only formed early in 1887, the June uprising was the result of long-smoldering tensions between different interest groups on the islands regarding broad questions of finance and governance. At the same time, however, it is impossible to understand the uprising, and the resulting changes in Hawaiian foreign policy, without reference to the economic causes that shifted the underlying balance of political power away from the monarchy and toward those who wanted closer relations with the United States. The cessation of Pearl Harbor, politically unacceptable in Hawaii less than fifteen years earlier, offers an illustration of Hirschmanesque effects: the transformation of domestic politics brought about by the pattern of international economic relations.

RECIPROCITY, REVOLUTION, AND ANNEXATION

The forces set in motion by reciprocity: the dramatic expansion of the sugar industry and related sectors, and their conditioning on the American market, continued to dominate the trajectory of Hawaiian politics after the bloodless revolution. This was made abundantly clear by the consequences of the McKinley Tariff of 1890, which eliminated all U.S. duties on sugar and gave a two cent per pound bounty to domestic producers. While not a violation of the reciprocity treaty, the measure with one stroke gutted its import, and hit the island like a tidal wave, throwing Hawaii into depression. The price of sugar in Honolulu fell by forty percent, and property values also declined precipitously. This agitated the still-simmering political tensions on the Islands. Things came to a head when Queen Liliuokalani, who had succeeded King Kalakaua upon his death in 1891, introduced a new constitution in an effort to reverse the political losses suffered by the Monarchy in 1887. This led to the overthrow of the Queen by the same elements that had formed the Hawaiian League and now favored the annexation of Hawaii by the United States. While

42. For an article-by-article comparison of the old and new constitutions, see FRUS, 804–17. The most important changes were to Articles 41 and 62. The revised Article 41 increased the power of the cabinet and made its members more accountable to the legislature. Changes to Article 62 expanded voting rights to include long-term residents. These changes reflected shifts in the balance of economic power on the island. Before these changes, residents who paid the vast majority of the island's taxes were not eligible to vote. See also Kuykendall and Day, *Hawaii*, 170; Stevens, *American Expansion*, 151–53; Tate, *Reciprocity or Annexation*, 198–200.

the United States appeared to support the revolutionaries, it did not agree to annex Hawaii until 1898.[43]

Some scholars have suggested (and it was the popular view at the time) that the annexationists were motivated by a desire to receive the U.S. sugar bounty, and that the Mckinley tariff thus caused the Hawaiian revolution.[44] This interpretation is not supported by the facts, and it fails to capture the broader range of issues at stake in Hawaiian politics.[45] Once again, however, as with 1887, even though the simple "sugar story" is too narrow, one cannot explain the 1893 revolution without an understanding of the political consequences of the changes in the domestic economy brought about by the pattern of Hawaii's external economic relations. In that sense, the rise of the sugar and attendant industries increased the power of those who saw Hawaii's destiny resting with some form of special relationship with the United States

AUSTRIA, CZECHOSLOVAKIA, AND THE *ANSCHLUSS* PROBLEM IN INTERWAR EUROPE, 1918–32

AUSTRIA WAS the focal point for two of the central security problems of interwar Europe. The first was the German problem, the second the collapse of the Habsburg Empire and central Europe's ensuing instability. The vast majority of Austrians and, at least later in the decade, Germans, favored the *Anschluss*, the political unification of the two states. *Anschluss* movements in Austria gained power throughout the 1920s, and German governments, which had been lukewarm in 1919, came also to champion the idea of union.

43. Stevens, *American Expansion*, 188, 192, 215–17. For the U.S., strategic concerns remained paramount throughout the 1890s as well. See, for example, Thomas A. Bailey, "The United States and Hawaii During the Spanish-American War," *American Historical Review* 36, no. 3 (April 1931): especially 560. Even passionate opponents of U.S. Hawaii policy and annexation recognized the strategic significance of the Islands. See, for example William H. Springer, "The Hawaiian Situation: Our Present Duty," *North American Review* 157, no. 445 (December 1893): 752.

44. Charles A. Beard and Mary R. Beard, *The Rise of American Civilization*, volume 2 (New York: Macmillan, 1927), 359–60; Scott Nearing and Joseph Freeman, *Dollar Diplomacy: A Study in American Imperialism* (New York: Viking, 1925), 75–76.

45. The revolutionaries did not expect to receive the sugar bounty, and many sugar producers opposed annexation because they feared becoming subject to U.S. labor exclusion laws. Political conflict in Hawaii centered around issues of general stability, property rights, taxation, domestic governance, and race relations. Most of these issues pertained to the functioning of the sugar and commercial economy, supporting the broad structural interpretation of the revolution. See Julius W. Pratt, "The Hawaiian Revolution: A Reinterpretation," *Pacific Historical Review* 1, no. 3 (September 1932): especially 278, 284, 286–87; William A. Russ Jr., "The Role of Sugar in Hawaiian Annexation," *Pacific Historical Review* 12, no. 4 (December 1943): 340, 350; Richard D. Weigle, "Sugar and the Hawaiian Revolution," *Pacific Historical Review* 16, no. 1 (February 1947): esp. 47, 53, 56–68.

Austria's socialists and pan-German nationalists, who together comprised approximately two-thirds of the parties and electorate, disagreed on almost every issue of policy except the *Anschluss*, which they sought with equal vigor, but for conflicting purposes.

Yet the unification of Austria and Germany did not occur in the 1920s for two reasons. The first was the opposition of France and Czechoslovakia, which, through their decisive roles in continental international relations between the two wars, did everything possible to prevent Austrian-German unification. The other and more complicated reason was the structure of Austrian domestic politics. The Christian Social Party was the only Austrian political party that did not favor unification with Germany, and yet it remained in power throughout the 1920s, "apparently deaf to all the agitation" for *Anschluss* and the demands of the two other major political groups, the socialists and the pan-German nationalists.[46] This section shows how the two reasons that Austrian-German unification did not occur became interconnected.

French and Czechoslovak opposition to *Anschluss* and the Christian Socials' consolidation of power in 1920s Austria, in a process that allowed them decisive influence on foreign policy making, were intimately connected through international finance. Czechoslovakia, with the help of France, persuaded the League of Nations to offer Austria a very large loan for economic reconstruction and stabilization. This loan and its terms, outlined in the Geneva Protocols of 1922, conclusively affected the balance of economic and political power in 1920s Austria. As a result of the politics and economics of the Geneva loan the Christian Socials and the social bases of their support, particularly the agricultural sector, consolidated their dominant position in the Austrian political economy.[47] Those states in opposition to *Anschluss* therefore, partially by altering the fortunes of economic groups that supported Austrian political parties, influenced the Austrian internal debate about its national interest with the timing and economic and political conditionality of financial flows. The strategy worked brilliantly, probably even more effectively than France and Czechoslovakia had hoped. The Austrian government, led by the Christian Socials, was able to oppose the groundswell of prounification sentiment in the 1920s in both Austria, where it was articulated by the socialists and nationalists, and Germany. The unification of Germany and Austria, as a result, had to wait until 1938, when it was accomplished by force.

---

46. M. Margaret Ball, *Post-war German-Austrian Relations: The Anschluss Movement, 1918–1936* (Stanford: Stanford University Press, 1937), 8–9.

47. These links are explicated clearly in Peter J. Katzenstein, *Disjoined Partners: Austria and Germany Since 1815* (Berkeley: University of California Press, 1976), chapter 6, esp. 159–61.

DEBATING THE NATIONAL INTEREST IN AUSTRIA: REMNANTS OF EMPIRE AND
GERMAN CULTURE

Austria immediately became one of Europe's most pressing security issues
when the Provisional Assembly of Austria, in November 1918, adopted a
resolution that explained to Europe, "German-Austria is a constituent part of
the German republic."[48] The victors of war, especially France, vetoed this political move.[49] The peace treaties then codified the separation of Germany and
Austria. The Treaty of Versailles included an article specifying Germany's
promise not to incorporate Austria into its state. The Treaty of St. Germain's
Article 88 outlined Austria's commitment not to give up its own sovereignty:
"The independence of Austria is inalienable otherwise than with the consent
of the Council of the League of Nations." The Austrian government, prevented by France from joining Germany, engaged independent statehood in
1919 unwillingly.

The Austria that emerged from, or rather was defined by, the ruins of the
Habsburg Empire was obsessed with the idea that it was not a viable political
or economic unit. The loss of a huge internal market and the dislocation of
interregional economic ties convinced Austrians that Austria could succeed
economically only as part of a larger economic unit, either in the form of a
unified German-Austrian state or a renewed confederation of the successor
states of the empire. Therefore, the idea of economic nonviability was tied to
the politics of the *Anschluss*.[50] Two aspects of Austria's interwar economy came
to affect its foreign policy consequentially. Austria, first of all, was short of
capital for investment and imports of food. The republic's new economy, second, was highly industrialized and, without a large internal market, needed to
export.[51]

In this period of rapid transition, however, Austria's future foreign economic interests, including the most important destination for Austrian exports,
were not clearly defined. In fact, the national interest was subject to intense

48. Quoted in Ball, *Post-war German-Austrian Relations*, 8–9.
49. Immediately after the war Britain and the United States were not particularly concerned about the Austrian *Anschluss*, but France was vehemently opposed.
50. Stefan Karner, "From Empire to Republic: Economic Problems in a Period of Collapse, Reorientation, and Reconstruction," in *Economic Development in the Habsburg Monarchy
and the Successor States*, ed. John Komlos (New York: Columbia University Press, 1990), 251–
69. See also Edward P. Keleher, "Austria's Lebensfähigkeit and the Anschluss Question,
1918–1922," *East European Quarterly* 23, no. 1 (March 1989): 71–83.
51. See W. T. Layton and Charles Rist, *The Economic Situation of Austria: A Report Presented
to the Council of the League of Nations* (Geneva: League of Nations, 1925); Kurt W. Rothschild,
Austria's Economic Development Between the Two Wars (London: Frederick Muller, 1947), especially chapter 2; and Rothschild, "Size and Viability: The Lesson of Austria," in *Economic
Consequences of the Size of Nations*, ed. E. A. G. Robinson (London: Macmillan, 1963), 168–81.

debate, and Austria's three main political groups expressed very different preferences for what were defined as the two alternatives, unification with Germany or with the successor states of Austria-Hungary.[52] The German alternative was much more popular. Both the socialists and the pan-German nationalists were strongly in favor of the *Anschluss*. The socialists consisted primarily of the industrial workers of Vienna and the several industrial centers in the provinces, and they viewed unification with Germany as a means for a rapid transition to socialism. After a brief coalition government with the Christian Socials from 1918–20, during which they were the dominant partners, the socialists remained outside of Austria's government. Significantly, however, the socialists were able to maintain the support of workers by highlighting social reforms enacted in those first years of the republic.[53] The working class and the socialists remained committed to unification with Germany throughout the period, and they consistently plead the economic case for the *Anschluss*, complaining that Austrian industry's narrow economic interests in the successor states should not outweigh the Austria's broad economic interest in a pan-German future.[54] The support of pan-German nationalists for unification was unwavering, as was, however, their opposition to socialists and their substantive ideology, apart from *Anschluss*.

The Christian Socials did not support the *Anschluss*, and throughout the 1920s, while they were the dominant party in all governing coalitions, they pursued the goal of political autonomy from Germany. The party, Catholic and conservative, drew its support from farmers[55] and financial and industrial

52. Party designations in interwar Austria can be confusing. The three main groups were the socialists (represented by the Social Democratic party), the conservative Christian Social party, and the pan-German nationalists (represented by several parties, including the Great-German party). Here we will refer to the socialists, the Christian Socials, and the pan-German nationalists. In general, the Christian Socials and pan-German nationalists remained in broad alignment against the socialists, whose fundamental political goals they both feared. Thus, the nationalists' opposition to socialism prevented their cooperation with the socialists.

53. The social reforms, which included wage increases and generous unemployment benefits, pushed the socialist government to run up huge budget deficits that lead, ultimately, to hyperinflation. The socialists, under Karl Renner, therefore also damaged the new state's credit reputation among the Allies, a process that further exacerbated Austria's persistent capital shortage during the interwar years. See Elisabeth Barker, *Austria, 1918–1972* (Coral Gables: University of Miami Press, 1973), 14, and chap. 2 more generally; and Katzenstein, *Disjoined Partners*, 157–58.

54. A memorandum from the Austrian Chamber for Workers and Employees to the League of Nations explained that a Danubian confederation of the Habsburg successor states, impossible because of politics, should be given up as a goal in favor of unification with Germany. "In some branches of industry," they complained, "there are close personal and material associations with the Succession States, which somewhat obscure specifically Austrian interests." This memorandum was included in the report of Layton and Rist, *Economic Situation of Austria*, 201–13, quote at 213.

55. Agriculture, already a traditional mainstay of the party, was further supported by protective tariffs and generous subsidies designed to encourage the development of Austrian

leaders. Finance and industry supported the party's stance against the socialists after 1920 and, as will be shown later, its support for Danubian economic cooperation as an alternative to unification with Germany. The Christian Socials, who never won a parliamentary majority in Austria's deadlocked and fragmented political system during the 1920s, managed effectively to rule throughout the 1920s. This effectiveness was based on the support of key sectors of the economy and, in the end, the decisive influence of Czechoslovak and French financial diplomacy.

The absence of influential economic pressure groups within the *Anschluss* movement demonstrates that, although many Austrian socialists viewed German unification as the solution to Austria's economic problems, the impetus toward Berlin was primarily political and cultural, not material.[56] This was because Austrian business and financial interests were concentrated not in Germany, but rather still in the Danube basin, even as post-Habsburg economic cooperation failed and close political ties to Germany were developed.[57] In 1919 the Habsburg successor states accounted for over 50 percent of Austrian imports, while German imports amounted to 34 percent of the total. By 1929 imports from Germany had fallen to 21 percent of the total, until they fell finally to less than 19 percent in 1933. Imports from the successor states, in contrast, remained steady at between 45 and 50 percent of total imports throughout the 1920s. Austrian exports told the same story. While Germany was the destination for 22 percent of Austrian exports in 1919, by 1933 Germany absorbed only 15 percent. The successor states accepted approximately 35 percent of Austrian exports throughout the interwar period.[58] German capital, moreover, held a negligible and declining place in the Austrian

agriculture after imports from agricultural regions of the former empire, including Hungary and Yugoslavia, declined dramatically after 1918. See Katzenstein, *Disjoined Partners*, 158. Also see Karl Bachinger, "Mittelstand und Bauernorganisationen als neue politische Kräfte in Österreich nach dem Ersten Weltkrieg," in *Die Auflösung des Habsburgerreiches: Zusammenbruch und Neuorientierung im Donauraum*, ed. Richard G. Plaschka and Karlheinz Mack (Vienna: Verlag für Geschichte und Politik, 1970), 462–67; and Frederick Hertz, *The Economic Problem of the Danubian States: A Study in Economic Nationalism* (London: Victor Gollancz, 1947), 118–23.

56. Katzenstein, *Disjoined Partners*, 146–48. See also Stanley Suval, *The Anschluss Question in the Weimar Era: A Study of Nationalism in Germany and Austria, 1918–1932* (Baltimore: Johns Hopkins University Press, 1974), 190–200.

57. For this conclusion, see Georges de Ménil and Mathilde Maurel, "Breaking Up a Customs Union: The Case of the Austro-Hungarian Empire in 1919," *Weltwirtschaftliches Archiv* 130, no. 3 (1994): 553–75; Herbert Matis, "Disintegration and Multinational Enterprises in Central Europe During the Post-war Years, 1918–1923," in *International Business and Central Europe, 1918–1939*, ed. Alice Teichova and P. L. Cottrell (New York: St. Martin's, 1983), 73–96; and Jürgen Nautz, "Between Political Disintegration and Economic Reintegration: Austrian Trade Relations with the Successor States After World War I," in *Economic Transformations in East Central Europe: Legacies from the Past and Policies for the Future*, ed. David F. Good (London and New York: Routledge, 1994).

58. Nautz, "Between Political Disintegration and Economic Reintegration," 265.

economy during the 1920s and 1930s. Although, to be sure, the problems of economic cooperation between the successor states had depressed the overall level of trade dramatically, the regional orientation of the Austrian economy remained Danubian and most certainly not German.[59]

Austrian industry therefore remained opposed to the *Anschluss* and various customs union schemes throughout the 1920s, although by the early 1930s the continuing problems of cooperation between the successor states had pushed Austrian industrial interests further toward Germany.[60] Business interests, which failed to find a permanent home in the three Austrian political groups but settled on the Christian Socials, remained in favor of an economic rapprochement among the successor states instead. Leadership of the struggle against the socialists, Alfred Diamant argues, "fell into the hands of Viennese industrialists, who also provided the funds to carry on the fight. As a result, the industrialists gained control of the Christian Social party and forced on the party an economic and social program favorable to big business."[61] In addition, Austrian industry was skeptical of proposals for German customs union, since they feared the prospects of competition with Germans in a unified market. By 1928 the difficulties of customs union negotiations caused their suspension, and in 1931 Austria's chambers of commerce disapproved of the creation of a unified Austrian-German market by a margin of four to one.[62]

Manufacturers' skepticism of a reorientation of the Austrian economy toward Germany was matched by the plain opposition of Austrian finance

59. See especially Nautz, "Between Political Disintegration and Economic Reintegration," 271; and de Ménil and Maurel, "Breaking Up a Customs Union." On the difficulties of cooperation there is a huge literature. See Leo Pasvolsky, *Economic Nationalism of the Danubian States* (New York: Macmillan, 1928); Ivan Berend and György Ránki, "Economic Problems of the Danube Region After the Break-up of the Austro-Hungarian Monarchy," *Journal of Contemporary History* 4, no. 3 (July 1969): 169–85; and Jürgen Nautz, *Die österreichische Handelspolitik der Nachkriegszeit, 1918 bis 1923* (Vienna: Böhlau, 1994). According to the League of Nations report, trade between the successor states had fallen to approximately 50 percent of the economic patterns before the war. See Layton and Rist, *Economic Situation of Austria*, 25–29.

60. On the orientation of Austrian industry, see Jürgen Nautz, "Die österreichische Wirtschaft und der Anschluss," in *Tirol und der Anschluss*, ed. Thomas Albrich, Klaus Eisterer, and Rolf Steininger (Innsbruck: Haymon, 1988), 385–402. On the late 1920s and 1930s when both industry and agriculture became more divided on the question of the *Anschluss*, see Suval, *Anschluss Question*, 187–89; Ball, *Post-war German-Austrian Relations*, 53, 137–41; and Hertz, *Economic Problem of the Danubian States*, 64, where he argues that every failure of Danubian cooperation encouraged the *Anschluss* movement.

61. Alfred Diamant, *Austrian Catholics and the First Republic: Democracy, Capitalism, and the Social Order, 1918–1934* (Princeton: Princeton University Press, 1960), 92.

62. Katzenstein, *Disjoined Partners*, 151; Rothschild, *Austria's Economic Development*, 72. More generally see Karl H. Werner, "Österreichs Industrie- und Aussenhandelspolitik, 1848 bis 1948," in *Hundert Jahre Österreichischer Wirtschaftswicklung, 1848–1948*, ed. Hans Meyer (Vienna: Springer, 1949), 359–471.

throughout the 1920s and 1930s.[63] Austria's first finance minister, Joseph Schumpeter, opposed the *Anschluss* and insisted that Vienna should and would remain the financial center of the successor states. At a press conference in 1919 Schumpeter argued that despite the nationalism of Czechoslovakia and the other successor states, Danubian economic unity would continue. "In this new organism," Schumpeter argued, "Vienna will have to continue as the financial center and the political separation will affect only marginally the purely economic relations." He followed these public comments with an address at the general meeting of the Vienna Industrial and Trade Association, where he explained that free trade and monetary union were in the interests of Austria and Viennese finance, because the "states of the Danube basin are undoubtedly dependent on close economic cooperation, whether they like it or not."[64] Such sentiments would not be enshrined in foreign policy until after 1920, however, when the Christian Socials emerged as the dominant party.

CZECHOSLOVAK FINANCIAL INFLUENCE ON AUSTRIAN POLITICS

The Christian Socials, without a parliamentary majority and despite strong public support for unification with Germany, maintained political power throughout 1920s in Austria, which they kept away from *Anschluss*. This is indeed a puzzle, the resolution of which is found in the financial diplomacy of Czechoslovakia and France. This financial diplomacy altered the economic and political balances of power in 1920s Austria in ways that allowed the Christian Socials and their constituents to consolidate their positions of dominance. All the political and economic background outlined above, including the persistent capital shortages, the material and social bases of the various parties, and the fragmentation of the political system, came into play. The Christian Socials were therefore able to turn their Danubian vision of Austria's national interests into political reality.

After the 1920 elections, when the socialists left the government and the Christian Socials formed a coalition with the pan-German nationalists as the minor partner, conservatives representing business interests came to power. In

---

63. See F. L. Carsten, *The First Austrian Republic, 1918–1938* (Aldershot and Brookfield, VT: Gower, 1986), 160. On the orientation of Austrian finance toward the successor states see Hans Kernbauer and Fritz Weber, "Multinational Banking in the Danube Basin: The Business Strategy of the Viennese Banks After the Collapse of the Habsburg Monarchy," in *Multinational Enterprise in Historical Perspective*, ed. Alice Teichova, Maurice Lévy-Leboyer, and Helga Nussbaum (Cambridge: Cambridge University Press; Paris: Éditions de la Maison des Sciences de l'Homme, 1986).

64. Quoted in Eduard März, *Austrian Banking and Financial Policy: Creditanstalt at a Turning Point, 1913–1923*, translated by Charles Kessler (New York: St. Martin's, 1984), 330–31.

May 1922 Ignaz Seipel became chancellor for the Christian Socials, dominating Austrian politics for the rest of the 1920s. Seipel, lamenting the sorry state of the Austrian economy, began to play on European fears of *Anschluss* in order to receive financial help from abroad. Although his coalition with the nationalists forced him to pay lip service to the long-term prospects of unification with Germany, Seipel remained opposed to *Anschluss* throughout the 1920s.[65] In order to emphasize the consequences for Europe of a failed Christian Social government, Austria circulated a memorandum that suggested that without foreign aid "the Austrian Government can no longer assure the functioning of the state."[66]

Czechoslovakia, the state in Europe with the most at stake in the Austrian question, responded.[67] The spread of the *Anschluss* movement in Austria alarmed the Czechoslovak government and its two dominant statesmen, President Thomas Masaryk and foreign minister, and later prime minister, Eduard Benes. Prague's newly dominant position in the central European economy gave its leaders some hubris, and Czechoslovak leaders very quickly after the war planned to influence Austrian domestic politics and prevent unification with Germany. In 1918 Masaryk sent a letter to Benes, in Paris at the time, and explained, "Vienna is in the hands of incapable people. The Viennese begin to realize this. Our influence will be considerable; we can bring it about that they will not desire to join Germany."[68]

In 1921 Benes, finally surmounting anti-Austrian public opinion in Czechoslovakia, concluded the Treaty of Lana with Austria, which soon received assurances of trade cooperation and a credit of 500 million crowns with which to purchase Czechoslovak coal and sugar.[69] When Chancellor Seipel arrived from Austria in August 1922, Masaryk and Benes assured him that Czechoslovakia would attempt to make the Austrian case for international financial help at the League of Nations meetings in September, although Czechoslovakia would,

65. Klemens von Klemperer, *Ignaz Seipel, Christian Statesman in a Time of Crisis* (Princeton: Princeton University Press, 1972). Seipel's eventual accommodation to ideas about unification in the early 1930s were a response to the repeated failures of his Central European initiatives, with the *Anschluss* remaining a last resort.

66. See the discussion of the memorandum in März, *Austrian Banking and Financial Policy*, 489–90.

67. Czechoslovakia would have been surrounded on three sides by a unified German-Austrian state, not to mention Prague's concerns regarding an increasingly dissatisfied and irridentist Hungary. See Felix John Vondracek, *The Foreign Policy of Czechoslovakia, 1918–1935* (New York: Columbia University Press, 1937), esp. 148, 173–81.

68. Quoted in Zygmunt J. Gasiorowski, "Czechoslovakia and the Austrian Question, 1918–1928," *Südost-Forschungen* 16, no. 1 (1957): 87–122, at 90.

69. See M. L. Flaningam, "A Survey of Czechoslovak-Austrian Tariff and Commercial Treaty Relations, 1919–1937," *Journal of Central European Affairs* 6, no. 1 (April 1946): 30–42. The Czech nationalists were opposed to the treaty.

they explained, have to insist on a thorough reorganization of Austrian finances and, possibly, financial control by the League itself.[70]

"Dr. Benes's unconcealed policy," the American minister in Prague relayed, "is to make Vienna increasingly dependent on Prague." The Czechoslovak government "counts on French assistance to further any designs to prevent Vienna from turning to Berlin." Jaroslav Preiss, the leading Czechoslovak financier, head of the Commercial Bank of Prague, and advisor to Masaryk and Benes, explained to the government that Prague should act decisively now. With the correct use of financial incentives, "a possibility offers itself to us of gaining influence, perhaps a decisive one, over Austria in the future." Czechoslovakia could "hook an anchor fast both in her economy and in her financial institutions."[71] At the least Czechoslovakia counted on using financial diplomacy to influence Austrian politics; at most Benes and Masaryk considered the possibility of their own union with Austria and perhaps the rest of the successor states, sponsored by France and under Prague's economic hegemony this time.[72]

France and Czechoslovakia ensured that the League's meetings on the Austrian situation in September 1922 would result in a loan package for Austria.[73] Somewhat surprisingly, Seipel arrived in Geneva for the meetings more conciliatory than he need have been, and he explained that the Austrian government would willingly submit to League supervision of any loan that was made.[74] The Geneva Protocols were quickly negotiated and signed in October 1922, and the League agreed to provide a loan of 650 million gold crowns, guaranteed in equal parts by Britain, France, Italy, and Czechoslovakia.

The provisions of the Geneva Protocols were remarkable. Austria's promise to balance its budget by 1924 and pursue an austerity package was the least interesting of the agreements. A Commissioner-General, appointed by the League, was to be based in Vienna to oversee the Austrian government's reforms. Further, Austria was not allowed to spend any of the loan funds with-

70. See F. Gregory Campbell, *Confrontation in Central Europe* (Chicago and London: University of Chicago Press, 1975), 114; Vondracek, *Foreign Policy of Czechoslovakia*, 193; and März, *Austrian Banking and Financial Policy*, 492.

71. The American minister and Preiss are quoted in Gasiorowski, "Czechoslovakia and the Austrian Question," 106, 107.

72. The evidence on these somewhat surprising plans by Benes and Masaryk seems quite clear. See Gasiorowski, "Czechoslovakia and the Austrian Question," 109–11; Campbell, *Confrontation in Central Europe*, 115; and Piotr S. Wandycz, *France and Her Eastern Allies, 1919–1925: French-Czechoslovak-Polish Relations from the Paris Peace Conference to Locarno* (Minneapolis: University of Minnesota Press, 1962), 351.

73. For a discussion of how Benes influenced the League loan and its terms, see Vondracek, *Foreign Policy of Czechoslovakia*, 195–97.

74. März, *Austrian Banking and Financial Policy*, 493.

out his express permission, and the Austrian parliament was required to pass a bill empowering Austrian governments for a period of two years to do whatever was necessary to create a reformed and balanced budget by 1924, creating a budgetary process that bypassed the Austrian parliament. The reforms included the dismissal of one-third of all civil servants, approximately 100,000 members of the Austrian bureaucracy. Austria also agreed, "in accordance with the terms of Article 88 of the Treaty of St. Germain, not to alienate its independence; it will abstain from any negotiations or from any economic or financial engagement calculated directly or indirectly to compromise this independence."[75]

The delegates in Geneva knew what the consequences of the loan would be. The strict austerity plan and resulting deflation would hurt the working class most, although the farmers not only avoided financial sacrifice but were promised an increase in agrarian tariffs.[76] Recalling that the narrow material interests of Austrian agriculture, finance, and industry were being represented by the Christian Socials, while the support of most of the population was divided between the socialists, supported by the working class, and the nationalists, supported by the professional class, helps clarify how the economic effects of the Geneva Protocols would soon translate into profound political effects as well. The Protocols thus "represented the culmination of Benes's policy of using Czechoslovak financial strength and Austrian weakness to erect more safeguards against an Anschluss."[77] The League's loan, in the words of E. H. Carr, was "a brilliant success" that "solved the Austrian problem for several years."[78]

CONSOLIDATING THE NATIONAL INTEREST, 1922–28: THE LOAN AND AFTER

From the perspectives of Czechoslovakia, France, and the Christian Socials in Austria, the details of the plan worked in their interests completely. The sectoral effects of the details of the Geneva Protocols decisively affected "the balance of power between the different *Lager* in Austrian politics."[79] The working class, the only organized economic group in favor of unification with

75. Quoted in Ball, *Post-war German-Austrian Relations*, 49.

76. See März, *Austrian Banking and Financial Policy*, 499.

77. Campbell, *Confrontation in Central Europe*, 116. See the discussion of Czechoslovak financial assistance both bilaterally and through the League in Robert A. Kann, "Czechoslovakia and Austria," in *Czechoslovakia, Past and Present*, Volume I, ed. Miloslav Rechcigl Jr. (The Hague and Paris: Mouton, 1968), 649–60.

78. E. H. Carr, *International Relations Between the Two World Wars, 1919–1939* (London: Macmillan, 1947), 64.

79. Katzenstein, *Disjoined Partners*, 159–60.

Germany and the social base for the socialist party, was hurt by the austerity policies and deflation, by the shift to more regressive taxation, and by the reversal of social services implemented by the socialists between 1918 to 1920. Not only did the financial policies therefore hurt the socialists' support, but the arrangements for budgetary policy making to bypass the parliament, the only place where the socialists continued to hold influence, also shifted power toward the Christian Socials. Chancellor Seipel's willingness to accept League supervision, in retrospect, seems also to have been part of his strategy of consolidating political power. In addition, the agreement to cut one-third of the bureaucracy directly harmed the social base of the pan-German nationalist parties, which were strong in the professional class and among state employees.[80]

The Christian Socials, however, managed to insulate their own social base, the farmers, from the effects of the financial austerity with the increase of agricultural tariffs, thus giving agricultural interests a better deal than they could have gotten through unification with Germany. The unemployment, resulting from deflation policies, that so affected the socialists and nationalists did not affect nearly as severely the Christian Socials. These effects were serious. At the beginning of 1922 there were 42,000 unemployed in Austria; by 1925 there were 176,000. These unemployed were not evenly distributed, with, for example, approximately 15,000 metal workers seeking unemployment relief, 12,600 from the machinery industries, and 32,000 from the building industry. Yet there were, at the same time, 126 unemployed agricultural workers, and only 4,200 from the foodstuffs sector.[81] Viennese finance, still allied with the Christian Socials, was relieved that the inflation had ended and that fiscal responsibility more austere than anywhere else in Europe reigned in Austria.

The political battle over ratification of the Geneva Protocols was intense. The socialists were fully aware of the political and economic implications of the loan, and, moreover, they explained them in detail to the Allies, who, as a result, were also informed of the consequences for Austrian domestic politics. The socialists accused the Christian Socials of "high treason," of "selling out" Austria.[82] The League sent a delegation to Vienna to gauge opposition to the loan, and, in interviewing Renner, a socialist leader, heard firsthand the reasons for the socialist opposition and, more importantly, a detailing of virtually all of

80. The political effects on the nationalists were no less profound. After the Christian Socials convinced the Great-German party to vote for ratification, "the Christian Socials managed to stigmatize that party as having voted against *Anschluss*, which permanently damaged its credibility in national politics." Katzenstein, *Disjoined Partners*, 160.

81. Layton and Rist, *Economic Situation of Austria*, 16, 52.

82. On the opposition of the socialists generally, see Barbara Jelavich, *Modern Austria: Empire and Republic, 1815–1986* (Cambridge: Cambridge University Press, 1987), 175–76.

the micro effects of the Geneva arrangements. Renner protested that Seipel "was making too much party capital out of the whole business." Renner then explained that the Geneva Protocols and their effects would harm the working class most, thereby reducing their political influence and economic prospects. This was in addition to the massive reductions in the bureaucracy and the party politics that would inevitably influence the implementation of the accords. The political effect of these changes, Renner made very clear, would be the reduction of the power of the socialists and the maintenance of the power of the Christian Socials.[83] The socialists were painfully aware that the "Geneva Bondage Treaty," the "road to Geneva," meant not only the end of the *Anschluss* project in the short term, but a reduction of their own political influence in the medium term.

UKRAINE, RUSSIA, AND THE PROBLEM OF ECONOMIC AUTONOMY, 1991–93

SINCE LATE 1991, when an independent Ukraine emerged from a collapsed Soviet Union, there have been two competing visions of the Ukrainian national interest. The first, outlined by nationally conscious Ukrainians, sees Ukraine's future in a new Central Europe and defines Russia as the state's central security threat, with economic autonomy from Russia as a fundamental strategic objective. The second, a reaction to the political orientation of Ukraine's nationalists, emphasized the continuity between the Soviet past and the sovereign present, defining a Eurasian Ukraine that maintains close economic, political, and cultural relations with Russia. Ukrainians who favor close relations with Russia tend to be in eastern Ukraine, where the content of national identity is more contested and, significantly, Ukraine's most important economic sector, its heavy industry, is located. Ukraine's inaugural independent government, under Leonid Kravchuk, clearly and aggressively adopted the first definition of Ukraine's national interest. Kravchuk's government, identifying its security threats in the east, implemented policies designed to enhance economic autonomy, which was supposed to be accomplished by a rapid reorientation of the economy toward the West. Influenced by the economic arguments of Ukrainian nationalists, the Ukrainian government assumed that Ukrainian economic independence would quickly follow its political independence, a transition that would ensure Ukraine a prosperous, stable future out-

---

83. For this quote and a discussion of the interview with Renner, see Carsten, *First Austrian Republic*, 52. For more on the socialists' arguments that the Christian Socials were using the loan to reduce the influence of the working class, see März, *Austrian Banking and Financial Policy*, 496.

side a Russian sphere of influence and, most importantly, a "return" to
Europe. Some observers in the West agreed. In 1990, as central authority in
the Soviet Union seemed increasingly precarious, the Deutsche Bank ranked
the 15 Soviet republics with regard to economic independence potential;
Ukraine was ranked first.[84]

Less than two years later, however, officials in Kiev had redefined Ukraine's
strategic interests and goals. This time organized interests in Ukraine's economy succeeded in influencing definitions of the Ukrainian national interest, as
Ukrainian industrialists demanded that Ukraine not leave the economic space
of the former Soviet Union. While in late 1991 economic cooperation with
Russia had been defined as a security threat, in 1993 the Ukrainian government
acknowledged that the lack of economic cooperation with Russia was a threat
to an independent, secure existence. This redefinition of the Ukrainian national
interest during 1992–93 resulted from the government's increasing awareness
of Ukrainian industry's dependence on Russian energy resources and markets,
and economic actors within Ukraine, in addition to actions by the Russian
government, helped convince President Kravchuk and his advisors to change
course. Patterns of Ukraine's foreign economic relations clarified the boundaries of the possible for postindependence Ukrainian foreign policy.[85] Although
Ukrainian foreign policy has been oriented toward integration with the West,
the costs of economic autonomy policies, determined to be unbearable in
1992–93, have been high enough to keep Ukraine's economic relations concentrated indisputably in the east.[86] The legacies of Soviet economic history,
clarified by economic crisis, by assertive industrialists, and by a Russian government desperate to keep Ukraine close, decisively raised the short-term costs

84. Jürgen Corbet and Andreas Gimmich, *The Soviet Union at the Crossroads* (Frankfurt:
Deutsche Bank, 1990). See also Gertrude Schroeder, "Economic Transformation in the
Post-Soviet Republics," in *Economic Transition in Russia and the New States of Eurasia*, ed. Bartlomiej Kaminski (Armonk, N.Y.: M. E. Sharpe, 1996), 11–41; and "On the Economic Viability of New Nation-States," *Journal of International Affairs* 45, no. 2 (winter 1992): 549–74, at
564–66.

85. This paper thus covers one part of the Ukrainian story; namely, the material pull back
toward Russia on Ukrainian foreign policy. This material pull results from regional divisions
in the Ukrainian economy and national identity that keep eastern Ukraine oriented toward
the Russian economy. For an explanation of why Ukrainian foreign economic policy was
oriented away from Russia in the first place and how the politics of Ukrainian nationalism
has prevented Ukraine from moving ever closer to Russia and has delegitimated certain
forms of cooperation with Russia, despite the concentration of Ukrainian material interests
in Russia and the former Soviet Union, see Rawi Abdelal, "Economic Nationalism After
Empire" (Ph.D. Dissertation, Cornell University, 1999), chap. 5.

86. Serhiy Tolstov, "Ukraine's Foreign Policy: Course Correction or Change of Priorities?" *Ukrainian Review* 42, no. 1 (spring 1995): 3–12. Larrabee notes the tension between
Ukraine's desire to "join all-European institutions on the one hand, and its close economic
dependence on Russia on the other." F. Stephen Larrabee, "Ukraine's Balancing Act," *Survival* 38, no. 2 (summer 1996): 143–65.

of economic change. Ukraine's nationalists and its first government underestimated these costs.

ENERGY, AUTONOMY, AND THE LEGACIES OF HISTORY

Ukraine is intensely dependent on Russian energy supplies, especially at the below-market prices offered by Russia even after 1991. Ukraine's debts to Russia and Russian companies for these energy supplies have been mounting relentlessly since late 1991. Russia supplies approximately 90 percent of Ukraine's oil consumption. For natural gas, which is the most commonly used form of energy in Ukraine, Ukraine relies on imports from Russia, for approximately 60 percent, and Turkmenistan, for another 20 percent. This energy dependence is the country's most glaring economic and strategic weakness.[87]

Ukraine's energy dependence on Russia has some straightforward political consequences, since Russia can, in theory, use this asymmetry of interdependence to coerce Ukraine. Ukrainian officials have been keenly aware of the problem. Evhen Baramikov, chief of interrepublic trade in the Ministry of the Economy, explained that although Russia "can last a year without our food," it "can halt Ukrainian industry in a day." The effects of a continued radical autonomy policy would ravage the Ukrainian economy, leaving Ukrainians to "eat our sugar while freezing in the dark."[88] Russian attempts to coerce Ukraine economically, however, have not been successful. The success of Russian influence is another matter.

This more significant consequence of Ukraine's energy dependence, its influence on debates about the national interest, is determined by Soviet economic history, and specifically by the path-dependences created by Soviet development policy. After the breakup of the Soviet Union Russia still did not charge members of the Commonwealth of Independent States (CIS) world prices for oil and natural gas. Therefore, Ukrainian industry was subsidized by Russian energy throughout the 1990s, although Russia has attempted slowly to raise CIS energy prices to world levels. Ukraine's heavy industry sector, its most successful during the Soviet period, is extremely energy inefficient and there-

---

87. See Erik Whitlock, "Ukrainian-Russian Trade: The Economics of Dependency," *RFE/RL Research Report* 2, no. 43 (29 October 1993): 38–42; also Evgeni Yasin, "The Economic Space of the Former Soviet Union, Past and Present," and Alexander Granberg, "The Economic Interdependence of the Former Soviet Republics," both in *Economic Consequences of Soviet Disintegration*, ed. John Williamson (Washington, D.C.: Institute for International Economics, 1993), 13–37 and 47–77.

88. Quoted in Chrystia Freeland, "Kiev Gripped in Russian Stranglehold—Ukraine's Economy Will Pay a Heavy Price for Defying Moscow," *Financial Times*, 23 July 1992.

fore depends not only on Russian energy, but also on Russian markets, in which, despite its high production costs, it is still competitive.

Prior to the Soviet Union's most extensive drives toward industrialization, Ukraine had its own energy industry, but this was phased out in favor of lower-cost alternatives in Russia and central Asia. Particularly since the 1960s Soviet planners allocated oil and gas to Ukraine's energy-intensive heavy industry at prices well below those of the world market. Ukrainian industry earlier had relied on coal, in which Ukraine is abundantly rich, for energy resources. The transition to plentiful and low-cost Russian oil and gas therefore integrated Ukraine's economy into the Soviet economy at higher levels than other allocation methods would have achieved.[89] This tight regional economic integration, furthermore, was a specific policy objective of Soviet strategists, who sought to tie the constituent republics closely together. They succeeded ingeniously in Ukraine, where the heavy industrial sector, the pride of Soviet economic planners, remains addicted to low-cost Russian energy. As Deputy Prime Minster for CIS Affairs Valentin Landik explained, "world prices for oil is death for us."[90]

The Russian government, and Russian energy conglomerates closely tied to it, had clarified the problem for Ukraine in political disputes, and although the Russian government was not able to extract significant political concessions, repeated energy and energy-debt crises during 1992 and 1993 helped to convince the Ukrainian government that it could not survive without economic cooperation with Russia. In addition, these energy crises, which had brought eastern Ukraine's heavy industry virtually to a standstill, helped mobilize the industrialists themselves to demand that Ukraine restore economic links with the CIS. Because Russian energy has been priced below the world market and credit terms have been liberal, in "a strictly economic sense, the energy trade with Russia is highly beneficial to Ukraine."[91] Implicit oil and gas price subsidies as well as implicit credit subsidies have continued, a fact that helps the Ukrainian economy while at the same time complicating attempts to reform its

89. See the discussion in Helen Boss, "Ukraine's First Year of Economic Statehood," in *Economic Transformation in East-Central Europe and the Newly Independent States*, ed. Gabor Hunya (Boulder: Westview, 1994), 243–75. See also Leslie Dienes, "Energy, Minerals, and Economic Policy," in *The Ukrainian Economy: Achievements, Problems, Challenges*, ed. I. S. Koropeckyj (Cambridge: Harvard Ukrainian Research Institute, Harvard University Press, 1992), 123–47; and Mariian Dolishnii, "Regional Aspects of Ukraine's Economic Development," in Koropeckyj *The Ukrainian Economy*, 290–311.

90. Quoted in John Lloyd, "Weak Ukraine Plays Into Russia's Hands: Economic Union Means Giving Moscow Control of Many of the Levers of Power," *Financial Times*, 17 September 1993.

91. Paul D'Anieri, "Dilemmas of Interdependence: Autonomy, Prosperity, and Sovereignty in Ukraine's Russia Policy," *Problems of Post-Communism* 44, no. 1 (January/February 1997): 16–26, esp. 18.

most energy-dependent industrial sectors.[92] These incentives and policies shaped the patterns of industrialization in Soviet Ukraine, patterns that will be one of independent Ukraine's most enduring Soviet legacies.[93]

UKRAINE'S BID FOR ECONOMIC AUTONOMY

Thus the government of Ukraine began 1992 with a politically independent state that was profoundly dependent economically on Russia, a fact that was considered by Kiev and nationalist groups in western Ukraine to be Ukraine's central security problem. During 1990 and 1991 the idea that Ukrainian economic independence would be rapidly and costlessly, possibly even lucratively, attained was widespread among Ukrainians. This was particularly true when *Rukh*, the broad-based movement for perestroika that transformed itself into a moderate nationalist movement, was most active in defining Ukrainian political debates. After Ukraine escaped the Soviet economic system that exploited them, the argument went, it would quickly reorient its trade toward the West, leaving economic ties with the East behind. The "breadbasket of Europe," rich in Donbas coal, and the soul, if not the heart, of Soviet industry, Ukraine would achieve economic autonomy from Russia quickly and dissociate itself from the Russian sphere of influence.[94]

In March 1992 Kravchuk outlined a new economic program, which the administration presented to the Ukrainian parliament in a closed session. The central goal of the program was neither growth, nor reform, nor development, but, instead, economic autonomy from Russia. In the proposal, "Principles of a National Economic Policy for Ukraine," the government lamented Ukraine's economic dependence on Russia, threatening that "the country's very independence is jeopardized." The policy response was to be a thoroughgoing structural transformation, the creation of a new Ukrainian currency, and reductions of imports from ruble-zone countries, through "economizing" and "reorientation toward new markets."[95] When the Ukrainian government began

92. Gregory V. Krasnov and Josef C. Brada, "Implicit Subsidies in Russian-Ukrainian Energy Trade," *Europe-Asia Studies* 49, no. 5 (July 1997): 825–43.

93. See Helen Boss and Peter Havlik, "Slavic (Dis)union: Consequences for Russia, Belarus, and Ukraine," *Economics of Transition* 2, no. 2 (June 1994): 233–54.

94. Orest Subtelny, *Ukraine: A History*, 2nd ed. (Toronto: Canadian Institute of Ukrainian Studies; University of Toronto Press, 1994), 589–93. See also the discussion of these popular preindependence ideas in Ustina Markus, "Shoring Up Russian Relations," *Transition* 1, no. 6 (28 April 1995): 55–58, at 56.

95. The report was reprinted in "L. Kravchuk's Report Had the Effect of an Exploding Bomb," *Komsomolskaia pravda*, 26 March 1992, in *Current Digest of the Post-Soviet Press*, 44, no. 12 (22 April 1992): 15–16. See also Chrystia Freeland, "Ukraine Plans to Sever Russian Economic Links," *Financial Times*, 24 March 1992.

making specific plans for the creation of a new currency in the summer of 1992, Moscow responded that all states outside the ruble zone would be charged world prices for oil, while those inside the ruble zone would continue to receive oil at below world prices.[96] Ukraine continued with its plans, however, leading Kravchuk to aver, "a single ruble—the same for all states? That is not a ruble zone, but a ruble state."[97]

By the end of the year, however, Ukraine was mired in a profound economic crisis. The Ukrainian economy had collapsed, in large part a consequence of the rupturing of economic ties with Russia and the rest of the Soviet Union. Fuel shortages, the closure of foreign markets that had only a year earlier been part of a single, all-union market, and the weak demand for Ukrainian goods in the West all called Ukraine's autonomy policy into question. No one was more upset or vociferous than Ukraine's industrialists, who had protested at the government's economic reorientation toward the West as soon as it had begun. Ukrainian officials had themselves begun to reëvaluate the autonomy policy, and Russian manipulation of Ukraine's energy supplies also helped to convince Ukraine of the medium-term permanence of its economic dependence.

Therefore, in the midst of economic crisis, convinced by Ukrainian industrialists and the Russian government, the Ukrainian government changed course. By late 1992 and early 1993, government officials in Kiev, "even the most anti-Russian," were forced to acknowledge that Russia, more than any Western state, was Ukraine's most important economic partner.[98] Without a cooperative economic relationship with Russia the Ukrainian state did not stand a chance at a stable, independent existence, and the realization by Kiev that it needed economic Russia as much as it needed independence from political Russia redefined the Ukrainian national interest.[99] Then prime minister Leonid Kuchma, asked how Ukraine's first year of economic independence had gone, noted the irony: "Strange as it may seem, the upshot has been an awareness of our economic dependence."[100] The Ukrainian government ended its radical

96. Chrystia Freeland, "Ukraine Threatens to Split CIS in Row With Russia," *Financial Times*, 19 June 1992. On Ukraine's political stance toward the ruble zone, see also S. M. Borisov, "Rublevaia zona bez nastoiashchego i budushchego?" (The ruble zone without a present and a future?), *Den'gi i kredit* no. 3 (March 1994): 12–18.

97. Quoted in the interview of Kravchuk by Stansilav Prokpuchuk, *Trud*, 19 January 1994, in Foreign Broadcast Information Service-Central Eurasia (hereafter FBIS-SOV)-94-014, 21 January 1994, 41–44.

98. Markus, "Shoring Up Russian Relations," 56.

99. See Aleksandr Golds, "Russia, Ukraine, CIS...," *Krasnaia zvezda*, 19 June 1993, in FBIS-SOV-93-118, 22 June 1993, 3–4.

100. Interview in *Komsomolskaia pravda*, 5 January 1993, in FBIS-SOV-93-005, 8 January 1993, 19–21.

autonomy policies and cut import and export quotas in May and June 1993, eliminated the value-added tax on trade with Russia and other CIS members in August 1993, and began cautiously to cultivate a new economic relationship with Russia. As Paul D'Anieri argues, "the policy of cutting ties with Russia has now been reversed as the price of economic independence has proved too high."[101] In May 1993 Kravchuk even negotiated and signed a declaration of intent to create a CIS economic union.[102]

In March 1993 President Kravchuk addressed the second congress of the Ukrainian Union of Industrialists and Entrepreneurs, the appropriate forum in which to reassess Ukraine's economic relationship with Russia, since these same industrialists had been clamoring for the restoration of economic links with Russia. This umbrella organization of industrialists, a union composed of over 14,000 collective and individual members representing various forms of ownership, had become more and more influential in government circles during the economic crises of 1992 and 1993. Kravchuk admitted that the government had overestimated the possibilities for economic independence, and he thereby acknowledged the political meaning of dependence on Russia. He explained, "we obviously overestimated the potential of our economy. We overlooked the fact that it was structurally incomplete."[103] The Ukrainian industrialists, for their part, announced that they would do all they could do restore economic links with Russia.[104]

Industrialists in Ukraine have lobbied for maintaining economic cooperation with Russia, particularly in the form of multilateral economic integration within the framework of the CIS. The economic interests of Ukrainian industry are concentrated in Russia and the CIS, where their traditional suppliers and markets remain. In addition, because they face such high production costs, resulting from the energy-inefficient development history of Soviet heavy industry, Ukrainian industrialists were keenly aware that they needed Russian markets to survive.

---

101. See D'Anieri, "Dilemmas of Interdependence," 21, where he describes the changes in foreign economic policy and assesses the reasons for them. It should be recognized, however, that Ukrainian nationalists continued to believe that autonomy was worth these costs.

102. Steven Erlanger, "Ex-Soviet Nations Agree to Form Economic Union," *New York Times*, 15 May 1993. Ukraine later that autumn refused to sign the common market treaty, opting instead to become an associate member.

103. Interfax, 6 March 1993, in FBIS-SOV-93-044, 9 March 1993, 36.

104. Vadim Bardin, "Russian-Ukrainian Thaw Will Be Shortlived," *Kommersant-Daily*, 9 March 1993, in FBIS-SOV-93-045, 10 March 1993, 49. Significantly for later developments, the author argued that the improvement in economic relations would not last, since it was the result only of Ukraine's recognition of its dependence, rather than the pursuit of mutually beneficial exchange.

Representatives of Ukrainian industrialist associations even began meeting with their Russian counterparts in order to discuss problems of Ukrainian-Russian cooperation and ways to maintain a single economic space in the former Soviet Union. Ukrainian industrialists and entrepreneurs, in the statement adopted to summarize such a conference in 1992, argued that it was "impermissible" for Ukraine to leave the CIS and its economic cooperation mechanisms.[105] At the same time that Ukrainian nationalists were demanding that Ukraine reorient toward the West and withdraw from the CIS completely, political parties with economic ties to labor and heavy industry in eastern Ukraine responded with equally vociferous calls to protect the CIS and historical economic relationships.[106] Particularly injured had been machine-building industries and the military-industrial complex in eastern Ukraine, where "industry simply cannot survive without the traditional economic links," because of those industries' close connections to other enterprises in Russia and the CIS for intermediate goods in their production runs.[107] In late 1994 the Ukrainian Union of Industrialists and Entrepreneurs met with its Russian and Belarusian counterparts in Minsk to coordinate their continuing attempts to influence the creation of a customs union in the CIS.[108] Even the Ukrainian agricultural sector, which is more efficient than Ukrainian industry, has remained oriented toward Russia and the CIS, primarily because their exports, despite their competitiveness, have also not penetrated Western markets.[109] These two sectors, heavy industry and agriculture, are indeed Ukraine's most important.

It was precisely these "industrialists and farmers," according to Kuchma, who "were the first to realize" that Ukraine needs economic cooperation with Russia, that "it cannot go on like this," with the Ukrainian economy separated from the economic space it had shared with Russia for so long.[110] Only in Rus-

105. Vladimir Kulagin, "Predprinimateli Rossii i Ukrainy vystupaiot protiv razrusheniia edinogo ekonomicheskogo prostranstva" (Entrepreneurs of Russia and Ukraine come out against destruction of the single economic space), *Izvestiia*, 21 October 1992.

106. See the discussion of the Civic Congress of Ukraine, the Ukrainian Labor Party, the All-Ukrainian Labor Collectives Council, and the Interregional Association of Industrialists in "Parties Oppose Call for Commonwealth Withdrawal," *Krasnaia zvezda*, 12 January 1993, in FBIS-SOV-94-008, 13 January 1993, 44.

107. Moscow television, 18 August 1993, in FBIS-SOV-93-162, 24 August 1993, 36–37.

108. Valentin Zhdanko, "Cooperation: Industrialists of Russia, Ukraine, and Belorussia Call For Further Integration," *Segodnia*, 14 December 1994, in FBIS-SOV-94-241, 15 December 1994, 2.

109. See Bartlomiej Kaminski, "Trade Performance and Access to OECD Markets," in *Trade in the New Independent States*, eds. Constantine Michaelopoulos and David Tarr (Washington, D.C.: World Bank/UNDP, 1994), 237–54.

110. Quoted in Viktor Drozd's interview with Leonid Kuchma, "Kakoe Obshchestvo My Stroim?" (What kind of society are we building?), *Pravda*, 9 July 1993.

sian and former Soviet markets could Ukraine find an outlet for its goods at acceptable prices. Kuchma, then prime minister, was one of the leading advocates of economic cooperation with Russia so that Ukrainian industry would survive its postindependence crises, and, having the ear of Kravchuk, he was able to clarify the costs of Ukraine's economic autonomy policies. As Kuchma later explained, he was only pragmatic, not pro-Russian, because of his encouragement of cooperation with Russia. "When I became Prime Minister of Ukraine," he insisted, "I went to Moscow because corn and sugar beets were lying ungathered in Ukraine's fields and the gas pumps were empty. So where should I have gone?"[111] Ultimately, Kuchma resigned as prime minister. His next position was as leader of the Ukrainian Union of Industrialists and Entrepreneurs, the same organization that had been lobbying for cooperation and maintenance of a common, post-Soviet economic space. Moreover, Kuchma, who had been the head of the largest nuclear missile plant in the USSR, located in eastern Ukraine, had strong historical ties to east Ukrainian industry.[112]

By the summer of 1993 the changing conception of Ukraine's economic relationship to Russia was apparent in Kravchuk's assessments of political events. "Our difficulties are primarily of an economic nature," Kravchuk explained. "Now we have created our own state, the people have created their own state. But the resources—those that used to belong to the whole country—have mainly remained in other states, in Russia to a very great extent."[113] Specifically, it was Ukrainian industry's, indeed Ukrainian society's, dependence on inexpensive Russian oil and gas that became most important over the course of Ukraine's first years of sovereignty. Oles M. Smolansky shows that the government's awareness of energy shortages and their devastating effects on Ukrainian industry led Kravchuk, "in a major about-face, publicly to express his administration's desire to establish close economic cooperation with Russia."[114] The pattern of Ukrainian foreign economic relations was a fundamental cause of the change in Ukrainian foreign policy, of Kravchuk's "swing

111. Quoted in Vladimir Skachko, "Exclusive: Both Kravchuk and Kuchma Know What They Will Do If They Win Election—Two Interviews At the Polls," *Nezavisimaia gazeta*, 28 June 1994, in *Current Digest of the Post-Soviet Press* 46, no. 26 (27 July 1994): 9–10.

112. Aleksandr Maslov, "Leonid Kuchma—New Leader of the Ukrainian Union of Industrialists and Entrepreneurs," *Kievskie novosti*, 17 December 1993, in FBIS-SOV-93-248, 29 December 1993, 37. Moreover, when Kuchma was elected president in 1994, the vote was split precisely along these regional, not ethnic, lines, with eastern and southern Ukraine supporting Kuchma and the renewal of economic ties with Russia.

113 Interview with Kravchuk on Moscow television, 24 August 1993, in FBIS-SOV-93-163, 25 August 1993, 32–33.

114. Oles M. Smolansky, "Ukraine's Quest for Independence: The Fuel Factor," *Europe-Asia Studies* 47, no. 1 (January 1995): 67–90, at 73.

to the East."[115] In 1995 Ukrainian prime minister Vitaly Masol reflected on the lessons of Ukraine's postindependence economic strategy and understated, "it is not so easy to leave the traditional economic zone."[116]

THE PRICE OF AUTONOMY

Russia failed in its attempts to exploit the coercive power inherent in its asymmetric economic relationship with Ukraine because Ukraine perceived (and continues to perceive) Russia as a security threat.[117] The Ukrainian government, under its first president, Kravchuk, was defiant, refusing to give in fully to Russian demands about the distribution of Soviet assets, control of the Black Sea Fleet, and basing rights in Sevastopol. Even after 1994 when Ukraine's second president, Kuchma, was elected on a platform of improved, or at least normalized, relations with Russia, the Ukrainian government has refused to accommodate specific Russian demands, especially when those demands are backed by economic power. In some ways Kuchma has been, contrary to many expectations, even more recalcitrant than Kravchuk on a number of contentious political issues, including multilateral political and economic integration within the CIS.[118] Neither the economic bullying underlying specific Russian demands, nor the election of a new, presumably more accommodating president led to changes in Ukrainian foreign policy. Moscow's most heavy-handed tactics did not force reversals in Kiev.

Clearly, however, Ukrainian foreign policy did change in 1992–93. The moderation of Ukraine's autonomy policies resulted from the way that patterns of economic relations with Russia influenced competing definitions of the na-

115. On Kravchuk's "swing to the east" and the influence of economic actors, see Lloyd, "Weak Ukraine Plays Into Russia's Hands."

116. Quoted in the interview with Masol in "Masol Discusses Energy, Closer CIS Ties," *Uryadovyi kurier*, 17 January 1995, in FBIS-SOV-95-017, 26 January 1995, 64–66.

117. Daniel Drezner, "Allies, Adversaries, and Economic Coercion: Russian Foreign Economic Policy Since 1991," *Security Studies* 6, no. 3 (spring 1997): 65–111, esp. 96–105. Compare Fiona Hill and Pamela Jewett, *"Back in the USSR": Russia's Intervention in the Internal Affairs Of the Former Soviet Republics and the Implications for United States Policy Toward Russia* (Strengthening Democratic Institutions Project, Kennedy School of Government, Harvard University, 1994), 66–85.

118. "Russia Frustrated with Ukraine, Belarus Leaders," Reuters, 9 July 1995. See Taras Kuzio, *Ukraine Under Kuchma: Political Reform, Economic Transformation, and Security Policy in Independent Ukraine* (New York: St. Martin's, 1997), esp. chap. 6. See also Alexander J. Motyl and Bohdan Krawchenko, "Ukraine: From Empire to Statehood," in *New States, New Politics: Building the Post-Soviet Nations*, ed. Ian Bremmer and Ray Taras (Cambridge: Cambridge University Press, 1997), 235–75; and P. Terrence Hopmann, Stephen D. Shenfield, and Dominique Arel, *Integration and Disintegration in the Former Soviet Union: Implications for Regional and Global Security* (Occasional Paper no. 30, Watson Institute for International Studies, Brown University, 1997).

tional interest. The cumulative effect of Russian energy manipulation has helped to convince Ukrainian political and economic actors that the Ukrainian economy is too dependent to exit fully the Russian sphere of economic influence. There are elements of both continuity and change in Ukrainian foreign policy since 1991. Ukrainian security policy is still oriented toward Western Europe. Ukraine's foreign economic policy orienation, however, is now divided between West and East, and economic and political relations with Russia have normalized. In this sense, Russia's broadest strategic goal with regard to Ukraine, that of keeping the second largest Soviet successor state politically and economically close, has already been achieved.[119] Although Russia was unable to coerce Ukraine on specific policies, it was able to prevent Ukraine from going the way of the Baltic republics, which are exiting the Russian sphere of influence and integrating with the European Union. The widely recognized continuity of foreign policy under Kravchuk and Kuchma, despite expectations to the contrary in 1993 and 1994, is based on the fact that the Ukrainian government had, by the 1994 presidential elections, already begun its economic rapprochement with Russia. Although much has been made of the "energy war" between Ukraine and Russia during 1993–94, a political-economic conflict in which Ukraine faced gas and oil cutoffs by Russia for nonpayment of debts, Russia's economic influence had by that time already persuaded Kiev to change its course.

HIRSCHMAN, INFLUENCE, AND INTERNATIONAL RELATIONS

National Power and the Structure of Foreign Trade is largely about Germany's interwar foreign policy, but the political behavior and phenomena elucidated by Hirschman are general. States, especially in their asymmetric relations, are willing to make economic sacrifices in order to advance strategic goals. The pattern of international economic relations affects the balance of political power within societies, and this in turn shapes foreign policy. The contours of commerce, once in place, may be difficult to alter, constraining strategic choice in the future. The cases considered above demonstrate how consequential for international politics these Hirschmanesque effects are.

Relations between the United States and the Hawaiian Kingdom offer an excellent illustration of Hirschmanesque forces at work. In the last quarter of the nineteenth century, U.S. goals with regard to the Islands were strategic, not

---

119. For a similar interpretation of recent Ukrainian-Russian relations, see James Sherr, "Russia-Ukraine *Rapprochement?*: The Black Sea Fleet Accords," *Survival* 39, no. 3 (autumn 1997): 33–50.

economic. Hawaii, on the other hand, was motivated principally by economics. To keep foreign powers out and increase American political influence the United States agreed to treaty of reciprocity from which the economic benefits accrued solely to Hawaii. The treaty, however, did change the balance of political power on the Islands, strengthening the hands of those forces who wanted closer ties with the United States

Competing definitions of the national interest in interwar Austria were competing definitions of the German problem in Europe. Although most Austrians and Austrian political elites supported the *Anschluss*, the only group of economic and political actors that opposed unification with Germany, the Christian Socials, maintained power throughout the 1920s. Two kinds of Hirschmanesque politics were at work. First, the Christian Socials defined their economic and political interests away from Germany and toward the Danubian basin because of the concentration of financial and industrial interests in the Habsburg successor states, contrasting with the paucity of economic links with Germany. Relying also for support from agriculture, which was protected by tariffs, the Christian Socials offered one of the political futures, independence, least popular in Austria. Austrian independence, however, was very popular outside of Austria, particularly in France and Czechoslovakia. Second, the Geneva loan and its stipulations, a clear financial power play by a Czechoslovak government very aware of Austria's capital shortage and domestic political debates, ensured that the definition of the Austrian national interest most preferred by Paris and Prague would win Austrian political battles throughout the 1920s. Not only did the pattern of Austrian foreign economic relations help determine internal political struggles, but the use of financial power by other states tipped the balance in favor of the Christian Socials, thereby further solidifying the Christian Socials' economic orientation toward Prague, and not Berlin.

Although the first independent Ukrainian government attempted to achieve quickly economic autonomy from Russia, the costs of the autonomy policies proved to be unsustainable. Soviet policy was a central cause of these high costs of autonomy, since planners had favored a tightly integrated regional economy based on the free flow of inexpensive Russian energy sources. Soviet industrialization policies therefore caused Ukrainian industry to be energy-inefficient and addicted to Russian raw materials, while at the same time they ensured that Ukraine would not have a thriving energy sector of its own, at least not one that could supply its heavy industry. Ukrainian industrialists themselves lobbied Kravchuk's government in order to clarify these high costs of autonomy, which created economic difficulties that were exacerbated by the industrialists' continuing dependence on Russian markets. The Russian government, finally, also tried to convince the Ukrainian government that it had not foreseen the true price of independence. Russia's manipulation of the economic incentives facing domestic economic actors within Ukraine did influence Ukraine's debate about its national interest. Ukraine moderated its economic autonomy policies, and economic cooperation came to be seen by Kiev as an inescapable component of Ukraine's medium-term foreign policy strategy.

National Power has been celebrated for explaining how divergent opportunity costs of exit can give states coercive power over others in asymmetric economic relations. Less attention has been given to Hirschman's arguments about the political influence accrued by economic relations. It is the latter, however, that is more profound for international politics. In most circumstances there is more than one plausible set of National Interests for a given country. Foreign policies, and the configurations of interests that underlie them, are not immutable, but emerge from domestic political struggles. International economic opportunities and the foreign economic policies of other states affect those struggles and, in turn, the trajectory of a state's foreign policy.

SLEEPING WITH THE (POTENTIAL) ENEMY:
ASSESSING THE U.S. POLICY OF ENGAGEMENT WITH CHINA

PAUL A. PAPAYOANOU AND SCOTT L. KASTNER

The simple truth is this: the direction China takes in the years ahead will be one of the most decisive factors that will determine whether the next century is one of conflict and cooperation. The emergence of China as a great power that is stable, open and nonaggressive; that embraces political pluralism and international rules of conduct; that works with us to build a secure international order—the emergence of *that* kind of China profoundly is in America's interest.

...the results are far from pre-ordained: inward looking isolation, or outward looking integration? As we create the structures and policies that will become the foundation for security and prosperity into the new century, one of our most critical challenges is to bring China into the effort as a stakeholder—to make the choices ourselves that will make it more likely China makes the right choices.

Samuel R. Berger, U.S. national security advisor, 6 June 1997[1]

China is increasingly seen to be the most significant and potentially troubling great power for the United States to deal with in the years to come. China's military and economic power are clearly substantial and increasing. In east Asia, China has the largest population and most land, and spends the greatest amount on defense expenditures. Its economy has grown rapidly for twenty years and now ranks as the world's third largest.[2] China also has the third largest nuclear arsenal and the largest army in the world. Its mili-

Paul A. Papayoanou is visiting assistant professor in the department of government, Harvard University, and Scott L. Kastner is a doctoral candidate, in the Political Science Department, University of California, San Diego.

For their comments, we thank Jean-Marc Blanchard, Avery Goldstein, Michael Gordon, Stephan Haggard, anonymous *Security Studies* reviewers, and the participants at the Workshop on Economic Power, Interdependence, and National Security held at the Mershon Center, Ohio State University, 3–4 April 1998.

1. "Building a New Consensus on China," Speech to Council on Foreign Relations, New York (http://www.whitehouse.gov/WH/EOP/NSC/html/speeches/ srb060697. html).
2. Defense and economic (Gross Domestic Product) figures are based on purchasing power parity.

tary expenditures are by some estimates growing about 10 percent per year. China's power capabilities clearly make it a serious potential challenger to the international status quo and to the United States.[3]

There are also reasons to be concerned about how China will use its capabilities in the years to come. China has significant territorial interests in Asia and broad geopolitical interests in the world that make conflictual scenarios quite possible. China's territorial interests overlap with those of twenty-four other countries, and threats or uses of military force in the Taiwan Straits in 1995–96 and 1999 as well as in the South China Sea in 1995[4] give reason to be wary of Chinese intentions. China has also engaged in the proliferation of weapons of mass destruction with rogue states such as Iran. China also has not been afraid to flex its muscles in noncooperative ways in international forums, as it did in the UN Security Council on the arms inspections dispute with Iraq in the winter of 1998 and over the military operation of NATO in Kosovo. Finally, because China is a nondemocracy there is reason to worry that its government can act recklessly in the international arena without regard for public accountability.[5]

Clearly China is, and will continue to be for some time to come, a great concern to U.S. administrations. The Clinton administration has chosen to pursue a policy of engagement with China, arguing that it is best to try to bring China into "the community of nations" rather than to contain and isolate it. Most importantly, the integration of China through a policy of engagement has meant the maintenance and expansion of American trade with, and the encouragement of investments in, China. There have been some limits to the administration's policy though, for a tough line has been taken toward China on membership in the World Trade Organization (WTO), on the piracy of intellectual property (for example, compact discs and videos), and on Chinese provocations in the Taiwan Straits. Nonetheless, while elements of containment exist in U.S. policy, the overall thrust has been to integrate China through increased trade and financial transactions.[6]

3. Gerald Segal, "East Asia and the 'Constrainment' of China," *International Security* 20, no. 4 (spring 1996): 107–35; Fareed Zakaria, "Let's Get Our Superpowers Straight," *New York Times*, 26 March 1997, A19; Avery Goldstein, "Great Expectations: Interpreting China's Arrival," *International Security* 22, no. 3 (winter 1997/98): 36–73.

4. This refers to China's seizing of Mischief Reef from the Philippines.

5. Segal, "East Asia and the 'Constrainment' of China"; Zakaria, "Let's Get Our Superpowers Straight"; and Goldstein, "Great Expectations."

6. For a concise overview of options for U.S. policy toward China in the 1990s, see Harry Harding, "The Debate Over America's Policy Toward China, 1989–97," in *China's Political Economy*, ed. Wang Gungwu and John Wong (Singapore: Singapore University Press, 1998), 277–90. Note that Harding draws a distinction between Clinton's early engagement policy and a deeper version of it, which he labels "integration." Integration seeks to incorporate China into world markets and institutions, which parallels our use of "engagement" in this

This article considers only the security implications of an engagement policy with China.[7] We focus specifically on the impact that deepening international economic ties will have on the direction of Chinese foreign policy and on U.S.-Chinese security relations. In short, we argue that a policy of engagement with China is likely to have beneficial consequences over the long term. Such a policy empowers more cooperative economic internationalists in China while a rigid containment policy would probably weaken those forces and might bring to the fore more conflictual political and economic interests. The risks of engagement are also limited in the near term. Because U.S. economic stakes in China are small, they do not carry the danger of tying the hands of U.S. leaders should the Chinese pursue conflictual policies that require the United States to balance against China. A policy of engagement thus promises greater benefits than containment, with few risks.

Our assessment draws on theory and salient historical examples. Theoretically, we argue that the cultivation of economic ties with nondemocratic great powers will help to elicit cooperative foreign policies in some cases. In other cases though, extensive economic ties may not constrain the leaders of non-democratic great powers to pursue cooperative policies. In fact, increased economic interaction may even generate domestic political dynamics that give rise to conflictual policies. What determines whether economic ties will influence a nondemocracy to pursue more cooperative than conflictual foreign policies is how much influence internationalist economic interests in the nondemocratic state have in the polity. If the dominant political coalition is comprised of groups with internationalist economic interests or if the leadership is autonomous yet committed to internationalization, the cultivation of economic ties should have positive effects. If internationalist economic concerns are not influential, economic ties are far from being a guarantee that a potential adversary will pursue cooperative foreign policies. In fact, domestic-oriented economic interests may feel threatened by an expansion of economic links. As a result, they may seek to assert political control to prevent a diminution of their economic benefits and political position, and this could lead to conflictual foreign policies. Understanding the dynamics economic ties generate in the do-

---

article. Another excellent review of the debate surrounding the engagement of China can be found in Michael Gordon, "American Economic Power and Future Great Power Rivals" (in progress), chap. 10.

7. Much of the debate centers around the effects of engagement versus containment on human rights in China. We do not address that issue, but see James Lilley, "Freedom Through Trade," *Foreign Policy*, no. 94 (spring 1994): 37–42; Bryce Harland, "For a Strong China," *Foreign Policy*, no. 94 (spring 1994): 48–52; Robert L. Bernstein and Richard Dicker, "Human Rights First," *Foreign Policy*, no. 94 (spring 1994): 43–47; and Wang Dan and Wang Juntao, "Jiang Zemin Shows His True Colors," *New York Times*, 27 July 1999, A23.

mestic political process of a nondemocratic state is therefore crucial to evaluating the relative merits of engagement and containment policies.

We also argue that if a democracy cultivates extensive economic ties with a nondemocratic potential adversary, that will generate domestic political constraints which will make it difficult for democratic leaders to balance against and deter such an adversary should the need arise. Democratic leaders should thus be cognizant that, while opening and closing economic ties are political decisions, creating extensive ties takes a long time and closing them is politically difficult once they are significant. Hence, leaders should have an eye on the long-term security implications of such policies.

After elucidating the analytical argument, we refer to two cases of nondemocratic powers that came to have extensive economic ties with democratic great powers: czarist Russia and its economic and political-military relationship with France in the late nineteenth and early twentieth centuries; and Wilhelmine Germany, which had extensive economic ties with Britain particularly, but also other great powers, before the First World War. These cases illustrate the argument and provide useful insight. We then explore the nature of China's political economy and its implications for Chinese foreign policy and U.S.-Chinese security relations, and assess the U.S. policy of engagement and policy recommendations.

The theoretical and historical discussions, together with an analysis of the Chinese political economy, help us evaluate whether U.S. foreign economic policies toward China are likely to influence Chinese foreign policy in a cooperative rather than conflictual direction. Our conclusion is that, while it is difficult to get a handle on the precise nature of the Chinese political economy, the United States should continue to pursue a policy of engagement with limits, at least into the near future. The Chinese leadership and a substantial portion of the "selectorate" in China appear to be committed to, or benefiting from, economic integration. Engagement thus fosters internationalist economic concerns and makes a conflictual foreign policy from China increasingly unlikely. Containment, by contrast, could weaken economic internationalists and strengthen inward-looking economic forces and those with aggressive motives, making a cooperative foreign policy much less likely. Moreover, we argue that the policy of engagement carries few risks in the short term. The small size of the U.S. economic stake in China means that U.S. leaders are unlikely to have their hands tied by economic interests in the United States if it is necessary to balance against Beijing, at least into the near future.

THE ANALYTICAL ARGUMENT

DRAWING ON liberal theories of economic interdependence and domestic processes, we focus on how domestic political institutions aggregate economic interests.[8] This process influences whether economic ties are seen as beneficial or pernicious, or whether they are inconsequential. In turn, this determines whether having extensive economic ties with other states will elicit more cooperative than conflictual policies. That is not to say that other factors do not influence foreign policies. They do. In fact, on core issues of national sovereignty, economic concerns will play little or no role. Nonetheless, we show that the role economic interests play in the political system generally has a substantial impact on whether states pursue more cooperative or conflictual foreign policies toward those with whom they have extensive economic ties.

In democracies, economic interest groups and society-at-large as voters are fairly powerful in relation to the state. The extent to which this is the case varies over time and across issues and types of democratic institutions. Nonetheless, state leaders in democracies will tend to be constrained to pursue policies that are largely consistent with the median preferences of vested interests. So as not to incur the wrath of voters, democratic leaders will also need to be concerned with the prospective adjustment costs to their economies that would be incurred in the event of a breakdown in economic ties, and they will have to be sensitive to the effects of costly security policies on their economies. Democratic states will, therefore, tend to pursue cooperative policies toward those with whom they have significant economic links.[9]

This will be true for certain nondemocracies as well. If the leadership is highly autonomous and sees internationalization as crucial to fulfill its economic or political goals, or if the most politically prominent societal groups have internationalist economic interests, nondemocratic leaders will be influenced in a strong, positive way by their states' economic ties. Leaders of such states will tend to pursue cooperative foreign policies with major economic partners, for that will help to achieve leadership goals that require internationalization or to preserve the stake that the dominant political coalition has in the economic ties. Below we discuss how this argument relates both to czarist

8. The argument in this section is adapted from Paul A. Papayoanou, "Interdependence, Institutions, and the Balance of Power: Britain, Germany, and World War I," *International Security* 20, no. 4 (spring 1996): 42–76; Paul A. Papayoanou, "Economic Interdependence and the Balance of Power," *International Studies Quarterly* 41, no. 1 (March 1997): 113–40; and Paul A. Papayoanou, *Power Ties: Economic Interdependence, Balancing, and War* (Ann Arbor: University of Michigan Press, 1999), chap. 2.

9. For evidence, see Papayoanou, "Economic Interdependence and the Balance of Power"; and Papayoanou, *Power Ties*.

Russia and present-day China. Czarist Russia in the late nineteenth and early twentieth centuries had a government that was quite autonomous from societal economic forces but its leadership had a high dependence on foreign capital to achieve its ambitious modernization goals and to finance its public debt. Contemporary China, we show, has a leadership that appears to be equally committed to internationalization. That leadership is not as autonomous as was czarist Russia's, but the "selectorate" in China seems, on balance, to consist more of internationalist than domestic-oriented economic interests.

In other nondemocracies, by contrast, internationalist economic concerns may play only a small role, if any, in the political process. In many authoritarian regimes, for instance, the leadership is quite autonomous from societal forces and sees nationalistic economic policies as best for development (for example, import substitution industrialization strategies). Also, in praetorian polities the institutional framework may not effectively assimilate struggles between competing groups; thus, narrow (economic or noneconomic) interest groups with disproportionate influence can capture national policy and shift it away from the preferences of median internationalist economic interests.[10] Under these types of nondemocracies, therefore, extensive economic ties will either not have political salience or will be seen as threatening by powerful domestic-oriented economic interests.

These states will thus be less inclined to pursue cooperative policies and are more likely to pursue conflictual policies even if strongly tied to other great powers in the international economy. If the political institutions have given disproportionate influence to domestic-oriented economic or other narrow interests over internationalist economic concerns, those interests may have an incentive and a substantial ability to influence the leadership to pursue a noncooperative foreign policy even if there are extensive economic ties to other great powers. Although a noncooperative foreign policy may cause the economic ties to be severed, the members of the dominant coalition would not pay the costs of that damage, and might even benefit from reduced international economic competition. As discussed below, Wilhelmine Germany is such an example. Before 1914 Germany pursued conflictual policies despite being highly dependent on the international economy because its political in-

---

10. Samuel P. Huntington, *Political Order in Changing Societies* (New Haven: Yale University Press, 1968), 81–82, 195–98; Michael Gordon, "Domestic Conflict and the Origins of the First World War," *Journal of Modern History* 46 (June 1974): 191–226; Jack Snyder, "Averting Anarchy in the New Europe," *International Security* 14, no. 4 (spring 1990): 5–41; and Jack Snyder, *Myths of Empire: Domestic Politics and International Ambition* (Ithaca and London: Cornell University Press, 1991).

stitutions gave domestic-oriented economic and military interests dispropor-tionate influence.[11]

This discussion leads to two concerns for a democracy considering culti-vating extensive economic ties with a nondemocracy. First, it is important to understand whether the institutions of the nondemocracy are likely to permit internationalist economic interests to wield significant influence in the political process or whether the leadership of the nondemocracy is committed to inter-nationalization. Second, democratic leaders should be concerned with the ef-fects that economic ties will have on their ability to balance a future threat from a nondemocracy. Vested interests with extensive ties to a state deemed by democratic strategists to be a threat, and political leaders with concerns about prospective adjustment costs, will fear that confrontational policies could lead to a severing of economic links. Democratic strategists may there-fore be constrained from balancing against a threat with which their state has extensive economic links. This was the case for British strategists in the period preceding 1914. As discussed below, they were constrained by internationalist economic concerns stemming from Britain's ties with Germany. As a result, Britain pursued an ambivalent "straddle strategy"[12] rather than a firm balancing effort that might have deterred the Germans from launching the Schlieffen Plan. For this reason, and because of the institutional biases of German politi-cal institutions, economic ties were not conducive to peace in 1914.

HISTORICAL PRECEDENTS

WE GROUND the analytic discussion with an examination of how economic ties influenced czarist Russia and its political-military relationship with France in the late nineteenth and early twentieth centuries, and Wilhelmine Germany and Anglo-German relations before 1914. These cases are useful analogues for the discussion of China's political economy, and its foreign pol-icy and relations with the United States.

Czarist Russia and Wilhelmine Germany are analogous to China today in several ways. Like China, neither can be considered to have been a full-fledged democracy.[13] Moreover, both undertook substantial efforts to modernize their

11. For a similar argument, see Norrin M. Ripsman and Jean-Marc F. Blanchard, "Commercial Liberalism Under Fire: Evidence from 1914 and 1936," *Security Studies* 6, no. 2 (winter 1996/97): 4–50.
12. Glenn H. Snyder, "The Security Dilemma in Alliance Politics," *World Politics* 36, no. 4 (July 1984): 461–95.
13. Wilhelmine Germany was what we call a pseudodemocracy, as discussed below.

economies, and international economic ties were integral to their economic development. Finally, the leadership in both countries wanted to modernize not only for economic reasons, but also because they felt it necessary to improve their relative political-military power. All of these characteristics apply to China today.

The Franco-Russian and Anglo-German dyads are also similar to the U.S.-Chinese relationship in at least two respects. First, these are all relationships among great powers. Second, they involve the cultivation of economic ties between a democracy and a nondemocracy.

Despite crucial similarities between czarist Russia and Wilhelmine Germany, and their economic ties with France and Britain respectively, the two countries pursued different foreign policies toward their major economic partners, with different implications. Czarist Russia agreed to political-military collaboration with France. Although it pursued some conflictual policies in the international arena and was seen as having some potential for recklessness, Russia was overall an accommodating ally for France. Wilhelmine Germany, by contrast, undertook highly conflictual policies in the international arena and was less than cooperative with Britain on security matters. Despite being the pivotal actor in balance-of-power politics in the decade preceding 1914, Britain pursued a somewhat ambivalent policy toward the Germans and its failure to attempt deterrence was a crucial reason for the outbreak of World War I.[14] An examination of why these particular foreign policies were pursued will provide clues that may be helpful for understanding the direction of China's foreign policy and U.S.-Chinese relations in the years to come.

The discussion that follows highlights that the particular institutional biases of czarist Russia and Wilhelmine Germany, not simply the fact that they were nondemocracies, affected the way in which economic ties influenced their foreign policies. The cases are not perfectly analogous since China's institutional biases are substantially different. While the czarist regime was almost completely autonomous from societal forces and Germany had some significant democratic characteristics, the Chinese polity is somewhere in between. Nonetheless, the examination of the historical record illuminates how particular institutional biases can influence the impact that economic ties have on foreign policies.

14. Sean M. Lynn-Jones, "Détente and Deterrence: Anglo-German Relations, 1911–1914," *International Security* 11, no. 2 (fall 1986): 121–50; Jack S. Levy, "Preferences, Constraints, and Choices in July 1914," *International Security* 15, no. 3 (winter 1990/91): 151–86; and Papayoanou, "Interdependence, Institutions, and the Balance of Power."

CZARIST RUSSIA AND FRANCE

In the late nineteenth century, the czarist government was committed to modernizing its economy and needed to finance a large public debt. Russia was thus highly dependent on access to foreign capital.

Germany had been the main banker financing Russian industrialization efforts and government debts until November 1887. At that time though, German chancellor Otto von Bismarck ordered the Reichsbank to stop accepting Russian bonds as collateral security for loans, and to inform its customers that Russian credit was not sound. The order led to a drop in Russian loan stock on the Berlin Bourse.[15]

French money was therefore essential for the Russian government to meet its financial needs and industrialization goals, and French bankers were ready, willing, and able to fill the void left by the Germans. After Bismarck's declaration, the chief financial houses of Paris formed a syndicate by which to bring French capital into the Russian market and to assist the czarist government. In November 1888 the first contract between French banks and the Russian government was signed, and two more loans were arranged in 1889 by the Paris Rothschilds. Three more loans followed in 1890. The terms of the deals made the Russian government's external indebtedness more manageable. Moreover, since Russia's system of taxation was ineffective and its available domestic capital insufficient to pursue industrialization, borrowing made that goal possible. Meanwhile, the deals were highly attractive for French investors since they provided high-interest yields and were considered very secure. Thus, these arrangements benefited both French bankers and the Russian government, and France replaced Germany as Russia's main creditor by the late 1880s, a position France held up to the First World War.[16]

15. Georges Michon, *The Franco-Russian Alliance: 1891–1917*, Translated by Norman Thomas (New York: Macmillan, 1929), 17–18; Alexander Gerschenkron, *Bread and Democracy in Germany* (1943; Ithaca: Cornell University Press, 1989), 44; David Calleo, *The German Problem Reconsidered: Germany and the World Order, 1870 to the Present* (Cambridge: Cambridge University Press, 1978), 14–16; John F. V. Keiger, *France and the Origins of the First World War* (London: Macmillan Press, 1983), 11; V. I. Bovykin, "The Franco-Russian Alliance," *History* 64 (1979): 24; Herbert Feis, *Europe: The World's Banker, 1870–1914* (New York: Council on Foreign Relations/Yale University Press, 1930), 213.

16. Michon, *The Franco-Russian Alliance*, 17–18; Rondo E. Cameron, *France and the Economic Development of Europe, 1800–1914: Conquests of Peace and Seeds of War* (Princeton: Princeton University Press, 1961), 73–74, 254, 300; Keiger, *France and the Origins of the First World War*, 11; Feis, *Europe: The World's Banker, 1870–1914*, 44–52, 210–15; George F. Kennan, *The Fateful Alliance: France, Russia, and the Coming of the First World War* (New York: Pantheon, 1984), 32–33, 75–76; Bovykin, "The Franco-Russian Alliance," 25; B. V. Anan'ich and V. I. Bovykin, "Foreign Banks and Foreign Investment in Russia," in *International Banking 1870–1914*, ed. Rondo Cameron and V. I. Bovykin (New York: Oxford University Press, 1991), 259; Clive Trebilcock, *The Industrialization of the Continental Powers, 1780–1914* (London and New York: Longman, 1981), 179–80.

As discussed, some nondemocratic regimes will not be sensitive to the effects of international economic ties, while others will. Czarist Russia was in the latter category. Although Russian leaders were not pressured by economic interest groups, they were keenly sensitive to the crucial role that international economic ties played in financing government debt and in achieving industrialization goals.

Russia's financial dependence on France was so great that Russia came to close ranks with France on security matters. Russia perceived Germany as having threatening intentions by 1891, and thought an attack was quite possible. The Russians, however, felt that France would probably fight on their side with or without an alliance, and so thought an ententelike understanding rather than an alliance was warranted. The Russians also feared that if an alliance were not secret, Germany might declare war preemptively. This possibility was ominous for the Russians, who felt they needed a couple of years to build up their forces to thwart an attack. Hence, state strategists in Russia were not convinced that an active and public balancing effort with France was prudent in the short run, though preparing to balance with a secret treaty could help achieve security beyond the near term. From a strategic point of view, therefore, the Russians were not nearly as keen about an alliance as were the French.[17]

Russia nonetheless tilted toward France and forged an alliance because of the breakdown of financial ties with Germany and because of Russia's financial dependence on France. Referring to Bismarck's 1887 order that prevented Russia from borrowing in Germany, Russian foreign minister Nikolai Giers told the German ambassador at St. Petersburg in 1893, "Bismarck drove us into the arms of France, especially through his financial measures."[18] Herbert Feis writes in his examination of the historical record, "A keen awareness of financial need and financial dependence...must have been among the influences which led the Czar to accept the understanding of August, 1891."[19] Also noteworthy in this regard, Giers wrote in a letter to Paris in 1891: "The cordial agreement which has so happily arisen between France and Russia, represents in our time a condition necessary not only in view of our common interests, but also for the establishment of a definite counter-weight to the influence of the League of the central powers, which will maintain the most beneficial bal-

17. Michon, *The Franco-Russian Alliance*, 19–20, 52; Keiger, *France and the Origins of the First World War*, 13; William Leonard Langer, *The Franco-Russian Alliance, 1890–1894* (1929; New York: Octagon, 1967), 181; Bovykin, "The Franco-Russian Alliance," 26.
18. Quoted in Feis, *Europe: The World's Banker, 1870–1914*, 214.
19. Ibid., 217.

ance of forces."[20] Giers apparently did not see the agreement of 1891 as primarily or exclusively a response to a security threat to the balance of power. Rather, he was alluding to a mutual economic stake as the basis for the relationship.

That the financial links mattered can also be seen in the ways that France successfully used the incentive of financial aid to reach agreeement on an alliance. The Russians had security concerns, but they were not as desirous of an alliance as were the French. As Feis writes, "It was no easy task for these two countries to find and define a jointly acceptable basis for alliance."[21] As a result, the French government conveyed to the Russians that French financial aid was virtually conditional upon an alliance. The French therefore used the incentive of financial ties to bind Russia militarily. French leaders saw that Russia's desire for money from France was so significant that they thought it could affect Russian strategic policy. They were right.[22]

WILHELMINE GERMANY AND BRITAIN

In the period leading up to 1914, Germany pursued highly conflictual policies despite having extensive ties in the international economy. This was because its pseudodemocratic political institutions gave prominence to aggressive socio-economic, political, and military forces, some of which perceived economic interdependence to entail pernicious effects, while internationalist economic interests with preferences for a more cooperative foreign policy were marginalized in the political process.

That Germany had extensive economic ties before 1914 is quite clear from the data. Germany was part of a highly integrated great power economy; one with significant factor-price equalization (that is, wholesale price levels were closely associated, indicating that economies responded very quickly to price changes in other economies). Moreover, Germany was becoming increasingly dependent on trade, which was 38 percent of its GNP in the years before the First World War.[23]

Germany had significant bilateral economic links with the European great powers as well, particularly Britain. One-fifth of Germany's enormous demand

20. Quoted in Bovykin, "The Franco-Russian Alliance," 26. Also quoted in Kennan, *The Fateful Alliance*, 57, though the translation differs slightly.

21. Feis, *Europe: The World's Banker, 1870–1914*, 214.

22. Ibid., 214–15, 217 n. 18.

23. Peter J. Katzenstein, "International Interdependence: Some Long-term Trends and Recent Changes," *International Organization* 29, no. 4 (autumn 1975): 1024; Richard Rosecrance, Alan Alexandroff, Wallace Koehler, John Kroll, Shlomit Lacqueur, and John Stocker, "Whither Interdependence?" *International Organization* 31, no. 3 (summer 1977): 425–71; Kenneth N. Waltz, *Theory of International Politics*, (Reading, Mass.: Addison-Wesley, 1979), 212.

for raw materials and foodstuffs was filled by the British Empire and financed by the City of London, and Lloyds of London insured much of the German merchant marine. Britain's trade with Germany was increasing in the period before World War I a greater proportion of total British trade than to become a trade with France, which was decreasing, while British trade with Russia was only about half of what it was with Germany from 1906 to 1913. In addition, Britain was the leading market for German exports—14.2 percent went to Britain in 1913—and Britain was a close second to the United States as Germany's most important bilateral trade partner in 1913. Although there were some rivalries and strains in the Anglo-German economic relationship, there was overall a high degree of complementarity and mutual benefit as Britain and Germany gained greatly from trade and financial ties.[24]

Why then did Germany pursue such conflictual policies before 1914? For that we turn to the role of Germany's political institutions.

From the 1870s to 1914 Germany's political structure was "an autocratic monarchy with a few parliamentary trimmings."[25] Although there was a legislature, including a popularly elected house, the Reichstag, it had no power to unseat government ministers, who were selected by the kaiser. Moreover, the kaiser had great authority over foreign affairs, including the right to wage war and supreme command of the armed forces. The legislature was not powerless, however. Laws needed a majority in both the Reichstag and the Bundesrat as well as the approval of the kaiser and chancellor to go into effect. Hence, tariffs, direct taxes, and the budget required legislative approval, so the executive branch was not simply free to do what it wanted on foreign economic and military procurement policies. Legislative power, however, favored the Bundesrat, which had the power to initiate bills and to block bills or amendments coming from the Reichstag. This was important since the Prussian government had ascendancy in the Bundesrat under the Constitution of 1871, and its interests were largely those of the Junkers, the landed aristocracy. Hence, the Reich government often had to reach agreements that were consonant with those agrarian interests.[26] Moreover, though elections to the Reichstag were by universal adult male suffrage, the "Government interfered notoriously in local

24. B. R.. Mitchell, *European Historical Statistics, 1750–1970* (New York: Columbia University Press, 1975), 526, 573; B. R. Mitchell, *European Historical Statistics, 1750–1970*, abr. ed. (New York: Columbia University Press, 1975/1978), 304, 307, 411, 416; Paul Kennedy, *The Rise of the Anglo-German Antagonism, 1860–1914* (London and Atlantic Highlands, N.J.: Ashfield, 1980), 294–95; Paul Kennedy, *Strategy and Diplomacy, 1870–1945: Eight Studies* (London: Fontana, 1983), 93–95.

25. V. R. Berghahn, *Germany and the Approach of War in 1914* (New York: St. Martin's, 1973), 9–11.

26. Gerschenkron, *Bread and Democracy in Germany*, 25; Berghahn, *Germany and the Approach of War in 1914*, 10–11.

campaigns, the undemocratic *Bundesrat* had an unlimited power of dissolution, and the electoral districts were increasingly malapportioned against the urban interest."[27]

It was, then, a governmental structure that gave prominence to the Junkers and to the kaiser and chancellor. They could not simply rule as they wished, but they had effective veto power. For that reason they had to form coalitions with other groups to pursue their goals, but coalitions that did not include the interests of the Junkers, kaiser, and chancellor either could not be realized or were doomed to failure. The German political system thus gave rise to a coalition of iron, rye, military, and kaiser—actors who had expansionist goals and saw economic ties to entail pernicious effects that could be mitigated only by transforming the nature of economic links with conflictual policies. As a result, interests opposed to democratization and free trade and in favor of conflictual policies were prominent. Internationalist economic concerns advocating more cooperative policies were largely shut out of the political system.[28]

This was manifest in the kaiser and Chancellor Bernhard von Bülow's world policy, *Weltpolitik*. This expansionist power policy sought to enhance Germany's international role by gaining access to overseas markets and raw materials, which would lead to self-sufficiency and greater levels of industrialization. They also had a belief that Germany would have to reduce its economic vulnerability and promote its growth by transforming economic relationships on the Continent through a customs union it would dominate, known as *Mitteleuropa*. In these ways, Germany could gain a measure of control over its economic destiny and augment its political power relative to other great powers, especially those on the Continent. These Weltpolitik and *Mitteleuropa* visions and the coalition forged by Wilhelm, Bülow, and Bülow's replacement as of

27. Ronald Rogowski, "Iron, Rye, and the Authoritarian Coalition in Germany After 1879" (paper prepared for delivery at the Annual Meeting of the American Political Science Association, Denver, Colorado, 1–5 September 1982), 9.

28. Snyder, *Myths of Empire*, 18, makes a coalitional argument similar to this argument, which is also found in Papayoanou, "Interdependence, Institutions, and the Balance of Power," and Papayoanou, *Power Ties*, chap. 2. He contends that logrolling is a function of the "distribution of power and interests in the society and on the character of its political institutions." He too applies this argument to Wilhelmine Germany. There is, however, a crucially important difference between the two arguments. Papayoanou points to these pseudodemocratic features, whereas he characterizes the political institutions as cartelized. For Snyder, cartelization is what is important because it gives prominence to concentrated interests that tend to logroll to pursue expansion and militarism. Papayoanou disagrees with this argument because concentrated interests do not necessarily have expansionist aims (and many in Wilhelmine Germany did not), so a cartelized system will not necessarily give rise to such a foreign policy. What is important is what *types* of concentrated interests have prominence under a particular set of political institutions, not whether there is cartelization.

1909, Theobald von Bethmann Hollweg, led to continued or increased tariffs the next few years and to a jump in defense expenditures from the 1890s on.[29]

The importance of political structure in determining such an outcome becomes more clear when one recognizes that many sectors in Germany disapproved of the tenor of German policy. In particular, the banks, export industry, and finished goods industry profited from, and lobbied for, strong economic links and better relations with other powers. These groups advocated peaceful approaches to altering the nature of their country's economic ties. In particular, good relations with Britain were a prerequisite for these groups.[30]

In contrast, the agrarians and heavy industrialists were generally in favor of higher tariffs and more aggressive security policies. They felt that maintaining German economic autonomy required Germany to alter the nature of economic ties by having a measure of political control, and this might entail war. Unlike the bankers, who expressed pessimism about financial difficulties, these groups were confident of Germany's ability to pay for war and felt that a compromise policy with Britain was merely wishful thinking.[31]

The more conflictual posture carried the day because the distribution of power in the German political system heavily favored the military, Junkers, and heavy industry. As they won out politically, military expenditures jumped dramatically, increasing from about 1.3 billion marks in 1911 to 2 billion marks in 1913, with much of the increase coming in the army as the Junkers successfully sought to bolster their positions in the German political system with greater expenditures on the army they dominated.[32]

All in all, Germany failed to pursue a cooperative foreign policy despite its economic dependence on Britain and other great powers. Its pseudodemocratic institutional structure gave prominence to forces that saw economic interdependence to have pernicious effects and conflictual policies as beneficial. Germany's political system gave the kaiser, chancellors, and the Junkers so much power that winning coalitions formed around their interests, while

29. Gerschenkron, *Bread and Democracy in Germany*, 58–61; A. J. P. Taylor, *The Course of German History: A Survey of the Development of Germany Since 1815* (1946; New York: Putnam, 1979), chaps. 8–9; Fritz Fischer, *War of Illusions: German Policies from 1911–1914* (New York: Norton, 1975), 11–12, 22–25, 33–35, 48–50, 137–38, 234, 237, 363; Immanuel Geiss, *German Foreign Policy, 1871–1914* (London: Routledge and Kegan Paul, 1976), chaps. 8–9; Eckart Kehr, *Economic Interest, Militarism, and Foreign Policy: Essays on German History*, ed. Gordon A. Craig, trans. Grete Heinz (Berkeley: University of California Press, 1977), chaps. 2, 55; Calleo, *The German Problem Reconsidered*, 20, chaps. 3–4; Kennedy, *The Rise of the Anglo-German Antagonism, 1860–1914*, chap. 13.

30. Fischer, *War of Illusions*, 22–25, 121, 134, 140, 199, 203, 231–36, 260; Kennedy, *The Rise of the Anglo-German Antagonism, 1860–1914*, 298–302.

31. Fischer, *War of Illusions*, 135, 140, 235, 265.

32. Alan C. Lamborn, *The Price of Power: Risk and Foreign Policy in Britain, France, and Germany* (Boston: Unwin Hyman, 1991), 119–20.

economic interests advocating cooperative foreign policies had little say in German politics.

British strategists, meanwhile, wanted to oppose firmly the threat they perceived from Germany. Economic ties, however, generated powerful domestic political constraints within Britain that limited the strategists' capacity to balance firmly against Germany and impelled them to pursue some conciliatory policies.

Britain's ambivalent straddle policy in the period leading up to August 1914 included entente balancing with France and Russia and a response to the German naval challenge. The ententes, however, were merely agreements to consult in a crisis; no commitments to come to the aid of France or Russia were made. While the naval buildup helped insure Britain's survival, it added little to the security of the Continent. Moreover, Britain failed to build up its army's resources or to undertake conscription, and was unwilling to commit to sending the expeditionary force to the Continent. Britain also pursued something of a détente with the Germans, negotiating over naval, political, economic, and colonial matters after 1911. In the crisis of July 1914, Britain pursued mediation and issued only a private, informal warning to Germany. British policy was, in short, a mix of balancing and conciliation.

British policy was the result of the fact that pressure groups, cabinet ministers, and members of Parliament whose interests were shaped in large part by economic interdependence were significant constraints on the strategists. Divisions in the cabinet were largely between the strategists and others in the cabinet, particularly those sensitive to international economic concerns. Those divisions constrained British strategists and even impelled them to pursue conciliatory policies. British policy was also influenced in important ways by direct pressure from economic interests in the policymaking process. In addition, cabinet and parliamentary political leaders had serious concerns about the costs to the British economy of a war, which would severely disrupt international economic relations. For such reasons, British leaders pursued the ambivalent straddle policy.[33]

The Germans' decision to risk launching the Schlieffen Plan was influenced strongly by their recognition of the power internationalist economic interests had in Britain. The mixed signals they saw coming from Britain's straddle policy also reinforced their beliefs about the significance of the constraints faced by British leaders. German leaders thus had somewhat optimistic expectations

---

33. On the British case, see Papayoanou, "Interdependence, Institutions, and the Balance of Power," 55–66; and Papayoanou, *Power Ties*, chap. 4, and the cites therein.

that Britain might stand on the sidelines long enough for a rapid military offensive to work.[34]

SUMMARY

The czarist Russia and Wilhelmine German cases show how nondemocracies can have different institutional biases that affect how economic ties are translated in the policy process and influence foreign policy. Leadership goals and the power of particularistic economic constituencies are crucial to determining whether nondemocracies opt for a cooperative foreign policy or a conflictual one. Economic ties may also constrain democratic strategists hoping to balance against a nondemocracy with which there are extensive links, as exemplified by the British case.

We now consider what these historical lessons and the theoretical argument tell us about the likely direction of China's foreign policy and U.S.-Chinese relations. This first requires an analysis of the nature of the Chinese political economy.

The Political Economy of China

IN 1977, on the eve of reforms that would spark two decades of extremely rapid growth and development, China was largely isolated from the world economy. Its total trade in that year was less than $15 billion, or 0.6 percent of total world trade.[35] By the 1990s, however, China had become a major participant in the world economy—in 1997, its total trade exceeded $325 billion, or 2.9 percent of world trade.[36] China's economy has achieved growth rates averaging nine percent for nearly twenty years, leading to improved living standards and making China an attractive site for investment from abroad. Yet few political reforms have accompanied these impressive economic advances as the Chinese Communist Party continues to control the political system without legal opposition.

Most in the United States who call for an end to the U.S. policy of engagement cite China's political system and its poor record on human rights. Recent revelations about Chinese espionage have also stirred up concerns about the

34. Papayoanou, "Interdependence, Institutions, and the Balance of Power," 71–74; Papayoanou, *Power Ties*, chap. 4.
35. Nicholas R. Lardy, *China in the World Economy* (Washington, D.C.: Institute for International Economics, 1994), 1–2.
36. International Monetary Fund, *Direction of Trade Statistics. Yearbook* (Washington, D.C.: International Monetary Fund, 1998).

implications for national security of the engagement policy.[37] Indeed, the analysis to this point suggests that the policy of engagement or its termination will have significant implications for China's foreign policy and U.S.-Chinese security relations. In order to understand those implications, however, the dynamics of the Chinese political economy should be analyzed. If the gains China reaps from deeper integration into the world economy are only a source of power, and not a constraint on future behavior, then the engagement policy may come back to haunt U.S. policymakers. Yet if deeper integration empowers vested interests with a strong stake in that integration and supports the leadership's economic goals, then Chinese decisionmakers will be less inclined to pursue conflictual political-military policies. An evaluation of the engagement policy requires an examination of the relative political influence of those who gain and lose in China from deepening exposure to the international economy.

In the discussion that follows we first consider the extent to which Chinese economic development has depended on integration into the world economy. We then examine the nature of the Chinese political system, focusing on identifying the officials to whom top Chinese leaders are accountable, the "selectorate." Next we discuss how various blocs within the selectorate are affected by integration into the world economy. There are considerable vested interests in internationalization throughout the Chinese selectorate, and on balance those interests probably outweigh domestic-oriented economic concerns. We also show that the highest leaders in China, including President Jiang Zemin and Premier Zhu Rongji, have made a strong commitment to continued economic reform. Their efforts necessitate the cultivation of international economic links. For these reasons, we conclude that as long as China's engagement in the world economy continues, Chinese leaders are unlikely to pursue a foreign policy that is so conflictual as to jeopardize China's economic links and reform efforts.

THE IMPORTANCE OF CHINA'S INTERNATIONAL ECONOMIC TIES

Deeper integration into the world economy, measured in both trade and foreign investment, has been a key ingredient in China's recent economic growth. In 1980, China's total trade amounted to only $38.1 billion, about fifteen percent of Chinese Gross Domestic Product (GDP) at official exchange rates.[38] By

---

37. See for example David E. Sanger with Frank Bruni, "Legislators Ask Pause in Relations With China," *New York Times*, 27 May 1999, A6.
38. Lardy, *China in the World Economy*, 15, 30.

1996, the value of China's foreign trade had grown to $290.1 billion, over forty one percent of GDP.[39]

Foreign direct investment (FDI) in China has also grown rapidly, particularly since the late 1980s. Before 1984, annual FDI in China amounted to less than $1 billion per year, or less than one percent of GDP.[40] By 1996, new FDI in China totaled nearly $42 billion, or six percent of GDP, and total accumulated FDI in China approached $177 billion by the end of that year.[41] Moreover, foreign-invested firms have been behind much of the expansion in China's exports. Although they produced just one percent of China's total exports in 1985, foreign-invested firms produced over forty one percent of China's total exports by 1996.[42] Relative to other countries at a similar stage of development, the importance of foreign investment to China's economy is large. By 1972, for example, total accumulated FDI in Japan amounted to less than $3.4 billion, while accumulated FDI totaled only $2.3 billion as of 1981 in South Korea. Furthermore, foreign-invested firms never produced more than eleven percent of total exports in Japan, Taiwan, or South Korea. Foreign investment, like trade, has clearly played a large role in China's economic development.[43]

Without question integration into the world economy has been of increasing importance to China's economy and is crucial to China's development prospects. How important the economic ties are perceived to be in China, however, and what role they will play in influencing Chinese foreign policy depends in part on the extent to which Chinese leaders are accountable to the actors who have gained from international economic ties. If leaders are autonomous from these forces and are not strongly committed to a reform policy that depends on integration into the world economy, then they will not be constrained from pursuing foreign policies that might endanger China's ties to the world economy. Indeed, the gains reaped from integration into the world economy might ultimately help finance a conflictual foreign policy in the future.

---

39. Calculated based on data in International Monetary Fund, *Direction of Trade Statistics*. It should be noted that these figures somewhat overstate China's dependence on foreign trade, since approximately one-half of the country's trade consists of imports processed into exports—such trade has a relatively limited effect on the domestic economy. See World Bank, *China 2020: Development Challenges in the New Century* (Washington, D.C.: International Bank for Reconstruction and Development/the World Bank, 1997), 85. Nonetheless, the rapid expansion of China's foreign trade is remarkable, and has certainly contributed substantially to the country's recent economic growth.

40. Lardy, *China in the World Economy*, 63–64.

41. *China Monthly Statistics* (Beijing: China Statistics Consultants Limited, June 1997); National Trade Data Bank and Economic Bulletin Board, product of Stat-USA, U.S. Department of Commerce (in www.stat-usa.gov).

42. *China Monthly Statistics*; Lardy, *China in the World Economy*, 71–72.

43. Lardy, *China in the World Economy*, 110–12.

TO WHOM ARE TOP CHINESE POLICYMAKERS ACCOUNTABLE?

Despite two decades of reforms that have transformed China into a largely market economy, the country maintains communist political institutions. The institutional framework clearly stipulates government subservience to the Chinese Communist Party, most notably through a nomenklatura system which ensures that *"[a]ll* positions of real importance in China fall under" party control.[44] The top leadership position within the Party is the general secretary, while the Standing Committee of the Politburo and the Politburo represent the Party's top collective organs.[45]

To determine what accountability, if any, the officials who sit in these high-ranking offices have, it is important to consider what actors select them. To whom do high level officials owe their positions? Though the Chinese Communist Party (CCP) constitution gives the Central Committee formal power to choose top party leaders, it is clear that selection authority also manifests itself in informal ways. Specifically, informal power has rested with retired party elders, the military, and the country's preeminent leader.[46]

During the 1980s and early 1990s, retired, high-ranking party elders held substantial authority within China's selectorate. Though officially retired, these elders continued to sit atop wide factional networks, and held a large degree of influence over appointment and dismissal decisions.[47] As members of the founding generation of the PRC have continued to pass away in recent years, however, the power of the elders has declined. In the years to come, the personal clout of newly retiring party leaders will certainly be smaller than that of the revolutionary elders. They will lack the prestige of having played a key role in the revolution. Moreover, unlike the revolutionary leaders who were able to create vast personal connections by serving in numerous bureaucracies and commissions, leaders in later generations have tended to advance within a single organization and thus have been unable to develop networks that are as extensive. The importance of personal authority is therefore shrinking.[48]

---

44. Kenneth Lieberthal, *Governing China: From Revolution through Reform* (New York: Norton, 1995), 209.

45. Susan L. Shirk, *The Political Logic of Economic Reform in China* (Berkeley: University of California Press, 1993), 70.

46. Shirk, *The Political Logic of Economic Reform in China*, chap. 4.

47. For example, Lowell Dittmer, "Patterns of Elite Strife and Succession in Chinese Politics," *China Quarterly* 123 (September 1990): 405–30.

48. Shirk, *The Political Logic of Economic Reform in China*, 73–74; see also, Suisheng Zhao, "The Structure of Authority and Decision-Making: A Theoretical Framework," in *Decision-Making in Deng's China: Perspectives from Insiders*, ed. Carol Lee Hamrin and Suisheng Zhao (Armonk, N.Y.: M. E. Sharpe, 1995).

The military, in addition to holding formal authority through its forty-two Central Committee seats, has also been an important group with informal authority in China's selectorate. On occasion, the People's Liberation Army (PLA) has been very active in Chinese politics. The military, however, has become involved politically only upon the initiative of high-ranking political leaders. Nonetheless, since leaders have at times used the PLA against their political opponents, having at least tacit military support has been crucial to any leadership contender. (Jiang Zemin has therefore been careful to prove himself a friend of the PLA.) As with the elders though, the informal influence of the military in the selectorate appears to be declining to some extent. The new generation of military leaders, like their political counterparts, simply lack the clout of the revolutionary generation. In addition, newer political leaders have more limited connections in the military, which makes it more difficult for them to involve the PLA in politics. Still, the PLA continues to play a prominent role in China's leadership selection process, a role that could intensify should Chinese politics become unstable.[49]

The preeminent leader also has informal leadership selection authority. Both Mao Zedong and Deng Xiaoping held considerably more sway over selection decisions than their formal positions might indicate. They certainly were able to veto any candidate to a top leadership position not acceptable to them.[50] Jiang Zemin, meanwhile, seems unlikely to be able to amass the personal authority of Deng in part because he has more limited personal connections (though he still wields considerable power).[51]

While informal lines of authority within the Chinese selectorate have been the most prominent source of leadership selection, the role of formal authority within the selectorate has been increasingly significant. Citing the tendency of elites to cater to constituencies within the Central Committee during the post-Mao era, evidence that the Central Committee acts as "the final veto gate in policy-making," and formal Communist Party rules, Susan L. Shirk argues that "it appears that the Central Committee is in the process of becoming the key group in the selectorate in China." The relationship between the Central Committee and the Politburo and its Standing Committee is one of "reciprocal accountability." While it is true that top Party leaders appoint the party, government, and military officials who sit on the Central Committee, members of

---

49. Ellis Joffe, "Party-Army Relations in China: Retrospect and Prospect," *China Quarterly* 146 (June 1996): 307–8; Shirk, *The Political Logic of Economic Reform in China*, 76; Richard Baum, "The Fifteenth National Party Congress: Jiang Takes Command?" *China Quarterly* 153 (March 1998): 155.

50. Shirk, *The Political Logic of Economic Reform in China*, 77.

51. Baum, "The Fifteenth National Party Congress," 149.

the Central Committee then have the authority (in conjunction with other members of the selectorate) to choose top Party leaders.[52]

In summary, a diverse range of actors possess at least some leadership selection authority in China; top party leaders and leadership contenders pursue policies that garner support among these actors—especially during times of leadership succession competition. While we have suggested that the role of informal selection authority appears to be declining, serious disagreements exist among scholars regarding the continued relative importance of formal and informal authority within the selectorate. Scholars in particular disagree over the extent to which the Central Committee wields real selection power.[53] Such disagreements should be kept in mind as we consider the international economic interests of different elements of the selectorate in the next section. To the extent constituencies that lose (gain) from international economic ties have more (less) power than we have suggested here, our conclusions should be tempered.

WHO IN THE SELECTORATE GAINS AND LOSES FROM INTEGRATION INTO THE WORLD ECONOMY?

Influential groups within the Chinese selectorate that have developed interests in continued integration into the world economy include many local officials, and even some central officials. The path of economic reforms in China has also weakened the resistance of some groups that once opposed deeper integration, such as interior provincial officials, and have undercut the influence of other opponents of integration, such as large state-owned enterprises (SOEs).

The group with perhaps the deepest interest in continued integration into the world economy is local party and government officials. These officials comprise a sizeable bloc within the Central Committee—thirty two percent of the members of the fifteenth Central Committee elected in September 1997 are local officials.[54] These officials have both indirect and direct interests in China's international economic ties.

Fiscal decentralization—a key component of China's economic reform strategy—has given local leaders a large stake in economic growth. Growth

52. Shirk, *The Political Logic of Economic Reform in China*, 72, 79–81.

53. Contrast, especially, Shirk, *The Political Logic of Economic Reform in China*, with Dali Yang, "Governing China's Transition to the Market: Institutional Incentives, Politicians' Choices, and Unintended Outcomes," *World Politics* 48, no. 3 (April 1996): 424–52; and Frederick C. Teiwes, "The Paradoxical Post-Mao Transition: From Obeying the Leader to 'Normal Politics,'" *The China Journal* 34 (July 1995): 55–94.

54. *China Monthly Data* (Hamburg: Institute of Asian Studies, December 1997).

enables such officials to expand their tax base and patronage opportunities.[55] Because deepening integration into the world economy has been an important source of economic growth in China, fiscal decentralization has given local officials a strong, indirect stake in China's foreign economic relations.

Since local regions have been given increasing autonomy to attract foreign investment over the course of the reform period, local officials are also realizing a more direct interest in China's ties to the international economy. In the late 1970s, Chinese leaders created four Special Economic Zones (SEZs) located in the Guangdong and Fujian provinces. The SEZs were encouraged to attract foreign direct investment, and were allowed to retain a generous portion of their foreign exchange earnings. The SEZs were highly successful, and thus gave officials from those provinces a vested interest in access to the world economy. Officials from other regions, seeing the benefits afforded by the SEZs, began to lobby for similar access. Central officials in 1984 awarded similar deals to fourteen coastal cities and Hainan Island, and even officials from inland provinces lobbied for the autonomy to attract foreign investment by the mid-1980s.

In the early 1990s the number of regions awarded special status continued to expand. Nearly two thousand Special Development Zones were established throughout China. These zones, which were more localized than the SEZs, were allowed to offer attractive terms to foreign investors. Budgetary difficulties at the local level have made local officials especially anxious to use their increased autonomy to seek expanded inflows of foreign investment. In particular, such officials have sought to convert unprofitable, locally controlled SOEs into foreign joint ventures to improve performance and relieve pressures on local budgets.[56]

Local officials with the deepest interest in continued access to foreign investment represent coastal provinces, for most foreign investment flows into coastal regions. In 1996 eighty-eight percent of FDI in China went to the nine

55. Shirk, *The Political Logic of Economic Reform in China.* See also Susan L. Shirk, "Internationalization and China's Economic Reforms," in *Internationalization and Domestic Politics,* ed. Robert Keohane and Helen Milner (Cambridge: Cambridge University Press, 1996).

56. Susan L. Shirk, *How China Opened its Door: The Political Success of the PRC's Foreign Trade and Investment Reforms* (Washington, D.C.: Brookings, 1994), 35, 38–39, 41; Dali Yang, "Reforms, Resources, and Regional Cleavages: The Political Economy of Coast-Interior Relations in Mainland China," *Issues and Studies* 27, no. 9 (September 1991): 56–58; Edward X. Gu, "Foreign Direct Investment and the Restructuring of Chinese State-Owned Enterprises (1992–1995): A New Institutionalist Perspective," *China Information* 12, no. 3 (winter 1997/1998): 46–47, 51, 55–56.

coastal provinces and three municipalities.[57] Officials representing inland provinces, however, also have a stake in continued access to foreign investments. A not insignificant amount of FDI flows into inland provinces, and these provinces have received considerable trickle-down benefits from foreign investments along the coast. Many enterprises and government organizations from inland areas have, for example, set up businesses in the SEZs along the coast.[58]

Important members of the selectorate have thus developed a strong stake in integration into the world economy. Before the 1980s, however, many officials opposed China's opening to the international economy, and some still do.

The major source of opposition to economic reform and to integration into the world economy early in the reform process came from inland provinces, heavy industry, and central planning agencies and industrial ministries. Inland provincial leaders were concerned that opening China to the world economy would widen income gaps between coastal and interior regions, since inland areas would benefit little from integration. Heavy industries were relatively uncompetitive on world markets, and so opposed the prospect of more stringent competition. The heavy industrial ministries that stood atop these industries naturally opposed China's increasing exposure to the international economy as well. Meanwhile, central officials—especially those in planning agencies—tended to oppose the overall reform program because it undercut their power.[59]

Do these constituencies in the selectorate continue to oppose integration into the world economy? If so, how powerful are they?

Interior provinces initially opposed many reform programs—particularly those that opened China's economy by giving preferential treatment to coastal areas. While coastal provinces benefited considerably from the SEZs and attracted the lion's share of foreign capital, interior provinces received few gains from integration into the world economy. Interior officials were thus concerned with growing regional income disparities. The problem was exacerbated by fiscal decentralization, which "undermined the ability of the central government to transfer resources from richer areas to poorer ones or across regions."[60]

---

57. *China Monthly Statistics.* The nine provinces and three municipalities are: Beijing, Fujian, Guangdong, Guangxi, Hebei, Hainan, Jiangsu, Liaoning, Shandong, Shanghai, Tianjin, Zhejiang.

58. Shirk, *How China Opened its Door,* 42.

59. Susan L. Shirk, "The Domestic Political Dimensions of China's Foreign Economic Relations," in *China and the World: Chinese Foreign Policy in the Post-Mao Era,* ed. Samuel Kim (Boulder: Westview, 1984), 57–81.

60. Yang, "Reforms, Resources and Regional Cleavages," 47–52.

Interior provinces constitute a significant part of the selectorate, holding 37 out of 193 seats in the Central Committee.[61] By the 1990s, however, interior provinces had fewer reasons to oppose integration than they did at the start of reforms. They were given more autonomy to attract foreign capital via Special Development Zones, and they received considerable trickle-down benefits from development along the coast. Hence, interior provinces began to "jump on the reform bandwagon" and lobby for access to the world economy themselves.[62] Nonetheless, given their geographical disadvantages in attracting foreign capital, support from interior provinces for the open policy is more lukewarm than that from coastal areas.

Local officials across China, including those who generally support and gain from China's internationalization, at times may have interests that conflict with such a policy. These officials are concerned, for example, with local unemployment rates, which can increase with deepening integration into world markets. Though protection remains high, China has begun to lift some of its barriers to imports. The average weighted tariff dropped from 28.1 percent to 19.8 percent in 1996, and China has pledged to lower it even further if and when it is granted entry into the WTO.[63] Yet lowering tariffs will bring stiffer foreign competition that will force many industries to downsize or shut down. In turn, the unemployment rate will go up in some regions. Officials from those regions will, no doubt, weigh such disruptions when considering their views on internationalization.

A second constituency that, for the most part, continues to oppose an open policy is heavy industry. China is relatively labor abundant and capital scarce, so its most competitive industries on world markets are thus labor-intensive light industries.

Yet heavy industry continues to constitute a large percentage of total industrial output: 55.6 percent of gross industrial output (at current prices) for the first five months of 1997, an even higher percentage than in 1985 (52.9 percent).[64] SOEs continue to produce a large portion of this heavy industrial output. In 1994 SOEs were responsible for 71 percent of total output in resource extraction and 65 percent of total output in utilities. In three scale-intensive industrial groups—metallurgy, chemicals, and transport machinery—SOEs produced 59 percent, 49 percent, and 51 percent of total output, respectively. SOEs

61. *China Monthly Data.*
62. Yang, "Reforms, Resources and Regional Cleavages," 55.
63. World Bank, *China 2020*, 85–88.
64. *China Monthly Statistics;* World Bank, *China 2020*.

produced 40 percent of total industrial output in 1994, and in 1996 employed 17 percent of the labor force.[65]

Heavy industry thus continues to produce a substantial portion of China's total output, and (especially large) SOEs are responsible for a large percentage of that heavy industrial output. Furthermore, since nearly all industrial ministries represent heavy industry in China, and since high ranking ministerial officials sit on the Central Committee, heavy industry has greater direct influence within the government and the selectorate than does light industry.[66] Since representatives of heavy industry and the SOEs are more likely to oppose integration into the world economy than are the representatives of other sectors, they remain important potential opponents of open policies. It is, of course, an oversimplification to say that all heavy industry interests oppose China's ties to the world economy—all sectors would gain from increased foreign investment—but resistance to integration into the world economy is likely from heavy industry. Moreover, this resistance is politically significant, for China's central government institutions give considerable representation to such interests.

Finally, various central government officials have at times opposed economic reforms in general, and integration into the world economy in particular. Fiscal decentralization and movement out of the planned economy have reduced the authority of many central government organs, particularly the State Planning Commission and the Ministry of Finance. The declining profitability of the SOEs (in response to increased international competition) has also undermined a major revenue source for the central government. Indeed, from 1978 to 1995, budgetary revenues dropped from 35 percent of GDP to 11 percent; 62 percent of the decline was the result of decreased revenues from industrial SOEs.[67] To the extent that integration into the world economy damages the competitiveness of SOEs, some central officials are likely to be opposed to open policies.[68]

---

65. Barry Naughton, (forthcoming); World Bank, *China 2020*, 29.

66. Shirk, *The Political Logic of Economic Reform in China*, 107–10.

67. World Bank, *China 2020*, 24.

68. Events during the post-Tiananmen conservative resurgence in China appear to underscore the concerns that financial and planning officials have had over China's reform program, and their identification with conservative efforts to roll back the reforms. Proposed policies at the time included strengthened planning, fiscal recentralization, and preferential policies for SOEs; planning and financial officials would, of course, have been among the major benefactors of such a program. Ultimately the program was defeated because of economic shortcomings, but also due to staunch opposition from provincial level officials. See Barry Naughton, *Growing out of the Plan: Chinese Economic Reform, 1978–1993* (Cambridge: Cambridge University Press, 1996), 277–83.

Recent events in China, however, suggest that concerns over budgetary revenues from SOEs are of less importance than in the past. China has recently embarked on a major fiscal rationalization program that entails a new tax system adopted in 1994. This tax system relies less on state industrial enterprises as revenue sources, spreading the tax burden more equally on all sectors and ownership forms. The system is also designed to lead to a gradual increase in central revenues.[69] Central officials, in short, are decreasingly dependent on the profits of SOEs for budget revenue. As such, they have less reason to abandon integrationist policies out of fear of SOE profitability. Moreover, as we note below, central leaders have recently embarked on a SOE restructuring drive. If the drive succeeds, the status of SOEs as cash cows for the central government will cease.

In sum, large constituencies within China's selectorate have a strong interest in China's continued integration into the world economy. Such groups would generally oppose policies that might put continued access to the world economy at risk. Still, some constituencies within China's selectorate are either opposed to, or ambivalent about, continued integration.[70] While the path of reforms in China has reduced the opposition to integration of some of these constituencies (such as interior provinces), and undercut the influence of others (such as SOEs), some interests in China (especially heavy industry) will continue to be hostile to increasing China's openness to the international economy. On balance though, it appears that substantial support from the selectorate exists for pursuing further internationalization.

THE CENTRAL LEADERSHIP, ECONOMIC REFORM, AND INTERNATIONALIZATION

The central leadership in China has made a clear commitment to continued economic reform and development. Such reform efforts would be significantly damaged should China pursue policies that undercut its international economic relationships, since China is increasingly integrated into world markets. Top leaders thus have a strong stake in China's continued integration into the world

69. Naughton, *Growing out of the Plan*, 293–94.
70. For example, in addition to those discussed, the PLA's preferences are ambiguous. Until recently, the PLA was heavily involved in business enterprises that in part benefited from economic integration. Beginning in 1998, however, the central leadership embarked on a campaign to separate the military from commercial pursuits, and it appears that the effort has been reasonably effective. As such, the PLA's direct stake in integrationist policies has probably declined to some extent. In recent years, however, the PLA's budget has increased partly because of the economic growth China has achieved due to successful internationalist policies. See Solomon M. Karmel, "The Chinese Military's Hunt for Profits," *Foreign Policy*, no. 107 (September 1997): 103–4, 109; and "No Longer the Army's Business," *Economist*, 8 May 1999.

economy. Recent statements and initiatives by President Jiang Zemin and Premier Zhu Rongji underscore their commitment to reform.

In the fall of 1997, for example, Jiang endorsed an effort to sell most of China's large SOEs, a plan that would effectively end the state's position as the primary owner of industry.[71] The plan certainly involves risks, including rising unemployment and opposition from conservatives. Jiang's backing of the plan shows that economic reform is a high priority for him.

Zhu Rongji has been even more explicit about his commitment to SOE restructuring. In a recent report he stated, "If we cannot achieve this goal [of solving SOE problems by the year 2000], it will prove that I am not worthy of leadership. Since I have been entrusted by the Party and the people for this task, I would have to admit my inability and resign. I would resign from the leadership group."[72] He further emphasized his commitment to continued economic reform in a March 1998 news conference in which he asserted: "No matter what is waiting in front of me—whether it be land mines or an abyss—I will blaze my trail."[73] In short, key elements of the Chinese leadership clearly place economic development and reform among their top priorities. As such, they are unlikely to favor policies that might put China's foreign economic ties, and thus its economy, at risk.

ECONOMIC TIES, THE DIRECTION OF CHINA'S FOREIGN POLICY, AND THE POLICY OF ENGAGEMENT

MANY OF THE key actors in the Chinese selectorate appear to have a strong stake in continued and robust foreign economic ties. Scholars such as Shirk argue that these officials have the power to select top leaders, so the leadership will generally prefer to follow policies that will not antagonize them.[74] As such, top leaders are unlikely to pursue policies that put China's foreign economic ties at risk. Shirk's view is debatable though. Some experts argue that the leadership possesses more autonomy.[75] Nonetheless, the leadership has demonstrated a strong commitment to economic reform in China. For its plans to succeed, integration is required. Hence, even if the top leaders'

---

71. Seth Faison, "Major Shift for Communist China: Big State Industries will be Sold," *New York Times*, 12 September 1997, 1.

72. "A Major Test for State Enterprise Reform," *Inside China Mainland* 20 (January 1998): 47.

73. Erik Eckholm, "New China Leader Promises Reforms for Every Sector," *New York Times*, 20 March 1998, A1.

74. Shirk, *The Political Logic of Economic Reform in China*.

75. For example, Yang, "Governing China's Transition to the Market."

autonomy from the selectorate is quite high, the leadership is unlikely to pursue policies that undermine foreign economic ties. There is thus good reason to expect that top Chinese policymakers will not pursue a conflictual foreign policy that could put China's international economic ties at risk.

Some qualifications are in order though. The most important concerns China's policies toward Taiwan. Since Beijing views Taiwan as a renegade province and has made reunification with the island a central tenet of its foreign policy since the 1950s, China's relations with Taiwan may constitute an exception. A declaration of Taiwanese independence would represent a monumental foreign policy failure for China and would lend greater legitimacy to separatist movements elsewhere on the mainland, such as in Tibet or Xinjiang.[76] As a result, Beijing might well pursue a military response even in the face of strong U.S. opposition and at the risk of jeopardizing economic ties with the United States and others in the world economy. As discussed above, on an issue of national sovereignty such as this, economic interests will clearly have less influence than they will have on the general direction of Chinese foreign policy and most other issues.

A second qualification concerns uncertainty about future political scenarios in Beijing. No guarantees exist that Chinese political institutions in 5, 10, or 25 years will resemble those of today or become more democratic. An economic crisis accompanied by social unrest, for example, might lead to greater PLA involvement in Chinese politics and even a coup.[77] Such a scenario would clearly change the political logic behind China's foreign policy.

It would be unwise, however, to conclude that the United States should end its engagement policy because Chinese politics *might* become destabilized and lead to a more conflictual foreign policy. Such a rationale for ending engagement holds the danger of self-prophecy. Doing so could help to usher in the type of crisis that would lead to a coup or hard-liner resurgence, and in turn, a less cooperative China. By contrast, engagement will further raise China's global economic stakes and likely broaden support for reform and further integration. This, in turn, would make China more cooperative on security issues.

Because there are uncertainties about China's future it is important to address another concern about engagement—whether U.S. leaders will have the capacity to balance against China should the need arise. As discussed, British strategists were unable to pursue firm balancing policies against Wilhelmine Germany before 1914 because internationalist economic concerns with strong

76. On the importance of Taiwan in China's strategic calculations, see Thomas J. Christensen, "Chinese Realpolitik," *Foreign Affairs* 75, no. 5 (September/October 1996): 37–52.
77. See, for example, Joffe, *Party-Army Relations in China*.

ties to Germany were constraining influences. Will this be a problem for the United States?

At present, the U.S.-Chinese economic relationship is asymmetric. China is highly dependent on the United States (especially with regard to trade), but China is not a very significant partner for the United States. 1996 figures show that trade with the United States amounted to 22.9 percent of total Chinese trade and 9.5 percent of Chinese GDP. At the same time, trade with China accounted for only 4.6 percent of total U.S. trade and 0.9 percent of U.S. GDP.[78] U.S. strategists are thus not likely to be highly constrained by economic interests with ties to China into the near future.

As economic ties grow, however, and the U.S. economy becomes more dependent on China, that may not be the case. Thus, over the next several years it is crucial that U.S. policymakers carefully monitor and analyze the dynamics of the Chinese political economy. If the balance of power within China begins to shift toward inward-looking concerns, a reevaluation of engagement policies would be in order. To ignore a reversal in the apparent trends in the Chinese political economy and continue with a policy of engagement could leave U.S. strategists constrained in the long term should the need to balance against China arise.

IMPLICATIONS FOR THEORY AND POLICY

THIS ARTICLE assesses the U.S. policy of engagement with China by employing theory, historical examples, and an analysis of the Chinese political economy. We argue that nondemocratic great powers are more likely to pursue cooperative policies with those to whom they have extensive economic ties when economic internationalists are politically prominent or when the leadership is committed to an expansion of international economic ties to achieve its goals. Conversely, when internationalist economic interests have little influence and the leadership pursues nationalist foreign economic policies, nondemocratic great powers are more likely to pursue conflictual foreign policies because economic ties will not be highly valued and may even be seen as pernicious. The argument is applied to the cases of czarist Russia and its relationship with France just before the turn of the twentieth century, Wilhelmine Germany and its relations with Britain up to the First World War, and China and its interactions with the United States today.

78. Euromonitor International, *International Marketing Data and Statistics* (London: Euromonitor Publications, 1998); International Monetary Fund, *Direction of Trade Statistics*.

Because a substantial portion of the Chinese selectorate benefits from integration into the world economy and the Chinese leadership has made a strong commitment to internationalist economic policies, we conclude that China is unlikely to pursue highly conflictual foreign policies that might put its ties at risk. Thus, a policy of engagement should help to elicit cooperation from China. The nature of China's political economy, however, is not entirely clear, and so there is some uncertainty about the course that Chinese foreign policy will take. The United States should therefore be prepared to use the stick as well as the carrot in case China is inclined to take actions that contravene American security interests. Maintaining a strong military presence in east Asia and bolstering security commitments to regional allies should thus be part of a guarded engagement policy, as it is at present. In so doing, the United States should be careful to avoid the adoption or appearance of a rigid containment policy. Such a policy, or the perception of one in China, would undercut the strength of economic internationalists in China, thereby reducing the prospects for a cooperative Chinese foreign policy in the years to come.[79]

Our analysis has significant implications for prominent theoretical arguments in the international relations literature as well. First, our analytical argument and policy prescriptions are in sharp contrast with realist conceptions. Realists would argue that since China is a potential enemy, the United States is likely to, or should, be reluctant to pursue open economic policies that can empower the Chinese. Doing so carries significant risks in a world in which relative gains matter.[80] Our analysis leads to a much different conclusion. It suggests that economic ties can improve the position of internationalist economic concerns within China and thus give rise to a more cooperative foreign policy. Empowering China, therefore, can yield positive security externalities.

Second, our argument suggests a refinement of the finding that regimes in transition from authoritarianism to democracy are war-prone. Edward Mansfield and Jack Snyder suggest that such states are war-prone because national leaders find it necessary to appeal to nationalist forces.[81] If a democratizing country, however, has extensive exposure to the international economy and constituents with a stake in economic integration wield considerable power in

79. For an alternative conception and analysis focusing on domestic politics, see David Shambaugh, "Containment or Engagement of China? Calculating Beijing's Responses," *International Security* 21, no. 2 (fall 1996): 180–209.

80. Joanne Gowa, *Allies, Adversaries, and International Trade* (Princeton: Princeton University Press, 1994); Waltz, *Theory of International Politics*; Joseph M. Grieco, "Anarchy and the Limits of Cooperation: A Realist Critique of the Newest Liberal Institutionalism," *International Organization* 42, no. 3 (summer 1988): 485–508.

81. Edward D. Mansfield and Jack Snyder, "Democratization and the Danger of War," *International Security* 20, no. 1 (summer 1995): 5–38; Edward D. Mansfield and Jack Snyder, "Democratization and War," *Foreign Affairs* 74, no. 3 (May/June 1995): 79–97.

the political system, nationalist appeals will be unattractive for political leaders and ineffective. Under those conditions, leaders will find it more useful to appeal to internationalists, and so a peaceful transition is quite possible. Thus, if China begins a process of democratization, its integration into the world economy should mitigate the impact of nationalist forces.[82]

This article thus challenges arguments, predictions, and prescriptions derived from theories that are purely systemic- or unit-level. Theoretically and empirically, international economic ties, domestic political processes, and security policies are shown to be integrally related. The analysis suggests that engaging a *potential* enemy will reap positive results under certain conditions. Such an important and counterintuitive conclusion points to the need for further study of the interconnections between domestic and international economic and security factors.

82. A similar argument about Russia's transition is made by Michael McFaul, "A Precarious Peace: Domestic Politics in the Making of Foreign Policy," *International Security* 22, no. 3 (winter 1997/98): 5–35.

THE TROUBLE WITH CARROTS:

TRANSACTION COSTS, CONFLICT EXPECTATIONS,

AND ECONOMIC INDUCEMENTS

DANIEL W. DREZNER

ARROTS ARE commonly used in domestic politics, as any study of legislative log-rolling, campaign finance, or political patronage would
attest. At the international level, the use of inducements to influence
individual officials in states or international organization is also rather
common, as the International Olympic Committee has recently discovered.[1] The theoretical literature suggests that inducements should be successful in altering the foreign policies of nation-states as well.[2] There have
been several prominent cases of financial inducements in world politics in
the past two decades. The United States greased the wheels of the Camp
David accords by promising billions in aid to Egypt and Israel. In 1990 the
Soviet Union agreed to a DM50 billion payment from Germany in return for
the Soviet withdrawal of troops from East Germany. From 1992 to 1994,
the United States used Nunn-Lugar funds to persuade Belarus, Ukraine,
and Kazakstan to relinquish their nuclear stockpiles.

Frequently, however, carrots are spurned. North Vietnam rejected Lyndon Johnson's covert offer of massive aid in return for halting the war in
Vietnam. The Reagan administration's attempt to trade arms for hostages

Daniel W. Drezner is assistant professor of political science at the University of Chicago.

This paper was prepared for the *Security Studies* Workshop on Economic Power, Interdependence, and National Security, held at the Mershon Center for International Relations,
Ohio State University, 2–5 April 1998. I am grateful to the participants of that conference,
and to the anonymous reviewers of *Security Studies*, for their helpful comments and suggestions. I am also grateful to Steve Chan for his observations on an embryonic version of this
paper.

1. Jere Longman, "Investigators Cite Cash Payments in Salt Lake City Bid for Olympics,"
New York Times, 8 January 1998, A1. See also Kimberly A. Elliott, ed., *Corruption and the Global
Economy* (Washington, D.C.: Institute for International Economics, 1999).
2. Robert Tollison and Thomas Willett, "An Economic Theory of Mutually Advantageous Issue Linkages in International Negotiations," *International Organization* 33, no. 4
(autumn 1979): 425–49; James Sebenius, "Negotiation Arithmetic: Adding and Substracting
Issues and Parties," *International Organization* 37, no. 2 (spring 1983): 281–316; James Fearon,
"Rationalist Explanations for War," *International Organization* 49, no. 3 (summer 1995): 379–
414.

with Iran did not produce substantial concessions. Russia chose not to accept Japan's offer of aid in exchange for returning the Kurile Islands. Pakistan refused U.S. offers of aid in return for not conducting nuclear tests. Despite famine conditions, North Korea rebuffed a South Korean carrot of food aid in return for permitting the reunion of family members split by the Korean War. The Clinton administration's attempt to use trade as a carrot for China to alter its human rights practices has proven futile.[3] Even more frequently, carrots are not proffered in situations where they are a clear option; instead, coercive tactics are used. To paraphrase Arthur Conan Doyle, this is a dog that rarely barks.

The existing literature on inducements is too small to be much of a guide for explanation. The work on carrots is paltry when compared to the literature devoted to economic or military coercion. Indeed, it is small enough to leave the definition of an intuitive notion somewhat unclear. It is telling that articles focusing on financial inducements talk about 'carrots' or 'bribes' while articles on other kinds of inducements talk about 'linkage.'[4] This paper will use a three-part definition of carrots or inducements. First, relative to the status quo, a carrot is a transfer of benefits offered by one actor, called the *sender,* to another actor, called the *receiver.* Second, the carrot comes with a clear quid pro quo; in return for the benefit, the receiver is expected to grant some concession to the sender.[5] Third, the sender's demanded concession is well-defined; the carrot is not proffered in the hopes of influencing the receiver country's policies over the long run.[6]

3. Randall Newnham, "How to Win Friends and Influence People" (paper presented at the International Studies Association annual meeting, Toronto, Canada, March 1997; Erik Eckholm, "Talks Between 2 Koreas Collapse in Mutual Blame," *New York Times,* 19 April 1998, 8; Robert Kagan, "The Price of 'Engaging' China," *New York Times,* 15 January 1999, A23.

4. David Baldwin, "The Power of Positive Sanctions," *World Politics* 24, no. 1 (October 1971): 19–38; T. Clifton Morgan, "Issue Linkages in International Crisis Bargaining," *American Journal of Political Science* 34, no. 2 (May 1990): 311–33; James D. Morrow, "Signaling Difficulties with Linkage in Crisis Bargaining," *International Studies Quarterly* 36, no. 1 (March 1992): 153–72; Eileen Crumm, "The Value of Economic Incentives in International Relations," *Journal of Peace Research* 32, no. 3 (summer 1995): 313–30; William J. Long, "Trade and Technological Incentives and Bilateral Cooperation," *International Studies Quarterly* 40, no. 1 (March 1996): 77–106; David Cortright, ed., *The Price of Peace: Incentives and International Conflict Prevention* (New York: Rowman and Littlefield, 1997).

5. Thus, the Marshall Plan does not qualify as a carrot, because there were no associated demands placed on it when it was first implemented. Demands made *after* 1949, using the Marshall Plan aid as leverage, would qualify as coercion relative to the status quo. See Helen Leigh-Phippard, "U.S. Export Controls and Aid to Britain, 1949–1958." *Diplomacy and Statecraft* 6, no. 3 (November 1995): 719–52.

6. For discussions of the use of inducements as a long-term strategy of increasing influence over the receiver, see Rawi Abdelal and Jonathan Kirshner, "Strategy, Economic Relations, and the Definition of National Interests," *Security Studies* 9, nos. 1/2 (autumn 1999– winter 2000): 119–56; and Paul A. Papayoanou and Scott L. Kastner, "Sleeping with the

The lack of any significant literature means that basic questions remain unaddressed. The literature suffers from Benjamin Most and Harvey Starr's criticism that the scholarly focus on foreign policy options has been too narrow. [7] In a disputed issue area, states are not limited to the choice of inducement or no inducement. They can also select other policy options, such as economic sanctions, threats of military force, attempts at diplomatic isolation, or doing nothing. Focusing only on carrots overlooks the fact that states can choose from a host of policy options and responses. Although more attention needs to be paid to the use of carrots, it also needs to be tied into the larger question of how states choose among their set of feasible influence policies.

This paper puts forward a rational choice explanation for the conditions when inducements are a feasible and preferable option. It does so by asking two questions. First, what prevents nation-states from using carrots more frequently? In other words, why are carrots not a ubiquitous feature of the international system? Second, how useful are carrots relative to other policy options? In other words, when will carrots be preferred over economic or military coercion?

This paper will argue that only under very special circumstances will states opt for the carrot as their preferred policy option, although it will emerge as a second-best option. Carrots are not feasible because of the high transaction costs involved in making political exchanges in an anarchic world. If actions are not observable or enforceable in international interactions, the costs of securing an agreement can outweigh the benefits of any inducement. Thus, carrots will be more likely and more successful in situations where transaction costs are reduced, such as between democratic dyads or within international regimes. Even in cases where the use of inducements is a feasible option, however, it may not be the sender's preferred choice. If the sender anticipates frequent conflicts with the receiver, it will be reluctant to proffer a carrot, for fear of weakening its bargaining position in the future. If a sender wants a concession from an adversarial receiver and coercion fails to generate compliance, the sender may then proffer a carrot as a second-best option. Even in cases where the two states

(Potential) Enemy: Assessing the U.S. Policy of Engagement with China," *Security Studies* 9, nos. 1/2 (autumn 1999–winter 2000): 157–87. Note that this distinction between short-term carrots and long-term engagement strategies corresponds to the distinction in the sanctions literature between economic warfare and economic coercion. See Robert Pape, "Why Economic Sanctions Do Not Work," *International Security* 22, no. 2 (fall 1997): 90–136.

7. Benjamin Most and Harvey Starr, "International Relations, Foreign Policy Substitutability, and 'Nice' Laws," *World Politics* 36, no. 3 (April 1984): 383–406. David Baldwin also makes this point in *Economic Statecraft* (Princeton: Princeton University Press, 1985).

have harmonious relations, senders may prefer using economic or military coercion instead of inducements as a method of extracting concessions, because it is more cost-effective. Ironically, a sender may choose to coerce an ally because previous inducements give it sufficient leverage to sanction.

There are several implications of this paper for both the theory and practice of foreign policy. Theoretically, it offers an additional explanation for the existence of the democratic peace. One of the reasons that democracies may choose not to fight each other is that the use of inducements is a more feasible option between these dyads. Relative to other dyads, democracies have a wider range of policy options, making the use of force less of a necessity. This article also suggests why states continue to use coercive tactics even though scholars remain pessimistic about their utility. Compared to inducements, even sanctions that fail to yield significant concessions might be preferable. The results also throw cold water on recent claims that inducements should be used more often in crisis situations.[8] Senders should consider other options before reaching for the bag of carrots.

This paper is divided into five sections. The next section examines why carrots are not a more common feature of world politics. It argues that high transaction costs prevent a genuine market for political concessions from developing. The third section of the paper considers how states choose among their policy options, and how states' expectations of future conflict affect those choices. Ironically, senders will prefer to sanction in cases where inducements have a better chance of success. The fourth section of the paper is a plausibility probe of the arguments developed here. It includes a statistical analysis of U.S. decisions to use carrots and sticks from 1950 to 1992, as well as a comparison of U.S. sanctions against South Korea in 1975 and inducements for North Korea in 1994 when both countries attempted to acquire nuclear weapons. The final section concludes.

WHEN ARE CARROTS FEASIBLE?

CARROTS HAVE been observed in international relations since the formation of the Delian League, and the anecdotal literature indicates that they have been used as a tool of statecraft ever since. Casual empiricism suggests, however, that at present the market for inducements in world

8. Leon V. Sigal, *Disarming Strangers: Nuclear Diplomacy with North Korea* (Princeton: Princeton University Press, 1998).

politics is remarkably thin. Klaus Knorr, writing in 1975, noted about inducements: "Surprisingly, the public record does not show this means... to have been practiced much in recent decades."[9] Unlike the frequent attempts to influence politicians at the domestic level, the market for purchasing influence in world politics remains underdeveloped. The question is, why? What prevents states from placing a well-defined price on all political assets? Why isn't there a more established international market for political concessions?

Transaction-cost economics provide several reasons for why markets fail to form, several of which apply to international relations.[10] For a market to exist, the costs of contracting between agents must be relatively small. If the costs of bargaining, monitoring, and implementing contracts between buyers and seller are too high, they can outweigh the utility derived from any exchange. Transactions costs are low when actions are both observable and enforceable. If contractual obligations are not directly observed, but rather outcomes related to those obligations are observed, the possibility of moral hazard arises. Agents can claim they have taken the agreed-upon action even if they have not, and attribute the absence of a desired outcome to other factors. A test-ban treaty, for example, is a contract signed by states pledging abstain from a specified action, the testing of nuclear weapons. The treaty is not perfectly monitored; nuclear tests are detected by observing seismic activity. This outcome (seismic activity) could be caused by an agent's actions (nuclear tests) or from some other form of activity (earthquake). Because actions are not perfectly observable, there is incentive for states to cheat. States could explode a nuclear device, and then claim that the outcome was caused by other factors, such as an earthquake.[11] When actions are not perfectly observable and verifiable, a receiver has the incentive to go back on a deal, and the sender will be tempted to cry foul even if the receiver honors a deal.

9. Klaus Knorr, *The Power of Nations: The Political Economy of International Relations* (New York: Basic Books, 1975), 163.

10. See Ronald Coase, *The Firm, the Market, and the Law* (Chicago: Chicago University Press, 1988); Oliver Williamson, *The Economic Institutions of Capitalism* (New York: Free Press, 1985), for introductions to transaction cost economics.

11. This is not a hypothetical example. In August 1997 the United States accused Russia of violating the comprehensive nuclear test-ban treaty after unusual seismic activity was detected in the Kara Sea. Despite angry Russian denials, the United States persisted in its claim for several months. The crisis was resolved only when outside experts, after examining the U.S. data, determined that a nuclear blast could not have caused the type of readings collected by the CIA. See R. Jeffrey Smith, "U.S. Formally Drops Claim of Possible Nuclear Blast," *Washington Post*, 4 November 1997, A2.

In some situations where carrots are considered, what the sender wants might not be under the full control of the receiving state. This could be due to domestic politics within the receiving country; some elements of a regime might be implacably opposed to the terms of any inducement and attempt to scuttle it. In other situations, the link between the agreed-upon action and the desired outcome might be more tenuous than the sender country perceives. In the Iran-Contra affair, the United States was offering carrots to Iranian moderates who claimed to have influence over Lebanese militias that held U.S. citizens. Since the link between the agreed-upon obligation (Iranian pressure on the militias to release the hostages) and the outcome (the actual release of the hostages) was not observable, the Iranians could always claim that they had honored the terms of the deal without too many hostages being released.[12] Without observable and verifiable actions, senders will be reluctant to proffer carrots, out of the fear that the receiver will exploit moral hazards.

Even if actions are perfectly observable, contracts must be enforceable. Unless exchanges are simultaneous, there is some juncture at which one side has what it wants and must decide whether to honor its part of the deal or act opportunistically and defect from the agreement. If one side in a transaction receives their desired ends before having to honor their part of the exchange, there is no incentive to honor an agreement in the immediate future. Consider the Framework Agreement between the United States and North Korea to eliminate the latter's nuclear weapons program. The key part of North Korea's concession, permitting inspections of all nuclear facilities to see if Pyongyang had attempted to manufacture nuclear weapons in the early 1990s, was delayed until the turn of the century. In the meantime, the country received fuel oil and Western investment for two civilian reactors. Having received significant benefits, there were indications in late 1998 that North Korea would renege on the agreement.[13]

Without some means of credible commitment, states always have the option of not honoring their agreements after payment has been delivered. It is often impossible to simultaneously exchange political assets such as territory, institutions, or weapons programs. Thus, senders proferring carrots must be wary of not receiving the demanded concession after making payment, ands receivers must be wary of making concessions before they have received the carrot. Since states can never fully trust each other is a world of anarchy, the problem of nonsimultaneous benefits, and the diffi-

12 See Theodore Draper, *A Very Thin Line: The Iran-Contra Affairs* (New York: Hill and Wang, 1991).
13 Robert Manning, "Time Bomb" *The New Republic*, 30 November 1998, 27–31.

culty of establishing credible commitments, prevents carrots from being more common.

In markets with a well-defined legal framework, contracts can be written to overcome problems of moral hazard and nonsimultaneous exchange. In an anarchic system, there is no legal recourse to force any country to honor the terms of such an agreement. The transaction costs posed by partially observable actions and unenforceable agreements prevent a full-fledged international market for political concessions from developing. This does not mean that the use of inducements never occurs. The prospect of mutually beneficial exchange still leads to some use of inducements in international affairs. Carrots are simply rarer than would be predicted in a world of perfectly observable and enforceable actions.

There are countervailing factors that can reduce the transaction costs of inducements and make their use more likely. Mechanisms for demonstrating credible commitments can reduce problems of moral hazard and opportunistic behavior. In a world of imperfect information, the best way to establish a credible commitment is to take positions that would lead to significant costs if the actor were to reverse its position. Game theory has demonstrated that in situations of imperfect information, the ability of actors to take potentially costly actions helps to separate actors capable of making credible commitments from those who cannot.[14] This point has also been made in the statecraft literature; David Baldwin notes in *Economic Statecraft*, "Other things being equal, it is always desirable to minimize costs; but other things are not equal. The selection of a costly method of conveying a signal may add credibility to the signal."[15] If a mechanism exists for actors to credibly commit, the transaction costs from nonsimultaneous exchange are significantly reduced.

The ability to provide verifiable information about actions and preferences also reduces the problem of moral hazard. If actions can be observed separate from outcomes then receivers have less of an incentive act opportunistically, and senders are thus more willing to offer an inducement in the first place. More information about actor preferences help reduce the transaction costs of bargaining in the first place. When there is more information about preferences and costs, bluffing, lowballing and other bar-

14. See Thomas Schelling, *The Strategy of Conflict* (Cambridge: Harvard University Press, 1960); A. Michael Spence, "Job Market Signaling," *Quarterly Journal of Economics* 87, no. 3 (August 1973).
    15. Baldwin, *Economic Statecraft*, 372.

gaining tactics are less useful. Game-theoretic models show that in a world of perfect information, bargains can be struck almost immediately.[16]

Transferring the lessons from the transaction cost literature to international relations, it becomes clear that carrots should be more likely and more successful between liberal democracies. Liberal democracies reduce the transaction costs of carrots in several ways. Democracies are more capable of making credible commitments than nondemocracies. This capability comes from two sources. First, democratic regimes face greater domestic audience costs from backing down from a commitment.[17] These costs could take the form of a drop in public or legislative support for a government, or more directly a leader's removal from office at the next election. This ability to generate political costs from breaking commitment makes it easier for democracies to make credible promises.

Another way that democratic regimes boost the ability to credibly commit is through the separation of powers. Democratic constitutions help to constrain foreign policy leaders from acting arbitrarily by granting powers to other branches of government. Ironically, constraints on a foreign policy leader's autonomy enhances that leader's ability to negotiate in good faith. Such constraints reduce the ability of states to act opportunistically after receiving the benefits from a political exchange. Governance structures that divide foreign policy powers provide a means of linking internal commitments that create the rule of law to the anarchic realm of the international system.[18] Historical studies of international finance reveal that national constitutions with well-defined separation of powers enabled states to acquire debt financing from international capital markets, because constraints on the head of state reduced the likelihood of government default.[19]

Overall, domestic audience costs and separation of powers enhance the ability of liberal democratic regimes to make credible commitments, reducing the transaction costs of exchange. This link between liberal democracies and credible commitments has found significant empirical support.

16. Ariel Rubinstein, "Perfect Equilibrium in a Bargaining Model," *Econometrica* 50, no. 1 (January 1982): 97–109.

17. James A. Fearon, "Domestic Political Audiences and the Escalation of International Disputes," *American Political Science Review* 88, no. 3 (September 1994): 577–92.

18. Peter Cowhey, "Domestic Institutions and the Credibility of International Commitments: Japan and the United States." *International Organization* 47 no. 2 (Spring 1993): 299–326.

19. Douglass North and Barry Weingast, "Constitutions and Commitment: The Evolution of Institutions Governing Public Choice in Seventeenth-Century England," *Journal of Economic History* 49, no. 4 (December 1989); François Velde and Thomas Sargent, "The Macroeconomic Causes and Consequences of the French Revolution," *Journal of Political Economy* 103 (1995).

Kurt Gaubatz has shown that between 1816 and 1965, democratic dyads were significantly more likely to honor their international obligations than nondemocratic or mixed dyads. Follow-up studies have confirmed Gaubatz's findings on the link between credible commitments and liberal democratic regimes.[20]

Finally, liberal democracies increase the amount of information about actors' preferences and actions. Most definitions of liberal democracy include the freedom of individuals to report on the government and to disseminate that information to all who wish to acquire it. This kind of information increases the transparency of state actions to the international system as well. Such transparency reduces the transaction costs of bargaining between democratic senders and receivers. It also enhances the effect of audience costs on credible commitment by permitting outsiders to gauge the magnitude of these costs.[21] Another way that democracies generate information is through the behavior of opposition parties. Opposition support of regime policies (or lack thereof) has been shown to convey crucial information about preferences and costs to other international actors. [22] Both means of providing information reduces the moral hazard problem that arises from unobservable actions.

These factors do not eliminate the transaction costs of carrots between democracies. In an anarchic world, even democratic governments can choose not to honor their commitments or conceal information from other countries. In general, however, the ability to make credible commitments and generate information about preferences allows democracies to reduce the transaction costs of international political exchange.

Thus, one would make two predictions about the relationship between regime type and the use of inducements. First, carrots are more likely to be proffered between democratic dyads than nondemocratic or mixed dyads. Reduced transaction costs between democracies makes senders more willing to consider inducements as an efficient way of obtaining political concessions. Democratic senders are also able to make their inducement offers more credible to receivers. Second, when carrots are proffered, they are more likely to succeed between democratic dyads than other types of dyads.

20. Kurt Taylor Gaubatz, "Democratic States and Commitment in International Relations," *International Organization* 50, no. 1 (winter 1996):109–39; William Reed, "Alliance Duration and Democracy: An Extension and Cross-Validation of 'Democratic States and Commitment in International Relations,'" *American Journal of Political Science* 41, no. 3 (July 1997),

21. Gaubatz, "Democratic States," 122.

22. Kenneth Schultz, "Domestic Opposition and Signaling in International Crises," *American Political Science Review* 92, no. 4 (December 1998):829–44.

The ability of democracies to make credible commitments reduces the likelihood of receivers acting opportunistically after receiving an inducement. Receiver suspicions of the sender backing down from its commitments are allayed if the sender is a democracy. Note that both these hypotheses apply to the dyadic level and not the monadic level. The problems of credible commitment and moral hazard are created if either side has less than perfect information about the other. Even if an authoritarian sender believes a democratic receiver will act in good faith, the reverse is not true. Between democratic dyads, carrots are more likely to be proffered, and they are more likely to succeed.

Another mechanism for reducing transaction costs between potential senders and receivers is the presence of international regimes. Neoliberal institutionalists have continually stressed that such regimes reduce transaction costs.[23] Regimes reduce transaction costs in three ways. First, they provide a routinized forum for negotiations. This reduces the costs of devising an agreement in the first place. Second, regimes lengthen the shadow of the future, which reduces the incentives to defect from agreed-upon contracts. The prospect of future exchanges can make actions enforceable, because of the ability of states to punish opportunistic actors with noncooperation in future rounds. Since reputation matters when there is repeated interaction, receivers that cheat will soon be unable to find a willing sender.[24] Third, international regimes increase the information available to all countries, either through active monitoring or acting as a clearing house for information collected by others. Historically, it has been shown that regimes that only provide information on compliance can encourage the rule of law, even if that entity lacks enforcement powers.[25]

International organizations can also generate information by converting a requested concession from an unobservable action to an observable commodity. Through the act of voting, international organizations provide a means for states to make transparent their preferences on an issue. Say, for example, that a sender is willing to use a carrot to ensure a receiver improves its relations with a third country. Without an international regime,

23. Robert Keohane, *After Hegemony* (Princeton: Princeton University Press, 1984), Robert Axelrod and Robert Keohane, "Achieving Cooperation under Anarchy: Strategies and Institutions," in *Cooperation Under Anarchy*, ed. Kenneth Oye (Princeton: Princeton University Press, 1986), 226–54.

24. David Kreps, "Corporate Culture and Economic Theory," in *Perspectives on Positive Political Economy*, ed. James Alt and Kenneth Shepsle (New York: Cambridge University Press, 1990), 90–143.

25. Paul Milgrom, Douglass North, and Barry Weingast, "The Role of Institutions in the Revival of Trade: The Law Merchant, Private Judges, and the Champagne Fairs," *Economics and Politics* 2, no. 1 (March 1990): 1–23.

the receiver might attempt to obfuscate the meaning of "improve". In an regime that requires states to vote their preferences, it becomes impossible for the receiving state to fudge the arrangement. Voting rights in international organizations can fuse actions and outcomes into a single commodity, eliminating the moral hazard problem.

The anecdotal literature on carrots shows that carrot are frequently associated with international regimes. As early as the mid-1700s, Great Britain bribed Saxony in order to buy the Saxon vote for a British electoral scheme in the Holy Roman Empire.[26] In this century, there are several examples of great powers using offers of aid to secure votes in international organizations. In 1961, the United States agreed to pay Haiti $5 million in airport facilities to secure its vote in the Organization of American States to expel Cuba from the organization. In the early 1980s, the United States made similar aid-for-vote deals with Argentina and Chile in the Inter-American Development Bank to deny Nicaragua access to credit. Great Britain agreed to contribute more to the European Community budget to acquire EC support for the Falklands War. The Soviets were very successful in the 1960s and '70s at using military aid and trade concessions to purchase UN General Assembly votes. In the lead-up to the Gulf War, the United States used inducements to persuade United Nations Security Council members to vote for the use of force; more recently, China has used offers of trade deals to persuade European countries not to vote against it in the UN Human Rights Commission.[27]

Carrots have also been observed in more arcane international regimes. The Montreal Protocol on the elimination of chloroflourocarbons explicitly includes funds for less-developed countries as a way of purchasing compliance with environmental regulations. Japan has increased its aid to Caribbean members of the International Whaling Commission in order to get enough votes to overturn the regime's ban on the hunting and killing of whales. One Caribbean diplomat defended the arrangement, stating, "Naturally we will discuss our needs with (the Japanese), and they will ask

26. George Liska, *The New Statecraft* (Chicago: University of Chicago Press, 1960), 53.

27. On Haiti, see Arthur Schlesinger, *A Thousand Days* (Cambridge: Houghton Mifflin, 1965), 782–83. On the early 1980s, see William Leogrande, "Making the Economy Scream: U.S. Economic Sanctions Against Sandanista Nicaragua," *Third World Quarterly* 17, no. 2 (March 1996): 329–48. On weapons proliferation from Eastern Europe, see Long, "Trade and Technology Incentives and Bilateral Cooperation." On the Falklands case, see Lisa Martin, *Coercive Cooperation* (Princeton: Princeton University Press, 1992), chap. 6. On the Soviet use of military aid, see Philip Roeder, "The Ties that Bind: Aid, Trade, and Political Compliance in Soviet-Third World Relations," *International Studies Quarterly* 29, no. 2 (June 1985): 191–216. On China's lobbying, see David Manasian, "The World is Watching: A Survey of Human Rights Law," *Economist*, 5 December 1998, 6.

us to support them in international organizations, as any other country would do."[28] While direct bribery of officials is illegal, it is an accepted practice to influence International Olympic Committee member votes about where to host the Olympics by pledging humanitarian aid to developing countries' athletic programs.[29] Cases of carrots being used to purchase concessions outside of an international organization framework are harder to find, however, and they have a more mixed record of success.[30]

The transaction costs of international political exchange prevent the use of economic inducements from being a more common occurrence. If states are unable to perfectly observe each others' actions, the prospect of moral hazard makes the use of carrots less likely and less successful when offered. The ability of states to act opportunistically, due to the absence of enforceable contracts, has the same effect. While transaction costs cannot be eliminated in an anarchic world, they can be reduced. Liberal democratic regimes can enable leaders to credibly commit and generate reliable information, reducing these transaction costs. International regimes can have the same effect, by routinizing bargaining procedures, extending the shadow of the future, and creating more reliable commodities in the form of votes.

WHEN ARE CARROTS PREFERABLE?

THE PREVIOUS section examined when carrots would be possible. In addition to carrots, however, states have other means of influence at their disposal, such as economic or military coercion. It is not enough to examine which variables make the use of carrots a feasible option; the context of alternative foreign policy options must be included to see whether the use of the carrot is the preferred option. The biggest criticism of the economic statecraft literature is that it fails to take into account how states choose among the range of policy alternatives.[31] This section analyzes how sender countries choose among their set of influence strategies: economic inducements, economic coercion, and military coercion.[32]

28. Mark Fineman, "Japan 'Buys' Pro-Whaling Votes with Caribbean Aid," *Denver Post*, 11 December 1997, 43A, 48A.

29. More recently, explicit bribes have also been observed. On the relationship between inducements and IOC votes, see Jere Longman, "Investigators Cite Cash Payments in Salt Lake City Bid for Olympics," *New York Times*, 8 January 1998, A1.

30. See Liska, *The New Statecraft*; and Cortright, *The Price of Peace*.

31. Baldwin, *Economic Statecraft*.

32. Two policy options will not be discussed: "doing nothing" and purely diplomatic efforts. Doing nothing is a viable policy option, but this has already been dealt with in the previous section, which asked whether proffering the carrot was preferable to the status quo.

A key difference between the carrot and the stick (be it economic or military) is that the stick is expensive when it fails, whereas the carrot is expensive when it succeeds. A successful threat of coercion is costless, because the receiver has acquiesced before the threat needs to be executed. A failed coercion attempt means that the receiver stands firm, and the sender incurs costs from implementing the threatened economic sanctions or military intervention. The reverse is true in the case of carrots. A successful inducement is costly but ensures that the sender will get the desired concession. A failed carrot is costless, although it forces the sender to contemplate its other alternatives. Thus, if both carrots and sticks are likely to succeed, senders will prefer sanctions over inducements, because the former are more cost-effective.

When is coercion is likely to succeed? The existing literature on economic statecraft does provide a guide as to when this condition will be met.[33] First, the demand must be specific and well defined. Second, the receiver must suffer greater opportunity costs of coercion than the sender, otherwise the threat of sanctions cannot be credible. Third, senders must anticipate enough conflicts in the future with the receiver to prefer incurring the costs of deadlock. When conflict expectations are high, senders are increasingly eager to sanction the receiver. The act of sanctioning can enhance a sender's reputation for tough bargaining, which can be useful in later conflicts. Any material concessions extracted from sanctions can also enhance the sender's bargaining position in the future. Heightened conflict expectations will increase the sender's concern about the material and reputational consequences of outcomes in the present. With adversaries, senders are willing to incur significant costs if sanctions hurt the receiver country even more.

The effect of conflict expectations, however, cuts both ways. The more conflicts that are anticipated, the less willing the receiver will be to concede to threats. Concessions can weaken a nation-state's material bargaining strength and its reputation. States will be concerned about the intrinsic value of the concession because of the possibility of today's concessions becoming tomorrow's leverage. A variety of demands could be used in this fashion. A sender may use economic coercion to secure military basing rights, and those bases are used in a later coercion episode to threaten the

---

The literature on purely diplomatic incentives and punishments is scant at best, but it does seem that this option is useful only for extremely minor affairs of state. See Joseph McKenna, *Diplomatic Protest in Foreign Policy* (Chicago: Loyola University Press, 1962).

33. The following is drawn from Daniel W. Drezner, *The Sanctions Paradox: Economic Statecraft and International Relations* (Cambridge: Cambridge University Press, 1999), chap. 2.

targeted country's territory. A demand for greater liberalization within the target regime might permit the sender country to exploit domestic divisions in a later dispute. Similarly, developing the reputation of conceding in the face of coercive pressure also will weaken one's bargaining position in future disputes. These concerns become more salient when more conflicts are expected in the future.

The effect of conflict expectations is paradoxical. With allies, senders have a higher threshhold to meet before coercion is an option, but once sanctions are threatened, they will lead to significant concessions. Receivers allied with the sender will care less about the long-run implications of acquiescing and more about the short-run costs and benefits of coercion. With adversaries, the reverse is true. Senders are more willing to threaten coercion, but are unlikely to extract any meaningful concessions. Indeed, conflict expectations lead to a paradox for the use of either incentives or sanctions. In the case of incentives, receivers will be the most eager to accept a carrot when they anticipate frequent conflicts with the sender, which is precisely the situation where senders are the most reluctant to proffer the carrot. When the sender and receiver anticipate frequent conflicts, they will be wary that any carrot proffered will strengthen the adversary in a future dispute. Before the First World War, for example, France refused to loan money to Germany for fear of strengthening its capabilities; Great Britain did not loan money to Russia because it did not want to strengthen Moscow's capabilities in imperial disputes.[34] In the late 1980s, U.S. policymakers did not extend large amounts of aid to Mikhail Gorbachev's regime in the Soviet Union in return for continued Soviet cooperation. The United States feared that this would allow the USSR to continue to subsidize regimes unfriendly to the United States, such as those in Cuba or Nicaragua. Another concern was that the money would lead to a Soviet economic turnaround, sparking a renewed cold war.[35] Thus, senders will prefer to use sanctions over inducements against adversaries because they anticipate frequent conflicts, but those expectations also make sanctions less effective and inducements more so.

Analyzing the choice between carrots and sticks at the decision-theoretic level further refines the conditions under which a carrot will be observed in international interactions. The sender's policy decision is dependent upon the expectations of future conflict. With adversaries, a sender will not proffer the carrot as its first policy option. It will resort to the carrot only after a

34. Liska, *The New Statecraft*, 49–50.

35. Michael Beschloss and Strobe Talbott, *At The Highest Levels* (New York: Little, Brown, 1993), 210–11, 377.

coercion attempt. This is true for two reasons. With adversaries, senders will be willing to absorb significant costs in order to coerce the receiver into conceding. Even if these expectations also reduce the likelihood that the receiver will make any substantial concessions, the sender will often prefer a stalemate.[36] In addition, threats or sanctions can blunt reputational implications of later offering a carrot. The threat of economic or military coercion can bolster a state's reputation as a tough bargainer. This reputation is further enhanced if economic sanctions are actually implemented. Sanctions also have the added benefit of reducing the receiver state's resources, making the postsanctions carrot a more palatable transfer.

With allies, the sender must look at the opportunity costs of coercion to see if coercion is a viable strategy. Because few conflicts are anticipated for the future, the sender will focus more on the immediate payoffs from its actions. With a coercive strategy, the sender must determine if the potential costs from coercion are small enough for it to be a credible threat to the receiver. If that criterion is met, the sender will prefer a coercive strategy; the successful coercion of allies is both costless and generates many concessions. If, for example, the sender had previously agreed to send foreign aid to the receiver, then the threat of an aid cutoff would not cost the sender anything, and generate significant concessions. If, however, that criterion is not met, then the sender will attempt to use the carrot. With reduced conflict expectations, the material or reputation effects are minor, paving the way for a carrot that enhances the utility of both the sender and receiver.

Once other policy options are included in the decision to proffer a carrot, there is a certain symmetry to great power decision making. With allies, if the great power has already extended aid or trade concessions to the receiver, it will first use economic coercion to extract the necessary concessions. Only if coercion is not a feasible option would a carrot be considered. With adversaries, the great power's first instinct is to use coercion, but due to heightened conflict expectations, sanctions are not likely to succeed. At that juncture, the sender must then choose between a carrot or stalemate. One could argue that the only difference between dealing with allies and adversaries is the sequencing of actions. With allies, the rewards are put in place first, and then used as leverage when a conflict arises. With adversaries, the conflict first arises, and if coercion fails, the sender then proffers the carrot. If force is not used, then regardless of the prior relationship, the

---

36. Drezner, *The Sanctions Paradox*, chap. 2.

outcome is the same; the receiver gets a reward, and the sender gets a concession. The only difference is the timing of the carrot and the stick.

States do not choose the carrot in a policy vacuum. Even if the carrot is a feasible option, they will opt for other forms of statecraft if they derive more utility from those options. Thus even if the transaction costs for carrots are minimal, sanctions could be preferred for several reasons. When conflict expectations are high, senders will prefer to sanction in order to improve its bargaining position in future conflicts, even though sanctions will not yield significant concessions. When conflict expectations are low, sanctions will still be preferred if the sender incurs minimal costs while imposing significant costs on the receiver. This is because sanctions against allies can yield significant concessions and are cheaper than carrots. Over time, senders will consider using inducements with adversaries only after sanctioning them; with allies, sanctions will often be imposed because of the use of a previous inducement.

From the previous two sections, one can derive the following testable hypotheses:

Hypothesis 1: Carrots are more likely to be observed between democratic dyads.

Hypothesis 2: Carrots are more likely to succeed between democratic dyads.

Hypothesis 3: Carrots are more likely to be observed within the framework of an international regime.

Hypothesis 4: Carrots are more likely to succeed within the framework of an international regime.

Hypothesis 5: Senders will proffer a carrot to an adversary only after they have threatened economic or military coercion first.

Hypothesis 6: Senders will coerce allies that have already received carrots related to the disputed issue.

PLAUSIBILITY PROBE

THE VARIOUS anecdotes in the previous sections suggest the existence of cases that support the theory developed here. Space constraints and limitations on data availability prevent a thorough statistical testing of all these hypotheses. Instead, this section offers a plausibility probe of some of these hypotheses. The results of the tests in this section can, at the very least, suggest that the theory developed here is worthy of further testing. The first part of this section uses chi-square tests to examine the effect of democratic regimes on the initiation and success of economic inducements. The second part of this section compares U.S. nonproliferation policy toward North Korea and South Korea to examine the sequencing of carrots and sticks.

To test for the effect of democracy on the use and success of inducements, I will use John Sislin's data set on American influence attempts from 1950 to 1992.[37] Sislin codes 191 attempts by the United States to use economic and military aid as a way to obtain concessions from other countries. These cases include episodes where the United States offered aid in exchange for a concession (a carrot) or cases where transfers were cut off unless the receiver acquiesced (a stick). The data set codes whether the United States used a threat of coercion or a promise of aid, and whether the influence attempt was successful. To my knowledge, this is the only data set that includes a substantial number of well-defined attempts to use inducements to extract concessions. Data on democratic regimes comes from Michael Doyle's well-known coding of regime types.[38]

Because transaction costs are expected to be lower between democratic regimes, the inducement option is predicted to be more attractive for the United States if the receiver is a democracy. Statistically, the United States should be more likely to offer carrots to other democracies than other regime types. The reduction in transaction costs also means that inducements offered to democracies should succeed more often than offers made to nondemocracies. If the transaction costs hypothesis is erroneous, there should be no correlation between the receiver's regime type and the decisions to use or accept the carrot.

The statistical results support the hypotheses about democratic regimes and the utility of inducements. Table 1 shows a tabular comparison of the receiver's regime type and the decision by the sender to proffer a carrot. The table shows that the United States was more than twice as likely to offer a carrot to a democratic receiver (58.8 percent) than a nondemocratic receiver (27.1 percent). The carrot was a more common option with democratic regimes than other types of regimes. Chi-square tests show this result to be statistically significant at the one percent level. To test for robustness, a multivariate logit regression was run to include control variables such as

37. John Sislin, "Arms as Influence: The Elusive Link Between Military Assistance and Political Compliance" (Ph.D. diss., Indiana University, September 1993); Sislin, "Arms as Influence: The Determinants of Successful Influence," *Journal of Conflict Resolution* 38, no. 4 (December 1994): 665–89.
38. Michael Doyle, "Liberalism and World Politics," *American Political Science Review* 80, no. 4 (December 1986): 1151–69; for cases between 1986 and 1992, I used Francis Fukuyama, *The End of History and the Last Man* (New York: Free Press, 1992), 49–50.

relative power, the receiver's perception of its security, declining U.S. hegemony, and the magnitude of the demand. The receiver's regime type remained positively correlated with the decision to proffer a carrot and statistically significant at the one percent level. The effect of the receiver's regime type on the likelihood of a carrot being proffered is consistent with the explanation developed here, statistically significant, and robust to the presence of control variables.

Table 1

REGIME TYPE AND THE DECISION TO USE A CARROT

	Coercion attempt	Inducement attempt	Total
Receiver is not a democracy	102	38	140
Receiver is a democracy	21	30	51
Total	123	68	191

Pearson chi-square	16.34	$P < 0.000$
Likelihood-ratio	15.90	$P < 0.000$
Gamma	0.586	

The statistical test for the second hypothesis, that carrots are more likely to succeed between democratic dyads, is shown in Table 2. This table looks only at the subset of cases where the United States offered an inducement in exchange for a political concession. Table 2 shows a tabular comparison of the receiver's regime type and whether the inducement offer was deemed successful or not. The results support the transaction cost approach. The failure rate for inducements with nondemocratic receivers (34.2 percent) is almost three times as high as the failure rate for democratic receivers (13.3 percent). The carrot was more successful between democratic dyads than mixed dyads. Chi-square tests show this result to be statistically significant at the five percent level. As with the first hypothesis, this result was checked for robustness by running a multivariate logit regression using the same set of control variables. The receiver's regime type remained positively correlated with the success of an inducement offer, and statistically significant at the five percent level. Thus, between democratic dyads, carrots are more likely to be proffered and, once proffered, more likely to be accepted.

Table 2

REGIME TYPE AND THE SUCCESS OF USING A CARROT

	Unsuccessful Inducement Attempt	Successful Inducement Attempt	Total
Receiver is not a democracy	13	25	38
Receiver is a democracy	4	26	30
Total	17	51	68

Pearson chi-square	3.897	P < 0.048
Likelihood-ratio	4.093	P < 0.043
Gamma	0.543	

To examine the relationship between conflict expectations, economic coercion, and the decision to use carrots, I now compare U.S. nonproliferation policies toward South Korea in the 1970s with U.S. policy toward North Korea in the 1990s. The previous section argued that due to conflict expectations one should observe senders using carrots with adversaries only after attempts at coercion. With allies, senders will choose to sanction if they have sufficient leverage, and that leverage emanates from preexisting flows of inducements. South Korea was a close ally and North Korea a bitter adversary of the United States. Therefore, one would expect to see the use of coercion against of South Korea, made possible by previous carrots; with North Korea, one would expect to see the immediate threat of sanctions, followed by an inducement offer due to the failure of sanctions to work.[39]

In early 1975 the U.S. intelligence community detected active efforts by the Republic of Korea (ROK) to acquire the necessary components to manufacture nuclear weapons. These components include a cadre of

39. For a much more comprehensive comparison of these cases, see Drezner, *The Sanctions Paradox*, chap. 8.

trained personnel, a delivery mechanism for the weapons, and a means to manufacture fissile material. South Korea wanted to purchase a plant to reprocess spent nuclear fuel into fissile urainium. One arms control analyst noted: "The reprocessing plant potentially would have given them fissionable material for weapons, but it was practically the last thing on the list of things they needed, from special machine tools to the nonnuclear component of weapons."[40]

The ROK had decided to start a nuclear weapons program following the articulation of the Nixon Doctrine, which required U.S. allies to shoulder more of their security burdens. To apply the doctrine to Korea, President Nixon had proposed in 1970 to withdraw a third of the troops—one division—from South Korean soil. The ROK reaction had been far from sanguine. The prime minister had threatened to resign, explaining, "We are not against the Nixon Doctrine in principle, but if North Korean Kim Il Sung miscalculates, the South Korean people will wonder if America will abandon its security treaty or come to our defense."[41] Over the next five years, the United States had refused to react to various acts of aggression by the North Korean regime. By 1975, Saigon had fallen and the United States was withdrawing from its bases in Thailand. The ROK desire for a credible deterrent had increased.

Starting in the summer of 1975, the United States entered into negotiations with South Korea to convince them to drop their nuclear weapons program. Six months later, in January 1976, the United States announced that Seoul had cancelled the purchase of the key components for a nuclear fuel cycle.[42] The available evidence strongly suggests that the South Koreans acquiesced due to economic coercion from the United States. In December 1975, the U.S. ambassador to South Korea cabled his superiors that he asked a senior ROK official, "whether Korea (is) prepared (to) jeapordize availability of best technology and largest financing capability which only the United States could offer, as well as vital partnership with the United States, not only in nuclear and scientific areas but in broad political and security areas."[43] Multiple press reports about the January 1976 reversal quoted anonymous officials as saying that if the South Koreans had not

40. Quoted in Robert Gillette, "U.S. Squelched Apparent South Korea A-Bomb Drive," *Los Angeles Times*, 4 November 1978, 1.

41. Quoted in Kwang-Il Back, *Korea and the United States* (Seoul: Research Center for Peace and Unification of Korea, 1988), 123.

42. Don Oberdorfer, "South Korea Cancels A-Plant." *Washington Post*, 30 January 1976, A1.

43. Quoted in Don Oberdorfer, *The Two Koreas: A Contemporary History* (Reading, Mass.: Addison-Wesley, 1997), 72.

acquiesced, the United States would have halted loans worth $275 million and loan guarantees worth $227 million from the U.S. Export-Import Bank. Washington also made it clear that it would withhold export licenses and block the South Korean purchase of a nuclear reactor from Westinghouse. In addition, the United States persuaded the Canadians to suspend their own reactor deal with Seoul unless the reprocessing plant was canceled.[44] Other U.S. officials stated that negotiators also threatened the South Koreans with stopping $275 million annually in U.S. military aid if the reprocessing plant went ahead as scheduled.[45]

The choice of coercion was not the only one available to the United States in this dispute. Indeed, South Korea strongly hinted that they were prepared to accept a carrot in exchange for abandoning their nuclear weapons effort. In December 1975, while the two countries were in negotiations, the South Koreans requested $1.5 billion in loans from the U.S. government for a new Force Improvement Program that would bolster their conventional military forces.[46] A key element of the ROK aid request was to have the ability to coproduce the M-60 tank as well as fighter and interceptor aircraft. The United States could have decided to use the aid request as a carrot to encourage ROK concessions. The conventional wisdom would expect this, since South Korea was such a close ally.[47]

The record shows the United States opted for the stick rather than the requested carrot. The Ford administration refused the December aid request, fearing it would destabilize the balance of power in the region. It also refused to sell F-16 aircraft and advanced rocket technology.[48] After 1975, U.S. military aid to South Korea never reached the levels of the early seventies.[49] Indeed, less than a week before South Korea's decision to acquiesce, President Ford announced an end to all free military assistance to South

---

44. On the reports of economic coercion, see David Burnham, "South Korea Drops Plan to Buy A Nuclear Plant From France," *New York Times*, 29 January 1976, A1; Oberdorfer, "South Korea Cancels A-Plant"; "Seoul Officials Say Strong Pressure Forced Cancellation of Plans to Purchase a French Nuclear Plant," *New York Times*, 1 February 1976, 11; Gillette, "U.S. Squelched Apparent South Korea A-Bomb Drive." On the amounts of U.S. aid to South Korea, see Clarence Long, "Nuclear Proliferation: Can Congress Act in Time?" *International Security* 1, no. 4 (January 1977): 56–57.

45. Leslie H. Gelb, "Nuclear Proliferation and the Sale of Arms," *New York Times*, 11 August 1976, 3; Gelb, "Conflict Continues over U.S. Effort to Halt Spread of Nuclear Weapons," *New York Times*, 24 August 1976, 4.

46. Don Oberdorfer, "Korea Asks $1.5 Billion in U.S. Loans for Arms," *Washington Post*, 29 December 1975, A2.

47. Virginia Foran and Leonard Spector, "The Application of Incentives to Nuclear Proliferation," in Cortright, *The Price of Peace*, 21–54.

48. See Back, *Korea and the United States*, 176–80; and Oberdorfer, "Korea Asks $1.5 Billion in Loans for Arms."

49. Drezner, *The Sanctions Paradox*, 275.

Korea, replacing it with loans.[50] The grant aid was never reestablished. Furthermore, American and Korean recollections of the negotiations do not jibe with the offer of any inducements. The South Koreans talked of "pressures bordering on threats" when discussing the incident. A State Department official described the U.S. bargaining strategy as follows: "We simply made the negative clear to them, that if they went forward with the reprocessing plant, Congress would insist on the termination of further military credit sales. And they understood this."[51]

There are three reasons why the United States rejected the carrot and opted for sanctions, all consistent with the theory of inducements developed here. First, one could argue that previous carrots to the South Korean regime had failed to prevent Seoul from trying to acquire nuclear weapons. When the original U.S. troop withdrawals were announced in 1970, the Nixon administration was concerned with assuaging Korean fears of abandonment. One of the ways the United States sought to allay these fears was through increased inducements. In 1971 both countries agreed that the redeployment of U.S. forces would be tied to an increased American appropriation of $1.5 billion in military aid to South Korea over the next five years. Despite this significant increase in U.S. aid, the South Korean regime, led by Park Chung Hee, still went forward with its nuclear weapons program. An additional carrot would have rewarded Park's decision to pursue a covert weapons program in spite of increased U.S. aid.

Second, the existing inducement flows to South Korea made the threat of coercion a credible and potent one for the United States. In addition to military aid, the United States had assisted South Korea in its attempt to diversify its energy needs away from oil. As early as 1967, the ROK government had expressed concern about its reliance upon energy imports. The 1973 energy shock, for example, had lowered ROK reserves to just two weeks of oil.[52] In that year South Korea relied on imports for more than half of its energy demands. By the mid-1970s, Seoul had an ambitious plan to switch their primary source of energy away from Middle East oil to nuclear power; by 2000, Seoul had hoped to rely on nuclear power for more than sixty percent of its electricity needs.[53] In support of the ROK project,

50. "Ford Plans to Cut Military Aid Grants," *New York Times*, 21 January 1976, 29.

51. Gelb, "Nuclear Proliferation and the Sale of Arms." On the South Korean reaction, see "Seoul Officials Say Strong Pressure Forced Cancellation of Plans to Purchase a French Nuclear Plant."

52. Mitchell Reiss, *Without the Bomb: the Politics of Nuclear Proliferation* (New York: Columbia University Press, 1988), 89.

53. Young-Sun Ha, "Republic of (South) Korea," in *Nuclear Power in Developing Countries*, ed. James Katz and Onkar Marwah (Toronto: Lexington Books, 1982), 235.

and as a form of export promotion, the United States had provided more than half a billion dollars in loans and loan guarantees for nuclear power projects.

Combined, the preexisting military and nuclear carrots made coercion a credible option. South Korea's immediate costs of sanctions would have been the disruption of the loans and loan guarantees. This was the equivalent of 3.4 percent of its gross national product in 1975, a considerable sum compared with other sanctions attempts. This understates the true cost of the sanctions, however. Because the United States had such a monopoly position in nuclear power in the 1970s, South Korea would have faced much higher costs to implement its energy diversification program without U.S. cooperation. The threat to suspend all trade in nuclear materials would have completely devastated ROK plans for energy autonomy. Because of previous carrots, the United States held significant economic leverage over South Korea.

Finally, because conflict expectations between the two countries were so minimal, the threat of sanctions could produce significant concessions. The Park regime perceived no threat from the United States. In 1975 the Korean foreign minister described the 1954 Mutual Security Treaty as the "mainstay of the Republic of Korea's security," and stated, "The most important and effective deterrent against any possible recurrence of major conflict on the Korean Peninsula is the firm commitment of the United States to the security of South Korea."[54] After the coercion event, Seoul was unwilling to comment publicly about U.S. pressure for fear of disrupting the alliance. The Koreans were concerned about the extent of the U.S. commitment, but at no time were they concerned that the United States would repeatedly coerce them in the future. Of the five states with interests in the region (the United States, the Soviet Union, China, Japan, North Korea) the United States represented the lowest perceived threat to ROK security in 1975. With such minimal conflict expectations, South Korea was more concerned with the immediate costs of sanctions than with the long-term material or reputational implications of acquiescing. Minimal conflict expectations, combined with the significant cost of sanctions created from previous inducements, made coercion the most attractive option to the United States. Consistent with the theory developed here, the sender chose to coerce its ally because that option was both feasible and preferable.

54. Quoted in Se-Jin Kim, ed., *Documents on Korean-American Relations, 1943–1976* (Seoul: Recearch Center for Peace and Unification, 1976), 19.

U.S. policy toward the Democratic People's Republic of North Korea (DPRK) in the 1990s contrasts sharply with its approach toward South Korea in the 1970s. The DPRK effort to develop nuclear weapons went into high gear following a series of diplomatic and economic reversals in the early 1990s. In 1990, the Soviet Union recognized South Korea over Pyongyang's vociferous objections. At the same time, China and the Soviet Union decided to stop trading with the DPRK on concessionary terms and insist on hard-currency payments. Most outside observers anticipated that North Korea would go the way of East Germany and be absorbed into the more populous and dynamic South Korea.

As its security grew ever more precarious, North Korea accelerated its nuclear program. In 1993, International Atomic Energy Agency (IAEA) officials, acting on information provided by U.S. intelligence, requested to inspect facilities suspected of producing plutonium. The North Koreans refused, and shocked everyone by announcing in March 1993 that it would withdraw from the Nuclear Non-Proliferation Treaty (NPT) in three months. Over the next eighteen months, Pyongyang repeatedly signaled to the United States that it would be willing to accept a "package deal" of inducements. In return for staying in the NPT and dismantling its nuclear weapons program, North Korea would require significant carrots, including Western investment into light-water nuclear reactors and increased trade with the United States.[55]

Given the extremely high expectations of future conflict shared by North Korea and the United States, the theory of inducements developed here would predict the United States would attempt to sanction first, and only offer inducements if the coercion attempt failed. This essentially describes the negotiations that occurred between March 1993 and October 1994. The immediate U.S. response to North Korea's threat to withdraw from the NPT was to threaten economic coercion. Just after the DPRK announcement, U.S. secretary of state Warren Christopher was quoted in the press as stating that sanctions would be the result if North Korea continued on its present path.[56] This was a bold statement, since the United States had no trade or aid to suspend with the DPRK. North Korea had been the target of comprehensive U.S. sanctions since the Korean War. If economic coercion was to be effective, the United States needed international cooperation. While

---

55. See Michael Mazarr, *North Korea and the Bomb: A Case Study in Nonproliferation* (New York: St. Martin's, 1995); Oberdorfer, *The Two Koreas*; Scott Snyder, "North Korea's Nuclear Program: The Role of Incentives in Preventing Deadly Conflict," in Cortright, *The Price of Peace*, 55–82; and Sigal, *Disarming Strangers*.

56. See Mazarr, *North Korea and the Bomb*, 111.

China, Russia, Japan, and South Korea all preferred the North Koreans not to have nuclear weapons, they also preferred an attempt at negotiations rather than an immediate rush to sanctions. After consultations with Seoul and Tokyo, the Clinton administration agreed to direct talks with the North Koreans to resolve the impasse. One U.S. official noted, "To some extent the diplomatic effort was forced on us by tactical considerations. The only way we could build a consensus at the U.N. Security Council to impose sanctions was to demonstrate that the North Koreans were unwilling to make a deal."[57]

The next year of negotiations played out in a manner consistent with an American preference for sanctions. Washington's strategy during the first round of negotiations, according to a State Department official, was one of, "showing the sticks first, and holding the carrots in reserve...the carrots were in a basket, and the basket was kept squarely on the floor behind him."[58] Most of these carrots, furthermore, were nothing new. They consisted mostly of promises not to attack North Korea, which had been made previously by the Bush administration. Throughout the negotiations, the United States retained a belligerent tone. On a visit to Seoul in July 1993, President Clinton warned Pyongyang that if North Korea developed nuclear weapons, "it would be the end of their country." Other U.S. officials made similar noises throughout the summer. In October, Defense Secretary Les Aspin told Japanese officials that negotiations would likely fail, and the result would be a sanctions attempt.[59] In June 1994, negotiations appeared to break down, and North Korea withdrew from the IAEA. In response, the United States, South Korea, and Japan issued a joint pledge to impose economic sanctions, and the United States redoubled its efforts to persuade the United Nations Security Council to mandate economic sanctions. Washington also dispatched more warships to the North Pacific in order to enforce a naval embargo.

Sanctions, even if they had been imposed by Japan and South Korea alone, would have imposed significant costs on North Korea. Pyongyang relied on transfers from ethnic Koreans living in Japan as a source for hard currency. These flows were estimated at somewhere between $600 million and $1.8 billion annually. The Japanese also represent North Korea's largest hard-currency export market; for example, ten percent of Japanese business

57. Quoted in Sigal, *Disarming Strangers*, 59.

58. Quoted in Snyder, "North Korea's Nuclear Program," 62.

59. Byung Chul Koh, "Confrontation and Cooperation on the Nuclear Peninsula," *Korean Journal of Defense Analysis* 6 (1994): 53–83. See also Mazarr, *North Korea and the Bomb*, 126–27.

suits are stitched in the DPRK.[60] By 1994, South Korea was also a significant export market. Roughly $200 million worth of goods were shipped to the ROK, making it Pyongyang's fourth largest trading partner. Sanctions would have disrupted this exchange. A naval embargo would have also frustrated North Korea's oil-for-arms trade with Iran and Libya. By the mid-1990s the DPRK military was selling roughly $500 million in ballistic missile technology to Middle Eastern customers.[61] Applying the most conservative estimate to Japanese transfers and exports, sanctions applied by Japan alone would have been the equivalent of 3.6 percent of North Korea's GDP. Adding in exports to South Korea, the figure jumps to 4.5 percent; a cutoff of the missile sales would have increased the amount to almost seven percent. The impact of sanctions against North Korea in 1994 would have been greater than South Korea's estimated costs of coercion in 1975. Furthermore, because of the peculiar nature of North Korea's economy, these sanctions would have hurt the DPRK elite much more than the average North Korean citizen.[62]

North Korea refused to acquiesce in the face of this pressure, however, because of its expectations of future conflict with the United States and South Korea. Evaluating the dispute, Paul Bracken noted:

> there are two "games" being played on the Korean peninsula. The first game is non-zero sum in character. It amounts to bargaining around a military and nuclear negotiation where the gains of one side do not necessarily come at the expense of the other. The second, and more important game, is zero sum. It is a game of control, and only one state can gain control of the entire Korean peninsula....it is the state-survival competition, rather than the one concerning nonproliferation and arms control, that shapes the dynamics of interstate relations among all affected parties....
>
> the immediate threat to North Korea is...strategic isolation leading to greater economic isolation, and opportunities for international intervention in Korean affairs. This is what is now happening, most notably with the pressure on the North to open suspect nuclear facilities to inspec-

60. For more on the Cho'chong'ryun, see Jennifer Lind, "Gambling with Globalism: Japanese Financial Flows to North Korea and the Sanctions Policy Option," *Pacific Review* 10, no. 3 (fall 1997): 391–406; "Kim Il Sung's Money Pipeline," *Time*, 13 June 1994, 27; and David E. Sanger, "North Koreans in Japan are Seen as Cash Source for Nuclear Arms," *New York Times*, 1 November 1993, 1.
61. Mitchell Reiss, *Bridled Ambition: Why Countries Constrain Their Nuclear Capabilities* (Washington: Woodrow Wilson Center Press, 1995), 232–33.
62. Vasily Mikheev "Reforms of the North Korean Economy: Requirements, Plans and Hopes," *Korean Journal of Defense Analysis* 5 (March 1993): 81–95.

tion by the IAEA. But such demands must surely be seen as only the first moves to open up the entire North Korean state.[63]

North Korea's specific concerns were that permitting inspections would give the United States valuable information about North Korea's defenses.[64] Such concerns were not just the product of North Korean paranoia. During its existence, North Korea had been the subject of no less than seven nuclear threats from the United States. In late 1991, as the crisis was heating up, JCS chairman Colin Powell told reporters about North Korea, "If they missed Desert Storm, this is a chance to catch a re-run." During a January 1992 trip to the DMZ, Bush administration officials told reporters that to answer the nuclear question, they would need a "mandate to roam North Korea's heavily guarded military sites."[65] Revelations that the United States used intelligence gathered from UNSCOM inspections of Iraqi facilities in planning Operation Desert Fox make North Korean suspicions quite plausible.[66] Because it was concerned about the material consequences of acquiescing to an adversary, North Korea preferred to stand firm in the face of both economic and military coercion.[67]

With conflict expectations preventing coercion from generating significant concessions, and after a year and a half of repeated threats to sanction, the Clinton administration finally opted for the carrot instead. In October 1994 the United States and North Korea signed a Framework Agreement. North Korea agreed to dismantle its gas-graphite nuclear reactors and submit to full IAEA inspections in exchange for a U.S. commitment to build two light-water nuclear reactors, supply Pyongyang with fuel oil while the reactors were built, and lift diplomatic and economic barriers to exchange. The cost of the carrots was estimated to be $5 billion, by far the largest foreign investment in North Korea's history.[68] Averaged out over the

63. Paul Bracken, "The North Korean Nuclear Program as a Problem of State Survival," in *Asian Flashpoint: Security and the Korean Peninsula*, ed. Andrew Mack (Canberra: Allen and Unwin, 1990), 86, 91.

64. "Nude, Absolutely Naked," *Far Eastern Economic Review*, 23 June 1994, 15.

65. Powell quoted in Sigal, *Disarming Strangers*, 31. Bush officials quoted in Bruce Cumings, *Korea's Place in the Sun: A Modern History* (New York: Norton, 1997), 469. On U.S. nuclear threats against North Korea, see Cumings, *Korea's Place in the Sun*, 450–70.

66. Tim Weiner, "U.S. Spied on Iraq under U.N. Cover, Officials Now Say," *New York Times*, 7 January 1999, 1.

67. There are indications that North Korea was prepared to make some concessions in the face of sanctions, but that the United States needed total acquiescence because of concerns about renewing the NPT in 1995. See Drezner, *The Sanctions Paradox*, chap. 8.

68. U.S. Senate, Committee on Armed Services (94th Congress, 1st session), *The Security Implications of the Nuclear Non-Proliferation Agreement with North Korea* (Washington: U.S. Government Printing Office, 1995), 18. Japan and South Korea agreed to finance significant portions of the reactor construction.

agreement's eight years, the deal injected capital investment equal to 2.8 percent of the gross domestic product of DPRK. The electrical power from the reactors had the potential to boost electrical output by 27.4 percent.[69]

U.S. defense secretary William Perry explanation of the administration's decision-making calculus fits very well with the theory of inducements presented here:

> While the United States and the international community were prepared to resort to sanctions if all other diplomatic remedies had failed, the outcome of a sanctions regime would have been highly unpredictable. Certainly, sanctions would have heightened tensions on the peninsula and would have obligated the United States and South Korea to take measures to prepare for military hostilities, especially in light of North Korean assertions that sanctions were tantamount to war.
>
> In general, our past experience shows that the North does not usually respond well to such blunt applications of pressure and, given the North's need to nurture its national pride, it is unlikely that the North would have acquiesced to U.S. demands after sanctions had been imposed.[70]

For the United States, the costs of implementing economic or military sanctions would have been considerable. North Korea had repeatedly stated that sanctions would be equivalent to war. The commander of U.S. forces in Korea estimated that a ground war would have cost over $1 trillion to all combatants; U.S. damages were estimated at $100 billion, with 80–100,000 U.S. soldiers dead. Plus, even if the United States was capable of defeating the North Korean regime, it would have been more costly to the United States than the DPRK. Washington would have had to bankroll some of the damage suffered by Seoul, as well as some of the costs of reunification. In a war, North Korea's costs would have eventually boomeranged back into the lap of South Korea and the United States.[71]

With no other feasible options available, the United States opted for the carrot, despite the high expectations of future conflict with North Korea. Policymakers in and out of the Clinton administration viewed the carrot as a second-best option that was preferable to war. As predicted by the transaction costs hypothesis in the case of mixed dyads, however, both sides have engaged in opportunistic behavior. Since the framework agreement

69. Council on Foreign Relations, *Success or Sellout? The U.S.-North Korean Nuclear Accord* (New York: Council on Foreign Relations, 1995), 7.

70. U.S. Senate, *Security Implications*, 94.

71. See John Burton, "Seoul on Hook of Unattractive Options," *Financial Times*, 6 June 1994, 6.

wassigned, the United States has held back agreed-upon shipments of fuel oil and refused to lift trade barriers with Pyongyang. North Korea, in response, has threatened to restart its nuclear weapons program.[72] The success of the inducement in this case is still an open question.

Like any plausibility probe, the empirical results are tentative. Data and space constraints prevent any testing of whether international regimes help to make inducements a more attractive policy option. Nevertheless, the results presented in this section are encouraging. Both the statistical results and the case studies support the theory of inducements developed here. Because of reduced transaction costs, carrots are more likely to be proffered and accepted between democratic dyads. Conflict expectations affect the sequencing of carrots and sticks. With allies, senders are likely to coerce receivers because they can use preexisting inducement flows as levers. With adversaries, senders will prefer to sanction first, because of the elevated expectations of future conflict. Because these expectations also sharply limit the concessions that could be extracted from a receiver, a sender will often choose to use inducements after coercion has failed.

CARROTS, STICKS, AND THE DEMOCRATIC PEACE

THIS ESSAY generates two reasons why carrots are not more common in international relations. First, there are situations where carrots are not a feasible option. The high transaction costs of trading political favors at the international level make the market for carrots remarkably thin. These transaction costs are even greater if the either the sender or the receiver is not a democracy, or if the carrot is proffered outside the framework of an international regime. Second, even if the carrot is a feasible option, there are still several roadblocks before a carrot is proffered and accepted. If conflict expectations are high, coercion is the preferred strategy. If conflict expectations are low, senders will still prefer to coerce if that option is feasible. These conditions severely circumscribe the possibilities of a successful carrot.

Despite these restrictions, it is possible to predict the use, success and sequencing of carrots. They are likely to be proffered if the sender and receiver are both democracies, because democratic regimes possess certain features that reduce the transactions costs of exchange. Inducements

---

72. Manning, "Time Bomb"; Philip Shenon, "North Korean Nuclear Arms Pact Reported Near Breakdown," *New York Times*, 6 December 1998, 16.

should be more common and more successful within the context of international regimes, because regimes also help to reduce transactions costs. Between allies, carrots should be observed, but just as often senders will use preexisting inducement flows as a means of coercion. Between adversaries, senders will prefer to sanction, and only turn to inducements as a second-best option. A plausibility probe of U.S. arms and aid transfers provides some initial support for this theory, as do case studies of U.S. nonproliferation policy toward North and South Korea.

The theoretical and empirical results have several implications. The theory of carrots developed here suggests why nation-states continue to employ economic or military coercion despite persistent doubts about its utility as a form of statecraft.[73] As David Baldwin has observed, influence strategies can only be judged in comparison to the likely success of other options.[74] Because the feasibility of carrots is sharply constrained, it is not surprising that economic coercion remains a popular course of action. The track record of economic or military coercion might not be sterling, but in many situations it is superior to an inducement-based approach. Furthermore, the theory developed here suggests how the use of carrots and sticks are intertwined. In some situations, the sender has an incentive to use inducements only after sanctions has been attempted. In others, the ability to use the stick can only occur if a previous carrot has been accepted. This equivalency suggests an international relations version of the Coase Theorem.[75] Regardless of the relationship between the sender and receiver, something is exchanged for a political concession.[76] Looking at either inducements or sanctions in a vacuum would be theoretically counterproductive.

Finally, this article also suggests another mechanism that helps to explain the democratic peace. Theories of the democratic peace have focused on normative and structural qualities of democratic regimes that make them less willing to go to war with each other. Indeed, one article argues that

---

73. For a pessimistic assessment of economic sanctions, see Pape, "Why Economic Sanctions Do Not Work"; T. Clifford Morgan and Valerie Schwebach, "Fools Suffer Gladly: The Use of Economic Sanctions in International Crises," *International Studies Quarterly* 41, no. 1 (March 1997): 27–50; Richard Haass, "Sanctioning Madness," *Foreign Affairs* 76, no. 3 (November/December 1997): 74–85. For a pessimistic assessment of military coercion, see Robert Pape, "Coercion and Military Strategy," *Journal of Strategic Studies* 15, no. 4 (December 1992): 423–75.

74. Baldwin, *Economic Statecraft*.

75. See Ronald Coase, "The Problem of Social Cost," *Journal of Law and Economics* 3, no. 1 (October 1960): 1–44.

76. This point is also made in R. Harrison Wagner, "Economic Interdependence, Bargaining Power, and Political Influence," *International Organization* 42, no. 3 (summer 1988): 461–83.

because of this preference, democracies will simply choose other means of coercion in dealing with each other.[77] The theory of inducements developed here offers an additional explanation. Democracies are less likely to go to war with each other because their ability to provide information and credibly commit gives them a policy alternative that other dyads lack. With the ability to use inducements, democracies are able to bargain efficiently without resorting to force. Surely availability of inducements is not the only explanation for the democratic peace, but it is an explanation that until now has been overlooked.

---

77. Patrick James and Glenn E. Mitchell, "Targets of Covert Pressure: The Hidden Victims of the Democratic Peace," *International Interactions* 21, no. 1 (March 1995): 85–107.

ASKING THE RIGHT QUESTION:
WHEN DO ECONOMIC SANCTIONS WORK BEST?

JEAN-MARC F. BLANCHARD AND NORRIN M. RIPSMAN

T HE PREVAILING view of economic sanctions is unquestionably negative. Most believe that neither the threat of economic sanctions nor sanctions themselves have the ability to compel meaningful changes in the political behavior of other states.[1] Indeed, in a recent commentary on economic sanctions in *Foreign Affairs*, Richard Haass lamented that, "with few exceptions, the growing use of economic sanctions to promote foreign policy objectives is deplorable."[2] Similarly, Robert Pape recently pronounced that both a major study supporting the efficacy of economic sanctions and the deductive case for expecting sanctions to be more effective in the future were "seriously flawed."[3]

Contemporary sanctions episodes lend credence to the long-running view that "economic sanctions have historically proven to be an ineffective means to achieve foreign policy objectives."[4] Nine years of the most universal

Jean-Marc F. Blanchard is visiting scholar in the department of political science, Villanova University; Norrin M. Ripsman is a visiting assistant professor in the Department of Political Science and a Faculty Fellow in the Centre for Foreign Policy Studies at Dalhousie University.

This a significantly revised version of a paper presented at the *Security Studies* Workshop on Economic Power, Interdependence, and National Security held at the Mershon Center, Ohio State University, 2–5 April 1998. We would like to thank workshop participants for their helpful suggestions. We would especially like to thank Dale Copeland, Peter Liberman, Edward Mansfield, Robert Pape, David Rowe, and two anonymous *Security Studies* reviewers for their extensive comments; and the Honorable Flora MacDonald and James Powell (Bank of Canada) for allowing us to interview them.

1. By economic sanctions, we mean a coercive foreign policy in which a state disrupts its normal economic relations with another state in order to achieve one of the following objectives: (1) to induce the targeted state to change its behavior; (2) to generate popular pressure on the government that causes it to change its policies; or (3) to provoke a coup or revolt that leads to the emergence of a new government that will act in accordance with the sanctioning state's wishes. This definition builds upon, but is substantially different from, George A. Lopez and David Cortright, "Economic Sanctions in Contemporary Global Relations," in *Economic Sanctions: Panacea or Peacebuilding in a Post–Cold War World?* ed. David Cortright and George A. Lopez (Boulder: Westview, 1995), 15, n. 3; and Robert A. Pape, "Why Economic Sanctions Do Not Work," *International Security* 22, no. 2 (fall 1997): 94.

2. Richard N. Haass, "Sanctioning Madness," *Foreign Affairs* 76, no. 6 (November/December 1997): 75.

3. Pape, "Why Economic Sanctions Do Not Work," 91.

4. Henry Bienen and Robert Gilpin, "Economic Sanctions as a Response to Terrorism," *Journal of Strategic Studies* no. 3 (May 1980): 89–98.

economic sanctions ever imposed have not compelled Iraqi leader Saddam Hussein to change his behavior.[5] Likewise, economic sanctions have not cowed Slobodan Milosevic, the president of the Federal Republic of Yugoslavia.[6] American threats to renounce China's most-favored-nation status have not changed Chinese policies on human rights or religious persecution. Finally, the threat of economic sanctions in the spring of 1998 compelled neither India nor Pakistan to refrain from nuclear testing.

Despite this poor record, governments, particularly the United States, are increasingly using economic sanctions in an effort to achieve their foreign policy objectives in the post–cold war era. The most important question for policymakers, then, is *when* do economic sanctions work best?

In this article we first address this question with a theoretical examination of the circumstances under which economic sanctions are likely to work best. Unlike most writers, our analysis does not focus on how states can maximize the economic pain imposed on a target state.[7] Although this is a pertinent issue, economic pain, even if extreme, is unlikely to result in changes in behavior if the right political conditions are not present.[8] As Robin Renwick puts it, "the idea of an automatic correlation between economic deprivation and the loss of the political will to resist it is, to say the least, questionable."[9] Hence, we dis-

---

5. On the use of sanctions against Iraq, see David E. Reuther, "UN Sanctions Against Iraq," in Cortright and Lopez, *Economic Sanctions*, 121–32; and Bashir Al-Samarrai, "Economic Sanctions Against Iraq: Do They Contribute to a Just Settlement?" in Cortright and Lopez, *Economic Sanctions*, 133–39.

6. On the use of economic sanctions against Serbia, see Susan L. Woodward, "The Use of Sanctions in Former Yugoslavia: Misunderstanding Political Realities," in Cortright and Lopez, *Economic Sanctions*, 141–51; and Sonja Licht, "The Use of Sanctions in Former Yugoslavia: Can They Assist in Conflict Resolution?" in Cortright and Lopez, *Economic Sanctions*, 153–60.

7. Johan Galtung, "On the Effects of International Economic Sanctions: With Examples From the Case of Rhodesia," *World Politics* 19, no. 3 (April 1967): 384–88; Klaus Knorr, "International Economic Leverage and Its Uses," in *Economic Issues and National Security* ed. Klaus Knorr and Frank N. Trager (Lawrence: Regents Press of Kansas, 1977), 103; Hanns Maull, "Oil and Influence: The Oil Weapon Examined," in Knorr and Trager *Economic Issues and National Security*, 259–88; Harry R. Strack, *Sanctions: The Case of Rhodesia* (Syracuse: Syracuse University Press, 1978); Donald Losman, *International Economic Sanctions: The Cases of Cuba, Israel, and Rhodesia* (Albuquerque: University of New Mexico Press, 1979); Miroslav Nincic and Peter Wallensteen, "Economic Coercion and Foreign Policy," in *Dilemmas of Economic Coercion*, ed. Miroslav Nincic and Peter Wallensteen (New York: Praeger, 1983), 11–13; Robert L. Paarlberg, "Using Food Power: Opportunities, Appearances, and Damage Control," in Nincic and Wallensteen *Dilemmas of Economic Coercion*, 131–53; and M. S. Daoudi and M. S. Dajani, eds., *Economic Sanctions: Ideals and Experience* (London: Routledge & Kegan Paul, 1983), 12–13.

8. For a similar observation, see Jonathan Kirshner, "The Microfoundations of Economic Sanctions," *Security Studies* 6, no. 3 (spring 1997): 41.

9. Robin Renwick, *Economic Sanctions* (Cambridge: Center for International Affairs, Harvard University, 1981).

cuss the political circumstances under which the economic harm resulting from sanctions is likely to cause the desired political changes.

The second section of this study involves detailed analyses of three cases where economic sanctions "worked." In order to avoid needless debate about whether or not our case selection is biased in one direction or another, we have selected three cases that both sanctions advocates and sanctions skeptics agree were successes.[10] These are: (1) the United Kingdom's use of economic sanctions in 1933 to compel the Soviet Union to release two British citizens convicted of espionage; (2) the employment of economic sanctions in 1979 by various Arab League states to force Canada to reverse its decision to move its embassy in Tel Aviv to Jerusalem; and (3) India's use of economic sanctions between 1989 and 1990 to distance Nepal from closer ties with China.

We focus exclusively on sanction successes because the extant literature relies almost entirely on failures, like sanctions against Italy in 1936, to determine when sanctions will work. Studies focusing on failures cannot examine how economic sanctions interact with other factors—for example, domestic political considerations—to achieve the desired result. Furthermore, these studies falsely assume that the absence of a particular condition in a case where sanctions failed implies that its presence would have resulted in the achievement of the declared political objective. Therefore, these studies must be balanced with analyses of sanctions successes.[11]

10. These cases are deemed successes by Gary Clyde Hufbauer, Jeffrey J. Schott, and Kimberly Ann Elliott, *Economic Sanctions Reconsidered*, 2nd ed., 2 vols. (Washington, D.C.: Institute for International Economics, 1990); Ivan Eland, "Economic Sanctions as Tools of Foreign Policy," in Cortright and Lopez, *Economic Sanctions*, 35; and Pape, "Why Economic Sanctions Do Not Work." Peter Wallensteen concurs that the 1933 case is one of the few cases where sanctions worked. See "Economic Sanctions: Ten Modern Cases and Three Important Lessons," in Nincic and Wallensteen, *Dilemmas of Economic Coercion*, 91, 96.

11. In our view, a sanction's success results in the achievement of the stated political objective. We recognize, of course, that sanctions may be used to accomplish secondary goals such as signaling moral reprobation, demonstrating resolve, or placating domestic groups. Nevertheless, the majority of policymakers, researchers, and international organizations are interested in the potential for sanctions to engender the desired political result. Furthermore, past some point, sanctions will lose their ability to achieve secondary purposes if they cannot achieve their primary ones. See, for example, Wallensteen, "Economic Sanctions," 92; Kimberly Ann Elliott, "Factors Affecting the Success of Sanctions," in Cortright and Lopez, *Economic Sanctions*, 52; and T. Clifton Morgan and Valerie L. Schwebach, "Fools Suffer Gladly: The Use of Economic Sanctions in International Crises," *International Studies Quarterly* 41, no. 1 (March 1997): 29. For good overviews of the secondary purposes of sanctions, see Nincic and Wallensteen, "Economic Coercion and Foreign Policy," 5–8; David A. Baldwin, *Economic Statecraft* (Princeton: Princeton University Press, 1985), esp. chaps. 7–8; Margaret P. Doxey, *International Sanctions in Contemporary Perspective* (New York: St. Martin's, 1987), 8–9, 144; Eland, "Economic Sanctions as Tools of Foreign Policy," 29–31; and David Rowe, "Economic Sanctions Do Work: Economic Statecraft and the Oil Embargo of Rhodesia," *Security Studies* 9, nos. 1/2 (autumn 1999–winter 2000): 254–87.

The three cases that we have selected have additional attributes that make them valuable to an analysis of the conditions that facilitate the attainment of political objectives with economic sanctions. Specifically, they encompass varying degrees of economic pressure from the modest (Arab sanctions against Canada) to the intense (Indian sanctions against Nepal). Furthermore, they involve diverse political goals ranging from the modest (release of British citizens) to the vital (loss of Nepalese sovereignty and foreign affairs independence).[12] To the extent that we can identify common threads in each of these disparate cases, our theoretical and policy argument is strengthened because it will be applicable across a wider range of cases.

Our findings are that economic coercion worked primarily because domestic and international political conditions existed that magnified the political costs of noncompliance for the target state.[13] The Soviet Union released the British citizens it had imprisoned primarily because it feared the incident would damage its fragile diplomatic relations with Great Britain and interfere with the establishment of relations with the United States. At the time, the presence of revisionist regimes in Germany and Japan required the Soviet Union to seek as many status quo allies as possible. Canada abandoned its planned embassy move because of American diplomatic pressure not to interfere in the Middle East peace process, fear that the action would undermine Canada's international role as an impartial participant in peacekeeping operations, domestic political support for the Arab position, and concern that the Arab states might grant diplomatic recognition to the Quebec separatist movement. Nepalese leaders complied with Indian pressure to reduce ties with China because the Indian embargo complicated an already unstable domestic political situation, strengthening the hands of the prodemocracy opposition. Absent these favorable political conditions, it is unlikely that economic sanctions alone would have brought about the desired results in any of the three cases.

WHEN DO SANCTIONS WORK BEST? A THEORETICAL ANALYSIS

MOST ANALYSES of when economic sanctions work focus on how a sanctioning state can maximize the economic pain that it inflicts on

---

12. The fact that the issue at stake was of paramount importance for Nepal undermines the potential counterargument that sanctions only work on trivial issues. We thank David Rowe and Bob Pape for their comments on this point.

13. In these cases, low political costs of compliance also facilitated the successful application of economic sanctions.

the sanctioned state.[14] This is sensible given that the standard theory of economic sanctions posits that high levels of economic suffering will result in political change. Furthermore, one of the most visible ways that sanctions seem to fail is through the sanctioned state's adoption of policy changes that blunt the economic costs imposed by sanctions. Traditionally, sanctioned states have engaged in smuggling, established resource conservation programs, developed new markets for their products, and created substitutes for embargoed goods.[15]

It is questionable to assume, though, that economic pain will always translate into political gain since there are a variety of techniques that policymakers can use to manage the political fallout resulting from economic distress. The leaders of a state can, for example, redirect the costs of sanctions away from their supporters on to opposition groups, as Iraqi and Haitian leaders did. Alternatively, policymakers can use coercive resources at their disposal such as special police forces or the army to suppress disenchanted groups that might press for political change. In this manner, Iraqi leader Saddam Hussein has employed his Republican Guard as well as his security forces to eliminate opposition groups and elites that favor different foreign and domestic policies.[16]

Moreover, as David Baldwin emphasizes, economic sanctions are merely one instrument in the national foreign policy toolbox.[17] They may be applied simultaneously with other political instruments of coercion to maximize not only the economic costs that will accrue to recalcitrant target states, but also the total political costs that these states face. Thus, when the United States imposed sanctions on Syria in 1986 for its role in sponsoring terrorism, it also withdrew its ambassador from Damascus to signal the risk of a serious diplomatic rupture between the two countries.[18] In fact, since economic sanctions are designed to influence target governments in large part by generating domestic political opposition to the proscribed policy, their political costs are more significant than their economic bite. The political costs of noncompliance with economic sanctions can be further enhanced by other international factors unrelated to their imposition or the policy choices of the sender state. Doubts about the legitimacy of its May

14. Galtung, "On the Effects of International Economic Sanctions," 384–85; Losman, *International Economic Sanctions*; Renwick, *Economic Sanctions*, 78–80; Daoudi and Dajani, *Economic Sanctions*, 13; and Hufbauer, Schott, and Elliott, *Economic Sanctions Reconsidered*, 98–103.

15. For a discussion of the ways states can escape vulnerability interdependence, see Jean-Marc F. Blanchard and Norrin M. Ripsman, "Measuring Economic Interdependence: A Geopolitical Perspective," *Geopolitics* 1, no. 3 (winter 1996): 231–41.

16. Eland, "Economic Sanctions as Tools of Foreign Policy," 34; and Reuther, "UN Sanctions Against Iraq," 127, 130.

17. Baldwin, *Economic Statecraft*.

18. Hufbauer, Schott, and Elliott, *Economic Sanctions Reconsidered*, vol. 2, 586.

1994 general elections, for example, led the government of the Dominican Republic to strive for international legitimacy by tempering its support for the military government in Haiti, which was the target of international economic sanctions at the time. This, in turn, increased Haiti's international isolation and increased the political costs of the sanctions it faced.[19] Our argument, therefore, is that the efficacy of economic sanctions should depend not on the economic pain they promise, but on the corresponding political costs that the target state faces if it refuses to comply with the sender's wishes as well as the political costs it will incur if it accedes to the sanctioning state's demands. We develop this argument in the next section.

THE NECESSARY CONDITION: HIGH POLITICAL COSTS

A S WE discussed above, other sanctions' analysts have tried, unsuccessfully, to correlate the effectiveness of economic sanctions with the economic costs that the sender country is able to impose on the target state.[20] In our opinion, their failure is not surprising, since they have neglected the essentially political nature of the policy changes that sanctions seek to achieve. Any assessment of the costs associated with sanctions must consider the attendant political costs, which are more important for target state calculations.[21]

We argue that the necessary condition for the successful application of sanctions is a high political cost for the target state if it persists in the offending policy. This political cost is affected by a variety of international and domestic conditions, which we discuss below. Without high political costs, there would be no reason for the target state to comply with the sanctioner's demands, regardless of the economic pain imposed. High political costs for noncompliance, however, do not guarantee success since the countervailing costs of complying with the sanctioner's demands also may be intolerable to the leadership of a state. As noted below, the cost of compliance is shaped *inter alia* by factors such as the overall domestic and international costs of changing behavior and the autonomy of the foreign security policy executive.

19. Claudette Antoine Werleigh, "The Use of Sanctions in Haiti: Assessing the Economic Realities," in Cortright and Lopez, *Economic Sanctions*, 161–72.

20. N. 7.

21. We demonstrate elsewhere, for example, that states take more notice of international strategic and domestic political considerations when making national security decisions than they do economic costs. See Norrin M. Ripsman and Jean-Marc F. Blanchard, "Commercial Liberalism Under Fire: Evidence from 1914 and 1936," *Security Studies* 6, no. 2 (winter 1996/97): 4–50.

POLITICAL COSTS OF NONCOMPLIANCE

The political cost that would accrue to the target government if it refused to comply with the sender's demands is far more important in determining the outcome of a sanctions episode than the prospective economic pain. The political cost is affected by a variety of domestic and international conditions, including the political sanctions imposed by the sender, the target state's international threat situation, the degree of third party political support, the degree of target state domestic stability, the strength of the existing opposition to the government, and the ability of the state to redirect the costs of sanctions to opposition groups.[22] The presence of these political conditions should greatly increase the probability that sanctions will achieve their objectives.

Compound sanctions. When states individually or jointly impose economic sanctions on another state, they may accompany these sanctions with other sanctions such as political and military sanctions. Specifically, they may embargo arms, threaten to bomb military targets in the targeted state, withdraw their ambassadors or other diplomatic representatives, expel the sanctioned state from an international organization, rally other states to join in political, military, and economic sanctions against the targeted state, and terminate cultural and sporting exchanges. In the late 1940s, for example, the Soviet Union and its Eastern bloc allies not only implemented economic sanctions against Yugoslavia for its unwillingness to follow the Kremlin line, but they also severed diplomatic ties, launched a propaganda war, closed the border, and massed troops along the frontier.[23] Similarly, in response to the Tiananmen massacre in 1989, the United States and certain European allies banned high level contacts with the Chinese in addition to imposing a variety of economic sanctions.[24]

Economic sanctions are more likely to achieve the desired political results when associated with other types of sanctions for several reasons. First, the noneconomic costs of noncompliance increase when economic sanctions are accompanied by other sanctions. This may be particularly important in cases where policymakers value the political status quo more than the economic

22. Of course, other variables may be salient. For instance, Morgan and Schwebach examine the relative military balance as a factor affecting the likelihood that economic sanctions will work. "Fools Suffer Gladly," 32–35. It may also matter if the sanctioning state is an ally of the sanctioned state since noncompliance in such circumstances may endanger the entire range of ties that typically exist between allies. For a discussion of this issue as it pertains to the use of economic incentives, see Daniel W. Drezner, "The Trouble with Carrots: Transaction Costs, Conflict Expectations, and Economic Inducements," *Security Studies* 9, nos. 1/2 (autumn 1999–winter 2000): 188–218.

23. Doxey, *International Sanctions in Contemporary Perspective*, 53–54; and Hufbauer, Schott, and Elliott, *Economic Sanctions Reconsidered*, vol. 2, 93–99.

24. Hufbauer, Schott, and Elliott, *Economic Sanctions Reconsidered*, vol. 1, 268–78.

one.[25] Second, the imposition of additional sanctions represents a forceful demonstration of resolve that should remove any doubts among policymakers in the sanctioned state about the seriousness with which the sender state views the dispute. Third, the joining of one or more forms of political sanctions with economic sanctions highlights a risk of escalation that may be absent when economic sanctions alone are imposed.

The target state's international threat situation. In an anarchic international system, states who are unable to guarantee their security with their own military capabilities must seek allies when they face international threats. They must enter into alliances and associations when necessary on the basis of international power considerations, regardless of ideological, historical or political differences that may make some alliances politically unpalatable. When states face an unfavorable international balance of power (or balance of threat), then, they should be more willing to settle their disputes with states who can enhance their security, even when that means complying with otherwise unacceptable political demands, since the failure to ally with a potential supporter can have disastrous consequences for national security.[26] This may explain, for example, why Israel—surrounded by hostile Arab states and in need of external support—withdrew from Gaza and Sharm-al-Sheikh following American threats of economic sanctions in 1957.[27] On the other hand, when states face rather stable external threat environments, they will not have this political incentive to satisfy a sanctioner's demands.

Third party support. In addition to appealing to third parties to help reduce the economic costs of economic sanctions, a target state will also seek diplomatic and political help in order to minimize the political costs associated with sanctions. It may ask third parties to exert pressure on the sanctioning state to end its economic assault, to defend it against sanctions in other spheres (for example, international organizations or international political meetings), and to contain the risk of escalation. Hence, it is reasonable to expect that the position of third parties will affect the potential of economic sanctions to achieve the preferred political ends.

If third parties are unwilling to offer support, economic sanctions are more likely to have the desired effect because the target will feel greater isolation. Furthermore, the sanctioned state might experience heightened concern that

25. South Africans, for instance, apparently were extremely distressed when they were banned from international sporting activities, since this form of shunning really made the average citizen feel like an international pariah. Eland, "Economic Sanctions as Tools of Foreign Policy," 33.

26. See Kenneth N. Waltz, *Theory of International Politics* (New York: McGraw Hill, 1979); and Stephen M. Walt, *The Origins of Alliances* (Ithaca: Cornell University Press, 1987).

27. Hufbauer, Schott, and Elliott, *Economic Sanctions Reconsidered*, vol. 2, 142.

the sanctioning state will be emboldened to inflict further or harsher sanctions. Finally, it may conclude that it lacks adequate political means to force the sanctioning state to end its economic sanctions. In this vein, it is suggestive that the Soviet Union/Russia's withdrawal of economic and diplomatic support from Cuba appears, in part, to have moved Fidel Castro to moderate his tone toward the United States and to pursue policies that were more in line with U.S. preferences.

Even worse perhaps, third parties may pressure the sanctioned state to comply with the sanctioning state's wishes in order to promote a variety of political objectives such as regional stability, its own security interests, the protection of an alliance, or the containment of the risks of war. In the mid 1970s, for example, South Africa, which had been an invaluable patron for Rhodesia, no longer proved willing to support the Ian Smith regime unconditionally and in fact pressured it to come to terms with black nationalist groups. This contributed significantly to the regime's decision to go to the bargaining table.[28] About ten years earlier, the United States had used a mixture of economic and political pressures to push its Southeast Asian ally Indonesia to stop its campaign to crush Malaysia, which had already implemented its own economic sanctions against Indonesia.[29]

Domestic political instability. Many writers have pointed to an unfavorable domestic political context as a factor that increases the prospect that economic coercion will yield the desired political outcome.[30] Numerous analyses of the efficacy of the economic sanctions regime imposed on Rhodesia, for example, highlight the bloody and economically costly guerrilla war against the white minority government as a variable that worked in tandem with economic sanctions to bring about a change in the policies of the Ian Smith regime.[31]

It is clear that a tumultuous domestic political situation makes it more difficult for policymakers to exploit rally-around-the-flag sentiments. Rally-around-the-flag sentiments make it easier for leaders to blunt the calls for political

28. Renwick, *Economic Sanctions*, 52–53; and Doxey, *International Sanctions in Contemporary Perspective*, 40.

29. Hufbauer, Schott, and Elliott, *Economic Sanctions Reconsidered*, vol. 2, 247–52.

30. See, for example, Knorr, "International Economic Leverage and Its Uses," 108; Richard Stuart Olson, "Economic Coercion in World Politics: With a Focus on North-South Relations," *World Politics* 31, no. 4 (July 1979): 487–88; Wallensteen, "Economic Sanctions," 109–11; Hufbauer, Schott, and Elliott, *Economic Sanctions Reconsidered*, vol. 1, 52–97; and Morgan and Schwebach, "Fools Suffer Gladly," 109–11.

31. Strack, *Sanctions*, 237–38; Losman, *International Economic Sanctions*, 122–23, 136; Renwick, *Economic Sanctions*, 50–51, 57–58; and Doxey, *International Sanctions in Contemporary Perspective*, 40. Baldwin suggests that economic sanctions may have helped to foster or intensify the guerrilla war. *Economic Statecraft*, 196–98.

change that may emerge as a result of economic pain created by sanctions.[32] Less well appreciated, however, domestic political divisions make it difficult for decisionmakers to mobilize the people to participate in strategies like material conservation programs that are designed to contain the distress resulting from economic sanctions. Furthermore, domestic political tensions create opportunities for the sanctioning state to exploit fifth columns or a fractured policy-making elite to put pressure on the leaders of a state to change their course.[33] Finally, domestic divisions may demand the time and energies of leaders to such an extent that they feel forced to comply with the sanctioning state's wishes in order to free themselves to focus fully on domestic political problems. Thus, sanctions should be more effective when applied against a country with an unstable domestic political landscape.

The opposition. Another domestic political variable that increases the chances that economic coercion will succeed is the existence of a strong political opposition prior to the application of sanctions. A strong political opposition improves the chances that economic sanctions will result in the desired political change for a number of reasons. For instance, a strong political opposition can insist on compliance with the sanctioning state's demands in return for its support on other facets of the government's political agenda. A strong opposition also may be able to mobilize disaffected elements in the general populace to rally for change. Furthermore, a strong political opposition may be able to offer bribes to pull supporters away from the ruling coalition and hence reduce the power of elements opposing compliance with the sanctioning state's wishes. At the extreme, a strong political opposition may be able to overthrow the existing government and to put in place a government that is more willing to comply with the wishes of the sanctioning state.

Redirection opportunities. In certain instances, policymakers will be able to redirect the costs of economic sanctions away from themselves and their supporters on to opponents.[34] In Rhodesia, for instance, black unemployment surged during the period of sanctions while whites were able to retain their jobs. In Iraq, Saddam Hussein kept food and medical supplies away from northern Kurdish and southern Shiite areas so that these resources could be used to

32. The seminal work on the rally-around-the-flag sentiment is undoubtedly Galtung, "On the Effects of International Economic Sanctions."
33. Rawi Abdelal and Jonathan Kirshner ("Strategy, Economic Relations, and the Definition of National Interests," *Security Studies* 9, nos. 1/2 [autumn 1999–winter 2000]: 119–56) demonstrates that domestic political instability facilitates and intensifies the penetration of external economic influences into the political sphere.
34. Eland, "Economic Sanctions as Tools of Foreign Policy," 32–33.

satisfy the needs of the populace in Baghdad.[35] Alternatively, policymakers may possess the capability to compensate themselves and their supporters for any economic losses that they suffer as a result of economic sanctions. In the face of American economic sanctions that significantly reduced foreign aid, trade, and the availability of currency, Panamanian General Manuel Noriega ensured that scarce cash resources were husbanded to pay his supporters in the military.[36]

If the costs of economic sanctions cannot be redirected, however, then there are three potential political consequences.[37] First, supporters may begin to pressure for political change and perhaps even shift to the opposition. Second, policymakers may find themselves less able to use their supporters to control or suppress opposition forces. For instance, army leaders or the military rank and file may become less willing to crack down on political opponents of the leadership. Third, supporters of the government may adopt new interests. In all three cases, the leaders of a state will discover themselves increasingly pressured to comply with the wishes of the sanctioning state.

CONFOUNDING FACTORS

In order for sanctions to achieve their purpose, the target government must face a high political cost if it persists in its offensive behavior. A high political cost, though, does not guarantee success since other factors may mitigate the effect of these political costs. For instance, if the domestic political costs of compliance are also extremely high, then policymakers may decide via a simple cost-benefit analysis to accept the high political costs associated with noncompliance. Below, we highlight two variables that we feel are particularly salient in determining when high political costs will promote the desired political outcomes: (1) the total domestic and international political costs of changing behavior; and (2) the autonomy of the executive.

Costs of changing behavior. Economic sanctions are more likely to induce policymakers to make the desired changes when the domestic political costs of compliance are low. If decisionmakers do not feel that compliance with the goals of the sanctioning state will damage their reelection chances, weaken their position in their respective political parties, decrease the depth of their

35. Strack, *Sanctions*, 237; Losman, *International Economic Sanctions*, 116; Renwick, *Economic Sanctions*, 52; and Reuther, "UN Sanctions Against Iraq," 127.

36. Kirshner, "The Microfoundations of Economic Sanctions," 50–56, esp. 56.

37. This is influenced by, but different from, Kirshner, "The Microfoundations of Economic Sanctions," 41. For a case where the costs of economic sanctions could not be redirected, see Kirshner's discussion of economic sanctions against the dictatorship of General Rafael Trujillo in the Dominican Republic (56–63).

support among key voter or support constituencies, or increase the political power of opposition groups, then, economic sanctions are more likely to achieve the desired effects.

The reasons for this are obvious. Decisionmakers are more likely to comply with the wishes of the sanctioning state if they would not risk their domestic political position by making the necessary policy changes. It would have been unreasonable, for instance, for the Clinton administration to have expected Benjamin Netanyahu to comply fully with American preferences regarding the Middle East peace process, despite the implicit threat of sanctions, if such compliance could have endangered his fractious conservative political coalition. Similarly, it would be illogical to expect Indian policymakers to abandon the country's nuclear weapons program in the face of American sanctions if it led to the defection of the political parties that sustain the power of the ruling coalition. By the same token, sanctions are more likely to be successful if the target's international position is not heavily compromised by compliance. In other words, if surrender would affect the sanctioned state's international prestige or its credibility with allies and foes alike, then it will be less likely to succeed, even if the political costs of noncompliance are also high.

Since there may be international political costs associated with compliance—for example, capitulation can damage a state's international prestige—it is more probable that a state will comply with a sanctioner's wishes when sanctions are accompanied by a face-saving way to back down.[38] Face-saving exits make it much more palatable for the leaders of a state to accept an otherwise unattractive policy option for two reasons. First, decisionmakers can claim that they made a trade-off that resulted in political gains when, in reality, they had to accept losses. In this regard, the experience of the Cuban Missile Crisis is instructive. Soviet Premier Nikita Khrushchev was able to agree to a potentially humiliating withdrawal of medium-range nuclear missiles from Cuba because of President John F. Kennedy's willingness to remove nuclear missiles from Turkey and to pledge that the United States would not again attempt to invade the Soviet client. Second, face-saving exits enable leaders to transform the apparent character of disputes from matters of vital interest to lesser issues. To illustrate this point, Chinese leaders released a number of leading dissidents to the United States in 1998 under the guise that they were sending them to the U.S. for medical care. Hence, the treatment of these individuals was effectively downgraded from a matter of national independence and sovereignty to a humanitarian issue.

---

38. On this point, see Baldwin, *Economic Statecraft*, 108–9.

Decision-making autonomy. As mentioned, the preeminent causal path of economic sanctions is through domestic opinion—that is, by generating opposition to and pressure on the political leadership in the legislature, key social groups and the public at large. To the extent that national leaders are insulated from domestic opinion by institutional, procedural or normative factors, the opposition caused by sanctions will not affect decision-making. In other words, the more structural autonomy a leader or an executive possesses, the less effective sanctions should be.[39] This may explain why eight years of excruciatingly painful sanctions on Iraq—where Saddam Hussein physically suppresses political opposition and where there is no genuine legislature with the political authority to challenge him—have had little impact on Iraqi behavior.

We argue that economic sanctions are likely to work best when there are high political costs to rejecting the demands of the sanctioning state. In the preceding section, we have identified six factors—some international and some domestic—that we believe will increase the political costs associated with economic sanctions if the targeted state persists in its undesired behavior, as well as two additional confounding factors. Whether or not these conditions truly result in a situation where the political costs of noncompliance are high is an empirical question that warrants verification through detailed case study. To this end, we test these propositions in the next section.

THREE ECONOMIC SANCTION SUCCESSES

IN THIS SECTION we examine three sanctions successes. The first involves the use of economic sanctions by the British in 1933 to force the Soviets to release two British citizens who were imprisoned for espionage. The second case concerns the imposition of economic sanctions in 1979 by various Arab states to induce Canada to reverse its announced plan to move the Canadian embassy in Israel from Tel Aviv to Jerusalem. The final case covers Indian efforts between 1989 and 1990 to use economic sanctions to compel Nepal to distance itself from China with whom it was forging increasing military links. In

39. For a discussion of structural autonomy, its determinants and its foreign security policy consequences, see Norrin M. Ripsman, "Democratic Institutions and the Governance of Foreign Security Policy: Peacemaking after Two World Wars" (Ph.D. diss., University of Pennsylvania, 1997). See also, Matthew Evangelista, "The Paradox of State Strength: Transnational Relations, Domestic Structures, and Security Policy in Russia and The Soviet Union," *International Organization* 49, no. 1 (winter 1995), 1–38; Susan Peterson, "How Democracies Differ: Public Opinion, State Structure, and the Lessons of the Fashoda Crisis," *Security Studies* 5, no. 1 (autumn 1995), 3–37; and Norrin M. Ripsman, "The Conduct of Foreign Policy by Democracies: A Critical Review" (paper presented at the Annual Meeting of the American Political Science Association, 1–4 September 1994).

each of these episodes we provide background on the case, identify the economic and political costs imposed on the sanctioned state, and, using our
theoretical framework, undertake an analysis of the reasons why economic
sanctions attained the desired political objectives.

BRITISH SANCTIONS AGAINST THE SOVIET UNION (1933)

On 12 March 1933 Soviet authorities arrested six British employees of Metro-
politan-Vickers Ltd., a British mechanical engineering firm, and subsequently
charged them with espionage and sabotage of Soviet electrical stations.[40] The
British government reacted with outrage that British subjects from a reputable
firm could be arrested on trumped-up charges by a foreign government. On 20
March 1933, His Majesty's Government suspended ongoing commercial negotiations with the USSR in an unsuccessful attempt to secure their release.[41] British ambassador to Moscow Sir Esmond Ovey escalated the pressure on 27
March, informing Soviet foreign minister Maxim Litvinov that action would be
taken against Soviet imports unless the Soviet government released the engineers without a trial. Litvinov rejected this proposal immediately, insisting that
the men would be tried in Soviet court.[42] The British Parliament consequently
passed legislation on 5 April granting the government the authority to impose
an embargo on Soviet imports if the prisoners were not released.[43]

The trial, which began on 12 April, was an open travesty of justice, with
obviously intimidated witnesses leveling incredible and often contradictory
charges at the accused.[44] The court reached its verdict on 19 April. Five of the
six British defendants were convicted. Two (Messrs. MacDonald and Thornton) received sentences of two and three years "deprivation of liberty"; the
others were expelled from the Soviet Union for a period of five years. In response, London authorized an embargo the following day. It prohibited the

40. See Lord Strang, *Home and Abroad* (London: Deutsch, 1956), 78–95.
41. See Undersecretary of State Sir Robert Vansittart to Soviet Ambassador to London
Ivan Maisky, 21 March 1933, *Documents on British Foreign Policy* (hereinafter *DBFP*), ed. E. L.
Woodward and Rohan Butler, 2nd Ser., vol. 7 (London: HMSO, 1958), 347.
42. Ovey to British Foreign Secretary Sir John Simon, 28 March 1933, *DBFP*, 2nd Ser.,
vol. 7, 374.
43. Simon to British Chargé d'Affairs in Moscow William Strang, 3 April 1933, *DBFP*, 2nd
Ser., vol. 7, 403.
44. At one point in the trial, one of the accused (Mr. MacDonald) recanted his confes-
sions and his guilty plea, which he claimed were false and had been obtained under duress.
The Court took an immediate and unscheduled recess, during which the prosecution issued
threats against his Russian housekeeper. When proceedings resumed, a subdued MacDonald
once again asserted that the charges against him were true. For details of this almost farcical
show trial, see Strang's reports from Moscow in *DBFP*, 2nd Ser., vol. 7, 423–91; and Robert
Conquest, *The Great Terror* (London: Macmillan, 1968), 553–56.

import of butter, wheat in grain, barley, oats, maize, poultry and game, raw cotton, petroleum and timber from the Soviet Union effective 26 April.[45] His Majesty's Government made it clear, both in Parliament and through the British Embassy in Moscow, that the embargo would last only until MacDonald and Thornton were safely returned to Great Britain.[46] The next day, Moscow retaliated against British imports, prohibiting Soviet organizations from placing orders in Great Britain and chartering British ships, restricting the use of British ports, and restricting British goods in transit through the Soviet Union.[47]

Soon after the verdict, Soviet ambassador to London Ivan Maisky and other unofficial People's Commissariat for Foreign Affairs sources hinted to the British that the Soviet Union was anxious to resolve the ensuing Anglo-Soviet dispute, but that it would take time and a concerted British effort to avoid public threats, which would make it difficult for the USSR to back down. In particular, they suggested a solution could lie in the ordinary appeal process, which could take a few months.[48] The foreign secretary, Sir John Simon, was cautiously optimistic, but emphasized that the embargo would not be withdrawn until MacDonald and Thornton were returned and the Soviet retaliatory embargo was lifted.

At the end of June, when Litvinov was in London for the World Economic Conference, he concluded an agreement with Simon to release the prisoners simultaneously with announcements from both governments lifting the countervailing embargoes and resuming bilateral trade negotiations. Thus, on 1 July 1933, the crisis was resolved as the Presidium of the Central Executive Committee commuted the prisoners' sentences to expulsion from the Soviet Union—ostensibly in response to their appeals—and the embargoes were lifted.[49]

Why were British trade sanctions successful in this case? An emphasis on the economic pain they would have caused, although considerable, is insufficient. To be sure, although there is little detailed information on Soviet trade dependence in this period, the evidence that is available indicates that Soviet sensitivity to a British embargo in 1933 was quite high. Great Britain was the leading market for Soviet exports. In the first three months of 1933, prior to

45. Simon to Vansittart, 19 April 1933, *DBFP*, 2nd Ser., vol. 7, 489.
46. Simon to Strang, 22 April 1933, *DBFP*, 2nd Ser., vol. 7, 500; and *Parliamentary Debates* (Commons), vol. 277, col. 264.
47. "Decree of the Foreign Trade Commissariat on Restrictions on Trade with Great Britain," 21 April 1933, *Soviet Documents on Foreign Policy* (hereinafter *SDFP*), ed. Jane Degras (London: Oxford University Press, 1953), vol. 3, 14.
48. See, for example, Strang to Simon, 19 April 1933, *DBFP*, 2nd Ser., vol. 7, 490; and Foreign Office Minute by Mr. L. Collier, 22 June 1933, *DBFP*, 2nd Ser., vol. 7, 565.
49. Simon to Strang, 22 June 1933, *DBFP*, 2nd Ser., vol. 7, 570–72; and "Tass Statement on the Raising of the Embargo on Anglo-Soviet Trade and the Release of the Imprisoned British Engineers," 2 July 1933, *SDFP*, vol. 3, 23.

the embargo, exports to Great Britain amounted to 18 million roubles or 22 percent of total Soviet exports.[50] While this percentage is high, these exports were even more significant than the amount indicates, since exports to Great Britain were the primary source of German currency with which the Soviet Union paid for its large trade imbalance with Germany, which for 1933 was estimated at around 650 million marks. Without these marks, it was likely that the Russians would have been unable to meet their payment schedules and the Germans had indicated that they did not wish to take inferior quality Russian goods as payment.[51]

The potential impact of British sanctions, if maintained for a prolonged period, was considerable. Nonetheless, despite this sensitivity the Soviets were hardly vulnerable to a disruption of trade with Great Britain, since none of the goods they imported from Great Britain were irreplaceable and, if the British Foreign Office's suspicion was correct, the currency supplied by exports to Great Britain could have been recouped by impending loans from or exports to the United States.[52]

The keys to the Soviet capitulation, however, were the powerful international political incentives for compliance with British demands that would have made outright defiance extremely costly for the Soviet Union. First and foremost, the threatening international environment that the Soviet Union faced in 1933 made it imperative to maintain good relations with as many "bourgeois" governments as possible. The Soviet leadership was very worried about Japanese expansionism in Asia, which began with the 1931 invasion of Manchuria. They feared that the Japanese would soon attack the Soviet Maritime Province and embroil them in a Russo-Japanese war they could ill afford and which they believed might draw in the other capitalist powers. Furthermore, Hitler's accession to power in January 1933 and his subsequent anticommunist rhetoric and domestic repression of German communists were considerable causes for alarm for the Russian leadership. Not only did it place an excessively anticommunist Great Power in central Europe, but it also deprived Soviet Russia of its primary "capitalist" ally since the Treaty of Rapallo. Under these troubling international circumstances, Litvinov's policy was to cooperate with as many of the status quo capitalist powers as possible to contain Germany and Japan. He certainly did not want to alienate Great Britain over the Metropoli-

50. Strang to Simon, 22 April 1933, *DBFP*, 2nd Ser., vol. 7, 498–99; and Max Beloff, *The Foreign Policy of Soviet Russia, 1929–1941*, vol. 1 (London: Oxford University Press, 1947), 41.

51. British Ambassador to Berlin, Sir Horace Rumbold to Undersecretary of State Sir Robert Vansittart, 16 November 1932, *DBFP*, 2nd Ser., vol. 7, 269–71; and Simon to Vansittart, 19 April 1933, *DBFP*, 2nd Ser., vol. 7, 489.

52. Foreign Office Memorandum by Sir Esmond Ovey, 2 April 1933, *DBFP*, 2nd Ser., vol. 7, 402.

tan-Vickers affair.[53] Therefore, the international threat situation heightened the political costs of noncompliance for the Soviets.

In light of the above, Soviet leaders had to be concerned about indications that the Anglo-Soviet dispute might result in the termination of diplomatic relations with Great Britain. Early in the crisis, Ovey warned Litvinov that "[the] question at issue was not one of sovereign rights but rather of whether the British public and His Majesty's Government could continue to consider Russia a country in which it was possible for an Englishman to live and trade with, or with which His Majesty's Government could maintain relations." He further cautioned that "there appeared good prospects of my being not only the ambassador who opened relations with the Soviet Government, but the ambassador who closed them."[54] While it was not the British Government's intention to threaten a diplomatic break overtly, they reinforced the ambassador's warning by recalling him to London for consultations on 29 March, where he remained for the duration of the crisis.[55] Because of this implicit threat of compound political sanctions, Soviet leaders had to be aware that they risked a serious diplomatic breach with the British if they did not reach a satisfactory resolution of the dispute.

A final important consideration was the effect the Anglo-Soviet dispute might have had on the prospects for American diplomatic recognition of the Soviet Union. As Strang observed, "[T]here is, of course, nothing that the Soviet Government more dearly desire in the international sphere than the establishment of diplomatic relations with the United States of America."[56] Recognition would not only help the USSR to improve relations with a Japanese rival in the Pacific, but would make it possible to raise additional loans and purchases to fuel the current Five-Year Plan.[57] Yet the summary arrest and trial of British workers aroused the concern of American companies such as General Electric, who were already operating in the Soviet Union, and strengthened the hands of the State Department, which was opposed to recognition. Notably, while recognition appeared to be imminent in early 1933, the American Under-secretary of State William Phillips told British sources in April that the Metro-

53. For an excellent analysis of the Soviet diplomatic predicament, see Strang to Simon, 4 June 1933, *DBFP*, 2nd Ser., vol. 7, 556–62. On the "Litvinov policy," see Henry L. Roberts, "Maxim Litvinov," in *The Diplomats, 1919–1939*, ed. Gordon A. Craig and Felix Gilbert (New York: Atheneum, 1965), 344–77, esp. 350–52.

54. Ovey to Vansittart, 17 March 1933, *DBFP*, 2nd Ser., vol. 7, 326–27.

55. Simon to Ovey, 29 March 1933, *DBFP*, 2nd Ser., vol. 7, 381.

56. Strang to Simon, 20 May 1933, *DBFP*, 2nd Ser., vol. 7, 547.

57. See, for example, Foreign Office Memorandum by Sir Esmond Ovey, 2 April 1933, *DBFP*, 2nd Ser., vol. 7, 402; and Adam B. Ulam, *Expansion and Coexistence* (New York: Praeger, 1968), 212.

236 POWER AND THE PURSE

politan-Vickers affair "put [the] clock right back."[58] Given the threatening
geopolitical context at the time, it was simply not worth jeopardizing American
diplomatic recognition to protect the minor amount of Soviet prestige at stake.

These powerful political incentives for compliance with the British demands
thus corresponded with a relatively low cost of capitulation. To be sure, the
Soviet leadership viewed the dispute in terms of Soviet sovereignty and prestige.[59] Nonetheless, in the final analysis, the release of two unimportant British
prisoners was not particularly damaging for the Soviet Union domestically or
internationally. The nature of the Soviet system and the Great Terror that Sta-
lin visited upon the country did not permit any meaningful domestic opposition to object to their release. Nor would capitulation have particularly detrimental effects on either the country's international standing or its international
security. Moreover, the Soviets compromised with the British in a manner that
mitigated any future fallout for Soviet prestige. Rather than giving in to British
pressure initially, the Russian government proceeded to hold a trial, find the
defendants guilty, sentence two of them to prison and imprison them, all in
open defiance of British threats. They further imposed a counter-embargo of
their own on British goods as soon as the British sanctions were announced.
Finally, when they released the prisoners after two months in prison, they did
so by commuting their original sentences from imprisonment to expulsion
from the Soviet Union. This was decided, ostensibly, in response to the customary Soviet appeal process, rather than to British pressure. While it was evident that the Soviet Union *was* bending as a result of British pressure, the
method by which the Soviets gave the British prisoners their freedom meant
that the total costs of compliance were minimized, since the government could
claim that legal, rather than international, factors resulted in their release.

The British embargo of Soviet exports had the maximum effect on Soviet
behavior, then, because there were corresponding and powerful international
political pressures—that is, the deteriorating Soviet international threat situation, implied threats of compound British diplomatic sanctions, and severe

58. British Ambassador to the United States Sir Ronald Lindsay to Simon, 25 April 1933,
DBFP, 2nd Ser., vol. 7, 508–09. On the uneasiness of General Electric, see Ovey to Vansittart, 13 March 1933, *DBFP*, 2nd Ser., vol. 7, 306.

59. The Soviet Government consistently treated the conflict as a matter of prestige and
national sovereignty. See, for example, "Statement by Litvinov to the British Ambassador on
the Arrest of British Engineers in Moscow: Tass Communiqué," 16 March 1933, *SDFP*, vol.
3, 9–10; and "Tass Communiqué on the Interview Between the Foreign Commissar and the
British Ambassador Concerning the Forthcoming Trial of the British Engineers," 30 March
1933, *SDFP*, vol. 3, 10. For this reason, Litvinov and others in the People's Commissariat for
Foreign Affairs frequently indicated to Strang and Ovey that the public British threats were
actually undermining the Soviet ability to compromise. See, for example, Strang to Simon, 28
April 1933, *DBFP*, 2nd Ser., vol. 7, 520; and Strang to Simon, 10 May 1933, *DBFP*, 2nd Ser.,
vol. 7, 541.

consequences for Soviet relations with the United States, an important third party—that promised high political costs if the Soviet Union failed to accommodate British demands and defuse the dispute. Furthermore, there were no domestic costs to surrendering to British demands. Although there were international costs affiliated with compliance, they were not great and were minimized by the way the Soviets released their captives.

It is conceivable, if unlikely, that the aforementioned political pressures and incentives might have compelled the Soviet leadership to repatriate the British prisoners even in the absence of British economic sanctions.[60] We are persuaded, however, that economic sanctions served as a signaling device to make Soviet leaders understand the political ramifications of their actions. Regardless, it is clear that sanctions alone—that is, without these high political costs—would not have yielded a Soviet capitulation.

ARAB SANCTIONS AGAINST CANADA (1979)[61]

During the Canadian election campaign in May 1979, the leader of the Progressive Conservative Party (PC), Joe Clark, promised to relocate the Canadian embassy in Israel from Tel Aviv to western Jerusalem. Clark made the pledge in order to garner the support of Jewish voters in key districts in Southern Ontario who had traditionally voted for Pierre Trudeau's Liberal party and to reward Israeli prime minister Menachem Begin for his efforts in sealing the Camp David Accord with Egypt.[62] After the elections, on 4 June, External Affairs Minister Flora MacDonald announced that Clark's newly elected Government would honor his campaign promise to relocate the embassy.[63] Since the embassy move would implicitly recognize the Israeli claim to all of Jerusalem as its undivided capital, her statement sparked angry protests from the Arab states. Within days, members of the Arab League threatened Canada with a variety of economic reprisals that would affect Canadian business with the

60. We thank one of the anonymous *Security Studies* reviewers for bringing this issue to our attention.

61. This case is based upon Norrin M. Ripsman and Jean-Marc F. Blanchard, "Canada At Bay: The Utility of Economic Sanctions in 1979" (unpublished manuscript; 1999).

62. Howard Adelman, "Clark and the Canadian Embassy in Israel," *Middle East Focus* 2, no. 5 (March 1980): 2–3; David B. Dewitt and John J. Kirton, *Canada as a Principal Power* (Toronto: Wiley, 1983), 396; George Takach, "Clark and the Jerusalem Embassy Affair: Initiative and Constraint in Canadian Foreign Policy," in *The Domestic Battleground: Canada and the Arab-Israeli Conflict*, ed. David Taras and David H. Goldberg (Kingston: McGill-Queen's University Press, 1989), 44; and Jeffrey Simpson, *Discipline of Power: The Conservative Interlude and the Liberal Restoration* (Toronto: University of Toronto Press, 1996).

63. "Canadian Embassy in Israel to Move to Jerusalem," Israel Home Service Newsreel Report, 5 June 1979, BBC Summary of World Broadcasts, ME/6135/A/9 from Lexis-Nexis.

Arab world, Canadian monetary relations with the Arab Monetary Fund (AMF) and Canadian imports and exports to the members of the Arab League.[64]

Following their vigorous remonstrations, the Canadian government began to equivocate. Three days after making her announcement about the proposed embassy relocation, MacDonald backpedaled, stating that "there is no for-rent sign out on the embassy in Tel Aviv." The external affairs minister emphasized that she would take no action regarding the embassy "precipitously and not in the near future."[65] Moreover, only two weeks later (23 June), Clark announced that he would suspend the proposed embassy move for one year while former Progressive Conservative leader and elder statesman Robert Stanfield toured the Middle East and prepared recommendations for the Canadian government on how it should proceed with the planned move.[66] Finally, on 29 October, a mere five months after the whole episode began, Clark announced that he was canceling the move in line with Stanfield's interim report, which concluded that relocating the embassy would have an adverse effect on the Middle East peace process.[67] In compliance with the Stanfield report's recommendations, Clark officially cancelled the move.

At first glance, it is plausible that the Canadian government backed down because of the potential economic costs of the threatened sanctions. At the time, Canada maintained extensive economic relations with the Arab world and had much to lose if they were to be disrupted.[68] Significantly, a disruption of Canadian trade with the members of the Arab League would have endangered the oil supplies that Canada received from the Middle East. In the period under study, Middle Eastern oil represented approximately 10-15 percent of total Canadian petroleum consumption.[69] An oil cutoff on its own would have

64. QNA (Doha), 8 June 1979 from FBIS-Middle East, 13 June 1979, A1; Gavin Bell, Reuters, 8 June 1979 from Lexis-Nexis; "Canada's Decision to Transfer Its Embassy to Jerusalem," BBC Summary of World Broadcasts, 9 June 1979, ME/6137/I from Lexis-Nexis; and Gulf News Agency (Manama) in Arabic, 9 June 1979 from FBIS-Middle East, 12 June 1979, C1.

65. Reuters, 7 June 1979 from Lexis-Nexis; and John Rogers, Reuters, 7 June 1979 from Lexis-Nexis.

66. "Israel Embassy Move Postponed," Facts on File World News Digest, 6 July 1979, 501 F1 from Lexis-Nexis.

67. For the text of Stanfield's final report and the former Conservative leader's reflections on his conclusions, see Tareq Ismael, ed., Canada and the Arab World (Edmonton: University of Alberta Press, 1985), 173–206.

68. For a comprehensive analysis of Canadian sensitivity, see Jean-Marc F. Blanchard and Norrin M. Ripsman, "Rethinking Sensitivity Interdependence: Assessing Trade, Investment, and Monetary Links between States," (paper presented at the 38th Annual Meeting of the International Studies Association, Minneapolis, Minnesota, 17–21 March 1998), 24–31.

69. Statistics Canada, Canada Yearbook 1980–1981 (Ottawa: Minister of Supply and Services, 1981), 494, 518–19; Ingrid Bryan, Economic Policies in Canada (Toronto: Butterworths, 1982), 79; and Takach, "Clark and the Jerusalem Embassy Affair," 155. Canadian policymakers were well aware of the importance of this oil. Howard Stanislawski, "Canadian Corpora-

significantly increased prices, but given the inflationary psychology afflicting Canada at the time and the lack of excess industrial capacity, an oil shock might have had unusually severe inflationary consequences.[70] Canada also was sensitive because the Arabs in both their public and private capacities had invested between C$3–C$4.5 billion in Canada.[71] If the Arabs pulled their investments out of Canada in order to sanction it, then Canada might have experienced balance-of-payments problems since it depended heavily on foreign capital to finance its large and persistent current account deficits.[72] The resulting depreciation of the Canadian dollar would have generated increased inflation, which was already a problem.[73] Finally, Canada was sensitive because it borrowed heavily from abroad to cover its current account deficits and its immense public debts.[74] Unfortunately for Canadian monetary officials, Canadian debt was increasingly denominated in foreign currency and a growing percentage of capital inflows were taking the form of portfolio or "hot money" investments.[75] If the members of the League of Arab States dumped their Canadian dollars or implemented sanctions that were deleterious to the health of the Canadian economy, then the Canadian dollar would definitely have experienced a significant decline in value. As noted, this would have had adverse inflationary consequences as well as increased the cost of servicing debt denominated in foreign currency.[76]

The Arab threat to implement economic sanctions, therefore, resonated because economic sanctions would have imposed meaningful—though not

---

tions and Their Middle East Interests," in Taras and Goldberg *The Domestic Battleground*, 70, 78.

70. Bank of Canada, *Annual Report of the Governor to the Minister of Finance and Statement of Accounts for the Year 1979* (Ottawa: Bank of Canada, February 1980), 6. On the Canadian capacity constraint problem, see idem. 11–15.

71. "Arab Anger at Canada," *Business Week*, 2 July 1979, 30 from Lexis-Nexis; and Takach, "Clark and the Jerusalem Embassy Affair," 155. We thank James Powell, Deputy Chief of the International Department at the Bank of Canada for his help in gauging this figure.

72. "Arab Anger at Canada," 30.

73. International Monetary Fund, *International Financial Statistics* 33, no. 7 (Washington, D.C.: International Monetary Fund, July 1980), 102–03; Statistics Canada, *Canada Yearbook 1980–1981*, 771; and Fred Lazar, "The National Economy," in *Canadian Annual Review of Politics and Public Affairs 1979*, ed. R. B. Byers (Toronto: University of Toronto Press, 1981), 128–29.

74. Bank for International Settlements, 50th Annual Report (Basle: Bank for International Settlements, June 1980), 94; International Monetary Fund, *Balance of Payments Yearbook*, vol. 31 (Washington, D.C.: International Monetary Fund, December 1980), 88–89; Statistics Canada, *Canada Yearbook 1980–1981*, 856, 859, 874–77; Lazar, "The National Economy," 133; and Bryan, *Economic Policies in Canada*, 10.

75. Bank of Canada, *Annual Report of the Governor to the Minister of Finance and Statement of Accounts for the Year 1978* (Ottawa: Bank of Canada, February 1979), 32–33; Statistics Canada, *Canada Yearbook 1980–1981*, 821, 857, 876; and International Monetary Fund, *Government Finance Statistics Yearbook* (Washington, D.C.: International Monetary Fund, 1981), 125–28.

76. Lazar, *The National Economy*, 130–31; and Bank of Canada, *Annual Report—1978*, 6–9.

extreme or disastrous—economic losses on Canada. It is not surprising, therefore, that leading Canadian businesses initiated a major lobbying campaign of their own to get the Clark government to reverse its plan to relocate the embassy. Bell Canada and Westinghouse Canada, for instance, warned that major contracts with Arab states (and hence thousands of Canadian jobs) were at risk. After the Arab Monetary Fund (AMF) decided to stop all financial dealings with Canada on 18 June, leading Canadian banks entered the fray, cautioning that Arab sanctions could have detrimental effects on Canadian banks as well as the Canadian economy.[77]

While Canadian sensitivity to Arab sanctions was reasonably high, it was the many corresponding political costs that compelled the Clark government to comply with Arab wishes. To begin with, the Arab states reinforced their economic threats with powerful political threats against the Canadian government. In the immediate aftermath of MacDonald's announcement, Arab ambassadors and foreign ministry officials warned of "profound" consequences for Arab-Canadian relations if the Canadian government went ahead with the embassy move. Moreover, they hinted that the proposed move would endanger Canada's special status as a UN peacekeeper—a prospect that alarmed Canadian policymakers.[78] Peacekeeping is one of the primary defense missions for the Canadian Armed Forces and an ideal source of prestige for a lesser international power. The idea of peacekeeping forces was, to a large degree, Canadian.[79] Ever since, the continued Canadian participation in UN peacekeeping efforts was a considerable source of pride to the country and lay at the core of the Canadian national identity.[80] Taking a heavily partisan stance in a complex international conflict, however, would undermine the reputation of impartiality that is necessary for participants in peacekeeping operations, particularly if

77. "Canadian Generators," CBC, 14 June 1979, BBC Summary of World Broadcasts, ME/W1037/A1/2 from Lexis-Nexis; "Arab Monetary Fund's action against Canada," 20 June 1979, BBC Summary of World Broadcasts, ME/6146/i from Lexis-Nexis; Ibrahim Noori, Reuters, 19 June 1979 from Lexis-Nexis; "Israel Embassy Move," The American Banker, 21 June 1979, 3 from Lexis-Nexis; Stanislawski, "Canadian Corporations and Their Middle East Interests," 75–79; and Takach, "Clark and the Jerusalem Embassy Affair," 157–58.

78. "Canadian Plan to Move Embassy from Tel Aviv to Jerusalem Opposed by Arab States," Xinhua General Overseas News Service, 8 June 1979 from Lexis-Nexis; MENA (Cairo), 7 June 1979 in FBIS-Middle East, 8 June 1979, D10–D11; and John Rogers, Reuters, 7 June 1979 from Lexis-Nexis.

79. Paul F. Diehl, International Peacekeeping (Baltimore: Johns Hopkins University Press, 1993), 30–31; and John English, The Worldly Years: The Life of Lester Pearson, 2 vols. (Toronto: Knopf Canada, 1992), 107–46.

80. David Cox, "Canada's Interest in Peacekeeping: Some Political and Military Considerations," in Peacekeeping: International Challenge and Canadian Response, ed. Alastair Taylor, David Cox and Jack L. Granatstein (Lindsay, Ont.: Canadian Institute for International Affairs, 1968), 41–62.

Arab states made good their threats to protest to the UN against Canadian involvement in Middle Eastern peacekeeping missions. Arab and American representatives, therefore, made this connection explicit to both Clark and MacDonald.[81] Hence, Clark's pledge threatened to undermine the pillar of Canadian foreign and defense policies since the mid-1950s.[82]

Even more serious were Arab threats to intervene in the most sensitive of Canadian internal political affairs—the status of Quebec. At a critical juncture for the French separatist movement in the province of Quebec, which was governed by the separatist Parti Québecois and would hold a referendum on withdrawal from the Canadian confederation the following year, the French Canadian press reported that René Lévesque's provincial government had struck a bargain with the Arab states, promising to withhold recognition of any Canadian embassy move provided that the Arab states would support the Québecois independence movement.[83] In essence, the Arab states threatened to strike at Canada's soft underbelly, promising to complicate federal government efforts to keep the Canadian confederation intact. Indeed, official Arab sources claimed that "it was the potential Arab political and not an economic threat that led to Canada reconsidering moving its embassy to Jerusalem."[84]

These political threats were reinforced by third party pressure from the United States and the European Community, who warned that if Canada moved its embassy in Israel it could harm on-going Middle East peace negotiations. While Clark had intended to move the embassy to win over the Canadian Jewish community, he certainly did not want to lend legitimacy to the Israeli claim to a united Jerusalem or prejudice the possibility of a negotiated settlement. Therefore, when Arab states, members of the European Community, and the United States, stressed that the proposed move could interfere with regional negotiations, the prime minister began to reconsider his plan.[85] It is significant in and of itself that the United States—Canada's most powerful and important ally—applied intense diplomatic pressure to persuade Clark to

81. Dusko Doder, "Arab Threat Reported in Canada Shift; Canada Reportedly Bows to Pressure from Arabs; Clark Delays Plan to Move Embassy to Jerusalem," Washington Post, 14 July 1979, A1 from Lexis-Nexis. See also, Andrew Malcom, New York Times Abstracts, 10 June 1979, 7 from Lexis-Nexis; and Simpson, *Discipline of Power*, 146.
82. This concern weighed heavily on the mind of the new External Affairs minister. Interview with the Honorable Flora MacDonald, 24 March 1998.
83. *Le Devoir*, 20 June 1979; and Takach, "Clark and the Jerusalem Embassy Affair," 154.
84. Ash-Sharq Al-Awsat in Arabic, 29 June 1979, 1 in FBIS-Middle East, 2 July 1979, A3; and Reuters, 30 June 1979 from Lexis-Nexis. In an interview on 24 March 1998, Miss MacDonald denied that this consideration influenced the embassy decision, but the government clearly has an interest in playing down the blackmail potential of the Quebec imbroglio.
85. Adelman, "Clark and the Canadian Embassy," 10; and Simpson, *Discipline of Power*, 146.

recant on his promise because of the negative effects that it might have on the Middle East peace process.[86] The American effort culminated in a meeting between American secretary of state Cyrus Vance and MacDonald at the United Nations, where the former expressed his country's grave reservations about the Canadian initiative.[87] President Carter reinforced this message personally when he met with Clark at the G-5 Tokyo Summit at the end of June.[88]

In addition to these international political pressures the Arab states exploited political divisions inside Canada and widespread opposition to the embassy move to their advantage.[89] Powerful groups opposed the government initiative at all levels of Canadian society. Significantly, the lay public—who saw the move as a "naked bribe for votes"—the media, academics, and the legislative opposition in the House of Commons all opposed the proposed embassy move.[90] Parliamentary opposition was particularly significant since the Conservatives possessed only the barest of majorities in the legislature and had to fear defeat in a motion of nonconfidence if they offended the opposition and could not muster a perfect turnout for a confidence vote.[91] The sum total of domestic opposition made it difficult for the new Government to get organized and tackle the political challenges that lay ahead of it. In an interview, MacDonald told us that she thus decided that it would be best to "put the issue on the back burner, where it belonged." She also said, "My concern at the moment was to get it off my desk. It was hampering things," such as preparations for the Tokyo economic summit, which was the Government's top priority.[92]

It is further significant that there was strong opposition to the embassy move within the Conservative government itself. Members of the PC as well as Clark's inner cabinet—including MacDonald, herself—opposed the planned embassy move. In fact, Finance Minister John Crosbie, who was the "strongman" of the inner cabinet, viewed the plan to move the embassy as "the silliest decision."[93] Thus, Clark had no strong reservoir of support in the

86. Andrew Malcom, New York Times Abstracts, 10 June 1979, 7 from Lexis-Nexis; and Henry Giniger, New York Times Abstracts, 24 June 1979, 8 from Lexis-Nexis.

87. Dewitt and Kirton, Canada as a Principal Power, 389.

88. Takach, "Clark and the Jerusalem Embassy Affair," 161.

89. Indeed, Clark recently informed us that "the factors which caused the creation of the Stanfield Commission, which led to a change in our position, were primarily domestic factors, in which international pressures played only an indirect role." Personal communication from the Right Honourable Joe Clark, 20 March 1998.

90. Simpson, Discipline of Power, 153, 159.

91. This lack of structural autonomy, engendered by small majority government, was illustrated poignantly in November, when the government was actually brought down in a vote of confidence over an economic issue.

92. Interview with the Honorable Flora MacDonald, 24 March 1998.

93. Simpson, Discipline of Power, 97, 153, 206.

government, his Cabinet, or the party to convince him to stay the course with his decision.

It is clear, then, that Arab threats to implement economic sanctions coincided with powerful international and domestic political conditions that amplified the pressure on Clark to back away from his pledge. At the same time, the costs of changing behavior were quite low. For the fledgling Conservative Government—which had been out of power since 1968 and was, consequently, struggling to stay on top of a complex domestic and international situation—the issue was "more or less an irritation that interfered with crucial matters" such as preparation for the Tokyo Summit.[94] Moreover, as mentioned, there was little support for the initiative among the Canadian electorate, and even Canadian Jews and Zionist organizations were lukewarm to the issue and proffered it only half-hearted support.[95] Thus Clark did not have to fear a domestic backlash if he backed down. Consequently, his government complied with the wishes of the Arab states.

We conclude, therefore, that economic sanctions worked in this case for several reasons. First, the threat of economic sanctions was associated with compound political sanctions that made the political costs of noncompliance high for Canadian policymakers. Second, important third parties (most prominently the United States) were not supportive of and, in fact, strenuously opposed the Canadian initiative. Third, domestic political factors, specifically divisions within Canada and the Canadian government, were conducive to the exercise of economic and political pressure by the Arab states. Fourth, the political opposition was strong. In addition to these incentives to capitulate, the Clark government's lack of executive autonomy as well as the low domestic and international political costs of retreat clinched the result.

These political considerations, though extremely powerful, would not have been sufficient to cause a Canadian reversal without the application of sanctions. In fact, sanctions served as both a lightning rod for domestic opposition to an unpopular policy and a dramatic signal of Arab discontent. Arab economic sanctions, therefore, heightened Clark's and powerful third parties' awareness of the political risks associated with the Canadian government's proposed policy. In this case, then, economic sanctions tapped into a conducive domestic and international political environment to produce the desired result.

94. Miss MacDonald stressed repeatedly to us that "other issues were much more important" than the embassy issue.
95. Takach, "Clark and the Jerusalem Embassy Affair," 164–66.

INDIAN PRESSURES AGAINST NEPAL (1988–90)

In June 1988 Nepal began to deepen its military ties with China by purchasing approximately $20 million of military equipment including light arms, ammunition, and sixteen antiaircraft guns. This action alarmed Indian decisionmakers since it has been Indian policy since 1940 on to preserve a dominant position in this Himalayan kingdom that adjoins India's powerful neighbor China.[96] Other sources of tension included the Nepalese government's requirement that Indian workers in Nepal obtain permits and Nepal's awarding of contracts to China to perform construction projects in strategic areas near the Indian border.[97] All these disputes were attributable to Nepal's intensifying desire to preserve its sovereignty and independence in the face of increasing regional assertiveness under the leadership of Rajiv Gandhi.[98]

To bring Nepal solidly back into the Indian sphere of influence, Indian leaders refused to renew two separate agreements signed in 1978 that governed trade and transit rights between the two states. [99] The Indians began to insist

96. "Nepal Buys Arms from China," *Kyodo News Service*, 8 September 1988 from Lexis-Nexis; and John W. Garver, "China-India Rivalry in Nepal: The Clash Over Chinese Arms Sales," *Asian Survey* 31, no. 10 (October 1991): 960–61. On the Sino-Indian competition over Nepal, see Devin T. Hagerty, "India's Regional Security Doctrine," *Asian Survey* 31, no. 4 (April 1991): 361; Garver, "China-India Rivalry in Nepal," 956–75; and Narayan Khadka, "Foreign Aid to Nepal: Donor Motivations in the Post–Cold War Period," *Asian Survey* 37, no. 11 (November 1997): 1044–61.

97. On these and other disputes between the two states, see "Nepal: King Birendra to Visit India, Review Ties," *Inter Press Service*, 14 September 1988 from Lexis-Nexis; "Indo-Nepal Pact Under Threat of Breakdown, Diplomats Say," *Reuters*, 23 February 1989 from Lexis-Nexis; Mahendra P. Lamba, "Indo-Nepalese Economic Relations," *Delhi General Overseas Service*, 12 May 1989 in FBIS-NES-89-091, 12 May 1989, 36; Niranjan Koirala, "Nepal in 1989: A Very Difficult Year," *Asian Survey* 30, no. 2 (February 1990): 137; and Leo O. Rose, "India's Foreign Relations: Reassessing Basic Policies," in *India Briefing, 1990*, ed. Marshall M. Bouton and Philip Oldenburg (Boulder: Westview, 1990), 63. On historical Indian sensitivities to events transpiring along the Sino-Indian frontier, see Jean-Marc F. Blanchard, "Borders and Borderlands: An Institutional Approach to Territorial Disputes in the Asia Pacific" (Ph.D. diss., University of Pennsylvania, 1998), chaps. 6–7.

98. Regarding Nepal's historical efforts to maintain a balance in its ties with India and China, see Lok Raj Baral, "Nepal's Security Policy and South Asian Regionalism," *Asian Survey* 26, no. 11 (November 1986): 1207–19. For details on India's new regional assertiveness, see Mark Fineman, "Trade Embargo Wreaks Havoc: Nepal Is Paying the Price for Standing up to India," *Los Angeles Times*, 10 April 1989, 1 from Lexis-Nexis; Rajendra Bajpai, "India, Nepal Still Split Despite Summit Agreement," *Reuters*, 27 August 1989 from Lexis-Nexis; and Druba Adhikary, "Nepal to Raise Trade War with India at Non-Aligned Summit," *Reuters*, 29 August 1989 from Lexis-Nexis.

99. The Indians also took a legalistic tack and accused Nepal of violating both the letter and spirit of their existing bilateral accords. Jeremy Gavon, "Nepal in Crisis as India Puts on Economic Squeeze," *Daily Telegraph*, 25 March 1989, 10 from Lexis-Nexis; "India and Nepal: The Parable of the Yam," *Economist*, 15 April 1989, 35 from Lexis-Nexis; "India: To Revive Talks with Nepal before NAM Summit," *Inter Press Service*, 22 August 1989 from Lexis-Nexis; and Druba Adhikary, "India-Nepal to Resume Trade Row Talks," *Reuters*, 27 December 1989 from Lexis-Nexis. For an evaluation of the merits of Indian claims, see Surya P. Subedi,

on *one* agreement while informing the Nepalese government that the existing treaties would expire on 23 March 1989. This was fundamentally unacceptable to the Nepalese who saw free transit as the inalienable and permanent right of a landlocked nation while trade was a matter subject to fluctuating economic interests that merited frequent renegotiation.

The expiration of the treaties meant, in the Indian view, that it no longer had to maintain its normal trade and transit arrangements with Nepal. Consequently, in late March, it closed all but two of its border crossings with Nepal and stopped shipments of fuel, salt, kerosene, medicines, and other essentials.[100] In early April, the Indians attempted to aggravate Nepal's economic suffering in two new ways. Although they continued to let goods from third parties pass into Nepal from India (with some interruptions), they closed the railway leading from the port of Calcutta to Nepal.[101] They also canceled several million dollars of trade credits that they had previously extended to Nepal on a routine basis.[102]

Even before Indian economic sanctions had begun to impose serious hardships on Nepal, the government confronted serious domestic problems. On 4 April a large student demonstration against Indian political and economic pressure turned into a violent antigovernment protest. The subsequent and harsh government crackdown intensified existing antigovernment sentiments and spurred new demands for democracy.[103] Over the next three months, the leading opposition group in Nepal, the Nepali Congress Party (NCP), and dissident members in Parliament joined the chorus demanding that the King Birendra implement political reforms and rectify the dreadful Nepalese

"India-Nepal Security Relations and the 1950 Treaty," *Asian Survey* 34, no. 3 (March 1994): 275–77.

100. "Nepal's Lifelines Squeezed in Trade Dispute with India," *Reuters*, 24 March 1989 from Lexis-Nexis; Gavon, "Nepal in Crisis as India Puts on Economic Squeeze"; "India Closes Most Roads to Nepal in Trade Dispute," *New York Times*, 26 March 1989, 8 from Lexis-Nexis; K. K. Sharma, "Delhi Tries to Shrug Off Nepal Bullying Charge," *Financial Times*, 18 May 1989, 6 from Lexis-Nexis; Bajpai, "India, Nepal Still Split Despite Summit Agreement," K. K. Sharma, "Bid to Break Indo-Nepal Impasse," *Financial Times*, 24 August 1989, 4 from Lexis-Nexis; and Adhikary, "Nepal to Raise Trade War with India at Non-Aligned Summit."

101. *Kathmandu External Service*, 4 April 1989 in FBIS-NES-89-064, 5 April 1989, 53; *AFP*, 16 April 1989 in FBIS-NES-89-074, 19 April 1989, 57; "Salt in the Wound," *Economist*, 20 May 1989 from Lexis-Nexis; and Garver, "China-India Rivalry in Nepal," 960. On the history of the Calcutta route and its importance, see Charles E. Stonier, "The Stranglehold on Nepal," *Journal of Commerce*, 10 October 1989 from Lexis-Nexis.

102. Rajendra Bajpai, "India Tightens Economic Noose on Nepal, Cancels Trade Credit," *Reuters*, 10 May 1989 from Lexis-Nexis.

103. Kedar Man Singh, Agence France Press (AFP), 4 April 1989 in FBIS-NES-89-064, 5 April 1989, 53.

economic situation and the trade war with India.[104] On 5 and 6 April 1990 massive numbers of protestors again took to the streets and clashed with the army. The army fired upon the protesters and killed hundreds, leading some members of the opposition to call for the outright abolition of the monarchy.[105] With this direct threat to the monarchy, the King capitulated. He dismissed the hated prime minister, agreed to legalize political parties, and dissolved the parliament, the Panchayat system of governance, and the Council of Ministers. He replaced it with a government more in tune with the people and the political opposition.[106]

In the face of intense domestic political pressure, the newly appointed government prepared to capitulate to India in order to restore political and economic order. On 17 April interim Prime Minister K. P. Bhattarai stated that his most important task was to restore ties with India. In line with this, he sent a letter to Indian prime minister V. P. Singh calling for a settlement of their dispute, a return to the pre-March 1989 status quo, and the conclusion of new trade and transit agreements. After Bhattarai visited New Delhi in early June, India agreed to lift its embargo and to open its trade ports with Nepal. For its part, Nepal abolished its work permit requirement for Indian nationals and, in a major concession, asked China to delay its last shipment of arms to Nepal. The agreement was not completely one-sided, allowing the Nepalese government a face-saving exit. India agreed to resume negotiations on trade and transit agreements, to provide certain favorable trade privileges, and to extend a large trade credit.[107]

Why did sanctions work against Nepal when the kingdom was defending its vital rights as a sovereign state? One plausible reason is that Nepal's economic health was highly dependent on Indian goodwill. India was Nepal's only supplier of a number of the aforementioned strategic goods, took 35–40 percent

104. *Delhi Domestic Service*, 19 June 1989 in FBIS-NES-89-120, 23 June 1989, 39; "Nepal's Government Attacked in Assembly over India Ties," *Reuters*, 4 July 1989 from Lexis-Nexis; and "Nepal: Uproar in the House as Impasse with India Continues," *Inter Press Service*, 11 August 1989 from Lexis-Nexis.

105. Michael Hutt, "Drafting the Nepal Constitution, 1990," *Asian Survey* 31, no. 11 (December 1991): 1021.

106. Niranjan Koirala, "Nepal in 1990: The End of An Era," *Asian Survey* 31, no. 2 (February 1991): 135–36; Hutt, "Drafting the Nepal Constitution," 1022–23; and Narayan Khadka, "Democracy and Development in Nepal: Prospects and Challenges," *Pacific Affairs* 66, no. 1 (spring 1993): 47. For a discussion of the political system in Nepal, see Narayan Khadka, "Crisis in Nepal's Partyless Panchayat System: The Case for More Democracy," *Pacific Affairs* 59, no. 2 (fall 1986): 429–54.

107. For discussions, see "India and Nepal Agree to be Friends Again," *Daily Telegraph*, 11 June 1990, 10 from Lexis-Nexis; Barbara Crossette, "India to Lift Embargo and Discuss Rift," *New York Times*, 12 June 1990, A12 from Lexis-Nexis; and Koirala, "Nepal in 1990," 138.

of Nepal's total exports, and was the only real transit point for foreign goods to enter landlocked Nepal. In addition, India sent large numbers of tourists, provided skilled laborers, and supplied employment opportunities for almost three million Nepalese workers.[108] Finally, the imbroglio with India threatened the lucrative Nepalese tourist industry, which was a critical source of foreign exchange for Nepal, one of the world's ten poorest countries.

Nepalese dependence on India is reflected by the fact that Indian economic sanctions began to bite quickly. Within two weeks after the expiration of the trade and transit agreements in March 1989, Nepal began to experience shortages of food (for example, sugar, rice, salt, and baby food), oil, kerosene, and medicine. In the capital, large percentages of public buses, taxis, and private vehicles were idled. Many Nepalese exporters found it to be prohibitively costly to export their goods through India due to new tariffs.[109] By July, the economic picture in Nepal was quite bleak. The government reported to the Parliament that the dispute with India had caused massive declines in GDP growth (from 5.3 to 1.5 percent), the stagnation of the construction, transportation, and trade industries, and double-digit increases in inflation.[110]

Although it is true that Nepal suffered economically from Indian sanctions, it is instructive that it did not capitulate until nearly fifteen months after India began to impose sanctions. In addition, more than six months before it complied with Indian demands, the Nepalese government had begun to tap into alternate sources of supply and alternative transportation routes that allowed it to minimize, though not eliminate, the economic pain resulting from Indian sanctions.[111] Since Nepal felt Indian economic sanctions fairly rapidly and since it appears that Nepal was beginning to stabilize its economic decline by the time it capitulated, we must look beyond the economic harm imposed by sanctions to understand why Nepalese policymakers took nearly fifteen months to accede to Indian demands

---

108. "India and Nepal: The Parable of the Yam"; "Indo-Nepal Pact Under Threat of Breakdown, Diplomats Say"; K. K. Sharma, "Landlocked Nepal Sets Sail on a Sea of Troubles," *Financial Times*, 12 April 1989, 5 from Lexis-Nexis; K. K. Sharma, "Nepal and India 'Willing to Hold Talks on Dispute'," *Financial Times*, 21 April 1989, 4 from Lexis-Nexis; and Hufbauer, Schott, and Elliott, *Economic Sanctions Reconsidered*, vol. 2, 628–29.

109. Jeremy Gavon, "Nepal Induces Rationing as Indian Sanctions Begin to Bite," *Daily Telegraph*, 6 April 1989, 11 from Lexis-Nexis; Sanjoy Hazarika, "India Presses and Nepalese Feel the Pinch," *New York Times*, 10 May 1989, 17 from Lexis-Nexis; and *AFP*, 13 May 1989 in FBIS-NES-89-092, 15 May 1989, 48.

110. *AFP*, 10 July 1989 in FBIS-NES-89-132, 12 July 1989, 79–80; and Koirala, "Nepal in 1989," 140–42.

111. "Nepal and India: Another Border," *The Economist*, 24 February 1990, 34 from Lexis-Nexis; Barbara Crossette, "A Cold Wind from India Makes Nepal Life Harder," *New York Times*, 15 November 1989, A4 from Lexis-Nexis; and Hufbauer, Schott, and Elliott, *Economic Sanctions Reconsidered*, vol. 2, 629.

Economic sanctions were effective in this case because the international and domestic political context imposed heavy political costs of noncompliance on the Nepalese government. On the international level, it was notable that Nepal could not rally any international organizations or foreign aid donors to its cause. Throughout the summer and fall of 1989, Nepal had appealed to international organizations for new grants and loans and discussed the consequences of the dispute with India at IMF and World Bank meetings. Unfortunately, the Nepalese proved unable to obtain any meaningful offers of political or economic assistance.[112] Indeed, international donors grew reluctant to provide aid to Nepal because of its political structure and pressed it to make major political and economic changes.[113]

Of greater consequence, China was not forthcoming with sufficient backing. Although Chinese leaders had helped Nepal since the beginning of the crisis by supplying fuel, opening several new border passes, giving free salt, and providing a multimillion dollar grant to Nepal, they were unwilling to do much more because of their own domestic economic problems at the time and improving Chinese relations with India.[114] Even on a rhetorical level, the best that Chinese Premier Li Peng could do was to call on India to be "magnanimous and generous" in its dealings with Nepal.[115] Later, during the height of the April 1990 protests, King Birendra appealed to the Chinese again, but was told that the Chinese government viewed the chaos in Nepal as strictly an internal affair.[116] This lack of third party support from international organizations and Nepal's most important neighbor made it difficult for the King to resist Indian pressure.

Far more important than the international context in this case, though, was the turbulent Nepalese domestic political context. Divisions in the country made it difficult for the government and the King to exploit rally-around-the-flag sentiments among the people. Although many segments of Nepalese society, including opposition leaders, blamed India for their economic problems

112. Druba Adhikary, "Nepal: Economy Near Shambles, Appeals for Help," *Inter Press Service*, 12 June 1989 from Lexis-Nexis; Druba Adhikary, "Nepal to Raise Trade War with India at Non-Aligned Summit," *Reuters*, 29 August 1989 from Lexis-Nexis; and Koirala, "Nepal in 1989," 139–40.

113. Sanjoy Hazarika, "Nepal Seeks Less Reliance on Foreign Economic Aid," *New York Times*, 7 May 1990, D5 from Lexis-Nexis; Hufbauer, Schott, and Elliott, *Economic Sanctions Reconsidered*, vol. 2, 628, 630; and Koirala, "Nepal in 1990," 134.

114. Garver, "China-India Rivalry in Nepal," 964–69; and John W. Garver, "China and South Asia," *Annals of the American Academy of Political and Social Sciences*, no. 519 (January 1992): 67–85.

115. "Li Comments on Chinese Arms for Nepal," *Kyodo News Service*, 21 November 1989 from Lexis-Nexis; and "Chinese Premier Asks India to be Generous over Trade Row," *Reuters*, 21 November 1989 from Lexis-Nexis.

116. Garver, "China-India Rivalry in Nepal," 971.

and felt Nepal had to stand up to Indian threats, many were simultaneously critical of the government.[117] Indeed, it was not clear that either the government or the King had any sort of mandate to wear the nationalist mantle.[118] In addition, the political crisis in Nepal coupled with the economic crisis came to threaten the monarchy itself rather than the Panchayat system alone. Finally, political problems in Nepal created openings for India to meddle in Nepal's internal affairs. Indian delegations not only attended the meetings of Nepalese opposition groups, but also gave vocal public support and perhaps even secret financial support to the NCP.[119] The King could not have looked on the prospect of Indian involvement in Nepal's domestic affairs except with the greatest concern given that on the previous occasion when India had meddled in Nepal's internal affairs, the prior regime had been overthrown.[120]

Some may argue that it was the economic sanctions which gave rise to the prodemocracy movement and led to the formation of a new government that was amenable to settlement with India on Indian terms.[121] Such a conclusion rests on an overly narrow and ahistorical reading of Nepalese domestic politics. In Nepal, opposition forces had long been disenchanted with the government. Corruption, decades of economic mismanagement, and the suppression of political rights since King Mahendra, King Birendra's father, had terminated constitutional rule in 1960 and, consequently, had created a strong undercurrent of support for major political, social, and economic reforms.[122] The growing opposition had tasted democracy in May 1980 during a national referendum on the Panchayat system and was hungrier than ever for political reform.[123] The prodemocracy movement received further boosts from the

117. Barbara Crossette, "Nepal's Economy is Gasping as India, a Huge Neighbor, Squeezes It Hard," *New York Times*, 11 April 1989, A12 from Lexis-Nexis; "Nepal: Uproar in the House as Impasse with India Continues"; Crossette, "A Cold Wind from India Makes Nepal Life Harder," A4; and Mark Fineman, "Trade Dispute with India Brings Economic Crisis: Nepalese Bracing for a 'Grim Year,'" *Los Angeles Times*, 14 April 1989, 18 from Lexis-Nexis.

118. Fineman, "Trade Dispute with India Brings Economic Crisis"; and Koirala, "Nepal in 1989," 139.

119. Koirala, "Nepal in 1990," 134–35; "MP's Deplore Nepalese Human Rights Violations," 30 March 1990 in FBIS-NES-90-062, 30 March 1990, 36; Adhikary, "Nepal: Economy Near Shambles"; and Garver, "China-India Rivalry in Nepal," 970.

120. Baral, "Nepal's Security Policy and South Asian Regionalism," 1210–11.

121. Hufbauer, Schott, and Elliott, *Economic Sanctions Reconsidered*, vol. 2, 630.

122. On these issues, see respectively Dor Bahadur Bista, "Nepal in 1988: Many Losses, Some Gains," *Asian Survey* 29, no. 2 (February 1989): 223–24; Shankar Sharma, "Nepal's Economy: Growth and Development," *Asian Survey* 26, no. 8 (August 1986): 897–908; Sukhdev Shah, "Nepal's Economic Development," *Asian Survey* 28, no. 9 (September 1988): 945–57; Narayan Khadka, "Nepal's Stagnant Economy: The Panchayat Legacy," *Asian Survey* 31, no. 8 (August 1991): 694–711; and Khadka, "Crisis in Nepal's Partyless Panchayat System," 429–54.

123. Khadka, "Crisis in Nepal's Partyless Panchayat System," 429–54.

large civil disobedience movement in Nepal in 1985, the staggering political changes sweeping the globe in 1989, particularly in eastern Europe, and a peaceful change of government in India in the same year.[124] This is not to say that the economic pain inflicted by Indian sanctions was irrelevant, but rather that it tapped into preexisting anger rather than created it. Economic sanctions worked in tandem with existing political discontent to bring about a change in government and compliance with Indian demands.[125]

Economic sanctions, thus, worked against Nepal because there was a favorable international and domestic political context that imposed heavy political costs of noncompliance on the Nepalese monarchy.[126] Specifically, Nepal largely complied with Indian requirements because it lacked third party support, confronted a divided country, and faced a strong domestic political opposition. Unfortunately for Nepalese leaders, there were no viable opportunities to redirect the brunt of the economic pain engendered by sanctions away from their supporters on to opposition groups. This was so because opponents of the regime were pervasive both geographically and politically. In other words, the opposition was present throughout the entire country and at all levels of society.

Nepalese policymakers could not have been pleased about acquiescing to Indian demands given that Nepalese elites themselves had initiated the crisis in order to assert their country's sovereignty and national independence. There were three factors, though, that made it easier for them to swallow the bitter pill of capitulation. First, the government did not suffer any domestic political costs from complying with Indian demands since influential groups and the mass public wanted the government to end the conflict with India. Second, any potential loss of face from complying was mitigated by Indian willingness to accept the principle of separate trade and transit agreements, which the Nepalese wanted from the start of the dispute. Third, the government lacked autonomy from societal forces—indeed, it owed its existence to their political activities—and hence was inclined to be responsive to them.

124. Koirala, "Nepal in 1989," 143; Koirala, "Nepal in 1990," 134; and Narayan Khadka, "Democracy and Development in Nepal: Prospects and Challenges," *Pacific Affairs* 66, no. 1 (spring 1993): 45–46.
125. Similar conclusions are implied by Koirala, "Nepal in 1990," 137; and Fred Gaige and Jon Scholz, "The 1991 Parliamentary Elections in Nepal: Political Freedom and Stability," *Asian Survey* 31, no. 11 (November 1991): 1041.
126. In a 1992 interview, King Birendra confirmed that political change—and the consequent policy surrender to India—occurred because "unforeseen economic factors and the question of political change within Nepalese society coincided with changes in the international arena which were unprecedented in recent history and monumental in scope and magnitude." Interview with King Birendra, *Independent*, 8 January 1992 quoted in Khadka, "Democracy and Development in Nepal," 46.

MAKING USE OF ECONOMIC SANCTONS IN THE CONTEMPORARY ERA

EIGHTY YEARS ago, Woodrow Wilson proclaimed "A nation that is boy-cotted is a nation that is in sight of surrender. Apply this economic, peaceful, silent, deadly remedy and there will be no need for force...it brings a pressure upon the nation which, in my judgment, no modern nation could resist."[127] Although writers have promoted Wilson's vision for decades, optimism about the potency of this "silent, deadly remedy" has degenerated over the course of the century into outright pessimism. Recognizing this growing disenchantment with sanctions, American UN ambassador Charles W. Yost sought to moderate expectations about what economic sanctions against Rhodesia could accomplish, stating that we should not demand more of sanctions than they could deliver.[128] It is far more important, though, to explain how we can increase the potential for economic sanctions to achieve the desired objective than to moderate our expectations.

In this article, we have developed such an explanation. We argued a priori that economic sanctions are likely to work best when the target state faces high political costs of noncompliance. Only when a state has powerful political incentives to comply with the sanctioning state's demands is it likely to change its behavior in response to sanctions. We also emphasized that high political costs of noncompliance are likely to push sanctioned states in the desired direction when the domestic and international political costs of changing behavior are low, and when executive autonomy is low. Our case studies support this theoretical analysis (see Table 1).

In each of the three cases that we examined, domestic and international political conditions ensured that the target state would pay a high political price if it refused to comply with the wishes of the sanctioning state. In the 1933 case, the Soviets risked their diplomatic ties with the British and impending relations with the United States at a time when the Soviet Union faced dangerous new threats on both its western and eastern flanks. In 1979, Canada faced third party pressure in the form of American diplomatic intervention and compound sanctions in the form of an Arab threat to Canadian participation in international peacekeeping operations. Domestically, sympathy for the Palestinian position and political instability in Quebec increased the political costs of noncompliance. Finally, Nepalese capitulation was achieved primarily be-

---

127. Saul K. Padover, ed., *Wilson's Ideals* (Washington, D.C.: American Council on Public Affairs, 1942), 108 quoted in Hufbauer, Schott, and Elliott, *Economic Sanctions Reconsidered,* vol. 1, 9.

128. The Department of State, *Bulletin,* 62 (13 April 1970), 507 quoted in Strack, *Sanctions: The Case of Rhodesia,* 251.

cause of domestic political factors, such as the preexisting political instability in Nepal and the power of the prodemocracy opposition. The lack of international third party support for Kathmandu further enhanced the political costs of sanctions.

Table 1

SALIENT FACTORS IN SANCTIONS SUCCESSES

	Great Britain/ Soviet Union	Canada/ Arab World	India/ Nepal
Compound sanctions	significant	highly significant	---------
High International Threat	highly significant	---------	---------
Third Party Behavior	significant	significant	significant
Domestic Instability	---------	significant	highly significant
Powerful Opposition	---------	highly significant	significant
Few Redirection Opportunities	---------	---------	significant
Low Costs of Compliance	significant	highly significant	significant
Low Structural Autonomy	---------	significant	significant

Furthermore, in each of the three cases that we have studied, the complicating factors that we enumerated amplified rather than diminished the effect of high political costs of noncompliance. In the case of the Soviet Union, the comparatively low domestic costs of retreat minimized the moderate international costs of changing behavior and thus facilitated compliance with British demands. Similarly, in the Canadian case, the costs of compliance were remarkably low and the face-saving cover of the Stanfield Report reduced them further. Furthermore, the low degree of structural autonomy that the Canadian government possessed amplified the domestic political costs of moving the embassy to Jerusalem. Finally, in the case of Nepal, there was a low domestic cost of exit and a new government possessing little if any autonomy from public pressures.

It should be noted that the political factors that conspired to produce compliance were different in each of the three cases. This leads us to conclude that it is the aggregate political costs that states face, rather than any particular source of these costs, that determine outcomes. Policymakers should take heart, therefore, that sanctions can be applied successfully in a variety of different domestic and international circumstances.

The lesson to be obtained from our study is that if leaders want to use economic sanctions effectively, they must make certain that the right political conditions are in place. To some extent this is in the sanctioner's control, since it can compound the effect of its sanctions by applying complementary diplomatic sanctions or by supporting opposition groups within the sanctioned state. Since, however, it is difficult to construct a viable political opposition or to shape a target state's international security environment, the sanctioning state will not have complete control over all the relevant factors that shape political cost. When the political conditions do not bode well for a strategy of economic coercion, policymakers must be prepared to use other policy instruments including, if necessary, force.

ECONOMIC SANCTIONS DO WORK:

ECONOMIC STATECRAFT AND THE OIL EMBARGO OF RHODESIA

DAVID M. ROWE

ECENT YEARS have witnessed a resurgence of scholarly interest in the
ability of states to use economic sanctions to achieve important policy
objectives.[1] This interest in the successful use of sanctions has been an
enduring theme of the sanctions literature and is driven by the desire to generate practical policy advice. By comparing past instances of success and failure,
scholars hope to discern the conditions under which policy makers can use
economic sanctions most successfully as an instrument of foreign policy.[2]

The soundness of the scholarly community's policy advice, however, relies
critically upon the accuracy of its assessments about the success or failure of
past uses of economic sanctions. Robert Pape, for example, strongly criticizes
an emerging optimism about the effectiveness of economic sanctions, arguing
that this optimism relies upon a misreading of the historical record that vastly

David M. Rowe is an assistant professor of political science at Ohio State University.

I thank David Bearce, Jean-Marc Blanchard, Pamela Camerra-Rowe, Patrick McDonald,
Edward Mansfield, Norrin Ripsman, the anonymous reviewers, and editors of *Security Studies*
for their comments.

1. See Gary Clyde Hufbauer, Jeffrey J. Schott, and Kimberly Ann Elliott, *Economic Sanctions Reconsidered*, 2nd rev. ed., 2 vols. (Washington, D.C.: Institute for International Economics, 1990), as well their first edition published in 1985; Jaleh Dashti-Gibson, Patricia Davis,
and Benjamin Radcliff, "On the Determinants of the Success of Economic Sanctions: An
Empirical Analysis," *American Journal of Political Science* 41, no. 2 (April 1997): 608–18; Robert
A. Pape, "Why Economic Sanctions Do Not Work," *International Security* 22, no. 2 (fall 1997):
90–136; Robert A. Pape, "Why Economic Sanctions *Still* Do Not Work," *International Security*
23, no. 1 (summer 1998): 66–77; Kimberly Ann Elliott, "The Sanctions Glass: Half Full or
Completely Empty?" *International Security* 23, no. 1 (summer 1998): 50–65; T. Clifton Morgan
and Valerie L. Schwebach, "Fools Suffer Gladly: The Use of Economic Sanctions in International Crises," *International Studies Quarterly* 41, no. 1 (March 1997): 27–50; David Cortright
and George A. Lopez, eds. *Economic Sanctions: Panacea or Peacebuilding in a Post–Cold War
World?* (Boulder: Westview, 1995).

2. See, for example, Jean-Marc Blanchard and Norrin M. Ripsman, "Asking the Right
Question: *When* Do Economic Sanctions Work Best," *Security Studies* 9, nos. 1/2 (autumn
1999–winter 2000): 219–53; Pape, "Why Economic Sanctions Do Not Work"; Hufbauer,
Schott and Elliott, *Economic Sanctions Reconsidered*, both editions. Although this method domi-
nates the literature, it is important to note that comparing the successfulness of past instances of economic sanctions is not the only method by which by which scholars may fruit-
fully study sanctions or generate sound policy advice about how policy makers should use
them. See especially Jonathan Kirshner, "The Microfoundations of Economic Sanctions,"
Security Studies 6, no. 3 (spring 1997): 32–64.

overstates the degree to which economic sanctions have actually achieved important foreign policy goals. Once Pape corrects for these errors, he finds little empirical justification for using economic sanctions to achieve important policy objectives.[3] Although David Baldwin reaches different conclusions about the likely utility of economic sanctions, he likewise argues that faulty analytical frameworks for assessing the past success of sanctions are one of the primary reasons why the utility of economic statecraft is systematically misrepresented in the literature.[4] These biased estimates, in turn, yield misleading policy prescriptions with potentially grave consequences. "In a world in which the stakes of statecraft have risen astronomically," Baldwin writes, "better understanding of all techniques of statecraft becomes imperative. If statesmen, indeed, are to choose war, this choice should be the result of reasoned assessment of alternative courses of action rather than the result of inadequate understanding of the range of policy options available to them."[5] In short, an accurate assessment of whether sanctions "work" in any individual case is not a peripheral concern to sanctions scholars. Rather, it is fundamental to their desire to generate sound policy advice about how and when to use this instrument of statecraft most wisely, for it is this knowledge that provides the basic building blocks from which scholars draw their recommendations.

Yet despite Baldwin's attempt in *Economic Statecraft* to establish a more systematic framework for assessing the utility of economic statecraft, most analyses continue to use oversimplified analytical frameworks likely to yield inaccurate assessments of sanctions. The most pervasive shortcoming remains the continued tendency of the literature to assess the successfulness of sanctions almost exclusively in terms of the publically stated demands of the sanctioning governments and then only over a narrow range of the target actors that these governments are seeking to influence.[6] This is a serious shortcoming. "To view the use of economic statecraft," Baldwin writes, "strictly in terms of securing compliance with explicit and publicly stated demands is to load the dice in

3. Pape, "Why Economic Sanctions Do Not Work"; and Pape, "Why Economic Sanctions *Still* Do Not Work."

4. David A. Baldwin, *Economic Statecraft* (Princeton: Princeton University Press, 1985): esp. 57–58.

5. Ibid., 373.

6. This is especially true of Hufbauer, Schott, and Elliott's study *Economic Sanctions Reconsidered.* See Baldwin, *Economic Statecraft*, 371. Since its initial publication in 1985, this Hufbauer, Schott, Elliott study has become the single most influential empirical analysis of economic sanctions and provides the empirical foundations for a number of subsequent studies, including Pape, "Why Economic Sanctions Do Not Work"; and "Why Economic Sanctions Still Do Not Work"; Dashti-Gibson et al., "On the Determinants of the Success of Economic Sanctions"; Lisa L. Martin, *Coercive Cooperation: Explaining Multilateral Economic Sanctions* (Princeton: Princeton University Press, 1992); George Tsebelis, "Are Sanctions Effective? A Game Theoretic Analysis," *Journal of Conflict Resolution* 34, no. 1 (1990): 3–28.

favor of failure. Third parties, secondary goals, implicit and unstated goals are all likely to be significant components of such undertakings."[7] The most critical component of any analysis of a sanctions episode is to measure the success of sanctions only in terms of the *entire* array of goals that states are trying to achieve and the targets they are seeking to influence.[8]

In this article, I seek to underscore the importance this point by reinterpreting one of most spectacular cases of the "failure" of economic sanctions: the British oil embargo of Rhodesia. The embargo was imposed within the context of a larger British strategy of economic sanctions intended to force Rhodesia's white minority government to accept eventual majority rule in this central African colony. Although the broader program of economic sanctions is now generally believed partially responsible for bringing majority rule to Rhodesia (Zimbabwe),[9] the oil embargo is widely perceived to have been a spectacular failure.[10] It collapsed shortly after its imposition, undermined by an impressive sanctions-busting campaign in which the subsidiaries of British and American oil companies supplied Rhodesia with this critical commodity.[11] The oil embargo thus stands as a compelling example of the futility of trying to control the behavior of private economic actors for political ends, and of using economic sanctions to pursue important foreign policy goals.

7. Baldwin, *Economic Statecraft*, 132.

8. Ibid., 371.

9. See, for example, William Minter and Elizabeth Schmidt, "When Sanctions Worked: The Case of Rhodesia Re-examined," *African Affairs* 87, no. 347 (April 1988): 207–37; Baldwin, *Economic Statecraft* 189–204; Hufbauer, Schott, and Elliott, *Economic Sanctions Reconsidered;* H. R. Strack, *Sanctions: The Case of Rhodesia* (Syracuse: Syracuse University Press, 1978). Studies that doubted the effectiveness of sanctions include Johan Galtung, "On the Effects of Economic Sanctions, With Examples From the Case of Rhodesia," *World Politics* 19, no. 3 (April 1967): 378–416; Donald Losman, *International Economic Sanctions: The Cases of Cuba, Israel and Rhodesia* (Albuquerque: University of New Mexico Press, 1979); Robin Renwick, *Economic Sanctions* (Cambridge: Harvard University Press, 1981). Pape reasserts the conventional wisdom that sanctions against Rhodesia failed (Pape, "Why Economic Sanctions Do Not Work").

10. See, for example, Martin Bailey, *Oilgate: The Sanctions Scandal* (London: Coronet Books, 1979); Commonwealth Secretariat, *Oil Sanctions Against Rhodesia* (London: Commonwealth Secretariat, 1979); Margaret Doxey, *International Economic Sanctions in Comparative Perspective* (London: MacMillan Press, 1987), 114; Losman, *International Economic Sanctions,* pp. 99–100; Arthur Jay Klinghoffer, *Oiling the Wheels of Apartheid: Exposing South Africa's Secret Oil Trade* (Boulder: Lynne Rienner, 1989), 84–85.

11. See, for example, *Sunday Times,* 27 August 1967. The role that British oil companies played in continuing to supply Rhodesia became a major political scandal in the late 1970s in Britain and was the subject of an intensive governmental inquiry. The inquiry's report is T. H. Bingham and S. M. Gray, Foreign and Commonwealth Office, *Report on the Supply of Petroleum and Petroleum Products to Rhodesia* (London: Her Majesty's Stationery Office, 1978). This report, hereafter referred to as the Bingham report, is an unrivaled source for studying the oil sanctions. It is not only exhaustive, but it also reproduces the major internal oil company documents on which its conclusions were based. See also, Bailey, *Oilgate* .

Drawing extensively on recently opened British government documents covering the critical first phase of the embargo, I will argue that the conventional interpretation of the embargo is highly misleading.[12] The conventional interpretation falsely assumes that the primary purpose of the embargo was to compel rapid capitulation by the white Rhodesian government and that the embargo's collapse represents a critical failure of policy. This view oversimplifies the complex range of goals that Britain pursued in the embargo, especially its need to accommodate substantial and conflicting economic and political interests in white and black Africa. The documents reveal that black Africa and the Commonwealth were primary targets of the embargo and that overriding goals of the embargo were to prevent the breakup up the Commonwealth and divert African political pressure for even more drastic — and in British eyes, more dangerous — actions against the colony. Equally important is the picture these documents provide of the complex strategic environment surrounding the oil embargo. For Britain's objectives in pursuing the embargo were shaped not only by its need to credibly demonstrate to black Africa and the Commonwealth its commitment to majority rule in Rhodesia, but also by its need to avoid the economic sanctions that other powers — especially South Africa — had threatened to impose against Britain should it carry its campaign against Rhodesia too far.

THE OIL EMBARGO IN CONTEXT

RHODESIA unilaterally declared its independence from Great Britain on November 11, 1965. Rhodesia's unilateral declaration of independence, or UDI, was intended to entrench Rhodesia's existing system of white minority rule, thus contradicting directly Britain's desire for eventual majority rule in the colony. Britain immediately responded by imposing a number of economic sanctions on the colony, including a complete ban on imports into British territories of Rhodesian tobacco and sugar, the exclusion of Rhodesia from the Sterling currency system and Commonwealth preference area, and a freeze on assets of the Rhodesian Reserve Bank held in London.[13]

Britain's major objective in implementing these sanctions was to return Rhodesia to constitutional rule and allow a resumption of "progress toward

12. British government documents from the Public Record Office (PRO) are identified using the PRO classification system. Unless otherwise indicated, U.S. government documents were released under the Freedom of Information Act and are available from the Lyndon Baines Johnson presidential library.

13. Doxey, *International Economic Sanctions*, 37.

majority rule as quickly as possible" by disillusioning Rhodesia's white community about the motives, politics, and performance of the Smith regime. At the same time, however, British policy was also constrained by a number of other important considerations. These included: the need to avoid stimulating "black/white conflict in Rhodesia" which would "seriously damage the prospects of a moderate multiracial settlement"; the need to satisfy black African opinion outside Rhodesia that Britain was strongly committed to creating an acceptable multiracial compromise but make clear that Britain would not confer immediate majority rule upon the colony; and the need to avoid actions that would precipitate economic war between Rhodesia and Zambia.[14]

Notably absent from Britain's initial sanctions against Rhodesia was the embargo of oil to the colony. This was surprising as many regarded oil as Rhodesia's achilles' heel. Rhodesia had no domestic sources of this mineral, and even though oil supplied only 27 percent of Rhodesia's energy needs, it was still Rhodesia's single most important import.[15] Oil was a critical input in several important economic sectors. It provided 100 percent of the energy required by the road transport industry. It also provided 70 percent of the requirements of commercial agriculture, which produced slightly over 20 percent of Rhodesia's GDP in 1965 and was the government's strongest constituency.[16] Finally, there are no ready substitutes for petroleum fuels. As a result, an effective oil embargo would not only bring critical sectors of the Rhodesian economy grinding to a halt, it would also create substantial political pressure on the Rhodesian government from its most important supporters.

An oil embargo, at first glance, also appeared easy to enforce and monitor. Five international oil companies—Shell, British Petroleum, Mobil, Caltex, and Total—supplied the Rhodesian market. Except for Total, these companies were headquartered in either Britain or the United States, which cooperated closely with Britain in the sanctions effort.[17] Moreover, at the time of UDI, oil

14. "Directive: Policy in Relation to Rhodesia," MISC.100/A/3, 19 November 1965, PRO CAB 130/254.

15. Sixty-three percent of Rhodesia's energy was from coal, which was also an important Rhodesian export. The remaining 10 percent of energy requirements came from hydroelectricity. W. J. Levy, Inc., *The Economics and Logistics of an Embargo on Oil and Petroleum Products for Rhodesia*, A Report Prepared for the United Nations Office of the Attorney General (New York: United Nations, 1966), 2. In fact, Rhodesia's limited dependence on oil-based energy sources led the UN study to conclude that: "on a siege basis, Rhodesia could probably make do to mid-year and even beyond....but if the decision were one of survival, the availability of oil, in itself, would apparently not be the decisive consideration" (Levy report, 29). Nonetheless, the economic and political pressure would be substantial.

16. Levy report, 3.

17 Total was a French oil company. Caltex was a joint venture between two U.S. companies, Standard Oil and Texaco. Besides Britain, the United States was the country which tried the hardest to make sanctions effective. Between 1969 and 1977, however, a glaring excep-

was imported into Rhodesia along a single route. Tankers carrying crude oil for the central African market would offload their cargoes at the Mozambican port of Beira. The crude was then pumped through a 189 mile pipeline to the Feruka refinery, just inside the Rhodesian border at Umtali, where it was refined into fuels, lubricants and solvents. Those were distributed throughout Rhodesia, Zambia and Malawi by the local subsidiaries of the five international companies. To most outside observers, applying effective oil sanctions seemed as easy as telling the oil companies to shut off the tap to Feruka.

Britain did not share this view. First, there were significant problems in implementing the embargo. A unilateral British effort would not halt the flow of oil to the colony. Even if the British companies, Shell and BP, ceased supplying Rhodesia, this would affect just over forty percent of Rhodesia's requirement, a breach that the other oil companies serving South Africa could easily fill.[18] Britain thus concluded that only a multilateral effort was likely to be effective in reducing the flow of oil to Rhodesia.

Yet even with substantial multilateral cooperation, the ultimate effectiveness of an oil embargo was questionable. The Beira-Umtali pipeline route was new, having first come on line in March 1965.[19] Previously, Rhodesia had been supplied with refined petroleum products via rail from the ports of Beira and Lorenço Marques. Closing the Beira pipeline would simply bring these earlier routes back into use.

Moreover, the Rhodesian oil market was small. In 1965, Rhodesia consumed approximately 400,000 tons of petroleum fuels and lubricants, making its market one-tenth the size of the South Africa's.[20] This meant that Rhodesia could easily draw its requirements from that market. Not only did South Africa possess ample stocks of oil that could cushion the impact of any embargo on Rhodesia, it also possessed the necessary refinery capacity and rolling railway stock to maintain a continual supply of petroleum products to the colony.[21] According to one British planning document, Britain should expect supplies to be made available through Mozambique and South Africa. South Africa received supplies of 4.5 million tons a year and its refineries "provide considerable help to Rhodesia."[22]

---

tion to this general rule was the Byrd amendment which enabled the United States to import Rhodesian minerals, especially chrome.

18. "Southern Rhodesia: Action in the Event of a UDI: Oil," MISC.84/15, 22 October 1965, 2, PRO CAB 130/245.

19. Bailey, *Oilgate*, 55.

20. Bingham report, 2.

21 "Southern Rhodesia: Action in the Event of a UDI: Oil," 2. See also Bailey, *Oilgate*, 132.

22. "Southern Rhodesia: Action in the Event of a UDI: Oil," 2. Likewise, according to an internal BP document which examined that company's role in busting the oil sanctions,

As a consequence, an effective embargo required not only the assistance of the home governments of the five oil companies serving the Rhodesian market, but the assistance of South Africa and Portugal (which administered Mozambique) as well. Although neither country welcomed the Rhodesian rebellion and the upsurge in black nationalism that would inevitably follow, neither would these countries cooperate with Britain by implementing sanctions. South Africa was already coming under international pressure because of apartheid. Portugal was tenuously clinging to its southern African colonies of Mozambique and Angola. Both countries realized that should sanctions succeed in bringing Smith to heel, they would become likely targets in the future. As a consequence, neither South Africa nor Portugal would support an embargo.[23]

The most Britain could hope for, then, was that South Africa and Portugal would remain neutral. Even if these states did not directly supply oil to Rhodesia, however, a policy of strict neutrality that allowed Rhodesian agents either to purchase oil in their markets, or to ship oil across their territories would cause the embargo to collapse. As one British study noted, Rhodesia's small oil market meant that "it would require only one loophole for operators seeking a quick profit to undermine the effectiveness of the embargo."[24]

The implication, of course, was that implementing an effective oil embargo against Rhodesia ultimately meant limiting supplies of oil to the whole of Southern Africa. Yet this strategy not only failed to offer a rapid resolution to the conflict, it was extremely risky. South Africa held oil stocks equal to six-months' normal consumption, only one month of which could keep the Rhodesian economy afloat for a year.[25] Moreover, cutting oil to southern Africa would force South Africa to abandon any pretense of neutrality and come down squarely on the side of Rhodesia, destroying any chance of forcing Smith from power. It would also widen the conflict by making South Africa a light-

---

"even a very substantial increase...in the quantities supplied to Rhodesia by South Africans purchasing oil from the Marketing Companies, could be concealed by changes in overall demand in South Africa or in the market shares of the Marketing Companies or by technical fluctuations in the pattern of imports caused, for example, by variations of stock or refinery shutdown periods...." The "Marketing Companies" are Shell and BP who operated jointly in southern Africa under a market-sharing agreement. British Petroleum, "Investigation into the Supply of Petroleum and Petroleum Products To Rhodesia," Memorandum Submitted by the British Petroleum Company Limited to The Bingham Inquiry, 27 September 1977, 34–35.

23. See, for example, U.S. National Security Council, "Study in Response to National Security Study Memorandum 39: Southern Africa," 9 December 1969, 45–46.

24. "Rhodesia: Oil Sanctions," Note by the Secretaries, MISC.100/D/11, 25 November 1965, PRO CAB 130/256.

25. "Rhodesia: Oil Sanctions," Note by the Chairman, MISC. 100/D, 26 November 1965, PRO CAB 130/254.

ning rod for further economic sanctions as well as force Britain to choose sides in a broader conflict between white and black Africa.[26] Finally, because South Africa was acutely sensitive to its dependence on imported oil, any British move to restrict South Africa's oil trade—even if the ultimate target of such restrictions were Rhodesia—would provoke South African retaliation, a factor that weighed heavily in British calculations. According to an assessment for the British cabinet, the major political objections to an oil embargo stemmed from South Africa's ability to retaliate against Britain. In fact, because the loss of markets and investments in South Africa would be "a serious blow" to the British economy, the cabinet had already decided to veto any mandatory UN resolutions calling for economic sanctions against South Africa because of apartheid.[27]

It was not, however, only South Africa's ability to retaliate against British economic interests that mitigated against an oil embargo. Rhodesia too could seriously damage British economic interests by imposing a series of countervailing, and equally crippling, sanctions against Zambia that would cause that country's economy to collapse and its copper mines to cease functioning. Because Zambia's sole source of petroleum products was the Feruka refinery, Rhodesia had made it very clear that any attempt to interfere with its own oil supplies would lead it to cut-off oil to Zambia.[28] In late September 1965, for example, Rhodesia's permanent secretary to the Ministry of Commerce and Industry told Peter Jameison, the general manager of Shell Rhodesia, that Rhodesia would not permit Zambia's petroleum supplies "to transit Rhodesia if crude supplies were denied to CAPREF [the Feruka refinery]."[29] Moreover, Rhodesia could also inflict serious harm on the Zambian economy by taxing heavily or denying Rhodesian exports of coal to Zambia, that country's primary source of energy. Finally, because Zambia's road and rail links to world

26. "Minutes on Economic Sanctions," by the minister of state (Roger Allen), 31 December 1965, and Addendum dated 16 November 1965, PRO FO 371/182045. Also, "Oil Sanctions Against Rhodesia," Note by the Foreign Office, 7 December 1965, PRO CAB 130/257.

27. "Rhodesia: Oil Sanctions," Note by the Secretaries, MISC.100/D/2, 22 November 1965, PRO CAB 130/256.

28. See, for example, "Rhodesia: Oil Sanctions." A Note by the chairman of MISC. 100/D, 26 November 1965.

29. Cable from Mr. P. M. Jameison, General Manager Shell Rhodesia, to Mr. de Bruyne, Shell regional coordinator for Southern Africa, 29 September 1965, quoted in Bingham report, 36. See also, "Rhodesia: Oil Sanctions," A Note by the chairman of MISC.100/D, 26 November 1965. CAPREF stands for the Central African Petroleum Refinery Company, the company which owned the Feruka refinery. CAPREF was itself a joint venture between the five international oil companies serving the Rhodesian market, American Independent Oil company and the Kuwait national petroleum company. Commonwealth Secretariat, *Oil Sanctions Against Rhodesia*, 8.

markets ran through Rhodesia, Rhodesia could effectively sever Zambia's trade.[30]

Rhodesia's ability to shut down Zambia's economy, especially its copper production, was a powerful deterrent to an oil embargo. Zambia supplied approximately 16 percent of the world's and 45 percent of Britain's copper imports.[31] Britain had no alternate sources of supply and feared that the cut-off of Zambian copper would lead to chaos on the London Metals Exchange and cause a rapid scramble for the "free supplies" on the spot market.[32] This not only threatened to impose substantial costs on British economic interests, with the "gravest repercussions on the United Kingdom's export effort and balance of payments position,"[33] it also threatened directly the interests of the United States government, which was increasing its demands for copper because of the escalating Vietnam war. As a result, the United States viewed an oil embargo of Rhodesia as reckless and initially refused to assist Britain should it seek to impose an embargo.[34] As a brief for British Cabinet ministers noted:

> An oil embargo, effective or not, would however put at risk the flow of copper from Zambia. The United States Government have told us that they regard continuing access for the world to Zambian copper supplies

30. A secret study of oil supplies to Rhodesia and Zambia by Louis Walker, managing director of Shell, South Africa lists six possible routes by which Zambia could be supplied with oil products. All were circuitous and extremely expensive. L. C. V. Walker, "Oil for Rhodesia and Zambia," internal Shell company document, 29 December 1965, reprinted in Bingham report, annex 2, 227–32. Once sanctions were imposed, Britain, the United States, and Canada supplied Zambia's oil requirements by airlifting and trucking drummed supplies in from Tanzania. This operation lasted until August 1968 when a pipeline linking Zambia to Tanzania was completed. Klinghoffer, *Oiling the Wheels*, 82.

31. See U.S. Department of State, "Outline of Rhodesian Problem," 1 December 1965, 3; also "Note by the Commonwealth Relations Office," Defence and Oversea Policy (Official) Committee, Subcommittee on Southern Rhodesia, O.P.D. (O)(S.R.)(65) 18, 2 June 1965, 4-5, PRO CAB 148/67.

32. "Submission to Ministers on Possible Action by the United Kingdom Government in the Event of a Unilateral Declaration of Independence by Rhodesia," Defence and Oversea Policy (Official) Committee, Subcommittee on Southern Rhodesia, Annex 4, PRO CAB 148/67.

33. "Note by the Commonwealth Relations Office," Defence and Oversea Policy (Official) Committee, Subcommittee on Southern Rhodesia, 2 June 1965, 4–5.

34. A cable from the State Department to the American Embassy London states "We are frankly dubious that the present U.K. program will produce a quick kill....We therefore think it would be wrong and dangerous in planning to assume efforts which would trigger the suspension of copper exports, since that suspension might prove to be long lasting....the U.K. should not take measures which would induce Rhodesia to act against Zambia..." Department of State, "Outgoing Telegram to American Embassy London," 4 December 1965, 4. The fear of Rhodesian retaliation against Zambia was not unfounded. One high-level businessman interviewed in January 1992 in Harare told me that the Smith government approached the Anglo-American company early in the crisis and asked it to "destroy" the Zambian economy. Anglo-American, which provided the bulk of Zambia's coal requirements, politely declined.

as far overriding in importance any possible advantages of denying oil to Rhodesia; and have warned us that we should not expect them to help us over the consequences for our own industry, for our balance of payments, and for our sterling, of an interruption in Zambian copper supplies.[35]

Finally, Britain also feared the longer term political ramifications of interfering with the free flow of oil in world markets. On the one hand, it was reticent to harm the commercial interests of the British oil companies in third countries. Oil company cooperation with the embargo could convey the message that they were really instruments of the British government, and not international companies committed to the free flow of commerce in world markets. This concern was especially acute for British Petroleum, in which the government held equity.[36] On the other hand, Britain was extremely wary of setting the precedent that the flow of oil could be openly interfered with for explicit political purposes. In particular, it feared that oil producing states might, in the future, begin to manipulate the flow of oil for their own political ends. According to a note by the Foreign Office, the security of Britain's energy supplies depended on the oil companies' existing right to decide where to export oil. An oil embargo would endanger this right and establish the "dangerous" precedent that states could overrule the commercial concerns of the companies and manipulate the flow of oil for their own political ends.[37]

Britain thus omitted an oil embargo from its initial package of sanctions not because it wanted to hold this weapon in reserve, one component of a strategy of graduated escalation in which it progressively widened the scope and impact of sanctions over time, but because an oil embargo was a politically provocative and dangerous policy which threatened many of Britain's broader political and economic interests.[38] Implementing an effective oil embargo against Rho-

35. "Brief for Ministers of State," For MISC.100/B Meeting, 29 November 1965, PRO FO 371/182043. See also, "Rhodesia: American Attitude," file JR 113134/2, West and Central African Department, 1 December 1965, PRO FO 371/182046.

36. See, for example, "Minutes of the Rhodesia Sub-Committee for Further Economic Measures," MISC 100/G/1st Meeting, 23 November 1965, PRO CAB 130/258.

37. "Oil Sanctions Against Rhodesia." Note by the Foreign Office, 7 December 1965. The dangers inherent in establishing the precedent that oil producing countries could determine the direction of exports was so high, that Britain consistently rejected using these countries as the first line of the embargo. British fears about the dangers of interfering with the oil trade were borne out in the oil shocks of the 1970s.

38. In fact, Britain's strategy was not to engage in a gradual escalation of the conflict, but to hit Rhodesia as hard and fast as possible. According to a policy directive: "Half-measures will not secure our objectives. The white population as a whole must be hit hard economically, politically and psychologically, so that they become convinced that continued support for Smith means an end to life in Rhodesia as they have known it. We therefore seek an immediate and painful dislocation of normalcy leading to rejection of the regime, with special

desia required not only shutting off the tap to Rhodesia, but to all of southern Africa. This, in turn, threatened to precipitate retaliatory measures by South Africa, Rhodesia, and (implicitly) by the United States. Britain's initial reluctance in imposing an oil embargo thus turned both on practical matters of implementation, and, ironically, on its own vulnerability to the economic "sanctions" that could be imposed by other powers. As a 12 November letter from George Brown to the prime minister noted:

> The main reasons [for not implementing an embargo] were that it would be seriously damaging to Zambia, that it was extremely dubious whether sufficient or effective cooperation would be secured from other governments to stop oil supplies and that South Africa could undermine any embargo....All this could spell serious dangers for our own economy.[39]

RETHINKING THE EMBARGO

THE BRITISH Cabinet revisited its decision not to impose an embargo as soon as Rhodesia declared its independence. It recognized that Britain's initial sanctions might not be sufficient to bring the rebellion quickly to an end and that even a partially effective oil embargo might be necessary to "divert the United Nations from military action."[40]

As Britain expected, pressure quickly built from black African states to take whatever action was necessary to end the Rhodesian Front's rebellion and to make an oil embargo the litmus test of Britain's commitment to majority rule. President Jomo Kenyatta of Kenya spoke for most of black Africa when he privately demanded of Prime Minister Harold Wilson "that the rebellion must be brought to an end by the British Government if necessary by the use of force," and "that Britain should demonstrate its continued determination to resist the entrenchment of the Smith regime by making an early start to impose

---

measures which will touch the convenience and pockets of the ordinary voter" ("Directive: Policy in Relation to Rhodesia," 19 November 1965, 2).

39. Letter from George Brown to the prime minister, 12 November 1965, PRO PREM 13/564. See also, "Action in the Event of a UDI: Oil."

40. See "Oil and Rhodesia" in file IOD 2241/1; and the minutes by D. M. March in file IOD 2241/1A, both in PRO FO 371/181592. Likewise, on 12 November George Brown wrote Prime Minister Wilson asking whether it would "not be wise to have another look at this [the decision not to impose an embargo] so that we can give some further guidance to the Foreign Secretary before we are finally committed" (Letter from George Brown to the prime minister, 12 November 1965).

an oil embargo."[41] On 20 November 1965 the UN Security Council sought to force Britain's hand by voting voluntary oil sanctions against the colony. On 5–6 December, the Organization of African States upped the ante by demanding that Britain impose stringent oil sanctions on Rhodesia within the next ten days. When Britain failed to do so, thirteen African states broke diplomatic relations with the country on 16 December 1965.[42] Also that day, some one-hundred delegates representing African countries walked out when Wilson spoke to the General Assembly of the United Nations. Britain's relations with Africa had reached their lowest point.[43]

Britain feared that the growing pressure for decisive British action would, if left unchecked, rapidly escalate into demands for mandatory United Nations resolutions to suppress the Rhodesian rebellion.[44] This created a significant dilemma for British policy. To veto any mandatory resolution in the UN would paint Britain as protecting white interests in Rhodesia at the expense of black. This would undermine the position of moderate and pro-British governments in Africa, especially Zambia's; fracture the Commonwealth; and transform the Rhodesia crisis into a wider confrontation between white and black Africa. Yet, allowing the United Nations to pass a mandatory resolution was scarcely more palatable to Britain. This course of action risked supplanting Britain's authority to manage the Rhodesia crisis as an internal matter; could easily accelerate rather than dampen demands for even more extreme measures against Rhodesia, especially if the initial measures did not produce immediate results; and threatened to broaden the conflict by generating substantial pressure to apply mandatory sanctions against South Africa and Portugal since these states were unlikely to comply with any mandatory economic or military measures aimed at Rhodesia. In short, Britain faced its "most serious crisis since Suez," with important ramifications for British power that reached far beyond its relationship with Rhodesia.[45]

Britain concluded that the best strategy to avoid this dilemma was to defuse the pressure for stronger action by increasing visibly the economic pressure on Rhodesia. Unless measures were soon taken that clearly indicated substantial economic harm on Rhodesia, political pressure would grow in the Security Council for more extreme mandatory resolutions that "would have grave im-

41. Letter from Jomo Kenyatta, president of Kenya, to Harold Wilson, prime minister of the United Kingdom, 19 November 1965, PRO PREM 13/546.

42. Klinghoffer, *Oiling the Wheels*, 80.

43. Bailey, *Oilgate*, 122–23.

44. See for example, Foreign Office, "Brief for talks with Mr. Mann of the United States Government," 29 November 1965, PRO FO 371/182039.

45. Thomas C. Mann, "Memorandum for the President on the Rhodesian Crisis," 22 December 1965.

plications for western interests and would be increasingly difficult to resist.[46] Most important, increasing pressure on Rhodesia meant instituting an oil embargo against the colony.[47] Because a unilateral embargo "would be an ineffective gesture and a dangerous one at that,"[48] however, Britain realized that an oil embargo would be possible *only* with U.S. assistance, and sought to convince the United States to support this change in course by arguing that the United States faced a similar dilemma in southern Africa.[49]

> The point is (reads one document) that we should try to persuade the Americans that it is in their interest to help us....The risk of racial war in Africa must be as unwelcome to them as to us. The...risk that South Africa will be brought in, with mounting pressure for economic sanctions against her too, is surly as alarming to them as to us. The possibility that the Smith regime might survive, with obvious consequences to American as well as British relations with African states must be almost as disturbing to them as to us. On the other hand, the chance that we may be able to take effective action jointly against Smith and in the defence of an African state, namely Zambia, should be helpful to the Americans in Africa.[50]

In early December, the United States dropped its reservations to an oil embargo in order to defuse growing tensions with Black Africa.[51] The final details were hammered out on 17 December. Britain, acting as the government de jure of Rhodesia, and supported by the United States, would announce an Or-

---

46. "Brief for talks with Mr. Mann of the United States Government."

47. Ibid. This document also states that Britain wanted to impose an oil embargo in order to achieve a "quick kill" and thus end the rebellion by creating a "revulsion of feeling in Rhodesia against the Smith regime which would enable the liberal White elements to take over." This statement, which suggests that the primary goal of the embargo was to quickly end the rebellion, must be carefully interpreted. The purpose of this document was to lay out the arguments that Britain would use to persuade the United States to cooperate in imposing an embargo; it is the only document I have located that suggests an embargo would actually produce Rhodesian capitulation. In fact, an accompanying document makes clear that there was no evidence that an embargo would do so. "Note to Minister of State," by Roger Allen, 29 November 1965, file JR 1071/6, PRO FO 371/182039. As I argue below, both Britain and the United States were highly skeptical that an embargo would end the rebellion and implemented the embargo largely for other reasons.

48. "Assessment of the Present Positions and Proposals for Further Action," Note by the chairman of MISC.100/G, MISC.100/B/15, 11 December 1965, PRO CAB 130/254.

49. "Anglo-American Consultations on Oil Sanctions," Note by the chairman of MISC.100/D, 27 November, 1965, MISC.100/B/9, PRO CAB 130/254.

50. "Note to Minister of State," by Roger Allen, 29 November 1965.

51. See Telegram no. 3249, From Washington to Foreign Office, 9 December 1965, PRO PREM 13/564. It reports a meeting with George Ball in which the United States signals that it has decided to support a voluntary oil embargo as well as an emergency airlift of oil to Zambia.

der in Council that banned the importation of petroleum products into Rhodesia while Zambia would be supplied with oil by a joint emergency airlift.[52]

Significantly, neither the United States (which played a follower's role) nor Britain believed the oil embargo would bring down the Smith regime. Although both sides hoped to impose significant economic costs on the Rhodesian economy and thereby increase the pressure on Smith to settle, they clearly recognized the geographic and strategic factors that made this outcome unlikely. They were under no illusions that the embargo would quickly end the rebellion. One U.S. State Department document doubted the effectiveness of an oil embargo because Rhodesia's "supplies could be obtained through oil brokers from other sources at slightly higher than world prices."[53] "Our and the UK estimates," reads another, "are that (an oil embargo) could not be effective, even with a naval blockade, since South Africa could pick up the slack."[54] A British assessment likewise notes, "although joint action with the U.S.A. should enable us to cut down supplies reaching Rhodesia via Beira we cannot hope that the ban will be complete."[55] According to another, "Oil sanctions would not be effective short of a naval blockade of southern Africa. Even then they would not, in the short term, bring down the illegal regime."[56] Still another states:

> No-one has yet indicated a method of producing a Rhodesia capitulation within a period of about three months other than by military sanctions. All the evidence is that an oil embargo would not do so. The Rhodesians have several weeks' supply in the pipeline, so that even if all their

52. Securing U.S. agreement in supporting an emergency (and very costly) airlift of oil to Zambia was a major achievement, as the United States was escalating the Vietnam conflict. Apparently, a major factor in the U.S. decision was the need to maintain access to Zambian copper, which the British fully exploited. According to one document regarding negotiating tactics, "the ultimate threat to copper production seems our best weapon and if we can satisfy the Americans that despite every effort on our part alone, there will still be a dangerous shortfall in P.O.L. supplies until surface routes are fully operative, we might get the right answer from them...." Telegraph No. 3289, From Washington to Foreign Office, 15 December 1965, PRO PREM 13/564. U.S. policy toward Rhodesia was guided by three principles: 1) that UDI was a British problem and the US should play a follower's role only; 2) that U.S. assistance to Britain should avoid committing U.S. troops to Africa or underwriting the pound; and 3) that given these limitations—and always in cooperation with Britain—the United States should take measures designed to pressure the Smith regime and to abate black African demands for more extreme action. U.S. Department of State, "Outline of Rhodesian Problem," 1.

53. "Memorandum for the President: Export Licensing for Southern Rhodesia," 18 November 1965, Attachment, 2.

54. U.S. Department of State, "Outline of Rhodesian Problem," 2.

55. "Assessment of the Present Position and Proposals for Further Action," Note by the Chairman of MISC.100/G, 11 December 1965, MISC.100/B/15, PRO CAB 130/254.

56. "Oil Sanctions Against Rhodesia," Note by the Foreign Office, 7 December 1965, PRO CAB 130/257.

sources of supply were cut off today oil sanctions would not begin to bite for six weeks or so at least. But all sources cannot be cut off today. Even if we blockaded Beira or blew up the pipeline to Umtali it is very probable that the Rhodesians could obtain supplies from South Africa (or possibly Angola).[57]

These pessimistic assessments raise an important puzzle. Why would Britain and the United States engage in an economically costly and politically risky oil embargo, given their well-grounded expectation that it would *not* end the Rhodesian rebellion? The answer is that the primary target of the oil embargo was not Rhodesia, it was Black Africa and the Commonwealth. Britain's initial sanctions had little immediate impact on Rhodesia.[58] This caused many to doubt the sincerity of Britain's commitment to majority rule and led them to demand more stringent action, including military intervention, to end the rebellion as quickly as possible. By imposing an oil embargo, Britain and the United States hoped to dissipate these growing pressures for more drastic action and thereby minimize the risks that the conflict would endanger their broader interests on the African continent. Only by undertaking an economically costly and politically risky strategy that imposed real and visible costs on Rhodesia could Britain and the United States credibly demonstrate to Black Africa and the Commonwealth that they were committed to ending the Rhodesian rebellion in a manner that ensured majority rule. As one set of British minutes noted, "The United States authorities agreed with us that no oil embargo against Rhodesia could be wholly effective, but they considered it politically and psychologically very important, and for this reason were prepared to cooperate with us."[59]

57. "Note to Minister of State," by Roger Allen, 29 November 1965.
58. In fact, Britain's most damaging sanction, the boycott of Rhodesian tobacco, which accounted for nearly one-third of Rhodesia's foreign exchange earnings, would not even begin to take effect until March 1966 when the current tobacco crop came to market.
59. Rhodesia: Steering Committee, "Note of a Meeting Held in the Minister of State's Room, Commonwealth Relations Office," 10 December 1965, MISC./100/ C/15th Meeting, 1, PRO CAB 130/255. Likewise, a memorandum for the U.S. president on export controls for Rhodesia noted that "the African states are watching carefully to see if we really mean it." It went on to state that moves to restrict Rhodesia's trade were important to "demonstrate to the world that we are supporting the British Government in trying to deal with the Southern Rhodesian crisis through non-military means and thus damp down the pressures building up in New York for more violent and drastic methods" (U.S. Department of State, "Memorandum for the President: Subject: Export Licensing for Southern Rhodesia," 18 November 1965).

THE OIL EMBARGO AGAINST RHODESIA

BRITAIN IMPOSED oil sanctions on Rhodesia on 17 December 1965. Securing US cooperation was an important achievement for Britain as the British and American oil companies supplied over ninety percent of the Rhodesian oil market.[60] Although it was skeptical that an oil embargo would force Rhodesia to renounce UDI, Britain needed to make the embargo as effective as possible in order to credibly demonstrate its commitment to ending the Rhodesian rebellion. In fact, its early efforts to stop the flow of oil to Rhodesia enjoyed a number of important successes.

One success was that the British and American oil companies that supplied Rhodesia proved extremely cooperative in implementing the sanctions. As early as 11 November 1965, the British government received indications that the British oil companies were quietly willing to institute a rationing system that limited supplies to South Africa in order to reduce the amount of oil that could reach Rhodesia.[61] The companies also informed Britain of tanker movements for the central and southern African markets during the planning of the embargo in late November and early December. British Petroleum even delayed the sailing of the tanker *British Security*, which was due in Beira in early December, and made contingency plans to divert its cargo at Britain's request.[62] Once the Sanctions Order was issued, Shell immediately diverted the tanker *Staberg* which was then underway for Beira with a cargo of crude.[63] By 20 December Louis Walker, the General Manager of Shell South Africa, had cabled Shell Centre London that "We have stopped despatch of products from

60. The market shares were: Shell Rhodesia (Pvt) Ltd. (39.1 percent); BP Rhodesia (Pvt) Ltd. (12.9 percent); Mobil Oil Southern Rhodesia (Pvt) Ltd. (20 percent); Caltex Oil Rhodesia (Pvt) Ltd. (20 percent); and Total Rhodesia (Pvt) Ltd. (8 percent). Shell and BP operated jointly in Southern Africa and were often referred to as the Consolidated Companies. Shell was the dominant partner in the relationship as it had operated longer in this region. The two companies, however, split equally their subsidiaries' earnings. See Bingham report, 2–11.

61. See "Oil Embargo Against Rhodesia," Note by P. H. Gore Booth, Foreign Office file IOD 2241/2, 15 November 1965, PRO FO 371/181592. In the note, Gore Booth writes that "when I had lunch with A.E.I. on 11 November, the Chairman, Mr. C. R. Wheeler, said that the oil companies were perfectly prepared to put into operation with great speed a rationing system which would cover not only Rhodesia itself but also South Africa and the Portuguese territories, the effect of which would be to impose a very considerable strain on South Africa if the latter were to give a priority to keep Rhodesia going."

62. See "Note for the Record: Oil for Rhodesia," 26 November 1965, PRO PREM 13/564. According to the note, "It is clear that B.P. have already moved a long way under our pressure....The ship [*British Security*] will not be loading until Sunday, and has thus already been delayed two days. This delay has enabled us to clear our possible lines of action with B.P., and the ship is now firmly under our control." This ship ultimately sailed and was the last tanker to offload its cargo at Beira.

63. Bailey, *Oilgate*, 126; Bingham report, 45.

Durban Refinery and also from Durban Lubricating Oil Blending Plant."[64] On 22 December, the British Ministry of Power noted that "Shell [have] all along cooperated closely with H.M.G. over the Rhodesia problem," and that "Shell have taken all necessary steps open to them to comply with the Order in Council."[65] On the American side, the United States ordered the Norwegian tanker *Tamarita*, which was chartered by Aminoil (the American Independent Oil Company) and bound for Beira, to discharge at the Kenyan port of Mombassa.[66] By late January, the State Department found that the American oil companies were "cooperating fully and have refused to sell oil to entrepreneurs for export to Southern Rhodesia."[67] Even more important, within South Africa itself, the South African subsidiaries had secretly agreed in February 1966 to limit the supplies of oil to the northern Transvaal to 115 percent of the previous year's supplies. This agreement would impede Rhodesia's ability to draw its supplies from this source as some outlets would run dry, and was reached without the knowledge of the South African government.[68]

Britain was also heartened by South Africa's position in the conflict. South Africa declared itself strictly neutral. Although it would not participate in the boycott, South Africa maintained that it would carry on only normal levels of trade with Rhodesia. This stance was interpreted by the British to mean that South Africa would continue to supply Rhodesia, but only with the few petroleum goods which were customarily supplied from the South African market.[69] Because Rhodesia received most of its major petroleum products via Beira and the Feruka refinery, the underlying message seemed clear: South Africa was unwilling to let itself become a major conduit through which oil sanctions could be busted.

The South African government's initial contacts with the oil companies' South African subsidiaries supported this interpretation. According to a Shell account of a 23 December 1965 meeting between the South African subsidiaries and the South African secretary of commerce and industry, the secretary told the oil companies that in order to preserve South Africa's neutrality they

64. Bingham report, 46.
65. "Rhodesia: Steering Committee: The Oil Embargo: Conflicts of Jurisdiction and Authority," Note by the Ministry of Power, 22 December 1965 MISC.100/C/11 (revised), PRO CAB 130/255.
66. Bailey, *Oilgate*, 126.
67. U.S. Department of State, "Rhodesia/Zambia Situation Report no. 17," Wednesday-Thursday, 26-27 January 1966, 3.
68. Telegraph No. 119, From Cape Town to Foreign Office, 16 February 1966, PRO PREM 13/1137.
69. Bingham report, 48. This was also the interpretation given by the United States. See U.S. Department of State, "Outgoing Telegram to American Embassy London, American Consulate Capetown, and American Consulate Pretoria," 28 December 1965.

should 1) continue supplying Rhodesia and Zambia at traditional levels; 2) not meet any requests for orders in excess of traditional commercial arrangements; 3) when approached by Rhodesian agents for products or quantities which exceeded traditional levels, to refuse supply and direct their agents to request the Rhodesian Government to approach the South African Government directly for assistance.[70]

Britain's confidence was also raised by reports from Rhodesia indicating that the oil sanctions were having a rapid and potentially severe economic impact. On 31 December 1965 the Beira pipeline shut down because the companies' storage tanks at Beira had run dry, stranding 14,000 tons of crude oil in the pipeline.[71] Lacking any further supplies of crude with which to push this oil through, Rhodesia could only acquire this oil by flushing the pipeline with seawater. Yet, this proved impossible when the Portuguese company controlling the pipeline refused to cooperate; flushing the oil with seawater threatened to seriously corrode the pipeline.[72] On 15 January 1966 the Feruka refinery ceased operating when its crude oil storage tanks ran dry.

Rhodesia's dwindling supplies of petroleum products forced it to ration supplies. On 27 December, it introduced its first rationing scheme which allowed motorists between three and five gallons of petrol per week, while exempting farmers and commercial vehicles using diesel fuel.[73] This scheme quickly proved unsatisfactory. On 6 January, a new scheme was announced which cut the basic petrol ration even further to between one and two gallons a week.[74] By 20 January, Rhodesia was again forced to reduce consumption. It cut the petrol allocation a further 25 percent while raising the price of fuel by 1d per gallon. Bulk purchasers of fuel were now receiving allocations of only 40 percent of normal consumption and licensed farmers became subject to diesel rations for the first time. They could now only draw 50 percent of their normal consumption of diesel.[75]

In reality, the embargo was slowly unraveling. One of the first indications of trouble came in late December when Mobil South Africa balked at an order by Mobil New York to cease pumping oil from the company's storage facilities at Beira. These facilities had been leased to CAPREF, the Rhodesian-registered

---

70. Cable from L. Walker, Shell South Africa to Shell London, 24 December 1965, reprinted in Bingham report, 47.

71. *Rand Daily Mail*, 3 January 1966. See also Bailey, *Oilgate*, 126–27 and Jorge Jardim, *Sanctions Doublecross: Oil to Rhodesia* (Lisbon: Intervençao, 1977), 32–34.

72. *Rand Daily Mail*, 6 January 1966.

73. *Rhodesia Herald*, 28 December 1965.

74. *Rand Daily Mail*, 7 January 1966.

75. *Rhodesia Herald*, 21 January 1966; *Rand Daily Mail*, 21 January 1966; and *Rhodesia Times*, 21 January 1966.

company which ran the Feruka refinery. Mobil South Africa argued that not only would it be breaching its commercial obligations to CAPREF (and thereby make itself vulnerable to legal action), but that it had been specifically warned by the South African government not to deny Beira storage to Rhodesia. Thus, ceasing to pump oil from Beira was not a realistic option for the company. Mobil New York accepted these arguments and allowed the pumping to continue. Although Britain was concerned that Rhodesia could now use Mobil Oil to pump bootleg supplies of crude through the pipeline, the event itself seemed to be of marginal importance as the storage tanks at Beira ran dry within a matter of days.[76] It was, however, an early indicator of both the difficulty which the parent oil companies would have in controlling their subsidiaries and the desire by South Africa not to see the oil embargo succeed.

In fact, South Africa's decision to limit trade with Rhodesia to normal levels of supplies arose not from a desire to remain neutral, but from two other factors. First, South Africa was uncertain what effect the Rhodesian purchase of South African petroleum products would have on its own level of supplies. By limiting sales to normal customers and quantities, it gave itself breathing space to clarify this issue. In his meeting with the oil companies, for example, the South African secretary of commerce and Industry did not actually prohibit the onward supply of Rhodesia from South African sources, but only required governmental approval before such sales were made. According to the Shell account of the meeting, the South African government would consider each request for purchase by Rhodesia on its merits and seek, in consultation with the oil companies, to make supplies available as long as it did not prejudice to South Africa's own stock and supplies.[77]

Moreover, by making oil company sales to Rhodesia contingent upon its approval, the South African government gave itself an important means by which it could influence Rhodesian behavior.

The second factor was South Africa's desire to avoid a major conflict with Britain. A serious row over Rhodesia would have injured both countries, as well as risked broadening the oil embargo to include South Africa. By taking a strict line early, South Africa retained the option of relaxing its position once Britain's position became clear.

76. Department of State, "Outgoing Telegram," 28 December 1965. See also Bingham report, 61–62, Jardim, *Doublecross*, 35–36, and "Rhodesia: Steering Committee, Minutes of a Meeting of the Committee held in the Minister of State's Room," Commonwealth Relations Office, 29 December 1965 MISC.100/C/24th meeting, 3, PRO CAB 130/255.

77. Cable from L. Walker to Shell London, 24 December 1965, reprinted in Bingham report, 47. See also Telegraph no. 49, From Cape Town to Foreign Office, 31 January 1966, in PRO PREM 13/1137.

By late January, South Africa began to probe the limits of British policy. On 21 January, it permitted small shipments of "gift petrol" to be sent northward from private groups which had sprung up to support Rhodesia's rebellion.[78] On 26 January South African prime minister H. F. Verwoerd stated in parliament that the government would not interfere with private individuals or oil companies that supplied Rhodesia.[79] At the same time, the government also began pressuring the South African subsidiaries of the oil companies to end the practice of conditional selling, in which oil was sold only with the proviso that it not be resold to Rhodesia. The oil companies balked at first, arguing that ending conditional sales risked an international crisis which might endanger South Africa's own supplies.[80] The British and American subsidiaries were acting under directives from the parent companies not to supply oil to Rhodesia; convincing the South African government that breaking the embargo was too risky was the simplest way to resolve the conflict between the legal obligations imposed on their parent companies and their own need to be responsive to the demands of the South African government.

The South African government seemed unconcerned by the risks associated with breaking the embargo. In a meeting with the oil companies on 25 January, Kotzenberg, South Africa's secretary of industry and commerce, characterized the oil companies' position as "rubbish," stating that "South Africa must call the bluff of the Western Nations."[81] Kotzenberg repeated this call three days later in another meeting with the oil companies. According to Shell's account of the meeting, Kotzenberg "took the attitude that our overseas suppliers would not in the ultimate refuse to supply us and he suggested that South Africa should call their bluff by helping Rhodesia on whatever scale was necessary."[82]

It was also clear that the South African government occupied a dominant position in any dispute over the supply of Rhodesia. The South African government was deeply disturbed by what it saw as foreign interference in the domestic affairs of South African companies. South Africa clearly distrusted these firms and closely monitored their activities. Shell and BP, for example, often communicated with their South African subsidiaries about the embargo

78. *Rand Daily Mail*, 22 January 1966.

79. *Rand Daily Mail*, 27 January 1966.

80. Bingham report, 54–55; also "Note of a Meeting with Representatives of Shell and BP about the Oil Position in South Africa and Southern Rhodesia," 19 April 1965 PRO POWE 63/206; Telegraph no. 49, Cape Town to Foreign Office, 31 January 1966.

81. Telegraph no. 49, Cape Town to Foreign Office, 31 January 1966.

82. Cable from L. Walker, Shell South Africa to Shell London, 28 January 1966, reprinted in Bingham report, 54–55. Also, Telegraph no. 49, Cape Town to Foreign Office, 31 January 1966.

via the British embassy in South Africa because they believed the South African government intercepted their intracompany communications.[83] In one instance when excessive sales caused a Shell station to run dry in the northern Transvaal, "Kotzenberg [the South African minister of commerce] had been on the 'phone within hours to the company to report that he had heard that one Shell station was refusing to supply and that this did not accord with the Government's position."[84] According to BP and Shell, "The South African government now considered that they [the oil companies] were not international companies but British and American companies who could not be relied upon to place South Africa's interests first."[85] The South African government also made clear that it could retaliate in any number of ways against a company which decided not to comply with its wishes.[86]

On 14 February the oil companies fell in line with South African policy by ending conditional sales.[87] The companies clearly recognized that as South African-registered subsidiaries, South African law and policies took precedence over home country directives and that the South African government gave them little choice but to toe the line. According to Louis Walker, General Manager of Shell South Africa, "if we really did carry out the spirit of the Order in Council we might as well shut up shop in South Africa...the Government would apply the sort of sanctions that Governments can apply very easily without ever having legislation, and there could be a serious confrontation."[88]

The trickle of refined oil products which had been flowing northward over the Beit Bridge (the only direct transportation link between South Africa and Rhodesia) became a torrent. In mid-February, *the Rand Daily Mail* estimated that over 35,000 gallons of petrol a day were crossing the border at Beit Bridge with an equal amount being shipped by rail via Mozambique.[89] By March, the

83. See, for example, "Brief for Lord Walston," no date (May? 1966), file JR 1531/33, PRO FO 371/188037.
84. F.S. Fielding, Record of a Conversation with Louis Walker, general manager of Shell South Africa, Johannesburg, 13 June 1966, file JR1531/129 in PRO FO 371/188039.
85. "Note of a Meeting with Representatives of Shell and BP about the Oil Position in South Africa and Southern Rhodesia," 19 April 1966, PRO POWE 63/206.
86. In a 1968 letter to the oil companies, for example, the South African minister of economic affairs reiterated the government's position, "I also wish to reaffirm the advice I have given to the oil companies on various occasions in the past...the Government will not hesitate to take legal action against them...in the event of the oil companies failing to comply strictly with the Government's verbal directive [prohibiting conditional sales]." Letter from the South African minister of economics to the managing directors of Shell South Africa and BP Southern Africa, October 1968, reprinted in Bingham report, 28–29.
87. *Rand Daily Mail*, 15 February 1966.
88. Bingham report, 118.
89. *Rand Daily Mail*, 16 February, 25 February. The oil companies believed that early press reports exaggerated the flow of oil. See Telegraph no. 119, Cape Town to Foreign Office, 16 February 1966, PRO PREM 13/1137.

British government estimated that Rhodesia was receiving 125,000–150,000 gallons per day, or between three-quarters and the whole of her petroleum requirements. Most oil now flowed into the colony via the Lorenco Marques railway. Britain suspected that the source this oil was the Sonarep refinery in Mozambique. The refinery would ship extra oil to normal bulk customers, such as large farms or mines, just inside the South African border. These customers would then reship the oil back to Mozambique and onward to Rhodesia, an arrangement that required the complicity of the South African Railways.[90]

In response, Britain sought to pressure South Africa to limit the flow to levels that had traditionally been supplied from the South African market. Unwilling to threaten South Africa directly, Britain sought to raise the specter of growing African pressure for mandatory UN sanctions and, implicitly, an embargo against South Africa if it did not comply in shutting off oil to Rhodesia. One plan suggested by Wilson in February 1966 was to encourage Kenyatta to make threatening public demands for a Chapter VII resolution. In this way, Britain could pressure South Africa but without making a direct threat that would endanger its own interests.[91]

The South African government, however, was unmoved. It made clear that it would not interfere with the flow of oil to Rhodesia. In (re)explaining his government's position that South Africa would only pursue normal trade with Rhodesia, Verwoerd told a campaign rally, "Normal trade means that everyone in competition tries to sell as much as he can.... If one sells more, it is not abnormal trade, but better trade. This must be quite clearly understood."[92] The supply of Rhodesia via the South African market was now assured.

In late March and early April 1966, the Rhodesian government sought to break the embargo for good by chartering the tanker *Joanna V* to put in a load of crude at Beira. Britain detected the tanker as it steamed toward Beira, and, after a flurry of diplomatic activity involving Greece, Panama (countries where the tanker was registered), South Africa and Portugal, was able to prevent it from offloading its cargo. Another tanker, however, the *Manuela* was already at sea and bound for Beira. On 7 April, invoking a threat to the peace, Britain tabled a resolution in the UN Security Council calling upon Portugal not to

---

90. "Rhodesia: Oil Leakages and Stocks in March," no date (April? 1966), POWE 63/226. The transshipment of oil to South Africa and then back to Rhodesia proved extremely expensive for Rhodesia. As busting the embargo became more routinized, this subterfuge was dropped and oil was shipped directly to Rhodesia from Lorenço Marques. See Bingham report,112–35.

91. J. Q. Wright to O. Forester, Commonwealth Relations Office, 16 February 1966, PRO PREM 13/1137.

92. *Rand Daily Mail,* 1 March 1966.

allow the delivery of oil to Rhodesia and permitting Britain to "prevent by force if necessary vessels reasonably believed to be carrying oil destined for Rhodesia."[93] The resolution, which passed on 9 April, was only the second occasion on which the United Nations had invoked mandatory sanctions under Chapter VII of the UN Charter, and the first time that a member had been authorized to use force to carry out the will of the Council.[94]

The UN resolution alarmed South Africa. Logically, the oil flowing from South Africa into Rhodesia via Mozambique was as much "a threat to the peace" as oil shipped directly to Rhodesia via the Beira pipeline.[95] It was thus a small step from the blockade of Beira to the blockade of Lorenço Marques, a major point of entry for oil bound for the northern Transvaal (and back to Rhodesia), and perhaps even a blockade of South Africa herself. After all, a comprehensive embargo of oil, including South Africa, was a major objective of the African states on the security council. "Why does Britain," queried the Ugandan delegate, "only concern itself with tankers and not with oil coming in from South Africa?"[96]

Nor could South Africa be certain that its strong economic ties with Britain would protect South African interests in the security council. The previous decade saw Britain's Africa policy shift away from protecting the settler interests that had become established under colonial rule toward accommodating the rise of African nationalism. "The wind of change," declared British prime minister Harold MacMillian in 1960 in Cape Town, "is blowing through the continent. Whether we like it or not, this growth of national consciousness is a political fact. We must accept it as a fact. Our national policies must take account of it."[97] Britain's growing responsiveness to African nationalism led South Africa to suspect that British policy was malleable; too easily influenced by pressures from Black Africa and elsewhere to be relied upon to protect South Africa's interests. As Verwoerd complained in a letter to Wilson, "the danger is great that other, particularly African, nations will seek further steps against Rhodesia, or that Britain, once again to avoid such intervention, will feel herself compelled to initiate more stringent measures. The same process

93. Robert C. Good, *U. D. I. The International Politics of the Rhodesian Rebellion* (Princeton: Princeton University Press, 1973), 139–40.

94. Ibid., 141. Under the Resolution, Britain diverted a second tanker, the *Manuela*, that had also been chartered to deliver oil to Beira for pumping to Rhodesia.

95. Ibid., 141.

96. Ibid.

97. Quoted in Larry W. Bowman, *Politics in Rhodesia: White Power in an African State* (Cambridge: Harvard University Press, 1973), 28.

could then follow against Portugal and South Africa."[98] Indeed, Britain consciously reinforced this assessment by often invoking the threat of "uncontrollable" pressures in the UN that would compel Britain to take action against South Africa should it fail to cooperate with the embargo.

Finally, and to nearly everyone's surprise, South Africa was alarmed because Britain had demonstrated that it *was* possible to achieve the level of multilateral cooperation necessary to severely restrict the flow of oil to southern Africa and thus impose severe economic damage on South Africa's economy. According to one assessment:

> As they (South Africa) know, we do not believe that the UN could impose effective economic sanctions right across the board against South Africa. But experience in Rhodesia has shown that an oil embargo would be likely to secure the collaboration of the major oil companies and a very wide measure of cooperation from the lesser companies and ship-owning states. Understandably, some oil would reach South Africa. But it would hardly be likely to be in quantities which would not seriously affect their economy.[99]

South Africa respond in two ways. Over the longer term, it sought to reduce its vulnerability to possible oil sanctions by engaging in a series of economically costly steps that included expanding its oil storage capacity to stockpile large reserves of crude, acquiring a small, nationally owned tanker fleet, and lessening its dependence on the British oil companies.[100] Over the shorter term, it sought to limit the scope and impact of the oil embargo by explicitly threatening to retaliate against British interests should Britain or the United Nations interfere with South African commerce. In a lengthy letter to Wilson on 15 April 1966, Verwoerd spelled out South Africa's position. South Africa, Verwoerd wrote, resented British efforts to force South African compliance with sanctions against Rhodesia and refused as a matter of principle to intervene in the affairs of other countries. It was especially concerned that Britain had involved the Security Council in a matter that was purely an internal British affair and would defend its own right of neutrality by whatever means necessary.

98. Text of a letter dated Pretoria, 15 April 1966, from Dr. the Hon. H. F. Verwoerd, M.P., prime minister of the Republic of South Africa to the Rt. Hon. H. Wilson, M.P., prime minister of Great Britain, PRO PREM 13/1140.

99. Telegraph no. 644, From Foreign Office to Cape Town, 4 April 1966, PRO PREM 13/1139.

100. Cabinet, Rhodesia: Committee on Economic Sanctions, "South African Oil Reserves," Note by the Foreign Office, R(S)(66)(43), 30 September 1966 PRO CAB 134/316.

If (Verwoerd wrote)... any action were now to be taken against South Africa, for example, the extension of an oil embargo against this country, such an attack on her sovereign rights would have to be opposed by all means at her disposal....and she would have to defend the freedom of the high seas for her transport as Britain would no doubt do under similar circumstances.

Any broadening of an oil embargo, or an embargo directed against South Africa to cover other trading commodities, would therefore have far reaching consequences for British-South Africa trade relations.

We are both familiar with the extent of our present mutual dependence on trade between our respective countries, as well as in wider economic and financial fields, including the contribution which South Africa is making to the stability of the Sterling area and the value of gold from South Africa for Western Nations....It is highly desirable that all this should not be affected.

For South Africa, if the test were to come, the choice would have to be between such advantages and her very existence. I therefore had to make quite clear how unavoidable our stand would have to be.[101]

Britain's initial response was contained in a personal telegraph from Wilson to Verwoerd. Wilson again invoked the specter of uncontrollable pressures that would lead Britain to act against South Africa. He strongly reiterated the point that South Africa's unwillingness to limit the flow of oil to Rhodesia to traditional, pre-UDI levels meant that South Africa was not neutral, but actively supported the rebellion. South Africa's stance was fueling extremist pressures in the United Nations and would ultimately lead to demands for mandatory sanctions against South Africa, demands that Britain could not veto.

A veto in these circumstances (Wilson wrote) would be interpreted as support for the illegal regime and would have the effect of swinging opinion in the whole of Africa, and indeed much more widely, away from the West....

I am well aware of the very important economic and financial links between our two countries and share your own evident strong wish to do nothing which would jeopardize these relations. But as you know we also have extensive economic interests in other parts of Africa, not least copper in Zambia. Moreover, we have to think of the safety and future of the substantial British communities in East and Central Africa, as well as elsewhere on the continent, and the maintenance of the common-

101. Text of a letter dated Pretoria, 15 April 1966, from Dr. the Hon. H. F. Verwoerd, M.P., prime minister of the Republic of South Africa to the Rt. Hon. H. Wilson, M.P., prime minister of Great Britain.

wealth which we believe has an important role to play in bringing together the developed and the developing nations of the world.[102]

Despite Britain's strong reply, the flow of oil from South Africa northward into Rhodesia continued unabated. In late spring, Britain estimated that Rhodesia was receiving between 250,000 and 320,000 gallons of oil per day, allowing Rhodesia to build stocks.[103] Britain was also told by Louis Walker, the general manager of Shell South Africa, that he suspected South Africa's national oil company, SASOL, played a major role in the trade.[104] By mid-year it was readily apparent that any efforts short of a major confrontation with South Africa would not stem the flow of petroleum products to Rhodesia. Not only could Rhodesia easily draw its supplies from the Transvaal, the oil companies had begun competing to supply the demand.[105] On 2 June Walker wrote to Dirk de Bruyne of Shell Centre London that Shell South Africa was under considerable commercial and political pressure. Any hopes by the British government that the oil companies would actively enforce the embargo were misplaced and Shell South Africa must be willing to supply any category of customer provided proper security for payment. "The meaning of this, of course," wrote de Bruyne, "is that the oil embargo has collapsed completely...."[106]

As Britain had foreseen, Rhodesia's ability to draw oil from the South African market fed pressures to extend the embargo. This led Britain to reexplore the possibility of imposing economic sanctions against South Africa. It ultimately decided, however, that the costs of doing so were too high, even if its failure to act made it the subject of sanctions by the Black African states. Although Britain's economic interests in Black Africa were comparable to its economic interests in South Africa, Britain believed that any sanctions im-

102. Telegraph no. 829, Foreign Office to Cape Town, prime minister's Personal Telegram, 18 April 1966. PRO PREM 13/1140.

103. From Foreign Office to Commonwealth Relations Office and Certain Missions, 24 May 1966, file JR1531/95 in FO 371/188039.

104. F. S. Fielding, Record of a Conversation with Louis Walker, general manager of Shell South Africa, Johannesburg, 13 June 1966, file JR1531/129 in PRO FO 371/188039. Walker also suspected Esso and Total of supplying Rhodesia. See Telegraph no. 454, Pretoria to Foreign Office, 14 May 1966 in file JR1531/66, PRO FO 371/188038. Suspicions at the role of the SASOL were also raised by the general manager of BP South Africa. See John Wilson to R. A. Farquharson, 19 August 1966, PRO FO 371/188039.

105. Mr. Dickenson, the general manager of the Consolidated Companies (Shell and BP) in Rhodesia, would later complain that during the first nine months of 1966 he did not receive "the support from Shell South Africa that other companies here were receiving from their Associates in South Africa." Letter from Dickenson to de Bruyne, August 1967, quoted in Bingham report, 76. Likewise, one Shell South Africa manager responded to initial internal reports that the company was supplying Rhodesia by saying that it was "high time that we caught up with the others...we can't see our share of the market going down the drain" (Bingham report, 119).

106. Letter from Walker to DeBruyne, 2 June 1966, Bingham report.

posed by Black Africa would be less costly than the economic warfare with South Africa. Black African sanctions would be far from universal, haphazardly enforced, and open to British retaliation. South Africa, on the other hand, could inflict deep and lasting economic damage on the British economy, including an immediate loss of £250 million a year on exports that could not be redirected; a fall in the supply of many commodities that would add considerably to Britain's import bill; a net annual loss of £60 million in investment income; and losses of £20 million in other invisible exports.[107] In fact, the scale of damage that South Africa could inflict on British interests was so great, that it concluded that South African retaliation was simply "too awful to contemplate."[108]

Not only was South Africa too important economically to risk a confrontation over Rhodesia, its threat to retaliate against an extension of the oil embargo was highly credible. This had a subtle but profound influence on British policy. Rather than seeking ways to pressure South Africa to limit the flow of oil to Rhodesia, Britain now sought to avoid a confrontation with South Africa at all costs, a point that it communicated to the British oil companies.[109] Not provoking South Africa had become the highest priority of Britain's Rhodesia policy. "In present circumstances," reads a Commonwealth Office memorandum to the British cabinet, "and indeed in any circumstances—this [confrontation with South Africa] is a price which we cannot afford to pay and we must at all costs insist that we are not drawn into economic warfare with South Africa."[110] In September 1966, the cabinet even concluded that economic warfare with South Africa "could be too high a price to pay even for holding the Commonwealth together."[111]

107. Cabinet, Rhodesia Talks, "Economic Implications of United Kingdom Policy in Southern Africa, Note by the Secretaries," 26 August 1966, PRO CAB 134/3167.

108. Note for the Prime Minister by J. Oliver Wright, 28 July 1966, in PRO PREM 13/1124. See also, for example, Cabinet, Rhodesia Talks, Minutes of a Meeting of the Committee held in the prime minister's Room, House of Commons, S.W.1., on Friday, 22 July 1966 at 2.30 P.M.; "Cabinet: Future Policy on Rhodesia," Memorandum by the Secretary of State for Commonwealth Relations, 30 July 1966; and Cabinet, Rhodesia Talks, Minutes of a Meeting of the Committee held at 10, Downing Street, S.W.1., on Wednesday, 31 August 1966 at 3.00 pm. PRO CAB 134/3167.

109. In May 1966, the Ministry of Power told Shell that the British government wished "not to 'rock the boat'" in any dealings with South Africa, information which Shell then passed to BP. Bingham report, 78-83.

110. Cabinet, Rhodesia, Memorandum by the Secretary of State for Commonwealth Affairs. C(66) 179, 9 September 1966, PRO CAB 129/127. The document also states: "Our policy should be to bring economic sanctions to the pitch of maximum effectiveness, only limited by the need to avoid confrontation with South Africa."

111. Cabinet, Rhodesia Talks, Minutes of a Meeting of the Committee held at 10, Downing Street, S.W.1., on Thursday, 8 September 1966 at 9.30 A.M., PRO CAB 134/3167.

Britain recognized that mandatory United Nations sanctions against Rhodesia were necessary to prevent the breakup of the Commonwealth, and, throughout the summer and fall of 1966, sought a formula that would permit mandatory sanctions against Rhodesia without provoking South Africa. One formula, secretly aired at the Commonwealth Prime Ministers Conference in September 1966, was to accept mandatory sanctions against selected Rhodesian exports, and, at a later stage, mandatory sanctions against Mozambique should it continue to supply oil to Rhodesia. Britain also made clear, however, that it would not permit sanctions against South Africa.[112] In later conversations with African leaders, Britain maintained that there was a clear distinction between sanctions against Rhodesia and enforcement measures against those states that failed to comply with UN resolutions. Britain conceded that it was prepared in the event of Portugal's and Mozambique's noncompliance to consider enforcement measures, including sanctions against them. It would not, however, accept such measures against South Africa.[113] Ultimately, this formula proved unworkable. It failed to satisfy African demands that oil be included in any mandatory measures voted in the United Nations. As a result, it would not dissipate the pressures to extend sanctions to South Africa, and could even intensify them.[114]

In November 1966, Britain took another tack. In this formula, Britain would sponsor a general resolution for mandatory sanctions against Rhodesia, but exclude any reference to oil. An amendment covering oil sanctions would then be inserted by a friendly African government, but the amendment would be carefully worded to omit any specific references to South Africa or Mozambique, instead calling on all countries to prevent "the participation by the nationals or vessels under their registration in the supply of oil and oil products to Rhodesia." Britain would also reassure South Africa, publically if necessary, that it would not be party to enforcement measures aimed at that state.[115] In early December, Britain's plan came to fruition. It tabled a proposal in the Security Council for mandatory sanctions against Rhodesia and accepted an amendment that covered imports of oil into the colony. In accepting the amendment, however, Britain also explained to the Security Council that the measures were aimed at Rhodesia only; it would not allow sanctions to escalate into confrontation with third countries. Privately, it explained to South Africa

112. Cabinet, Rhodesia, Memorandum by the Secretary of State for Commonwealth Affairs. C(66) 179, 9 September 1966.

113. "Talking Points on Oil Sanctions for Special Representative's Conversations with African Leaders," no date (October/November? 1966), PRO PREM 13/1142.

114. Cabinet, "Rhodesia: Mandatory Sanctions," Memorandum by the Secretary of State for Commonwealth Affairs, C(66)173, 25 November 1966, PRO CAB 129/127.

115. Ibid.

that Britain was not "prepared to engage in a full confrontation" with that country.[116] On 16 December the UN Security Council voted mandatory sanctions, including oil, against Rhodesia. Resolution 232 obligated all members of the United Nations to halt the flow of oil to Rhodesia, but it was—by design—a resolution lacking enforcement mechanisms.

Despite Britain's unwillingness to publically restrict the flow of oil to southern Africa, it still sought to intensify the oil embargo through more covert mechanisms. Throughout the first two years of the embargo, the British government explored various options for limiting Rhodesia's ability to draw oil from the South African market with the tacit cooperation of the oil companies. Its latitude for action, however, was severely constrained by its overriding need to avoid a confrontation with South Africa. As a consequence, any options which involved even the slightest change in the oil companies' traditional commercial practices were ruled out as they would come to the attention of the South African government. Moreover, even if Britain and the British oil companies could agree on a scheme, there was no guarantee that it would be implemented by the lower level staff in South Africa. Rhodesia's defiance of Britain was very popular in South Africa—a local depot manager was more likely to turn the blind eye to a shipment bound for Rhodesia than to follow a company directive whose intent was to end the Rhodesian rebellion.[117] As a result, Britain's objectives in the oil embargo underwent a subtle but profound change. If it could not prevent oil from reaching Rhodesia, it at least had to insure that the oil Rhodesia obtained was not *British* oil. According to Lord Thomson, foreign and commonwealth secretary at the time:

> So it was against this background that we (the government) came increasingly to the conclusion...that we couldn't bring the Rhodesian Government to an end by sanctions, unless we were prepared to apply them to South Africa. We were under no circumstances willing to do that, and therefore...we came to the conclusion, I think, that the best we could make of a bad job in this respect was to be in a position to say at least there was no oil from British oil companies reaching Rhodesia.[118]

Moreover, this "cosmetic" arrangement to ensure that Rhodesia did not receive British oil was very important and useful to the British government for protecting the country's broader national interests. Lord Thomson testified

116. Record of a Conversation Between the prime minister and the South African ambassador at 10 Downing Street at 12.15 P.M. on Tuesday, 13 December 1966, PRO PREM 13/1142.
117. Bingham report, 71.
118. Testimony of Lord Thomson to Bingham Inquiry, Bingham report, 105.

further that British efforts to prevent British oil from reaching Rhodesia were extremely important for British credibility. It would "have done immense harm to the United Nations and elsewhere," Thompson testified, "if it could be shown that the British government knowingly allowed oil from companies operating under British legal authority to reach Rhodesia. To be able to say that no British oil was reaching Rhodesia was critical to the British diplomats conducting diplomacy in the United Nations and world capitals."[119]

Britain's new attitude was a recognition of the limits of its own policies, and it did little else to stop the flow of oil to Rhodesia. Its initial skepticism had proved correct—the oil embargo would not bring the Rhodesian rebellion to an end. The embargo collapsed for a number of reasons, among them the difficulty of controlling the foreign subsidiaries of the oil companies and the connivance of South Africa and Portugal in busting the sanctions. The most important, however, was South Africa's threat to retaliate against any measure which affected its own supplies of oil. This not only allowed South Africa to bust sanctions with impunity, it also undermined any attempts by the oil companies and their South African subsidiaries to limit the flow of oil to Rhodesia. Because supplying Rhodesia would not precipitate a crisis between Britain and South Africa, these companies no longer had any real basis for defying South African edicts. Louis Walker, the general manager of Shell South Africa testified to the Bingham inquiry that Britain's desire to avoid a confrontation with South Africa at all costs played a key role in his shift in emphasis away from his early actions to impede the flow of Shell product into Rhodesia to simply staying within the letter of the law.[120] As a result, commercial concerns came to dominate the oil companies' actions; enforcing the oil embargo was now simply a matter of style over substance.

ASSESSING THE RHODESIAN OIL EMBARGO

THE OIL embargo did not bring majority rule to Rhodesia. By the time mandatory sanctions were imposed in December 1966, sufficient quantities of oil were flowing into the colony, supplied largely by the subsidiaries of the British and American oil companies. Clearly there is a strong basis for the conventional interpretation that the embargo stands as a compelling example of the futility of trying to control the behavior of private economic actors for

119. Ibid., 107.
120. Bingham report, 118–19.

political ends, and of using economic sanctions to pursue important foreign policy goals.

Yet the conventional interpretation of the oil embargo is highly misleading.[121] The British oil companies cooperated closely with Britain in the first months of the embargo and supplied Rhodesia only after ordered to do so by the South African government. Even then they covertly explored with Britain ways to limit the flow of oil. That oil continued to reach Rhodesia rested as much on Britain's unwillingness to provoke South Africa as it did the commercial interests of the oil companies serving the Rhodesian market.

Moreover, Britain's early success in enlisting the cooperation of the oil companies also demonstrated that it was possible to control the flow of oil to southern Africa. South Africa distrusted the oil companies with good reason. It threatened retaliatory sanctions against Britain not because the embargo could not be effective, but because it could. It also reacted to the embargo by undertaking a series of economically costly steps to lessen its vulnerability to possible oil sanctions directed against it. Unlike many scholars of sanctions, South Africa harbored no illusions about the potential of sanctions to impose significant and harmful economic and political penalties.

The conventional wisdom is also misleading in classifying the embargo as a failed influence attempt. Britain used the oil embargo to defuse powerful political pressures for even stronger, and more unwelcome actions against Rhodesia and even South Africa, and to prevent a breakup of the Commonwealth. These were important British goals, even more important than ending the Rhodesian rebellion. That they were largely achieved is remarkable and must

121. Even the statement that the oil embargo did not bring majority rule to Rhodesia deserves further scrutiny. The embargo made oil significantly more expensive to Rhodesia and proved a significant drag on the Rhodesian economy. This intensified Rhodesia's difficulties in the late 1970s in battling its nationalist guerilla movements, which is often offered as the primary reason for Rhodesia's acceptance of majority rule. According to a U.S. Central Intelligence Agency cable, "The costs of waging the war against the black nationalist guerrillas *and* the high cost of petroleum products have drained the country's economy" (U.S. Central Intelligence Agency, Intelligence Information Cable, "Assessment of Rhodesia's Economic Situation," [DOI: 1978], 14 March 1978, [emphasis added]). A 1979 report identifies a "increases in petroleum prices" as a key problem for Rhodesia and then notes that "Economic sanctions are a far greater problem for the economy than the military threat...the economy is approaching a point at which the damage done will become virtually irreversible" (U.S. Central Intelligence Agency, Intelligence Information Report, "Prospects for the Rhodesian Economy in 1979," 18 April 1979). Both documents were obtained by the author under the Freedom of Information Act. These contemporary analyses contradict Pape's recent assertions that military force, not economic sanctions, alone was responsible for majority rule and that the decline in economic growth after 1975 was "a result of the war, not sanctions" (Pape, "Why Economic Sanctions Do Not Work," 118–19). In fact, Pape's general assessment that sanctions against Rhodesia were a clear failure is based on a highly selective and unbalanced interpretation of the historical evidence. He neglects to cite, for example, the most comprehensive post-independence analysis of sanctions—Minter and Schmidt, "When Sanctions Worked."

be credited in no small part to the oil embargo. One cannot assert that the embargo failed to achieve important British foreign policy objectives.

Finally, the oil embargo also contradicts in another way the conventional wisdom that sanctions almost never work. One cannot accurately analyze the Rhodesian oil embargo without reference to South Africa's role in determining the extent to which Britain could use the embargo to pressure the Rhodesian government. South Africa asserted its influence by allowing oil to transit its territory, by ordering the local subsidiaries to supply Rhodesia, and by explicitly threatening retaliatory sanctions against Britain. South Africa's ability to use this threat to set the parameters of Britain's Rhodesia policy thus represents a stunning, and previously unrecognized, instance of the successful use of economic sanctions.

One cannot draw sound policy recommendations for how and when policy makers should use economic sanctions from the study of a single episode. One can, however, draw several important implications from the oil embargo for how scholars should think about economic sanctions.

First, the oil embargo underscores the necessity of gauging the success of sanctions only against the *entire* array of objectives that policy makers seek. The oil embargo did not end the Rhodesian rebellion. Yet it is wrong to argue that embargo failed because it did achieve two even more important British goals, preserving the Commonwealth and defusing pressure for more extreme action against the colony, goals that were largely the reasons why Britain (with the cooperation of the United States) imposed the embargo. To argue that the oil embargo failed would not only misrepresent the purposes and outcome of the embargo, it would deny important information to policy makers about the ability to use economic sanctions as credible signals in an international environment rife with "cheap talk" and opportunistic and deceptive behavior.

Second, the oil embargo demonstrates that scholars cannot assume the goals and targets in any influence attempt are unproblematic. Most analyses of the Rhodesian case assume that ending the Rhodesian rebellion was the primary purpose of the oil embargo because this was the primary purpose of Britain's larger package of economic sanctions. Yet, Britain (and the United States) doubted that the embargo would end the rebellion and took this economically and politically costly step largely to demonstrate their commitment to bringing about majority rule in Rhodesia. Nor can one assume that Rhodesia was the primary target of the influence attempt simply because it was the country whose oil was being embargoed. No attempt by Britain or the United States to convince Black Africa and the Commonwealth of their commitment to majority rule would have been credible in the absence of severe penalties against Rhodesia. It was only by making the embargo as effective as possible in imposing visible economic costs on Rhodesia that Britain and the United States could credibly demonstrate their commitment. The first and most important step in any analysis of a sanctions episode, then, is to accurately describe the structure of goals that states seek to achieve and the targets they seek to influence.

Third, this case demonstrates that our knowledge about the universe of sanctions is limited. The most comprehensive listing of sanctions is offered by Hufbauer, Schott, and Elliott.[122] This data has become the empirical foundation of a number of important studies about sanctions.[123] Yet my study has identified at least three instances of economic sanctions that fit their definition of an economic sanction, but are not within their data set.[124] These include the United States' implicit threat to deny assistance to Britain should its policies disrupt the supply of Zambian copper; Rhodesia's threat to retaliate against Zambia in the event of an oil embargo; and South Africa's threat to retaliate against Britain should its trade be disrupted. The first two were at least partially successful in shaping British policy regarding the oil embargo, while South Africa's threat against Britain can only be regarded as a major and successful threat of economic sanctions. To their credit, Hufbauer, Schott, and Elliott recognize their data does not include instances such as South Africa's, where sanctions are threatened or applied in relative secrecy.[125] Yet this raises serious concerns about potential selection biases in the data set; for it may be that most successful uses of sanctions never become public because targeted countries adjust their behavior before sanctions are actually announced or implemented. At a minimum, this ambiguity about the actual universe of sanctions cases should encourage a little humility among scholars about making blanket statements that "economic sanctions do not work."[126]

Finally, the experiences of the oil embargo contradict the assertion that sanctions are only likely to be effective (and, by implication, should only be used) when the stakes are low, or, in other words, for issues that "do not affect the target country's territory, security, wealth, or the regime's domestic

122. Hufbauer, Schott, and Elliott, *Economic Sanctions Reconsidered.*

123. See n. 6.

124. In fact, given that the primary purposes of the oil embargo differed from the general package of sanctions against Rhodesia, it comprises a fourth case of sanctions not picked up by the Hufbauer, Schott and Elliott study. Hufbauer, Schott, and Elliott define economic sanctions as "the deliberate government inspired withdrawal or threat of withdrawal, of 'customary trade or financial relations. 'Customary' does not mean 'contractual'; it simply means the level that would have probably occurred in the absence of sanctions" (Hufbauer, Schott, and Elliott, *Economic Sanctions Reconsidered*, 1985 ed., 2).

125. Ibid., 3.

126. For example, Pape, "Why Economic Sanctions Do Not Work."

security."[127] What is striking about the oil embargo is how high the stakes were for all countries involved with it, targets and senders alike. Moreover, British policy was responsive to South Africa's threatened sanctions precisely because South Africa could credibly threaten to impose severe economic damage on Britain, while black Africa could not.

The oil embargo thus stands as a compelling example, not of the abject failure of economic sanctions to achieve important foreign policy goals, but as a number of important successes. It demonstrates, moreover, the critical need of scholars to understand better the entire array of objectives that states seek whenever they use sanctions. Only then can scholars gauge accurately the success of individual uses of sanctions and, in turn, use this knowledge across cases to generate sound policy advice about how and when to use economic sanctions most wisely.

127. Pape, "Why Economic Sanctions Do Not Work," 109.

Economic Statecraft, Interdependence, and National Security:

Agendas for Research

Michael Mastanduno

THE ABILITY to attract the devotion of younger scholars is one key indicator of the intellectual appeal of a set of research questions in the study of international relations. By this measure, the intersection of economic and national security issues is among the most prominent agendas in the field today. The same could not be said twenty-five years ago. At that time, international relations scholarship proceeded along two separate tracks. Security studies emerged after the Second World War as a distinct subfield of international relations, and during the 1970s the "new" subfield of international political economy arose to analyze a suddenly politicized world economy. International relations scholars were typically trained and worked in one subfield or the other, and there was not a great deal of intellectual engagement across the divide.

Today, the dividing line between international political economy and security studies has all but disappeared. There exists a renewed interest in virtually every aspect of the intersection of the two concerns.[1] This includes, at the systemic level, studies of the international security consequences of economic interdependence, and of the political and security foundations for increased economic interaction among states. At the level of the individual unit, there is renewed attention to how economic and defense policies interact to produce the grand strategies of major powers. Work is accumulating on the use of economic statecraft to achieve strategic objectives and on the use of security strategies (for example, conquest, alliances) to satisfy economic aims. International relations specialists are drawing on microeconomic models to explain security outcomes, and are beginning to borrow concepts from security studies (for example, the balance of power, the security dilemma) to explain outcomes in international political economy.

Michael Mastanduno is professor of government at Dartmouth College.

1. For an elaboration of this argument and the relevant source references, see Michael Mastanduno, "Economics and Security in Statecraft and Scholarship," *International Organization* 52, no. 4 (autumn 1998): 825–54.

The articles in this special issue are at the center of the revival of interest in the intersection of economics and security. They are written by younger scholars with a sensitivity both to broader theoretical concerns and to the importance of conducting careful empirical research. Their contributions can be grouped into three major categories. Some of the articles focus on the extent to which negative economic sanctions can be used to further the core national interests of states. Others emphasize the potential of economic inducements, or positive economic sanctions, to be a key national security instrument. In the third category are studies that explore the intervening variables that link economic interdependence to the existence of peace or military conflict among major powers.

Significant scholarly progress is being made in each of these three areas. In what follows, I frame the central issues specific to each and explore the particular contributions made by the articles in this special issue. A reading of the individual essays and a comparison across them raises both new arguments and fruitful conceptual and empirical questions. A concluding section highlights several themes emerging from the volume as a whole, which are relevant to the study of economic and security interactions.

NEGATIVE ECONOMIC SANCTIONS: ASKING THE RIGHT QUESTIONS

THE STUDY of negative economic sanctions, or economic coercion, has long been crucial to any understanding of the relationship between economic interdependence and national security. Over the years, scholars have vacillated between optimism and skepticism on the utility of negative sanctions. The period following the First World War was one of highest expectations. Framers of the League of Nations hoped that economic coercion could deter military aggression.[2] Their desire to find a substitute for war was understandable in light of the horrible experience of the First World War and their belief that peace was a worthy international objective in and of itself.[3] Many scholars and policymakers believed that economic sanctions were a credible alternative to military force because states had become increasingly interdependent and

2. Article 16 of the League Covenant reflected this sentiment. See Margaret P. Doxey, *International Sanctions in Contemporary Perspective*, 2nd ed. (London: Macmillan, 1996), 3–4.
3. John Foster Dulles summarized this perspective in 1932: "The great advantage of economic sanctions is that on the one hand they can be very potent, while on the other hand they do not involve that resort to force which is repugnant to our objective of peace" (Dulles is quoted in Mark Brawley, "Globalization, Democratization, and the Paradoxical Future of Economic Sanctions" [paper prepared for the conference on international order in the 21st century, McGill University, May 1997, 18–19]).

would be reluctant to risk the disruption of trade and financial flows to their economies.[4]

The dramatic failure of League sanctions against Italy, after its invasion of Ethiopia in 1935, cast doubt both on the League and on the efficacy of the economic instrument. That episode took on significance as one of the "classic cases" invoked by scholars after the Second World War to develop a new skepticism about the utility of economic sanctions. The League experience, coupled with other salient cases of failure—U.S. sanctions against Cuba, UN sanctions against Rhodesia, NATO sanctions against the Soviet Union and China, Arab sanctions against Israel—pointed scholars writing during the 1960s and 1970s to the more pessimistic consensus that economic sanctions might cause economic disruption and pain but were unlikely to lead to meaningful political change in the behavior or composition of a target government.[5]

A revisionist challenge to this pessimistic assessment arose during the 1980s. David Baldwin reconceptualized the scholarly literature and argued that the use of economic sanctions—more generally economic statecraft—typically involved multiple objectives and targets, and that the assessment of success or failure could only be made convincingly by comparing the costs and benefits of economic statecraft to that of other forms of statecraft.[6] Baldwin did not claim that economic sanctions were likely to succeed. His conceptual framework and reconsideration of classic cases, however, did suggest that the economic instrument was considerably more useful than scholars generally acknowledged. The empirical analyses by Gary Clyde Hufbauer, Jeffrey Schott, and Kimberly Ann Elliott reached a similar conclusion. Their study of what they considered to be the full array of economic sanctions cases from 1914 to 1990—114 cases in all—found that economic sanctions were at least partially successful in 40 of them, or about one-third of the time.[7] Although the success rate was highest in the two decades following the Second World War and de-

4. These ideas are reviewed in William J. Barber, "British and American Economists and Attempts to Comprehend the Nature of War, 1910–1920; and Neil de Marchi, "League of Nations Economists and the Ideal of Peaceful Change in the Decade of the 'Thirties," in *Economics and National Security: A History of Their Interaction*, ed. Craufurd D. Goodwin (Durham: Duke University Press, 1991), 61–86 and 143–78.

5. Representative examples of the postwar consensus include Donald Losman, *International Economic Sanctions: The Cases of Cuba, Israel, and Rhodesia* (Albuquerque: University of New Mexico Press, 1979); Klaus Knorr, *The Power of Nations: The Political Economy of International Relations* (New York: Basic Books, 1975); and Johann Galtung, "On the Effects of International Economic Sanctions: With Examples from the Case of Rhodesia," *World Politics* 19, no. 3 (April 1967): 378–416.

6. David A. Baldwin, *Economic Statecraft* (Princeton: Princeton University Press, 1985).

7. Gary Clyde Hufbauer and Jeffrey Schott, with the assistance of Kimberly Ann Elliott, *Economic Sanctions Reconsidered: History and Current Policy* (Washington, D.C.: Institute for International Economics, 1985).

clined sharply during the 1970s and 1980s, the overall picture painted by Hufbauer, Schott and Elliott suggested there was no basis for the popular and scholarly claim that sanctions never work.[8]

In scholarship, as in physics, every action produces a reaction. In 1997 Robert Pape challenged the methods and results of Hufbauer, Schott and Elliott in an effort to reassert the more pessimistic scholarly consensus. He argued that sanctions do not work and that policymakers should not employ them to achieve major foreign policy goals.[9] Pape's critique inspired a response from Elliott defending the case selection and findings of *Economic Sanctions Reconsidered*, and one from Baldwin suggesting that Pape overstated his case by stacking the deck conceptually and empirically in favor of sanctions failure.[10]

Broad assessments of and debates over whether sanctions "work" play a useful role in scholarship. They prompt us to review our assumptions, reconsider established habits, and renew the search for empirical evidence. Baldwin's work has profoundly influenced how the current generation of scholars approaches the study of economic statecraft and sanctions.[11] Whether or not one agrees with him, Pape's more recent frontal assault has forced a reexamination of particular sanctions cases and of an aggregate database that has served for more than a decade as a benchmark for scholars and policymakers seeking, sometimes uncritically, a summary assessment of the utility of sanctions. The article in this special issue by David Rowe is both inspired by the methods of Baldwin and responsive to the challenge posed by Pape.

A general debate pitched at the level of whether sanctions "work," however, is at this point bound to be inconclusive. Given the current state of knowledge, it is premature to pronounce generally that "sanctions fail," or for that matter, that "sanctions work." Any general debate over the utility of economic sanctions has an irresolvable quality similar to concurrent debates in the field over whether institutions matter, whether realism is dead, or whether rational choice is necessarily the method of choice.

A more productive course at this stage is for sanctions scholars to focus on a series of more conditional questions and issues. As Richard Haass noted recently, "the answer to the question 'Do sanctions work?' must necessarily be

8. See Kimberly Ann Elliott, "The Sanctions Glass: Half Full or Completely Empty?" *International Security* 23, no. 1 (summer 1998): 50–65.

9. Robert A. Pape, "Why Economic Sanctions Do Not Work," *International Security* 22, no. 2 (fall 1997): 90–136.

10. Elliott, "The Sanctions Glass"; and David A. Baldwin, "Evaluating Economic Sanctions," *International Security* 23, no. 2 (fall 1998): 189–95.

11. See, for example, Lisa L. Martin, *Coercive Cooperation: Explaining Multilateral Economic Sanctions* (Princeton: Princeton University Press, 1992); and the contributions in Richard N. Haass, ed., *Economic Sanctions and American Diplomacy* (New York: Council on Foreign Relations, 1998).

'It depends.'"[12] The contributors to this special issue proceed in that spirit. As Jean-Marc Blanchard and Norrin Ripsman note explicitly, the more pertinent question is not "do economic sanctions work", but rather, under what conditions are sanctions likely to be a more or a less effective instrument of statecraft.[13] The answer to that question, of course, requires analyses of a range of conceptual and empirical issues. The following set is not intended to be exhaustive, but reflects my sense of the most pressing concerns given the state of the literature and the current international context. A review of these "right questions" underscores the need for skepticism regarding general pronouncements and also highlights the significant challenges and opportunities awaiting scholars working at this intersection of economic interdependence and national security.

IDENTIFYING OBJECTIVES

Baldwin's argument on the need to recognize that multiple objectives are at play in any sanctions attempt is compelling. The identification of sender objectives is obviously crucial to any assessment of the utility of economic sanctions in any particular case. Scholarly assessments of the effectiveness of Western sanctions against the Soviet Union during the cold war differed widely depending on whether damaging the Soviet economy, delaying improvements in Soviet military capabilities, or influencing Soviet foreign policy behavior were judged to be primary or secondary objectives.[14]

The recognition of multiple objectives, however, raises new challenges for sanctions analysis. It may be true, as Baldwin and others have pointed out, that to focus only on the publicly stated objective or on the most ambitious one in a given sanctions episode sets the threshold for success too high and is likely to bias results in the direction of failure. An appreciation of multiple objectives, on the other hand, may tempt one to set the threshold too low and bias findings in favor of success. A creative analyst who looks deeply enough at any sanctions attempt is likely to find *some* objective that was satisfied, however modest. This is all the more likely once we accept that sanctions attempts have multiple audiences and targets as well as multiple objectives. To make a per-

---

12. Richard N. Haass, "Introduction," in Haass, *Economic Sanctions and American Diplomacy*, 4.

13. Jean-Marc F. Blanchard and Norrin M. Ripsman, "Asking the Right Question: *When Do Economic Sanctions Work Best?*" *Security Studies* 9, nos. 1/2 (autumn 1999–winter 2000): 219–53.

14. See Michael Mastanduno, *Economic Containment: CoCom and the Politics of East-West Trade* (Ithaca: Cornell University Press, 1992).

suasive case, it quickly becomes imperative to sort out primary objectives and targets from secondary and even tertiary ones.

Blanchard and Ripsman recognize this problem, and provide the insight that sanctions will lose their ability to serve secondary objectives if they consistently fail to satisfy primary ones. They imply, however, that identifying primary objectives is not problematic. One needs to focus on "the stated political objective" and to assess the ability of sanctions to "engender the desired political result."[15] The desired political result may be uncontroversial in some cases, but is certainly not in others. One could certainly make the case that the stated purpose or desired result of U.S. sanctions in 1980 was to drive the Soviets out of Afghanistan. Because that goal was so ambitious as to be unrealistic, however, some analysts have concluded that the *primary* objectives were to punish the Soviet Union, and, by signaling an end to business as usual, to deter the Soviets from future adventurism in the region.[16]

David Rowe's contribution to this volume demonstrates how much is at stake in the identification of objectives. The oil embargo directed at Rhodesia is generally acknowledged to be a failure because it is associated with an apparent primary objective—the rapid capitulation of Smith's minority regime. Rowe makes a strong case that the primary target was not Rhodesia but Black African states, and that the primary objectives were to preserve the British Commonwealth and deflect demands for more dramatic (that is, military) action against Rhodesia.[17] This reevaluation of objectives leads to the conclusion that the oil embargo was a success rather than a failure, and on an issue of considerable national security significance to Great Britain. The use of previously unexplored primary sources justifies and lends credibility to Rowe's reinterpretation. Perhaps the most important implication of Rowe's study is that the debate over the utility of sanctions in any particular case must first be a debate over objectives.

UNDERSTANDING ECONOMIC PRESSURE

Economic sanctions typically involve the application of economic pressure to produce some type of political result—a change in the current or future behavior of a target government, or perhaps a change in the target government

15. Blanchard and Ripsman, "Asking the Right Question."

16. For discussion, see Baldwin, *Economic Statecraft*, 263–68; and Kim Richard Nossal, "International Sanctions as International Punishment," *International Organization* 43, no. 2 (spring 1989): 310–22.

17. David Rowe, "Economic Sanctions Do Work: Economic Statecraft and the Oil Embargo of Rhodesia Reconsidered," *Security Studies* 9, nos. 1/2 (autumn 1999–winter 2000): 254–87.

itself. The most familiar logic of sanctions suggests that more economic pain is better. The more damage can be inflicted on the target economy, the more likely that the target government will capitulate, either on its own or as a result of political pressure imposed by a deprived population. Students of sanctions have observed, however, that this typical logic is flawed and may even be, in Galtung's word, naïve.[18] Economic pain does not necessarily translate into political gain because sanctions may create a "rally around the flag" effect, as in Castro's Cuba, or because elites may be able to shift the incidence of sanctions and insulate key supporters from their effects, as in Saddam Hussein's Iraq.

The observation that there is no predictable relationship between economic pain and political influence opens two important research issues. The first, addressed by Blanchard and Ripsman, involves the *conditions under which* economic pressure translates into political change. Their central insight is compelling: the key to an effective translation is not the extent of economic pressure, but the existence of favorable political conditions.[19] They focus not on the economic costs to the target but on the international and domestic political costs of compliance and noncompliance. Blanchard and Ripsman point us in the right direction, even though at this stage their framework is fairly indeterminate. They offer eight crosscutting factors that affect how a target government will weigh the relative costs of compliance or noncompliance. An important next step will be to develop operational measures of these cost factors so that their argument will be testable in cases beyond those which they use to illustrate it.[20]

If there is no linear relationship between economic pain and political change, then policymakers would be prudent to reconsider the common practice of using economic sanctions as an "assured destruction" instrument to pummel a target into submission. Assured destruction is costly. The current cases of sanctions against Iran and Iraq, and the bickering they have inspired among the major powers, demonstrate that comprehensive trade, financial, and investment sanctions can harm the senders as well as the target. The more important problem is that assured destruction may be counterproductive. During the 1990s, the international community became far more sensitive to the humanitarian consequences of economic sanctions and no longer imagines

18. Galtung, "On the Effects of International Economic Sanctions," 388–89.

19. A version of this argument is offered by Jonathan Kirshner, "The Microfoundations of Economic Sanctions," *Security Studies* 6, no. 3 (spring 1997): 32–64.

20. Blanchard and Ripsman's analysis also raises the important issue of *how much* economic pain is needed to trigger the political effects on which they focus. It may be, and their analysis of the British-Soviet case suggests this, that even fairly modest economic sanctions can serve "as a signaling device" to make target leaders "understand the political ramifications of their actions" (237).

them as a benign or peaceful alternative to military force.[21] Sanctions harm the civilian population of a target, treating it, in effect, as "the enemy" in an effort to exert pressure on the real enemy, the target government. Resourceful target regimes, however, may insulate themselves from the effects of sanctions, and may, as Saddam Hussein has, manipulate the plight of their beleaguered populations to gain domestic and international political advantages. The result, in Bruce Jentleson's words, is the "neutron bomb problem": sanctions end up destroying the civilian economy but leave the regime standing.[22]

This predicament leads to a second policy-relevant research problem: the extent to which economic sanctions can be targeted with greater precision directly against offending regimes and their supporters. As the humanitarian costs of comprehensive sanctions have become more apparent, the idea of employing "smarter" or "designer" sanctions to avoid collateral damage has become increasingly popular.[23] Designing designer sanctions, however, is no simple task. First, it requires a detailed understanding not only of the domestic economy and political system but also of the personal and business connections among elites in societies (for example, Iran, Libya, Iraq, China) that are hardly transparent. This is a significant challenge for intelligence analysts in government, and comparative politics and political economy experts in political science. Second, designer sanctions require a greater appreciation than we currently have of the differential characteristics and impacts of different sanctions instruments.[24] Trade sanctions may harm populations more than regimes. Financial sanctions may have greater potential to harm elites, but must be deployed quickly and decisively before funds are moved out of reach. We know relatively little about the exercise and distributional consequences of monetary sanctions.[25] Third, selective sanctions are more difficult to devise and imple-

21. See John Mueller and Karl Mueller, "Sanctions of Mass Destruction," *Foreign Affairs* 78, no. 3 (May/June 1999): 43–53; and Gideon Rose, "Haiti," in Haass, *Economic Sanctions and American Diplomacy*, 57–84.

22. Bruce W. Jentleson, "Economic Sanctions and Post–Cold War Conflict Resolution: Challenges for Theory and Policy" (paper prepared for the Committee on International Conflict Resolution, National Academy of Sciences, September 1997), 73.

23. For example, Gary Clyde Hufbauer and Elizabeth Winston, "Smarter Sanctions: Updating the Economic Weapon" (unpublished paper, Institute for International Economics, May 1997). An earlier example of this approach in a specific case context is Charles M. Becker, "Economic Sanctions Against South Africa," *World Politics* 39, no. 2 (January 1987): 147–73.

24. Becker argued that divestment from South Africa would provide a windfall to white supporters of the regime, but that a ban on *new* investments and on high technology exports would harm white supporters and help black opponents by increasing the demand for unskilled labor. See Becker, "Economic Sanctions Against South Africa."

25. Jonathan Kirshner's recent book goes far to rectify this problem. Kirshner, *Currency and Coercion: The Political Economy of International Monetary Power* (Princeton: Princeton University Press, 1998).

ment than are comprehensive sanctions. As the United States and its CoCom allies learned, once the decision is make to control transactions selectively, determining what is to be controlled becomes an ongoing and often intractable problem politically and conceptually.[26]

EXPLAINING MULTILATERAL COORDINATION

There is almost universal agreement in the sanctions literature that multilateral sanctions are superior to unilateral ones. Multilateral sanctions allow the senders to maximize the effectiveness of economic pressure, whether selective or comprehensive. They maximize the political isolation of the target government, and make it more difficult for that government to evade sanctions by relying on third parties for political and economic support. Multilateral coordination also makes it easier for sender governments to maintain domestic support for sanctions; private firms are less likely to grumble about lost market opportunities if their international competitors are constrained as well.

There is less agreement, however, on the explanation for effective multilateral coordination. For some, effective coordination is a function of the international distribution of power. As hegemony declines, so too does the effectiveness of cooperation.[27] For others, international institutions are the critical explanatory variable.[28] Still others highlight the influence of shared norms in developing and sustaining an international consensus for sanctions.[29] International security threats and their ability to create a shared sense of interests constitute yet another plausible explanation.[30]

Even with additional research, it is unlikely that one explanatory factor will emerge as the uncontested winner. It is all the more unlikely when one considers that the most prominent explanations are drawn from competing paradigms in international relations theory, paradigms to which many scholars have enduring commitments. The challenge for scholarship is less to determine the last variable standing, and instead to explore the interactions among what

---

26. Mastanduno, *Economic Containment*, esp. chap. 6.

27. Kenneth A. Rodman, "Sanctions at Bay? Hegemonic Decline, Multinational Corporations, and U.S. Economic Sanctions Since the Pipeline Case," *International Organization* 49, no. 1 (winter 1995): 105–37; and Bruce W. Jentleson, *Pipeline Politics: The Complex Political Economy of East-West Energy Trade* (Ithaca: Cornell University Press, 1986).

28. See Martin, *Coercive Cooperation*; and Edward D. Mansfield, "International Institutions and Economic Sanctions," *World Politics* 47, no. 4 (July 1995): 575–605.

29. Audie Klotz, *Norms in International Relations: The Struggle Against Apartheid* (Ithaca: Cornell University Press, 1995).

30. Michael Mastanduno, "Trade as a Strategic Weapon: American and Alliance Export Control Policy in the Early Postwar Period," *International Organization* 42, no. 1 (winter 1998): 121–50.

many would agree are key variables. An understanding of the interplay between power and international institutions, for example, might be helpful in understanding why some sanctions initiated by the same sender in the same time frame command more multilateral support than others.

ASSESSING TARGET VULNERABILITY

Are some target countries more susceptible to economic pressure than others? Students of sanctions typically answer in the affirmative by focusing on political and economic characteristics. Size matters; states with larger economies are said to be less vulnerable that states with smaller ones. The former are more self-sufficient and also likely to be more powerful politically. This logic is plausible, although it should be noted that small, dependent targets often resist sanctions effectively. The cases of Cuba, Israel and Rhodesia illustrate that even vulnerable economies can find external protectors, exploit political integrative effects, and substitute domestic production for sanctioned imports.[31] The small may in general be more vulnerable than the large, but variations across states with small, dependent economies suggest again that analyses of different political circumstances are crucial for explanation.

The most familiar political distinction among targets is between democracies and nondemocracies. Democracies are more vulnerable because the state is more responsive to society, and thus is more sensitive to political pressure from societal groups facing sanctions-induced deprivation. Authoritarian regimes, in contrast, are more insulated from societal pressure. Again, the logic is plausible but the argument does not go far enough. Nondemocratic regimes can face domestic political opposition that is more or less powerful. Democratic states also can respond to sanctions, as they typically do to war, with political integration rather than disintegration.

Formal political structures are less important than the interests and influence of domestic political actors, and the relationships between those actors and the state. As Jentleson puts it, the key is the ability of domestic actors to act as "transmission belts," carrying the economic effects of sanctions into the political process of the target state.[32] Business and political elites can play that role, depending on whether they view sanctions as a threat to their international connections or as an opportunity to profit by breaking sanctions or exploiting the black market. Sanctions can strengthen domestic opposition groups by granting them greater international legitimacy (the ANC in South

31. Losman, *International Economic Sanctions*.
32. Jentleson, "Economic Sanctions and Post–Cold War Conflict Resolution," 21.

Africa is a good example); they can weaken opposition groups if the regime is able to use the imposition of sanctions effectively as a rationale for domestic repression. In any event, the research strategy is to get "underneath" the formal political structure to assess the impact of sanctions on particular domestic actors and on the relationships among the state, its supporters, and its opponents.[33]

A second useful way to think about target vulnerability is in terms of international relationships. The research of Hufbauer, Schott, and Elliott, among others, has suggested that sanctions are likely to be more effective against allies than against adversaries. Daniel Drezner develops this point conceptually and empirically.[34] He argues that adversaries are less likely to concede because they anticipate future conflicts with the sender state. They worry, more so than the allies of sender states, about the relative gains and reputational consequences of capitulation.

These insights on the relevance of reputation, relative gains, and future expectations are significant. Generalizations about allies and adversaries, however, may be more questionable. There are circumstances in which allies are sensitive to relative gains; consider the potential for a "hegemonic transition" between the United States and Japan during the late 1980s.[35] One can easily conceive of circumstances in which the absolute power differential between two adversaries is sufficiently large so that the weaker party has little reason to be concerned about the *relative* gains consequences of sanctions episodes. (Can Cuba's defiance of U.S. sanctions really be driven by a concern that capitulation will make the United States a more formidable adversary than it already is?) Allies also worry, just as adversaries do, about their bargaining reputations. Allies may not expect future wars against each other, but they certainly do not anticipate harmony either. Longstanding U.S.-Japan and U.S.-European Union trade conflicts offer ample evidence that allies on either side of the bargaining table worry that backing down in one round will lead to a weaker position in the next. The history of U.S. efforts to use economic sanctions to coerce its

33. Examples of this kind of analysis include Kirshner, "The Microfoundations of Economic Sanctions"; Becker, "Economic Sanctions against South Africa"; and, although more focused on the sender side, Anton Lowenberg and William Kaempfer, *International Economic Sanctions: A Public Choice Perspective* (Boulder: Westview Press, 1992).

34. Daniel W. Drezner, "Allies, Adversaries, and Economic Coercion: Russian Foreign Economic Policy Since 1991," *Security Studies* 6, no. 3 (spring 1997): 65–111; and Drezner, "The Trouble with Carrots: Transactions Costs, Conflict Expectations, and Economic Inducements" *Security Studies* 9, nos. 1/2 (autumn 1999–winter 2000): 188–218.

35. See Michael Mastanduno, "Do Relative Gains Matter? America's Response to Japanese Industrial Policy," *International Security* 16, no. 1 (summer 1991): 73–113; and more generally, Joseph M. Grieco, *Cooperation Among Nations: America, Europe, and Non-Tariff Barriers to Trade* (Ithaca: Cornell University Press, 1990).

more dependent allies to back U.S. foreign policy initiatives (for example, the Battle Act, the Siberian pipeline, the Iran and Libya Sanctions Act) is characterized by target defiance rather than compliance. In each of these prominent conflicts the United States backed down rather than risk an escalation of conflict that might jeopardize future alliance relations.[36]

INTEGRATING INSTRUMENTS OF STATECRAFT

An important insight of the revisionist literature is that economic sanctions should be viewed in the context of other instruments of statecraft. For many analysts, this has meant treating economic sanctions as alternatives to military force or diplomacy. Baldwin's framework suggests this by calling for a comparative analysis of the costs and benefits of economic statecraft, military statecraft, diplomacy, and perhaps propaganda in any foreign policy influence attempt. The Hufbauer, Schott and Elliott study seeks to isolate and estimate the particular contribution of economic sanctions to foreign policy outcomes. Pape's reexamination of their cases is explicit in treating sanctions as a stand-alone foreign policy instrument. He notes in response to Elliott that "both studies seek to identify the effectiveness of economic sanctions not as a complement but as a substitute for other instruments of statecraft."[37]

There may be merit in treating sanctions "on their own," but it is as important if not more so to conceive of them as complements to other means of statecraft. This is a case of practice preceding theory. More often than not, policymakers treat economic sanctions as part of a package of foreign policy measures.[38] Nonetheless, scholarly analysis thus far has not addressed systematically the *interaction* of sanctions and other instruments of statecraft.

Consider, for example, some of the ways sanctions and military force might interact to produce a foreign policy outcome. Sanctions may have the potential to "soften" the military and technological capabilities of a target in the event that war becomes necessary. By the same token, the use of military force to degrade a target's economic and military infrastructure may help to make subsequent sanctions efforts more effective. The imposition of economic sanc-

---

36. On the Battle Act and pipeline conflicts, see Jentleson, *Pipeline Politics*; and Mastanduno, *Economic Containment*. On the U.S. decision to forego sanctions under the Iran-Libya Sanctions Act, see Statement by the Secretary of State, "Iran and Libya Sanctions Act (ILSA): Decision in the South Pars Case," London, United Kingdom, 18 May 1998.

37. Robert A. Pape, "Why Economic Sanctions *Still* Do Not Work," *International Security* 23, no. 1 (summer 1998): 66–77, cite at 69.

38. Blanchard's and Ripsman's discussion of "compound sanctions" suggests this. See "Asking the Right Question: *When* Do Economic Sanctions Work Best?" *Security Studies* 9, no. 1 (autumn 1999): 228–64.

tions may pave the way politically for the use of force; in the Iraq case, without the prior imposition of sanctions it would have been more difficult to convince wavering members of the international coalition to support to escalation to war. In the Rhodesian case, Rowe's evidence suggests that the oil embargo both enhanced the effectiveness of an internal military insurgency and enabled Britain to deflect pressure for external military intervention.

It is also instructive to analyze the interplay of sanctions and diplomacy. Too often, diplomacy is given limited analytical attention because it is considered too weak as an *alternative* to force or even sanctions. If the focus is on the interaction of instruments of statecraft, however, the role of diplomacy becomes more appreciated. Stephen John Stedman argues that sanctions alone obviously did not produce the Dayton Accords, but sanctions did provide a valuable bargaining chip in separating Milosoviec from the Bosnian Serbs and prodding him to accept the Accords.[39] Blanchard and Ripsman show how the threat of Arab sanctions against Canada was reinforced by a diplomatic threat to meddle in Canadian internal affairs by supporting the Quebecois independence movement.[40] The Nixon administration adjusted economic sanctions against the Soviet Union but simultaneously initiated a diplomatic opening to China to signal the Soviet leadership that it favored détente, but only conditionally. Along similar lines, a U.S. administration hoping to mitigate the humanitarian effects of sanctions while still holding Iraq's feet to the fire might consider lifting sanctions selectively while thawing relations with Iraq's enemy, Iran.

DEVELOPING THE DATA BASE

Any effective effort to generalize about the utility of economic sanctions requires some agreement on the universe of relevant cases. Hufbauer, Schott, and Elliott provided a useful first cut at establishing a large-N data base. As more attention is devoted to their data in particular and the study of sanctions more generally, however, it has become apparent that scholars are far from agreement on what constitutes the boundaries of the subject matter.

Kirshner complains that existing data sets generally ignore monetary sanctions; his own work analyzes dozens of cases.[41] Drezner contends that existing data sets focus mostly on cases involving adversaries and tend to downplay

39. Stephen John Stedman, "The Former Yugoslavia," in Haass, *Economic Sanctions and American Diplomacy*, 177–96, at 187.

40. Blanchard and Ripsman, "Asking the Right Question: *When* Do Economic Sanctions Work Best?" *Security Studies* 9, nos. 1/2 (autumn 1999–winter 2000): 219–53.

41. Kirshner, *Currency and Coercion*, 7.

cases involving allies.[42] Rowe, in reexamining the Rhodesia case, uncovers a "new" case: South Africa's use of economic coercion against Britain. Rawi Abdelal and Kirshner similarly bring "new" cases to light in their study of positive sanctions.[43] Some scholars believe cases of trade disputes and economic warfare should not count as economic sanctions; others point out that trade disputes typically involve efforts by one state to change the political behavior of other states.[44] Compelling a government to let more goods in is arguably as much a political act as compelling a government to let more people out.

Disagreements over what constitutes a relevant case reinforce the point that any definitive assessment of the utility of sanctions remains premature. That is less a failure of scholarship than a reflection of the fact that economic sanctions are complex and multifaceted instruments of statecraft, and that we are still relatively in the early stages of comprehending their workings. The discussion above suggests there are not one but many right questions and answers to be had in studying the causes and consequences of negative sanctions.

THE REDISCOVERY OF POSITIVE ECONOMIC SANCTIONS

"IT IS NOT that political scientists have said wrong things about the role of positive sanctions in power relations; it is just that they have said little." David Baldwin made that observation in 1971 and it remained accurate for roughly the next twenty years.[45] In the decade since the end of the cold war, however, positive economic sanctions have been rediscovered. Empirical research, particularly by younger political scientists, has accumulated. It is striking that half of the contributions to this special issue focus their central arguments on the use by states of economic incentives or rewards to achieve political objectives.[46]

---

42. Drezner, "Allies, Adversaries, and Economic Coercion," 110–11.

43. Rawi Abdelal and Jonathan Kirshner, "Strategy, Economic Relations, and the Definition of National Interests," *Security Studies* 9, nos. 1/2 (autumn 1999–winter 2000): 119–56.

44. Baldwin, "Evaluating Economic Sanctions," 190–91.

45. David A. Baldwin, "The Power of Positive Sanctions," *World Politics* 24, no. 1 (October 1971): 19–38, cite at 19.

46. See the following articles in *Security Studies* 9, nos. 1/2 (autumn 1999–winter 2000); Drezner, "The Trouble with Carrots: Transactions Costs, Conflict Expectations, and Economic Inducements" (188–218); Dale C. Copeland, "Trade Expectations and the Outbreak of Peace: Détente 1970–74 and the End of the Cold War 1985–91" (15–58); Abdelal and Kirshner, "Strategy, Economic Relations, and the Definition of National Interests" (119–56); and Paul A. Papayoanou and Scott L. Kastner, "Sleeping with the (Potential) Enemy: Assessing the U.S. Policy of Engagement with China" (157–87).

This renewed interest in positive sanctions is in large part a reaction to developments in international politics. Recent studies highlight the key role economic inducements played in the cold war settlement, and in particular in the reunification of Germany. Patricia Davis shows how Germany, beginning in 1969, used economic statecraft to build the political foundation for a rapprochment with one of its most distrustful neighbors, Poland.[47] When Germany finally seized the opportunity to reunify in 1989, a reassured Poland did not stand in the way. Randall Newnham makes a complementary argument in his recent study of German-Russian relations.[48] The Federal Republic of Germany used a steady stream of economic inducements over two decades to inculcate Soviet dependence on German commerce and credits and to signal Germany's benign foreign policy intentions. In the crucial endgame of the cold war, Gorbachev counted on Germany, more so than any other Western state, to provide much-needed economic support. The German government responded at critical moments with food aid and sizable economic credits. The clinchers, which paved the way for Russian acquiescence to unification on Germany's terms, included a five billion deutsche mark credit, a willingness to allow Russia to buy goods from the eastern zone of Germany with rubles rather than hard currency, and a commitment to provide financial support for the Red army in the German Democratic Republic and for its postunification resettlement in Russia.[49]

Each of these books argues that positive sanctions were effective, and on matters of "high politics." Reunification was arguably postwar Germany's most important national security achievement. Other, recent studies that make similar claims about the pivotal role of positive economic statecraft in the pursuit of core national security objectives by great powers include Lars Skalnes' examination of economic discrimination in nineteenth century French, interwar British, and postwar American grand strategy; William Long's analysis of positive economic incentives in U.S.-Chinese relations; Paul Papayounou's work on the use of economic ties to establish the credibility of balancing strategies in relations among the major powers during the nineteenth and twentieth

47. Patricia A. Davis, *The Art of Economic Persuasion: German Economic Diplomacy* (Ann Arbor: University of Michigan, forthcoming).

48. Randall E. Newnham, *Deutsche Mark Diplomacy: Economic Linkage in German-Russian Relations* (Penn State University Press, forthcoming).

49. Ibid., chap. 3. The credit was the largest offered to the Soviet Union in its seventy-year history. Newnham traces the development of the reunification for economic benefits deal and describes its culmination in the Gorbachev-Kohl "walk by the Rhine" at the Bonn Summit in June 1989.

centuries; and Dale Copeland's account of the role of trade expectations in Gorbachev's strategy for peace and the end of the cold war.[50]

It is not surprising that this wave of literature has peaked during the post–cold war era. During the cold war, the two dominant powers were largely self-sufficient and economically independent of each other. The study of super-power (and inter-bloc) economic interaction emphasized negative sanctions. After the cold war, the major powers once again are economically interdependent. Economic relations are matters of high politics, and any effective understanding of great power politics requires an understanding of positive economic statecraft and the links between economics and security. U.S.-Soviet summits used to focus on arms control and the management of political competition; U.S.-Russian summits now focus more on economic reform, currency crises, and the management of IMF conditionality. America's relations with China, Japan, and the European Union similarly reserve an important place for economic inducements.[51] As the articles in this special issue attest, international relations specialists are responding to the new international setting by resurrecting classic writings (for example, the work of Albert Hirschman) and reexamining historical eras (for example, the interwar period, the late nineteenth century, and the 1970s) in which economic inducement strategies figured prominently in the great power game. The research agenda is taking shape as follows.

STRATEGIES AND CASES

Positive economic sanctions can be defined as the provision or promise of economic benefits to induce changes in the behavior of a target state. It is important to distinguish two types of positive statecraft. The first involves the promise of a well-specified economic concession in an effort to alter specific foreign or domestic policies of the target government. I call this version tactical linkage; others refer to "carrots," or "specific positive linkage."[52] A second version, which I term structural linkage and which others refer to as "general positive linkage" or "long-term engagement," involves an effort to use a steady

50. Lars S. Skalnes, *When International Politics Matters: Grand Strategy and Economic Discrimination* (Ann Arbor: University of Michigan Press, forthcoming); William J. Long, "Trade and Technology Incentives and Bilateral Cooperation," *International Studies Quarterly* 40, no. 1 (March 1996): 77–106; Paul A. Papayounou, *Power Ties: Economic Interdependence, Balancing, and War* (Ann Arbor: University of Michigan Press, 1999); and Dale C. Copeland, "Trade Expectations and the Outbreak of Peace."

51. Mastanduno, "Economics and Security in Statecraft and Scholarship."

52. Mastanduno, *Economic Containment*, 52–57; Drezner, "The Trouble with Carrots: Transaction Costs, Conflict Expectations, and Economic Inducements"; and Newnham, *Deutsche Mark Diplomacy*, chap. 1.

stream of economic benefits to reconfigure the balance of political interests within a target country. Structural linkage tends to be unconditional; the benefits are not turned on and off according to changes in target behavior. The sanctioning state expects instead that sustained economic engagement will eventually produce a political transformation and desirable changes in target behavior.

What can be said about the frequency of these two versions of positive statecraft? Drezner observes that carrots are "not a ubiquitous feature of the international system." He argues that specific positive linkage is uncommon in international politics because of the high transactions costs associated with exchanging economic benefits for political concessions. Sticks tend to be more cost effective, and policy makers prove more willing to resort to them even though they do not always yield significant concessions.[53]

The previous discussion of negative sanctions suggests that we should be cautious in concluding that specific positive linkage is uncommon. In the case of negative sanctions, the harder analysts looked, the more cases they "discovered." The same is likely to be true for specific positive linkage, and here political scientists have only begun to investigate. A cursory examination of the empirical literature on postwar U.S. foreign policy points to the basis of what could become a substantial data base. Cases might include the U.S. offer of sizable postwar reconstruction loans to Great Britain, France, and the Soviet Union (accepted in two cases in exchange for political concessions, rejected in the third); the Marshall Plan, which might count as one or multiple cases; the offer of economic aid to Egypt and Israel to facilitate the Camp David Accords; the easing of export controls to induce the Soviet Union to press North Vietnam to accept the Paris Peace Accords; numerous attempts to use trade and financial incentives to discourage nuclear proliferation; the offer of increased U.S. coal exports in 1982 to tempt West European states away from the Soviet gas pipeline deal; the liberalization of high technology exports to strengthen Iraq's position in the Iran-Iraq war; and the purchase of MIGs from Moldova in 1997 to assure that Iran would not gain access to them.[54] The economically powerful United States might resort to tactical linkage most

---

53. Drezner, "The Trouble with Carrots: Transactions Costs, Conflict Expectations, and Economic Inducements," 190. Baldwin intuits the opposite: positive sanctions are more costly than negative when they succeed, while negative are more costly when they fail. Since the probability of success of influence attempts in international politics is relatively low, we should expect to states to use carrots more than sticks. Baldwin, "The Power of Positive Sanctions," 28–29.

54. Some of these influence attempts succeeded while others failed. All but the last case are relatively familiar. On the last, see Steven Lee Myers, "U.S. Is Buying MIGs so Rogue Nations Will Not Get Them," *New York Times*, 5 November 1997, A1.

frequently, but other states employ this instrument as well. Examples include Japan's use of economic inducements to Arab states during the 1973 oil crisis; Japan's offer of economic incentives to bring territorial concessions from Russia; Germany's use of credits and trade expansion to influence Poland's treatment of ethnic Germans; and Germany's use of food aid during 1989–90 to keep reunification talks with Russia on track. The latter two examples suggest that specific positive linkage attempts can be embedded in long-term engagement strategies. The more carefully we examine the historical record, the more cases—successes and failures—we are likely to find.[55]

The same point holds for structural linkage, or long-term engagement. The universe of relevant cases is still largely unexplored, perhaps, as Abdelal and Kirshner point out, because the focus in the literature on coercion "has given the illusion that few states have employed Hirschmanesque [positive engagement] strategies."[56] Their contribution to this special issue explores three "new" cases of general positive linkage. There are numerous others across time and space including Germany's interwar relationships with central European countries; Germany's cold war relationships with Poland and the Soviet Union; U.S. cold war strategy toward Western Europe and Japan; the Nixon-Kissinger détente strategy; Great Britain's interwar relationship with the Commonwealth; France's late nineteenth century relationship with Russia; and America's post–cold war approach to Russia and China.[57]

It may be, as Baldwin has pointed out, that researchers typically have tended to overestimate threats (negative sanctions) relative to promises (positive sanctions) in the study of international politics.[58] Now that political scientists are trying to overcome this bias and focus attention on the positive side, the building of a data base for specific and general positive sanctions, in the spirit of that created by Hufbauer, Schott, and Elliott for negative sanctions, would be an important next step.

55. IMF demands that debtors make well-specified political and economic changes in order to receive "conditional" financial rewards constitute multiple examples of specific positive linkage.

56. Abdelal and Kirshner, "Strategy, Economic Relations, and the Definition of National Interests," 121.

57. In addition to sources previously cited, see Robert G. Gilpin, *U.S. Power and the Multinational Corporation* (New York: Basic Books, 1975); and Lars S. Skalnes, "Grand Strategy and Foreign Economic Policy: British Grand Strategy in the 1930s," *World Politics* 50, no. 4 (July 1998): 582–616.

58. His reasoning is that the failed influence attempts are more common than successful ones in international relations. The failure of negative attempts leads us to "see" the imposition of sanctions; the failure of positive attempts leads us to "see" nothing, that is, no economic benefits are forthcoming. See Baldwin, "The Power of Positive Sanctions," 30–31.

DOMESTIC POLITICS AND LONG-TERM ENGAGEMENT

Specific positive sanctions and long-term engagement are each informed by a different logic. Specific sanctions operate at a more immediate level: The sanctioning state calculates that the provision of a particular type of economic reward will be sufficient to convince policymakers in the target state to reconsider their existing foreign or domestic policies. Long-term engagement works at a deeper level. The sanctioner provides a stream of economic benefits over time, and those benefits gradually transform domestic political interests in the target state. Those domestic political changes lead to a redefinition of the target's national interest and corresponding changes in target policies.

Analyses of long-term engagement converge on this crucial insight. The genesis of the idea can be traced to Albert Hirschman. As Abdelal and Kirshner point out, *National Power and the Structure of Foreign Trade* is best remembered for its arguments about economic coercion between stronger and weaker states.[59] The important part of Hirshman's argument, however, is found at the domestic level. Asymmetrical interdependence leads to changes in domestic interests in the weaker state. Over time, domestic coalitions that favor interdependence with the stronger state will form and strengthen, and will exert influence over the policy of the weaker state in a direction preferred by the sanctioning state.[60]

Hirschman's insight has been picked up and developed in the new literature on economic engagement. Skalnes offers the hypothesis, supported in his cases, that states will use economic discrimination (that is, provide economic rewards) to shore up domestic support in an ally for an alliance.[61] Newnham argues that general positive linkage is most effective when it leads to a redefinition of a target state's self interest, and claims this transformation took place in Russia as a result of interdependence with Germany.[62] Abdelal and Kirshner are explicit in applying Hirschman's insight directly in very different political and historical contexts. They show that domestic political interests in nineteenth century Hawaii, interwar Austria, and postwar Ukraine were each transformed by economic interaction with more powerful states.[63] Papayounou and

---

59. Abdelal and Kirshner, "Strategy, Economic Relations, and the Definition of National Interests," 119.
60. Hirschman, *National Power and the Structure of Foreign Trade,* 28–29.
61. Skalnes, *When International Politics Matters,* chaps. 2 and 7.
62. Newnham, *Deutsche Mark Diplomacy,* chap. 1.
63. Abdelal and Kirshner, "Strategy, Economic Relations, and the Definition of National Interests." Scott James and David Lake, without the emphasis on Hirschman, make a similar argument about the reconfiguration of U.S. domestic political coalitions in the nineteenth century as a result of increased trade with Great Britain after the repeal of the Corn Laws.

Kastner propose an important modification to the Hirschman argument, that is, that long-term engagement will influence a nondemocracy to be more accommodating in its foreign policy only if internationalist economic interests have more domestic political clout than nationalists.[64]

Arguments linking economic engagement to target domestic politics raise both analytical and policy challenges. The analytic is to assess accurately the balance of domestic forces and the impact of interdependence on their political fortunes. This is generally difficult, though easier to do retrospectively than prospectively. Both the Abdelal-Kirshner and Papayounou-Kastner contributions proceed with some degree of confidence in their assessments of how interdependence affected domestic politics in historical cases. In their analysis of contemporary China, however, the latter authors become more circumspect, claiming only that internationalist interests "probably" outweigh nationalist ones.[65] They are somewhat uncertain in identifying the preferences of the major domestic players, the impact of interdependence on them, and the resulting balance of domestic forces. They conclude that engagement is the desirable strategy for the United States but that it must be reassessed if the domestic balance in China shifts in favor of nationalist interests.

The implications of their analysis for foreign policy making is profound. Increased interdependence is likely to lead to foreign policy benefits only if internationalist forces are in control. If nationalist forces prevail, however, then interdependence produces a counterproductive effect: the dominant nationalists perceive it as threatening and prompt the target state to respond with a confrontational rather than cooperative foreign policy. The problem for policymakers in the sanctioning state, of course, is that they must decide whether to employ the engagement strategy without full knowledge of which set of domestic interests is in control, and likely to remain in control, of target politics.

International relations theorists might recognize this problem as an economic statecraft version of the security dilemma. Building one's arms to increase security might provoke an otherwise peaceful, status quo-oriented state; not arming might give the initiative to a seemingly peaceful state masking revi-

See James and Lake, "The Second Face of Hegemony: Britain's Repeal of the Corn Laws and the American Walker Tariff of 1846," *International Organization* 43, no. 1 (winter 1989): 1–29.

64. Papayounou and Kastner, "Sleeping with the (Potential) Enemy: Assessing the U.S. Policy of Engagement with China." They also argue that interdependent democracies will be more consistent in pursuing accommodating foreign policies. It is worth noting that democracies similarly can be divided into economic nationalist and internationalist camps, and the latter do not always win. For an illustration, see Jeff Frieden, "Sectoral Conflict and Foreign Economic Policy, 1914–1940," *International Organization* 42, no. 1 (winter 1988): 59–90.

65. Papayounou and Kastner, "Sleeping with the Potential Enemy."

sionist intentions. Similarly, economic engagement might strengthen a potential adversary and provoke it to behave confrontationally, while the failure to
engage might condemn an internationalist or reform-minded coalition to domestic defeat. The consequences of miscalculation in the context of Hirschman's argument are less severe, because he focused on economic interdependence between powerful and weak states. In the contemporary international
system, the stakes are higher. Economic engagement is the preferred strategy
of the United States in relations with two large, potential challengers, Russia
and China. It has, in effect, replaced arms control as the principal means to
improve relations among competitive major powers.

Two additional problems at the domestic level further complicate the strategy of long-term engagement. First, even if policymakers correctly assess the
balance of domestic forces in the target, they may not be able to control the
effects of interdependence on target politics. As the Asian financial crisis of
1997–98 demonstrated, interdependence can be painful and disruptive, particularly in countries where domestic institutions are not fully prepared to
manage its consequences. Even when internationalists seem to be in control,
economic crises triggered by a too rapid increase in interdependence could
lead to a conservative backlash, nationalist resentment, and a more aggressive
foreign policy to deflect attention from domestic economic austerity. This is
clearly a concern in Western relations with Russia at the end of the 1990s, and
it has the potential to be a problem in future relations with China.

A second set of problems relates to domestic politics within the sanctioning
state. An effective strategy of economic engagement requires a patient, sustained commitment on the part of the sanctioning state. As Copeland demonstrates, this is not always easy to attain, particularly in relations with a potential
or actual adversary.[66] During the early 1970s, the Nixon-Kissinger engagement
strategy was supported by U.S. business but ultimately frustrated by domestic
interest groups who distrusted Soviet foreign policy and objected to Soviet
domestic (human rights) policy. Efforts by the United States to engage China
during the 1990s have similarly been complicated by the political initiatives of
the human rights lobby, the Taiwan lobby, advocates of religious freedom and
opponents of child labor and other forms of political and economic repression. Long-term engagement may prove difficult to carry out, especially for a
democracy.

If a state manages to pursue the strategy effectively, domestic politics could
create an alternative dilemma, that of "self-containment." Papayounou and
Kastner point out that economic engagement creates vested interests in the

---

66. Copeland, "Trade Expectations and the Outbreak of Peace."

sanctioner as well as in the target. The deepening of interdependence has the potential to tie the hands of sanctioning state policy officials, should they decide in the future that they need to abandon engagement and adopt a more confrontational foreign policy strategy.

POSITIVE AND NEGATIVE ECONOMIC STATECRAFT

The revival of interest in positive sanctions naturally raises the issue of the relationship between positive and negative means of economic statecraft. We can conceive of positive and negative measures as substitutes or complements. As substitutes, a key concern is whether there are circumstances under which positive economic sanctions are likely to perform more effectively than negative ones.

Drezner's article takes up this question, and, drawing on his transaction costs argument, suggests that positive sanctions are most likely to be effective among democracies and in the context of international regimes.[67] In overall terms, however, he is skeptical of the prospects for positive sanctions, arguing that policymakers will resort more regularly to negative sanctions because they are more cost effective. Carrots also subject the sanctioning state to potential blackmail, since the state that hands out bribes in one context is likely to be pressured to do the same in others.

Although these arguments are plausible, it is possible to build an alternative, intuitive case for the expected utility of positive sanctions. Threats tend to inspire resistance and resentment in the target government; a typical response to the promise of rewards is hope and expectation.[68] Negative sanctions often produce the "rally around the flag effect." Positive sanctions do not, and have the potential to undermine the target government by creating transnational coalitions between the sanctioner and target at the societal level. Positive sanctions encourage the target government to cooperate with the sanctioner on other issues; negative sanctions create a reluctance to cooperate. With negative sanctions, multilateral cooperation is a necessity and there are strong incentives for third parties to break the embargo in order to gain above normal profits. Positive sanctions do not require multilateral support, and alternative economic partners typically cannot gain by undercutting the sanctions. Business interests in the sanctioning state tend to mobilize against negative sanctions. They are likely, however, to support positive ones that coincide with their natural interest in expanding economic interaction.

67. Drezner, "The Trouble with Carrots: Transaction Costs, Conflict Expectations, and Economic Inducements."
68. See Baldwin, "The Power of Positive Sanctions," 27–36.

This "debate" over the relative utility of positive sanctions ultimately must be resolved empirically. Studies of economic statecraft, however, to this point have not focused their research to provide a systematic answer. Empirical studies of negative sanctions, if they compare alternatives, tend to focus on economic vs. military coercion. The new literature on positive statecraft, in part reacting to the preponderance of attention to negative sanctions, has tended to focus research on "showcasing" the effectiveness of economic inducements in carefully selected case studies. With positive statecraft now sharing the central stage, the time is right for more systematic comparisons of positive and negative means of influence.

Positive and negative sanctions can also usefully be considered as complementary instruments of statecraft. Positive economic sanctions can set up the threat or use of negative ones by developing the economic dependence of the target on the sanctioner. Similarly, negative sanctions can structure opportunities for the use of positive ones. Once negative sanctions have been in place, lifting them is a change from the status quo for which sanctioning states can derive some concession in return. The United States used this tactic in 1980 to facilitate the return of hostages from Iran, and Western states employed it against Milosoviec in the context of the Dayton Accords of 1995.[69] The long-standing U.S. embargo of Cuba holds open this possibility as well.

It is attractive in principle, but difficult in practice, to move frequently between positive and negative sanctions in relations with the same target over time. Kissinger recognized the attraction during the early 1970s, and hoped the United States could constrain Soviet foreign policy through the conditional application of carrots and sticks. To pull off such a strategy requires both effective control of policy-making machinery and the support of the sanctioning state's business sector. By the latter part of the 1970s, it was clear that the U.S. executive had neither. As Copeland notes, Congress used the Jackson-Vanik Amendment to impose its own negative sanctions agenda on the Soviets in defiance of the executive. For its part, the U.S. business community refused to support what it termed derisively "lightswitch diplomacy." U.S. firms resented a political strategy that left their business prospects hostage to the short-term vagaries of U.S. and Soviet foreign policy, and that earned them reputations as unreliable suppliers. The clear lesson from this case is that over the long term it is easier to implement a strategy of either positive or negative sanctions than a complicated mixture of the two.

69. On the Iran case, see Robert Carswell, "Economic Sanctions and the Iranian Experience," *Foreign Affairs* 61, no. 1 (winter 1981–82): 247–65.

INTERDEPENDENCE, WAR, AND PEACE: WHICH INTERVENING VARIABLES?

THE PREVIOUS section discussed the renewal of positive economic sanctions at the level of state strategy or foreign policy analysis. It is important to consider the systemic implications as well. If economic interdependence can be used to strengthen alliances and improve relations with adversaries, does its presence lead more generally to peaceful relations among major powers?

There are paradigmatic answers to this long-standing question.[70] Liberals argue that economic interdependence decreases incentives for conflict and war by tying peoples more closely together and increasing the costs of economic disruption to high or prohibitive levels. States eventually come to recognize that they can no longer afford war because it jeopardizes the economic benefits of interdependence. Realists, in contrast, generally argue that economic interdependence is more likely to lead to state conflict. It heightens the potential for political friction and exposes the vulnerabilities of insecure states in an anarchic setting. A second line of realist argument suggests that liberals are overly optimistic because economic interdependence has no systematic effect on the occurrence of war and peace.[71]

International relations scholarship paid scant attention to this question during the cold war. Students of international political economy generally focused on economic interdependence without reference to interstate conflict, while students of national security focused on conflict without much concern for the consequences of economic interdependence. With the revival of interest in the intersection of economics and security, the causal relationship between interdependence and conflict is once again a central concern. An examination of the emerging literature suggests two points.

First, and not surprisingly, we can find empirical support for either liberalism or realism. Edward Mansfield reinforces the liberal view with his finding that since 1850 the level of international trade has been inversely related to the occurrence of major power wars.[72] Support is also offered by John Oneal and Bruce Russett's study of the 1950–86 period, which found a significant correlation between increased interdependence and democracy, on the one hand, and a reduction in the likelihood of military conflict, on the other.[73] On the

---

70. See Michael W. Doyle, *Ways of War and Peace* (New York: Norton, 1997).

71. See Barry Buzan, "Economic Structure and International Security: The Limits of the Liberal Case," *International Organization* 38, no. 4 (autumn 1984): 597–624.

72. Edward D. Mansfield, *Power, Trade and War* (Princeton: Princeton University Press, 1994).

73. John R. Oneal and Bruce Russett, "The Classic Liberals Were Right: Democracy, Interdependence, and Conflict, 1950–1985," *International Studies Quarterly* 41, no. 2 (June 1997): 267–94.

realist side of the ledger, Ann Uchitel concluded from her study of the inter-war period that dependence on strategic mineral imports did create incentives for offensive strategies and expansionary foreign policies.[74] Blanchard and Ripman's 1995 study found in a similar vein that the costs of disrupting inter-dependence (that is, perceived strategic vulnerabilities) did not restrain coun-tries from going to war.[75] Peter Liberman confounds liberal expectations by finding that wars do pay economically: "ruthless invaders can successfully ex-ploit industrial societies, at least for short periods of time."[76] In her survey of twenty recent studies of interdependence and conflict, Susan McMillan reports that ten studies support the liberal position, four support the realist, and six come up with mixed results. She concludes that it would be premature to de-clare liberalism the theoretical winner because too many major questions re-main unanswered.[77]

Second, and more importantly, the recent literature has begun to move us beyond the liberal-realist debate in a search for the intervening variables that help to explain the circumstances under which economic interdependence leads to war or peace. The contributors to this special issue take up that chal-lenge, with a recognition that the causal links between interdependence and security are neither simple nor self-evident. Although different authors place their bets on different intervening variables, their most powerful common finding is that an understanding of economic interaction is crucial to the analy-sis of great power security relationships.

Papayounou emphasizes both domestic interests and foreign policy strate-gies.[78] He argues that extensive economic ties between status quo powers will lend credibility to balancing strategies and thus to the maintenance of peace. Extensive ties between status quo and revisionist powers will undercut the credibility of balancing and increase the chances of conflict. The mechanism driving this process is found at the domestic level. Domestic interests favoring economic interdependence will push the state toward firmer balancing com-

74. Ann Uchitel, "Interdependence and Instability," in *Coping With Complexity in the Inter-national System,* ed. Jack Snyder and Robert Jervis (Boulder: Westview, 1993).

75. Jean Marc F. Blanchard and Norrin M. Ripsman, "Commercial Liberalism Under Fire: Evidence from 1914 and 1936," *Security Studies* 6, no. 2 (winter 1996/97): 4-50.

76. Peter Liberman, *Does Conquest Pay? The Exploitation of Occupied Industrial Societies* (Princeton: Princeton University Press, 1996).

77. Susan M. McMillan, "Interdependence and Conflict," *Mershon International Studies Re-view* 41, Supplement 1 (May 1997): 33-58, cite at 43. Perhaps more revealing is her observa-tion that "analysis undertaken in the liberal tradition seems to support liberalism's hypothe-. ses," while "studies taking a more realist perspective indicate no systematic relationship" between interdependence and peace (p. 52).

78. Papayounou, *Power Ties,* and "Interdependence, Institutions, and the Balance of Power," *International Security* 20, no. 4 (spring 1996): 42-76.

mitments in relations with status quo allies and toward self-containment in relations with revisionist challengers.

Copeland's search for intervening variables leads not to the level or extent of interdependence, but to the expectations policymakers have about their future trade prospects.[79] High levels of interdependence can lead to either peace or war, depending on whether future expectations are optimistic or pessimistic. Copeland's insight contributes to an understanding of how economic and security factors interacted to produce the First World War, and suggests that economic factors were crucial to the resolution of the U.S.-Soviet conflict, despite low levels of interdependence. Papayounou and Copeland are each self-conscious in straddling the liberal-realist divide, and each seeks to establish the primacy of economic relations in great power politics.

Edward Mansfield, John Pevehouse, and David Bearce address the interdependence-security link by directing attention to yet another variable, the form of commercial interdependence. They find that trade institutions, in particular preferential trade arrangements (PTAs), decrease the likelihood of security conflict among sovereign states.[80] Their argument builds on that of Copeland in that they stress the expectation of a stream of future benefits as a key reason why members of PTAs are likely to maintain cooperative security relations. The extensive literature on PTAs during the 1990s has focused mostly on the economic and sometimes political consequences of economic integration; Mansfield, Pevehouse, and Bearce place this prominent feature of the contemporary world economy squarely at the intersection of economics and security.

Peter Liberman's contribution challenges Copeland's findings and provides yet another cut at the central question. Whether or not interdependence leads to peace for Liberman depends not on trade expectations but on the perception of the offense-defense balance.[81] Interdependence leads to conflict when major powers are both trade dependent and facing a security situation of defense dominance. The need to prepare for the possibility of a protracted conventional war raises the stakes and exposes the vulnerabilities of trade dependent states. Liberman's argument is doubly significant: by emphasizing the interplay of economic and security factors, he forces us to rethink key findings in both the offense-defense literature and the interdependence-conflict literature.

79. Dale C. Copeland, "Economic Interdependence and War: A Theory of Trade Expectations," *International Security* 20, no. 4 (spring 1996): 5–41.

80. Edward D. Mansfield, Jon C. Pevehouse, and David H. Bearce, "Preferential Trade Agreements and Military Disputes," *Security Studies* 9, nos. 1/2 (autumn 1999–winter 2000): 92–118.

81. Peter Liberman, "The Offense-Defense Balance, Interdependence, and War," *Security Studies* 9, nos. 1/2 (autumn 1999–winter 2000): 59–91.

These four studies help to raise the debate over interdependence and war to a more sophisticated level. They demonstrate that the set piece battles between the liberal and realist positions are no longer productive, and they open new questions to help establish the research agenda for the next phase of scholarship. Papayounou's argument, for example, reminds us of the need, and the difficulty, of distinguishing status quo and revisionist states. Hans Morgenthau observed some fifty years ago that the "fate of nations" hinged on the ability to make that distinction.[82] We can all agree that interwar Germany was a revisionist state, but what about contemporary Russia or China? Copeland's model prompts the question of how trade expectations operate in a multilateral as opposed to bilateral setting. In the early 1970s, why were the Soviets willing to make political concessions for U.S. trade, when Western Europe and Japan were willing and eager to step in as substitute partners? The same question is relevant to Copeland's more provocative argument that Gorbachev abandoned the Soviet empire and ended the cold war essentially on the expectation of future trade with the United States. The preliminary findings of Mansfield, Pevehouse, and Bearce suggest that states *within* a PTA will be less war-prone toward each other; an equally pressing question, given developments in the contemporary world economy, is whether and under what conditions the co-existence of multiple PTAs increases the incentives for peace or war.

Economic interdependence is typically operationalized in terms of the level of trade. The focus on trade expectations and PTAs yields new insights, and also raises the question of whether different types or forms of economic interdependence will have different effects on the prospects for war and peace. Lenin, after all, built his theory of imperialism and intercapitalist war more on the investment imperatives of capitalist states than on their levels of trade. In the current world economy, international finance may have eclipsed international trade as the principal source of political tensions among sovereign states. Classic liberal thinkers believed that capital mobility led to peace, by making it more difficult for rulers to seize wealth by capturing territory.[83] The recent Asian crisis and Russian default suggest the potential for a different logic and outcome—capital mobility creates economic crisis and domestic disruption, leading to more nationalistic foreign policies. Liberman notes that peacetime trade barriers are unlikely to weigh heavily on security calculations because their impact on wealth is gradual.[84] The impact of financial crises tends to be

82. Hans J. Morgenthau, *Politics Among Nations: The Struggle for Power and Peace*, fifth ed (New York: Knopf, 1978), 67–68.

83. Albert O. Hirschman, *The Passions and the Interests* (Princeton: Princeton University Press, 1977).

84. Liberman, "The Offense-Defense Balance, Interdependence, and War," 68.

more immediate, and, depending on how the initial shocks are handled and whether and how they spread, are potentially more profound politically.

THE ENDURING SIGNIFICANCE OF ECONOMICS AND SECURITY

THE ARTICLES in this special issue contribute significantly to the revival of work at the intersection of economics and security. They enhance our understanding of the effectiveness of negative economic sanctions, the role and potential of positive sanctions, and the relationship between economic interdependence and military competition. In conclusion I offer several brief observations inspired by the collection as a whole that are relevant to the future study of economics and security.

The first concerns the manner in which research problems are framed. It is often tempting to strive for definitive "yes or no" answers or to declare paradigmatic winners and losers. The authors in this volume show alternatively that scholarly progress can be made effectively, if less dramatically, by asking and answering conditional questions. The payoff from framing research questions at a more intermediate level is especially evident in the work linking interdependence to war and peace. It also comes across in the efforts to assess the utility of positive and negative economic sanctions.

A second observation concerns the role of domestic politics. It is perfunctory at this point to claim that the study of any aspect of international relations *should* be integrated with that of domestic politics. The articles above demonstrate that the study of economic statecraft *must* proceed not only with an appreciation of the domestic level of analysis but with a sophisticated understanding of it. Economic sanctions involve the exploitation of power asymmetries, but the effectiveness of sanctions, that is, whether those asymmetries can be exploited, depends vitally on how their effects are transmitted domestically. This is true of both positive and negative sanctions, although the mechanics of transmission are somewhat different. The study of economic statecraft has now progressed to the point at which effective research requires the skills of the comparativist are as much as those of the international relations specialist.

Third, the articles in this issue highlight that the practice of economic statecraft has always been and remains a matter of high politics. The cold war international system was more an aberration than the norm. The particular features of that system—two, economically independent superpowers locked in ideological rivalry and nuclear competition—prompted scholars to underplay economic statecraft and the links between economics and security. In the more "normal" international environment after the cold war, the integral role of economics in great power politics is more readily apparent. Economic instruments and relations are at the forefront of post–cold war U.S. relations with status quo powers such as Japan and Germany, potentially revisionist challengers such as China and Russia, and regional revisionists such as Iraq and Serbia.

Finally, this special issue offers a refreshing reminder that international relations did not begin in 1945. The revival of interest in economics and security has prompted these scholars to rediscover the experience of the interwar era, the late nineteenth century, and other periods in the search for relevant patterns and insights. The results contained herein indicate that the effort will remain a fruitful one.

BIBLIOGRAPHY

Allison, Graham T. *Essence of Decision: Explaining the Cuban Missile Crisis.* Boston: Little and Brown, 1971.

Anderson, Kym, and Richard Blackhurst. "Introduction and Summary." In *Regional Integration and the Global Trading System*, edited by Kym Anderson and Richard Blackhurst. New York: Harvester Wheatsheaf, 1993.

Angell, Norman. *The Great Illusion.* 2nd. ed. New York: Putnam's Sons, 1933.

Arad, Ruth, Seev Hirsch, and Alfred Tovias. *The Economics of Peacemaking.* New York: St. Martin's, 1983.

Art, Robert J. "Bureaucratic Politics and American Foreign Policy: A Critique." *Policy Sciences* 4, no. 4 (December 1973): 467-90.

Axelrod, Robert, and Robert Keohane. "Achieving Cooperation under Anarchy: Strategies and Institutions." In *Cooperation Under Anarchy*, edited by Kenneth Oye. Princeton: Princeton University Press, 1986.

Baldwin, David A. *Economic Statecraft.* Princeton: Princeton University Press, 1985.

———. "Interdependence and Power: A Conceptual Analysis." *International Organization* 34, no. 4 (Autumn 1980): 471-506.

———. "The Power of Positive Sanctions." *World Politics* 24, no. 1 (October 1971): 19-38.

———. "Security Studies and the End of the Cold War." *World Politics* 48, no. 1 (October 1995): 117-41.

———., ed. *Neorealism and Neoliberalism: the Contemporary Debate.* New York: Columbia University Press, 1993.

Barber, William J. "British and American Economists and Attempts to Comprehend the Nature of War, 1910-1920." In *Economics and National Security: A History of their Interaction*, edited by Craufurd Goodwin, 61-86. Durham, NC: Duke University Press.

Barbieri, Katherine. "Economic Interdependence: Path to Peace or Source of Interstate Conflict." *Journal of Peace Research* 33 (1996): 29-49.

———. "Explaining Discrepant Findings in the Trade-Conflict Literature." Paper presented at the 1996 annual meeting of the International Studies Association, San Diego, CA.

———. "International Trade and Conflict: The Debatable Relationship." Paper presented at the annual meeting of the International Studies Association, Minneapolis, March 1998.

Beck, Nathaniel, and Richard Tucker. "Conflict in Space and Time: Time-Series-Cross-Section Analysis with Binary Dependent Variable." Paper presented at the 1996 annual meeting of the American Political Science Association, San Francisco, CA.

Beck, Nathaniel, and Jonathan N. Katz. "The Analysis of Binary Time-Series-Cross-Sectional Data and/or the Democratic Peace." Paper presented at the 1997 annual meeting of the Political Methodology Group, Columbus, OH.

Beck, Nathaniel, Jonathan N. Katz, and Richard Tucker. "Beyond Ordinary Logit: Taking Time Seriously in Binary Time-Series Cross-Section Models." *American Journal of Political Science*, 42, no. 4 (October 1998): 1260-88.

Becker, Gary S. "A Theory of Competition Among Pressure Groups for Political Influence." *Quarterly Journal of Economics* 98, no. 3 (August 1983): 371-400.

Betts, Richard K. "Should Strategic Studies Survive?" *World Politics* 50, no. 1 (1997): 7-33.

Bhagwati, Jagdish. "Regionalism and Multilateralism: An Overview." In *New Dimensions in Regional Integration*, edited by Jaime de Melo and Arvind Panagariya, 22-51. New York: Cambridge University Press, 1993.

Bhagwati, Jagdish, and Arvind Panagariya. "Preferential Trading Areas and Multilateralism — Strangers, Friends, or Foes?" In *The Economics of Preferential Trade Agreements*, edited by Jagdish Bhagwati and Arvind Panagariya, 1-78. Washington, D.C.: AEI Press, 1996.

Bhagwati, Jagdish, and Hugh Patrick, eds. *Aggressive Unilateralism: America's 301 Trade Policy and the Politics of International Trade*. Ann Arbor: University of Michigan Press, 1990.

Bienen, Henry, and Robert Gilpin. "Economic Sanctions as a Response to Terrorism." *Journal of Strategic Studies* 3, no. 2 (May 1980): 89-98.

Blainey, Geoffrey. *The Causes of War*. 3rd ed. New York: Free Press, 1988.

Blanchard, Jean-Marc F. "Borders and Borderlands: An Institutional Approach to Territorial Disputes in the Asia Pacific." Ph.D. diss., University of Pennsylvania, 1998.

Blanchard, Jean-Marc F., and Norrin M. Ripsman. "Measuring Economic Interdependence: A Geopolitical Perspective." *Geopolitics and International Boundaries* 1, no. 3 (Winter 1996): 231-241.

————. "Rethinking Sensitivity Interdependence: Assessing Trade, Investment, and Monetary Links between States." Paper presented at the 38th Annual Meeting of the International Studies Association, Minneapolis, Minnesota, 17-21 March 1998.

Brawley, Mark. *Liberal Leadership: Great Powers and Their Challengers in Peace and War*. Ithaca: Cornell University Press, 1993.

Bremer, Stuart A. "Dangerous Dyads: Conditions Affecting the Likelihood of Interstate War." *Journal of Conflict Resolution* 36, no. 2 (June 1992): 309-41.

Brodie, Bernard. "Strategy as a Science." *World Politics* 1, no. 4 (July 1949): 467-88.

————. *Strategy in the Missile Age*. Princeton: Princeton University Press, 1959.

Brooks, Stephen, and William Wohlforth, "Why Identities Change: Material Forces, Identity Transformation, and the End of the Cold War." Paper delivered at the annual convention of the American Political Science Association, Boston, September 1998.

Brown, M. Leann. *Developing Countries and Regional Economic Cooperation*. Westport, CT: Praeger, 1994.

Buck, Philip W. *The Politics of Mercantilism*. New York: Henry Holt, 1942.

Bueno de Mesquita, Bruce, and David Lalman. *War and Reason: Domestic and International Imperatives*. New Haven: Yale University Press, 1992.

Bull, Hedley. "Strategic Studies and Its Critics." *World Politics* 20, no. 4 (1968): 593-605.

Buzan, Barry. "Economic Structure and International Security: The Limits of the Liberal Case." *International Organization* 38, no. 4 (Autumn 1984): 597-624.

————. *People, States, and Fear: An Agenda for International Security Studies in the post-Cold War Era*. Boulder, Co.: Lynne Reinner, 1991.

Caporaso, James A. "False Divisions: Security Studies and Global Political Economy." *Mershon International Studies Review* 39, no. 1 (April 1995): 117-22.

Carr, E.H. *The Twenty Years' Crisis: 1919-1939*, 2nd ed. New York: Harper and Row, [1939] 1946.

Caves, Richard E., and Ronald W. Jones. *World Trade and Payments*, 4th ed. Boston: Little-Brown, 1985.

Christensen, Thomas J. "System Stability and the Security of the Most Vulnerable Significant Actor." in *Coping with Complexity in the International System*, edited by Robert Jervis and Jack Snyder. Boulder, Co.: Westview, 1993.

Coase, Ronald. *The Firm, the Market, and the Law*. Chicago: University of Chicago Press, 1988.

————. "The Problem of Social Cost." *Journal of Law and Economics* 3, no. 1 (October 1960): 1-44.

Condliffe, J.B. "Economic Power as an Instrument of National Policy." *American Economic Review* 34, no. 1 (May 1944): 305-14.

————. *Markets and the Problem of Peaceful Change*. Paris: League of Nations, 1938.

Cooper, Richard N. *The Economics of Interdependence*. New York: McGraw-Hill, 1968.

Copeland, Dale C. "Economic Interdependence and War: A Theory of Trade Expectations." *International Security* 20, no. 4 (spring 1996): 5-41.

————. "Economic Interdependence and the Future of U.S.-Chinese Relations." Paper presented to the conference on "The Emerging International Relations of the Asia-Pacific Region," Dartmouth College, October 1998, organized by John Ikenberry and Michael Mastanduno.

————. "Modeling Economic Interdependence and War." Paper delivered at the annual meeting of the American Political Science Association, Chicago, August 1995.

Cortright, David, ed. *The Price of Peace: Incentives and International Conflict Prevention*. New York: Rowman and Littlefield, 1997.

Cowhey, Peter. "Domestic Institutions and the Credibility of International Commitments: Japan and the United States." *International Organization* 47, no. 2 (Spring 1993): 299-326.

Crumm, Eileen. "The Value of Economic Incentives in International Relations," *Journal of Peace Research* 32, no. 3 (1995): 313-30.

Daoudi, M.S., and M.S. Dajani, eds. *Economic Sanctions: Ideals and Experience*. London: Routledge & Kegan Paul, 1983.

de Marchi, Neil. "League of Nations Economists and the Idea of Peaceful Change in the Decade of the 1930s." In *Economics and National Security: A History of their Interaction*, edited by Craufurd Goodwin, 143-78. Durham, NC: Duke University Press, 1991.

de Melo, Jaime, and Arvind Panagariya. "Introduction." In *New Dimensions in Regional Integration*, edited by Jaime de Melo and Arvind Panagariya, 3-21. New York: Cambridge University Press.

de Melo, Jaime, and Arvind Panagariya, eds. *New Dimensions in Regional Integration*. New York: Cambridge University Press, 1993.

Destler, I.M. *American Trade Politics: System Under Stress*. Washington, D.C.: Institute for International Economics, 1992.

——. "Foreign Policy Making with the Economy at Center Stage." In *Beyond the Beltway*, edited by Daniel Yankelovich and I.M. Destler, 26-42. New York: Norton, 1994.

Diebold, William, Jr. "The Changed Economic Position of Western Europe: Some Implications for United States Policy and International Organization." *International Organization* 14, no. 1 (winter 1960): 1-19.

Diehl, Paul F. *The Dynamics of Enduring Rivalries*. Urbana: University of Illinois Press, 1998.

——. ed. *International Peacekeeping*. Baltimore: Johns Hopkins University Press, 1993.

Dixon, William. "Democracy and the Peaceful Settlement of International Conflict." *American Political Science Review* 88, no. 1 (March 1994): 14-32.

Dominquez, Jorge I., ed. *International Security and Democracy*. Pittsburgh: University of Pittsburgh Press, 1998.

Domke, William J. *War and the Changing Global System*. New Haven: Yale University Press, 1988.

Doxey, Margaret P. *International Sanctions in Contemporary Perspective*. New York: St. Martin's Press, 1987.

Doyle, Michael. "Liberalism and World Politics." *American Political Science Review* 80 (December 1986): 1151-69.

——. *Ways of War and Peace: Realism, Liberalism, and Socialism*. New York: Norton, 1997.

Drezner, Daniel W. "Allies, Adversaries, and Economic Coercion: Russian Foreign Economic Policy Since 1991." *Security Studies* 6, no. 3 (spring 1997): 65-111.

——. *The Sanctions Paradox: Economic Statecraft and International Relations*. Cambridge: Cambridge University Press, 1999.

Dunn, Frederick S. "The Scope of International Relations." *World Politics* 1, no. 1 (October 1948): 142-46.

Duvall, Raymond, P. Terrence Hopmann, Brian Job and Robert Kudrle. "The Economic Foundations of War: Editor's Introduction." *International Studies Quarterly* 27 (1983).

Earle, Edward Mead. "Adam Smith, Alexander Hamilton, Friedrich List: The Economic Foundations of Military Power." In *Makers of Modern Strategy from Machiavelli to the Nuclear Age*, edited by Peter Paret, 217-61. Princeton: Princeton University Press, 1986.

Eichengreen, Barry, and Jeffrey A. Frankel. "Economic Regionalism: Evidence from Two 20th Century Episodes." *North American Journal of Economics and Finance* 6, no. 2 (1995): 89-106.

Eichengreen, Barry, and Douglas A. Irwin. "The Role of History in Bilateral Trade Flows." In *The Regionalization of the World Economy*, edited by Jeffrey Frankel, 33-57. Chicago: University of Chicago Press, 1998

Eland, Ivan. "Economic Sanctions as Tools of Foreign Policy." In *Economic Sanctions: Panacea or Peacebuilding in a Post-Cold War World?*, edited by David Cortright and George A. Lopez, 29-42. Boulder: Westview, 1995.

Elliott, Kimberly Ann. "Factors Affecting the Success of Sanctions." In *Economic Sanctions: Panacea or Peacebuilding in a Post-Cold War World?*, edited by David Cortright and George A. Lopez, 51-59. Boulder: Westview, 1995.

Encarnation, Dennis. *Rivals Beyond Trade: America Versus Japan in Global Competition.* Ithaca: Cornell University Press, 1992.

Evangelista, Matthew. "The Paradox of State Strength: Transnational Relations, Domestic Structures, and Security Policy in Russia and The Soviet Union." *International Organization* 49, no. 1 (winter 1995): 1-38.

Evans, Peter. *Dependent Development: The Alliance of Multinational, State and Local Capital in Brazil.* Princeton: Princeton University Press, 1979.

Fearon, James. "Domestic Political Audiences and the Escalation of International Disputes." *American Political Science Review* 88, no. 3 (September 1994): 577-92.

———. "The Offense-Defense Balance and War Since 1648." Unpublished manuscript, University of Chicago, April 1997.

———. "Rationalist Explanations for War." *International Organization* 49, no. 3 (Summer 1995): 379-414.

———. "Threats to Use Force." Ph.D. diss., University of California Berkeley, 1992.

Feis, Herbert. *Europe, the World's Banker, 1870-1914.* New Haven: Yale University Press, 1930.

———. *The Road to Pearl Harbor.* Princeton: Princeton University Press, 1950.

Fernández, Raquel. "Returns to Regionalism: An Evaluation of Nontraditional Gains from Regional Trade Agreements." Typescript, World Bank, 1998.

Frankel, Jeffrey. "Is Japan Creating a Yen Bloc in East Asia and the Pacific?" In *Regionalism and Rivalry: Japan and the United States in Pacific Asia*, edited by Jeffrey A. Frankel and Miles Kahler, 53-85. Chicago: University of Chicago Press, 1993.

————. ed. *The Regionalization of the World Economy*. Chicago: University of Chicago Press, 1998.

Frankel, Jeffrey, Ernesto Stein, and Shang-jin Wei. "Trading Blocs and the Americas: The Natural, the Unnatural, and the Super-natural." *Journal of Development Economics* 47, no. 1 (June 1995): 61-95.

Friedberg, Aaron. "The Strategic Implications of Relative Economic Decline." *Political Science Quarterly* 104, no. 3 (autumn 1989): 401-32.

————. *The Weary Titan: Britain and the Experience of Relative Decline, 1895-1905*. Princeton: Princeton University Press, 1988.

Frieden, Jeffry A., and Ronald Rogowski, "The Impact of the International Economy on National Policies." In *Internationalization and Domestic Politics*, edited by Robert O. Keohane and Helen V. Milner, 25-49. Cambridge: Cambridge University Press, 1996.

Fukuyama, Francis. *The End of History and the Last Man*. New York: Free Press, 1992.

Galtung, Johan. "On the Effects of International Economic Sanctions: With Examples From the Case of Rhodesia." *World Politics* 19, no. 3 (April 1967): 378-416.

Gardner, Richard M. *Sterling-Dollar Diplomacy: Anglo-American Collaboration in the Reconstruction of Multilateral Trade*. Oxford: Clarendon Press, 1956.

Garrett, Jeffrey, and Barry Weingast. "Ideas, Interests, and Institutions: Constructing the European Community's Internal Market." In *Ideas and Foreign Policy: Beliefs, Institutions, and Political Change*, edited by Judith Goldstein and Robert O. Keohane, 173-206. Ithaca: Cornell University Press, 1993.

Gartzke, Erik. "Kant We All Just Get Along? Opportunity, Willingness, and the Origins of the Democratic Peace." *American Journal of Political Science* 42, no. 1 (January 1998): 1-27.

Gasiorowski, Mark. "Economic Interdependence and International Conflict: Some Cross-national Evidence." *International Studies Quarterly* 30, no. 1 (March 1986): 22-38.

Gasiorowski, Mark, and Soloman W. Polochek, "Conflict and Interdependence: East-West Trade and Linkages In the Era of Détente." *Journal of Conflict Resolution* 26, no. 4 (December 1982): 709-29.

Gaubatz, Kurt Taylor. "Democratic States and Commitment in International Relations." *International Organization* 50, no. 1 (Winter 1996): 109-39.

Gilpin, Robert. "Economic Interdependence and National Security in Historical Perspective." In *Economic Issues and National Security*, edited by Klaus Knorr and Frank N. Trager, 19-66. Lawrence, Kan.: University of Kansas Press, 1977.

————. *The Political Economy of International Relations*. Princeton: Princeton University Press, 1987.

————. *U.S. Power and the Multinational Corporation*. New York: Basic Books, 1975.

————. *War and Change in World Politics*. Cambridge: Cambridge University Press, 1981.

Glaser, Charles. "Realists as Optimists: Cooperation as Self-Help." *International Security* 19, no. 3 (Winter 1994/95): 50-90.

———. "The Security Dilemma Revisited." *World Politics* 50, no. 1 (October 1997): 171-201.

Glaser, Charles, and Chaim Kaufmann. "What is the Offense-Defense Balance and How Can We Measure It?" *International Security* 22, no. 4 (spring 1998): 44-82.

Gochman, Charles S., and Zeev Maoz. "Militarized Interstate Disputes, 1816-1976." *Journal of Conflict Resolution* 28, no. 4 (December 1984): 585-615.

Goertz, Gary, and Paul F. Diehl. "The Empirical Importance of Enduring Rivalries." *International Interactions* 18, no. 2 (1992): 151-63.

———. "Enduring Rivalries: Theoretical Constructs and Empirical Patterns." *International Studies Quarterly* 37, no. 2 (June 1993): 147-72.

———. "The Initiation and Termination of Enduring Rivalries." *American Journal of Political Science* 39, no. 1 (February 1995): 30-52.

Goldstein, Avery. "Great Expectations: Interpreting China's Arrival." *International Security* 22, no. 3 (winter 1997/98): 36–73.

Gordon, Lincoln. "Economic Aspects of Coalition Diplomacy—The NATO Experience." *International Organization* 10, no. 4 (November 1956): 529-43.

Gordon, Michael. "American Economic Power and Future Great Power Rivals." In progress.

———. "Domestic Conflict and the Origins of the First World War." *Journal of Modern History* 46, no. 2 (June 1974): 191–226.

Gourevitch, Peter. *Politics in Hard Times*. Ithaca: Cornell University Press, 1986.

Gowa, Joanne. *Allies, Adversaries, and International Trade*. Princeton: Princeton University Press, 1994.

Grieco, Joseph M. "Anarchy and the Limits of Cooperation: A Realist Critique of the Newest Liberal Institutionalism." *International Organization* 42, no. 3 (summer 1990): 485-507.

Gurr, Ted Robert, Keith Jaggers and Will H. Moore. "Polity II: Political Structures and Regime Change." Inter-University Consortium for Political and Social Research no. 9263, Ann Arbor, MI, 1989.

Haas, Ernst. *The Uniting of Europe: Political, Social, and Economic Forces, 1950-1957*. Stanford: Stanford University Press, 1958.

Haass, Richard. "Sanctioning Madness." *Foreign Affairs* 76, no. 6 (November/December 1997): 74-85.

Halliday, Fred. *The Making of the Second Cold War*. London: Verso, 1983.

Hanlon, Joseph. *Beggar Your Neighbor*. London: Villiers Publications, 1986.

Hawtrey, Ralph. *Economic Aspects of Sovereignty*. London: Longman, Greens and Company, 1930.

Heckscher, Eli F. *Mercantilism*, 2 vols. London: George Allen, 1931.

Hirschman, Albert O. *National Power and the Structure of Foreign Trade*, Berkeley: University of California Press, [1945] 1980.

———. *The Passions and the Interests*. Princeton: Princeton University Press, 1977.

Hoffman, Stanley. *Primacy or World Order–American Foreign Policy since the Cold War.* New York: McGraw Hill, 1978.

Hopf, Ted. "Polarity, the Offense-Defense Balance, and War." *American Political Science Review* 85, no. 2 (June 1991): 475-93.

Hufbauer, Gary Clyde, Jeffrey J. Schott, and Kimberly Ann Elliott, *Economic Sanctions Reconsidered*, 2nd ed., 2 vols. Washington, D.C.: Institute for International Economics, 1990.

Huntington, Samuel P. *Political Order in Changing Societies.* New Haven: Yale University Press, 1968.

————. *The Soldier and the State: The Theory and Politics of Civil-Military Relations.* Cambridge: Harvard University Press, 1957.

Huth, Paul, and Bruce Russett. "General Deterrence between Enduring Rivalries." *American Political Science Review* 87, no. 1 (March 1993): 61-73.

Ikenberry, G. John, David Lake, and Michael Mastanduno, eds. *The State and American Foreign Economic Policy.* Ithaca, NY: Cornell University Press, 1988.

Iklé, Fred. *Every War Must End*, rev. ed. New York: Columbia University Press, 1991.

Irwin, Douglas A. "Multilateral and Bilateral Trade Policies in the World Trading System: An Historical Perspective." In *New Dimensions in Regional Integration*, edited by Jaime de Melo and Arvind Panagariya, 90-119. New York: Cambridge University Press.

Jaggers, Keith, and Ted Robert Gurr. "Tracking Democracy's Third Wave with the Polity III Data." *Journal of Peace Research* 32, no. 4 (1995): 469-82.

James, Patrick, and Glenn E. Mitchell. "Targets of Covert Pressure: The Hidden Victims of the Democratic Peace." *International Interactions* 21 (March 1995): 85-107.

Janis, Irving L. *Groupthink: Psychological Studies of Policy Decisions and Fiascoes*, 2nd ed. Boston: Houghton Mifflin, 1982.

Jervis, Robert. "Cooperation under the Security Dilemma." *World Politics* 30, no. 2 (January 1978): 167-214.

————. "International Primacy: Is the Game Worth the Candle?" *International Security* 17 (1993):52-67.

————. *The Meaning of the Nuclear Revolution: Statecraft and the Prospect of Armageddon.* Ithaca, N.Y.: Cornell University Press, 1989.

————. *Perception and Misperception in International Politics.* Princeton: Princeton University Press, 1976.

————. "Perception, Misperception, and the End of the Cold War." In *Witnesses to the End of the Cold War*, edited by William C. Wohlforth. Baltimore: Johns Hopkins University Press, 1996.

Johnson, Chalmers, and E.B. Keehn. "The Pentagon's Ossified Strategy." *Foreign Affairs* 74 (1995): 103-14.

Johnson, Robert H. *Improbable Dangers: U.S. Conceptions of Threat in the Cold War and After.* New York: St. Martin's Press, 1994.

Jones, Daniel M., Stuart A. Bremer, and J. David Singer. "Militarized Interstate Disputes, 1816-1992: Rationale, Coding Rules, and Empirical Patterns." *Conflict Management and Peace Science* 15, no. 2 (fall 1996): 163-213.

Kaiser, David E. *Economic Diplomacy and the Origins of the Second World War.* Princeton: Princeton University Press, 1980.

Kaldor, Mary. *The Disintegrating West.* New York: Hill and Wang, 1978.

Kapstein, Ethan. *The Political Economy of National Security.* New York: McGraw-Hill, 1992.

Kapstein, Ethan, and Michael Mastanduno, eds. *Unipolar Politics: Realism and State Strategies After the Cold War.* New York: Columbia University Press, forthcoming.

Katzenstein, Peter J. *Disjoined Partners: Austria and Germany Since 1815.* Berkeley: University of California Press, 1976.

————. "International Interdependence: Some Long-term Trends and Recent Changes." *International Organization* 29, no. 4 (autumn 1975): 1021-34.

————. ed. *Between Power and Plenty: Foreign Economic Policies of Advanced Industrial States.* Madison: University of Wisconsin Press, 1978.

Kennedy, Paul. *The Rise and Fall of the Great Powers: Economic Challenge and Military Conflict from 1500 to 2000.* New York: Random House, 1987.

Keohane, Robert. *After Hegemony.* Princeton: Princeton University Press, 1984.

————. "Economic Liberalism Reconsidered." In *The Economic Limits to Modern Politics,* edited by John Dunn, 165-94. Cambridge: Cambridge University Press, 1990.

————. "Reciprocity in International Relations." *International Organization* 40, no. 1 (winter 1986): 1-27.

————. "The Theory of Hegemonic Stability and Changes in International Economic Regimes, 1967-1977." In *Change in the International System,* edited by Ole Holsti, Randolph Siverson, and Alexander George, 131-62. Boulder, Colo.: Westview Press, 1980.

Keohane, Robert O., and Helen V. Milner, eds. *Internationalization and Domestic Politics.* Cambridge: Cambridge University Press, 1996.

Keohane, Robert O., and Joseph Nye. *Power and Interdependence.* Boston: Little Brown, 1977.

————. eds. *Transnational Relations and World Politics.* Cambridge, Mass: Harvard University Press, 1972.

Keynes, John Maynard. *The Economic Consequences of the Peace.* New York: Harcourt, Brace, Howe, 1920.

Kindleberger, Charles P. "Group Behavior and International Trade." *Journal of Political Economy* 59, no. 1 (February 1959): 30-47.

————. *The World in Depression, 1929-1939.* Berkeley: University of California Press, 1973.

Kirshner, Jonathan. *Currency and Coercion: The Political Economy of International Monetary Power.* Princeton: Princeton University Press, 1995.

———. "The Microfoundations of Economic Sanctions." *Security Studies* 6, no. 3 (spring 1997): 32-64.

———. "Political Economy in Security Studies After the Cold War." *Review of International Political Economy* 5, no. 1 (spring 1998): 64-91.

Kissinger, Henry. *Nuclear Weapons and Foreign Policy.* New York: Harper and Row, 1957.

Koslowski, Rey, and Friedrich V. Kratochwil. "Understanding Change in International Politics: The Soviet Empire's Demise and the International System." *International Organization* 48, no. 2 (spring 1994): 215-247.

Knorr, Klaus. "The Bretton Woods Institutions in Transition." International Organization 2, no. 1 (1948): 19-38.

———. "International Economic Leverage and Its Uses." In *Economic Issues and National Security*, edited by Klaus Knorr and Frank N. Trager. Lawrence: The Regents Press of Kansas, 1977.

———. *The Power of Nations: The Political Economy of International Relations.* New York: Basic Books, 1975.

———. *The War Potential of Nations.* Princeton: Princeton University Press, 1956.

Knorr, Klaus, and Frank N. Trager. *Economic Issues and National Security.* Lawrence: University Press of Kansas, 1977.

Krasner, Stephen. "American Policy and Global Economic Stability." In *America in a Changing World Political Economy*, edited by William Avery and David Rapkin, 29-48. New York: Longman, 1982.

———. *Defending the National Interest: Raw Materials Investments and U.S. Foreign Policy.* Princeton: Princeton University Press, 1978.

———. "State Power and the Structure of International Trade." *World Politics* 28, no. 3 (April 1976): 317-47.

———. ed. *International Regimes.* Ithaca: Cornell University Press, 1983.

Krause, Keith, and Michael Williams. "Broadening the Agenda of Security Studies: Politics and Methods." *Mershon International Studies Review* 40, no. 2 (October 1996): 229-54.

Kreps, David. "Corporate Culture and Economic Theory." In *Perspectives on Positive Political Economy*, edited by James Alt and Kenneth Shepsle, 90-143. New York: Cambridge University Press, 1990.

Krugman, Paul. "The Move to Free Trade Zones." In *Policy Implications of Trade and Currency Zones*, edited by Federal Reserve Bank of Kansas City, 7-41. Kansas City, MO: Federal Reserve Bank, 1991.

———. "Regionalism versus Multilateralism: Analytical Notes." In *New Dimensions in Regional Integration*, edited by Jaime de Melo and Arvind Panagariya, 58-79. New York: Cambridge University Press, 1993.

Kupchan, Charles A. *The Vulnerability of Empire.* Ithaca: Cornell University Press, 1994.

Kydd, Andrew. "Game Theory and the Spiral Model." *World Politics* 49, no. 3 (April 1997): 371-400.

Labs, Eric J. "Beyond Victory: Offensive Realism and the Expansion of War Aims." *Security Studies* 6, no. 4 (summer 1997): 1-49.

Lake, David A. "Anarchy, Hierarchy, and the Variety of International Relations." *International Organization* 50, no. 1 (Winter 1996): 1-33.

————. *Entangling Relations: American Foreign Policy in Its Century.* Princeton: Princeton University Press, 1990.

————. *Power, Protection, and Free Trade: International Sources of U.S. Commercial Policy, 1887-1939.* Ithaca, NY: Cornell University Press, 1988.

Lawrence, Robert Z. *Regionalism, Multilateralism, and Deeper Integration.* Washington, D.C.: Brookings, 1996.

Layne, Christopher. "From Preponderance to Offshore Balancing: America's Future Grand Strategy." *International Security* 22, no. 1 (Summer 1997): 86-124.

————. "The Unipolar Illusion: Why New Great Powers Will Rise." *International Security* 17, no. 4 (Spring 1993): 5-51.

Lebow, Richard Ned, and Janice Gross Stein. *We All Lost the Cold War.* Princeton: Princeton University Press, 1994.

Leffler, Melvyn. *A Preponderance of Power.* Stanford: Stanford University Press, 1992.

Lenin, V.I. *Imperialism: the Highest Stage of Capitalism.* New York: International Publishers, 1916.

Leonard, Robert J. "War as a 'Simple Economic Problem': The Rise of an Economics of Defense." In *Economics and National Security: A History of their Interaction,* edited by Craufurd Goodwin, 261-83. Durham, NC: Duke University Press, 1991.

Levy, Jack S. "The Causes of War: A Review of Theories and Evidence." In *Behavior, Society, and Nuclear War,* edited by Philip E. Tetlock et al., 209-313. New York: Oxford University Press, 1989.

————. "Historical Perspectives on Interdependence and Conflict." Paper presented at the Annual Meeting of the International Studies Association, Minneapolis, Minnesota, March 1998.

————. "The Offensive/Defensive Balance of Military Technology: A Theoretical and Historical Analysis." *International Studies Quarterly* 28, no. 2 (June 1984): 219-238.

————. "Preferences, Constraints, and Choices in July 1914." *International Security* 15, no. 3 (Winter 1990/91): 151–86.

Levy, Jack S., and Lily Vakili. "Diversionary Action by Authoritarian Regimes." In *The Internationalization of Communal Strife,* edited by Manus Midlarsky. London: Routledge, 1992.

Levy, Philip I., and T. N. Srinivasan. "Regionalism and the (dis)advantage of Dispute-Settlement Access." *American Economic Review (Papers and Proceedings)* 86, no. 2 (May 1996): 93-98.

Liberman, Peter. *Does Conquest Pay? The Exploitation of Occupied Industrial Societies.* Princeton: Princeton University Press, 1996.

————. "Trading with the Enemy: Security and Relative Economic Gains." *International Security* 21, no. 1 (summer 1996): 147-75.

Lieberman, Eli. "What Makes Deterrence Work? Lessons from the Egyptian-Israel Enduring Rivalry." *Security Studies* 4, no. 4 (summer 1995): 851-910.

Lipson, Charles. International Cooperation in Economic and Security Affairs. *World Politics* 37, no. 1 (October 1984): 1-23.

Liska, George. *The New Statecraft.* Chicago: University of Chicago Press, 1960.

Long, William J. "Trade and Technological Incentives and Bilateral Cooperation." *International Studies Quarterly* 40, no. 1 (March 1996): 77-106.

Lopez, George, and David Cortright. "Economic Sanctions in Contemporary Global Relations." In *Economic Sanctions: Panacea or Peacebuilding in a Post-Cold War World?*, edited by David Cortright and George A. Lopez. Boulder: Westview, 1995.

Lynn-Jones, Sean M. "Détente and Deterrence: Anglo-German Relations, 1911–1914." *International Security* 11, no. 2 (fall 1986): 121–50.

———. "Offense-Defense Theory and Its Critics." *Security Studies* 4, no. 4 (summer 1995): pp. 660-91.

———. "Rivalry and Rapprochement: Accommodation Between Adversaries in International Politics." Ph.D. diss., Harvard University, in progress.

Lynn-Jones, Sean, and Joseph Nye, Jr. "International Security Studies: A Report of a Conference on the State of the Field." *International Security* 12, no. 4 (Spring 1988): 5-27.

Machlup, Fritz. *A History of Thought on Economic Integration.* New York: Columbia University Press, 1977.

Mallery, Otto. *Economic Peace and Durable Union.* New York: Harper, 1943.

Mandelbaum, Michael. *The Nuclear Revolution.* Cambridge: Cambridge University Press, 1981.

Mansfield, Edward D. *Power, Trade, and War.* Princeton: Princeton University Press, 1994.

———. "The Proliferation of Preferential Trading Arrangements." *Journal of Conflict Resolution* 42, no. 5 (October 1998): 523-42.

Mansfield, Edward D., and Rachel Bronson. "Alliances, Preferential Trading Arrangements, and International Trade." *American Political Science Review* 91, no. 1 (March 1997): 94-107.

Mansfield, Edward D., and Helen V. Milner. "The New Wave of Regionalism." *International Organization* 53, no. 3 (summer 1999): 589-627.

———. eds. *The Political Economy of Regionalism.* New York: Columbia University Press, 1997.

Mansfield, Edward D., and Jon Pevehouse. "Trade Blocs, Trade Flows, and International Conflict." *International Organization* 54, no. 4 (Autumn 2000), forthcoming.

Mansfield, Edward D., and Jack Snyder. "Democratization and War." *Foreign Affairs* 74, no. 3 (May/June 1995): 79–97.

———. "Democratization and the Danger of War." *International Security* 20, no. 1 (summer 1995): 5–38.

Mansfield, Edward D., Helen V. Milner, and B. Peter Rosendorff. "Why Democracies Cooperate More: Electoral Control and International Trade Agreements." Paper presented at the 1998 annual meeting of the American Political Science Association, Boston, MA.

Martin, Lisa. *Coercive Cooperation*. Princeton: Princeton University Press, 1992.

Mason, Edward. 1949. "American Security and Access to Raw Materials." *World Politics* 1, no. 2 (January 1949): 147-60.

Mastanduno, Michael. "Do Relative Gains Matter? America's Response to Japanese Industrial Policy." *International Security* 16, no. 1 (summer 1991): 73-113.

————. *Economic Containment: CoCom and the Politics of East-West Trade*. Ithaca: Cornell University Press, 1992.

————. "Preserving the Unipolar Moment: Realist Theories and U.S. Grand Strategies After the Cold War." *International Security* 21, no. 4 (Spring 1997): 49-88.

Maull, Hanns. "Oil and Influence: The Oil Weapon Examined." In *Economic Issues and National Security*, edited by Klaus Knorr and Frank N. Trager, 259-88. Lawrence: The University Press of Kansas, 1977.

McClaren, John. "Size, Sunk Costs, and Judge Bowker's Objection to Free Trade." *American Economic Review* 87, no. 3 (June 1997): 400-20.

McFaul, Michael. "A Precarious Peace: Domestic Politics in the Making of Foreign Policy." *International Security* 22, no. 3 (winter 1997/98): 5–35.

McKenna, Joseph. *Diplomatic Protest in Foreign Policy*. Chicago: Loyola University Press, 1962.

McMillan, Susan M. "Interdependence and Conflict." *Mershon International Studies Review* 41, suppl. 1 (May 1997): 33-58.

Mearsheimer, John. "Back to the Future: Instability in Europe After the Cold War." *International Security* 15, no. 1 (summer 1990): 5-56.

————. *Conventional Deterrence*. Ithaca: Cornell University Press, 1983.

————. "Disorder Restored." In *Rethinking America's Security*, edited by Graham Allison and Gregory F. Treverton. New York: Norton, 1992.

————. "The False Promise of International Institutions." *International Security* 19, no. 3 (winter 1994/95): 5-49.

Medlicott, W.M. *The Economic Blockade*, 2 vols. London: HMSO, 1952-1959.

Milgrom, Paul, Douglass North, and Barry Weingast. "The Role of Institutions in the Revival of Trade: The Law Merchant, Private Judges, and the Champagne Fairs." *Economics and Politics* 2, no. 1 (March 1990): 1-23.

Milner, Helen V. "The Political Economy of U.S. Trade Policy: A Study of the Super 301 Provision." In *Aggressive Unilateralism: America's 301 Trade Policy and the Politics of International Trade*, edited by Jagdish Bhagwati and Hugh Patrick, 163-80. Ann Arbor: University of Michigan Press, 1990.

————. *Resisting Protectionism*. Princeton: Princeton University Press, 1988.

Milward, Alan. *War, Economy and Society, 1939-1945*. Berkeley: University of California Press, 1977.

Mirowski, Philip. "When Games Grow Deadly Serious: The Military Influence on the Evolution of Game Theory." In *Economics and National Security: A History of their Interaction*, edited by Craufurd Goodwin, 227-55. Durham, NC: Duke University Press, 1991.

Mitrany, David. *The Problem of International Sanctions.* London: Oxford University Press, 1925.

———. *A Working Peace System.* Chicago: Quadrangle, 1964.

Moran, Theodore. "Grand Strategy: The Pursuit of Power and the Pursuit of Plenty." *International Organization* 50, no. 1 (Winter 1996): 175-205.

Morgan, T. Clifton. "Issue Linkages in International Crisis Bargaining." *American Journal of Political Science* 34, no. 2 (May 1990): 311-333.

Morgan, T. Clifton, and Valerie Schwebach. "Fools Suffer Gladly: The Use of Economic Sanctions in International Crises." *International Studies Quarterly* 41 (March 1997): 27-50.

Morgenthau, Hans J., and Kenneth Thompson, *Politics Among Nations, 6th ed.* New York: Alfred Knopf, 1985.

Morrow, James. *Game Theory for Political Scientists.* Princeton: Princeton University Press, 1994.

———. "Signaling Difficulties with Linkage in Crisis Bargaining." *International Studies Quarterly* 36, no. 2 (June 1992): 153-172.

Morse, Edward. *Modernization and the Transformation of International Relations.* New York: Free Press, 1976.

———. "The Transformation of Foreign Policies: Modernization, Interdependence, and Externalization." *World Politics* 22, no. 3 (April 1970): 371-92.

Most, Benjamin, and Harvey Starr. "International Relations, Foreign Policy Substitutability, and 'Nice' Laws." *World Politics* 36, no. 3 (April 1984): 383-406.

Muir, Ramsay. *The Interdependence World and its Problems.* Boston: Houghton Mifflin, 1933.

Nathan, James A., and James K. Oliver. *Foreign Policy Making and the American Political System.* Boston: Little and Brown, 1987.

Nau, Henry. *Trade and Security: U.S. Policy at Cross-Purposes.* Washington, DC: AEI Press, 1995.

Newnham, Randall. "How to Win Friends and Influence People." Paper presented at the International Studies Association annual meeting, Toronto, Canada, March 1997.

Nincic, Miroslav, and Peter Wallensteen. "Economic Coercion and Foreign Policy." In *Dilemmas of Economic Coercion*, edited by Miroslav Nincic and Peter Wallensteen, 1-15. New York: Praeger, 1983.

Nordlinger, Eric. *Isolationism Reconfigured: American Foreign Policy for a New Century.* Princeton: Princeton University Press, 1995.

North, Douglass, and Barry Weingast. "Constitutions and Commitment: The Evolution of Institutions Governing Public Choice in Seventeenth-Century England." *Journal of Economic History* 49, no 4 (December 1989): 803-32.

Nye, Joseph S, Jr. *Bound to Lead: The Changing Nature of American Power* (New York: Basic Books, 1990.

————. "Neorealism and Neoliberalism." *World Politics* 40, no. 2 (January 1988): 235-51.

————. *Peace in Parts: Integration and Conflict in Regional Organization.* Boston: Little and Brown, 1971.

Odell, John S. "Military-Political Conditions and International Economic Negotiations." Unpublished manuscript, University of Southern California, Los Angeles.

Olson, Richard Stuart. "Economic Coercion in World Politics: With a Focus on North-South Relations." *World Politics* 31, no. 4 (July 1979): 471-94.

Oneal, John, Francis Oneal, Zeev Maoz, and Bruce Russett. "The Liberal Peace: Interdependence, Democracy, and International Conflict, 1950-1985." *Journal of Peace Research* 33, no. 1 (1996): 11-28.

Oneal, John, and Bruce Russett. "The Classical Liberals Were Right: Democracy, Interdependence, and Conflict, 1950-1985," *International Studies Quarterly* 41, no. 2 (June 1997): 267-94.

————. "Is the Liberal Peace Just an Artifact of the Cold War?" Paper presented at annual meeting of International Studies Association, Minneapolis, March 1998.

Osgood, Robert E. (eds), *NATO: The Entangling Alliance.* Chicago: University of Chicago Press, 1962.

Oye, Kenneth (ed.), *Cooperation Under Anarchy.* Princeton: Princeton University Press, 1986.

Paarlberg, Robert L. "Using Food Power: Opportunities, Appearances, and Damage Control." In *Dilemmas of Economic Coercion,* edited by Miroslav Nincic and Peter Wallensteen, 131-53. New York: Praeger, 1983.

Papayoanou, Paul A. "Economic Interdependence and the Balance of Power." *International Studies Quarterly* 41, no. 1 (March 1997): 113–40.

————. "Interdependence, Institutions, and the Balance of Power: Britain, Germany, and World War I" *International Security* 20, no. 4 (spring 1996): 42–76.

————. *Power Ties: Economic Interdependence, Balancing, and War.* Ann Arbor: University of Michigan Press, 1999.

Pape, Robert. "Coercion and Military Strategy." *Journal of Strategic Studies* 15 (December 1992): 423-475.

————."Why Economic Sanctions Do Not Work." *International Security* 22, no. 2 (fall 1997): 90-136.

Patterson, Gardner. *Discriminating in International Trade: The Policy Issues, 1945-65.* Princeton: Princeton University Press, 1966.

Peterson, Peter, and James Sebenius. The Primacy of the Domestic Agenda. *In Rethinking America's Security,* edited by Graham Allison and Gregory Treverton, 57-93. New York: Norton, 1992.

Peterson, Susan. "How Democracies Differ: Public Opinion, State Structure, and the Lessons of the Fashoda Crisis." *Security Studies* 5, no. 1 (autumn 1995): 3-37.

Pollard, Robert. *Economic Security and the Origins of the Cold War, 1945-1950*. New York: Columbia University Press, 1985.

Pollins, Brian. "Conflict, Cooperation, and Commerce." *American Journal of Political Science* 33, no. 3 (August 1989): 737-61.

Polochek, Soloman. "Conflict and Trade." *Journal of Conflict Resolution* 24, no. 1 (March 1980): 55-78.

————. "Conflict and Trade: An Economics Approach to Political International Interactions." In *Economics of Arms Reduction and the Peace Process*, edited by Walter Isard and Charles H. Anderton. Amsterdam: North Holland, 1992.

Polochek, Soloman, and Judith McDonald. "Strategic Trade and the Incentive for Cooperation." In *Disarmament, Economic Conversions, and Peace Management*, edited by Manas Chatterji and Linda Rennie Forcey. New York: Praeger, 1992.

Pomfret, Richard. *Unequal Trade: The Economics of Discriminatory International Trade Policies*. Oxford: Basil Blackwell, 1988.

————. *The Economics of Regional Trading Arrangements*. New York: Oxford University Press, 1997.

Posen, Barry. *The Sources of Military Doctrine: France, Britain, and Germany Between the World Wars*. Ithaca: Cornell University Press, 1984.

Posen, Barry, and Andrew Ross. "Competing U.S. Grand Strategies." In *Eagle Adrift: American Foreign Policy at the End of the Century*, edited by Robert J. Lieber, 100-34. New York: Longman, 1997.

Powell, Robert. "Nuclear Brinkmanship with Two-Sided Incomplete Information." *American Political Science Review* 82, no. 1 (March 1988): 155-78.

Prestowitz, Clyde, Jr. *Trading Places: How We Are Giving Our Future to Japan and How to Reclaim It*, 2nd ed. New York: Basic Books, 1990.

Quester, George. *Offense and Defense in the International System*. New York: Wiley, 1977.

Reed, William. "Alliance Duration and Democracy: An Extension and Cross-Validation of 'Democratic States and Commitment in International Relations.'" *American Journal of Political Science* 41, no. 3 (July 1997): 1072-78.

Renwick, Robin. *Economic Sanctions*. Cambridge: Center for International Affairs, Harvard University, 1981.

Reiss, Mitchell. *Without the Bomb: the Politics of Nuclear Proliferation*. New York: Columbia University Press, 1988.

————. *Bridled Ambition: Why Countries Constrain Their Nuclear Capabilities*. Washington: The Woodrow Wilson Center Press, 1995.

Ripsman, Norrin M. "Democratic Institutions and the Governance of Foreign Security Policy: Peacemaking after Two World Wars." Ph.D. diss., University of Pennsylvania, 1997.

————. "The Conduct of Foreign Policy by Democracies: A Critical Review." Paper presentedat the Annual Meeting of the American Political Science Association, September 1994.

Ripsman, Norrin M., and Jean-Marc F. Blanchard. "Commercial Liberalism under Fire: Evidence from 1914 and 1936." *Security Studies* 6, no. 2 (winter 1996-97): 4-50.

Risse-Kappen, Thomas. "Ideas Do not Float Freely; Transnational Coalitions, Domestic Structures, and the End of the Cold War." *International Organization* 48, no. 2 (spring 1994): 185-214.

Robbins, Lionel. *The Economic Causes of War.* London: Jonathan Cape, 1939.

Rock, Steven R. *Why Peace Breaks Out: Great Power Rapprochement in Historical Perspective.* Chapel Hill: University Of North Carolina Press, 1989.

Roeder, Philip. "The Ties that Bind: Aid, Trade, and Political Compliance in Soviet-Third World Relations." *International Studies Quarterly* 29, no. 2 (June 1985): 191-216.

Rogowski, Ronald. *Commerce and Coalitions: How Trade Affects Domestic Political Alignments.* Princeton: Princeton University Press, 1989.

———."Iron, Rye, and the Authoritarian Coalition in Germany After 1879." Paper prepared for delivery at the Annual Meeting of the American Political Science Association, Denver, Colorado, 1–5 September 1982.

Ropke, Wilhelm. *International Economic Disintegration.* London: William Hodge, 1942.

Rosecrance, Richard. "A New Concert of Powers." *Foreign Affairs* 71, no. 2 (Spring 1992): 64-82.

———. *The Rise of the Trading State.* New York: Basic Books, 1986.

———. "War, Trade, and Interdependence." In *Interdependence and Conflict in World Politics*, edited by James N. Rosenau and Hylke Tromp. Aldershot, Eng.: Averbury, 1989.

Rosecrance, Richard, and Arthur Stein, eds. *The Domestic Bases of Grand Strategy.* Ithaca: Cornell University Press, 1993.

Rosecrance, Richard, Alan Alexandroff, Wallace Koehler, John Kroll, Shlomit Lacqueur, and John Stocker. "Whither Interdependence?" *International Organization* 31, no. 3 (summer 1977): 425–71.

Ruggie, John G. "The Past as Prologue? Interests, Identity, and American Foreign Policy." *International Security* 21, no. 4 (Spring 1997): 89-125.

Rubinstein, Alvin. "Soviet and American Policies in International Economic Organizations." *International Organization* 18, no. 1 (Winter 1964): 29-52.

Rubinstein, Ariel. "Perfect Equilibrium in a Bargaining Model." *Econometrica* 50 (1982): 97-109.

Russett, Bruce. "The Mysterious Case of the Vanishing Hegemony; or, is Mark Twain Really Dead." *International Organization* 39, no. 1 (January 1985): 207-31.

Russett, Bruce, John Oneal, and David Davis. "The Third Leg of the Kantian Tripod for Peace: International Organizations and Militarized Disputes, 1950-1985." *International Organization* 52, no. 3 (summer 1998): 441-67.

Sagan, Scott D. *Moving Targets: Nuclear Strategy and National Security.* Princeton: Princeton University Press, 1989.

————."The Origins of the Pacific War." In *The Origin and Prevention of Major Wars*, edited by Robert Rotbert and Theodore Rabb, 323-52. Cambridge: Cambridge University Press, 1989.

Sagan, Scott D., and Kenneth N. Waltz. *The Spread of Nuclear Weapons: A Debate*. New York: W.W. Norton & Co., 1995.

Sayrs, Lois. "Reconsidering Trade and Conflict: A Qualitative Response Model with Censoring." *Conflict Management and Peace Science* 10 (1988): 1-19.

————. "Trade and Conflict Revisited: Do Politics Matter?" *International Interactions* 15 (1989): 155-75.

Schelling, Thomas C. *Arms and Influence*. New Haven, Conn.:Yale University Press, 1966.

————. *The Strategy of Conflict*. Cambridge: Harvard University Press, 1960.

Schmitter, Phillipe. "Three Neo-Functionalist Hypotheses about International Integration." *International Organization* 23, no. 2 (winter 1969): 327-60.

Schroeder, Gertrude. "On the Economic Viability of New Nation-States." *Journal of International Affairs* 45, no. 2 (winter 1992).

Schultz, Kenneth. "Domestic Opposition and Signaling in International Crises." *American Political Science Review* 92 (December 1998): 549-74.

Shambaugh, David. "Containment or Engagement of China? Calculating Beijing's Responses." *International Security* 21, no. 2 (fall 1996): 180–209.

Sebenius, James. "Negotiation Arithmetic: Adding and Subtracting Issues and Parties." *International Organization* 37, no. 2 (Spring 1983): 281-316.

Segal, Gerald. "East Asia and the 'Constrainment' of China." *International Security* 20, no. 4 (spring 1996): 107–35.

Serra, Jaime, Guillermo Aguilar, Jose Cordoba, Gene Grossman, Carla Hills, John Jackson, Julius Katz, Pedro Noyola, and Michael Wilson. *Reflections on Regionalism*. Washington, D.C.: Brookings, 1997.

Silberner, Edmund. *The Problem of War In Nineteenth Century Economic Thought*. Princeton: Princeton University Press, 1946.

Singer, J. David, and Melvin Small. "Correlates of War Project: International and Civil War Data, 1816-1992." Inter-University Consortium for Political and Social Research no. 9905, Ann Arbor, MI, 1994.

Singer, J. David, Stuart Bremer, and John Stuckey. "Capability Distribution, Uncertainty, and Major Power War, 1820-1965." In *Peace, War, and Numbers*, edited by Bruce Russett, 19-48. Beverly Hills: Sage, 1972.

Sislin, John. "Arms as Influence: The Determinants of Successful Influence." *Journal of Conflict Resolution* 38, no. 4 (December 1994): 665-89.

————. "Arms as Influence: The Elusive Link Between Military Assistance and Political Compliance." Ph.D. dissertation, Indiana University, September 1993.

Skalnes, Lars. *When International Politics Matters: Grand Strategy and Economic Discrimination*. Ann Arbor:University of Michigan Press, forthcoming.

Small, Melvin, and J. David Singer, "Formal Alliances, 1816-1965: An Extension of the Basic Data." *Journal of Peace Research* 6, no. 3 (1969): 257-82.

————. *Resort to Arms: International and Civil Wars, 1816-1980*. Beverly Hills: Sage, 1982.

Smith, Peter H., ed. *The Challenge of Integration: Europe and the Americas*. New Brunswick: Transaction Publishers, 1993.

————. "The Politics of Integration: Concepts and Themes." In *The Challenges of Integration*, edited by Peter H. Smith,1-14. New Brunswick: Transaction Publishers, 1993.

Snyder, Glenn H. *Deterrence or Defense*. Princeton: Princeton University Press, 1961.

Snyder, Glenn H. "The Security Dilemma in Alliance Politics." *World Politics* 36, no. 4 (July 1984): 461–95.

Snyder, Jack. "Averting Anarchy in the New Europe." *International Security* 14, no. 4 (spring 1990): 5–41.

————. *The Ideology of the Offensive: Military Decision Making and the Disasters of 1914*. Ithaca: Cornell University Press, 1984.

————. *Myths of Empire: Domestic Politics and International Ambition*. Ithaca: Cornell University Press, 1991.

Staley, Eugene. *War and the Private Investor*. Chicago: University of Chicago Press, 1935.

Stein, Arthur. 1984. "The Hegemon's Dilemma: Great Britain, the United States, and the International Economic Order." *International Organization* 38, no. 2 (Spring 1984): 355-86.

Stern, Paula. *Water's Edge: Domestic Politics and the Making of American Foreign Policy*. Westport: Greenwood, 1979.

Stevenson, David. *The First World War and International Politics*. New York: Oxford University Press, 1988.

Strange, Susan. "International Economics and International Relations: A Case of Mutual Neglect." *International Affairs* 46, no. 2 (April 1970): 304-15.

Thompson, William R. "Principal Rivalries." *Journal of Conflict Resolution* 39, no. 2 (June 1995): 195-223.

Tollison, Robert, and Thomas Willett. "An Economic Theory of Mutually Advantageous Issue Linkages in International Negotiations." *International Organization* 33, no. 4 (autumn 1979): 425-49.

Trachtenberg, Marc. "Strategic Thought in America, 1952-1966." *Political Science Quarterly* 104, no. 2 (Summer 1989): 301-44.

Tyson, Laura D'Andrea. *Who's Bashing Whom? Trade Conflict in High Technology Industries*. Washington, D.C.: Institute for International Economics, 1992.

Uchitel, Anne. "Interdependence and Instability." In *Coping with Complexity in the International System*, edited by Jack Snyder and Robert Jervis, 243-64. Boulder: Westview, 1993.

Ulam, Adam B. *Expansion and Coexistence*. New York: Praeger, 1968.

Ullman, Richard. "Redefining Security." *International Security* 8 (1983):129-53.

Van Evera, Stephen. "The Cult of the Offensive and the Origins of the First World War." In *Military Strategy and the Origins of the First World War*, edited by Steven E. Miller, 58-107. Princeton: Princeton University Press, 1985.

———. "Offense, Defense, and the Causes of War." *International Security* 22, no. 4 (spring 1998): 5-43.

———. "Primed for Peace: Europe after the Cold War." In *The Cold War and After*, edited by Sean Lynn-Jones and Steven E. Miller. Cambridge: MIT Press, 1993.

Viner, Jacob. *The Customs Union Issue*. New York: Carnegie Endowment for International Peace, 1950.

———. *International Economics*. Glencoe, Ill.: The Free Press, 1951.

———. "Power Versus Plenty as Objectives of Foreign Policy in the Seventeenth and Eighteenth Centuries." *World Politics* 1, no. 1 (October 1948): 1-29.

Wagner, R. Harrison. "Economic Interdependence, Bargaining Power, and Political Influence." *International Organization* 42, no. 3 (summer 1988): 461-83.

Wallander, Celeste. *Balancing Acts: Security, Institutions, and German-Russian Relations after the Cold War*. Ithaca: Cornell University Press, 1998.

Wallensteen, Peter. "Economic Sanctions: Ten Modern Cases and Three Important Lessons." In *Dilemmas of Economic Coercion*, edited by Miroslav Nincic and Peter Wallensteen, 87-129. New York: Praeger, 1983.

Wallerstein, Immanuel. *The Modern World System: Capitalist Agriculture and the Origins of the European World-Economy in the Sixteenth Century*. New York: Academic Press, 1974.

Walt, Stephen M. *The Origins of Alliances*. Ithaca: Cornell University Press, 1987.

———. "The Renaissance of Security Studies." International Studies Quarterly 35 (June 1991): 211-39.

Waltz, Kenneth N. "The Emerging Structure of International Politics." *International Security* 18, no. 2 (fall 1993): 45-80.

———. "The Myth of National Interdependence," in *The International Corporation*, edited by Charles P. Kindleberger, 205-23. Cambridge: MIT Press, 1970.

———. "The Stability of a Bipolar World." *Daedalus* 93 (1964):881-909.

———. *Theory of International Politics*. Reading, Mass.:Addison-Wesley, 1979.

Wendt, Alexander. "Anarchy is What States Make of It." *International Organization* 46, no. 2 (spring 1992): 391-425.

Whalley, John. "Why Do Countries Seek Regional Trade Agreements?" In *The Regionalization of the World Economy*, edited by Jeffrey Frankel, 63-83. Chicago: University of Chicago Press, 1998.

Williamson, Oliver. *The Economic Institutions of Capitalism*. New York: Free Press, 1985.

Wilson, Charles. *Mercantilism*. London: Wyman, 1958.

Wohlforth, William C. "The Perception of Power: Russia in the Pre-1914 Balance." *World Politics* 39, no. 3 (April 1987).

Wolfers, Arnold. *Discord and Collaboration: Essays on International Politics*, 353-81. Baltimore: Johns Hopkins University Press, 1962.

————. "National Security as an Ambiguous Symbol." *Political Science Quarterly* 67, no. 4 (December 1952): 481-502.

Wohlstetter, Albert. "The Delicate Balance of Terror." *Foreign Affairs* 37 (1959): 211-34.

World Trade Organization. *Regionalism and the World Trading System.* Geneva: World Trade Organization, 1995.

Yarbrough, Beth V., and Robert M. Yarbrough. *Cooperation and Governance in International Trade: The Strategic Organizational Approach.* Princeton: Princeton University Press, 1992.

————. "Dispute Settlement in International Trade: Regionalism and Procedural Coordination." In *The Political Economy of Regionalism*, edited by Edward D. Mansfield and Helen V. Milner, 134-63. New York: Columbia University Press, 1997.

INDEX

CPSIA information can be obtained at www.ICGtesting.com
Printed in the USA
LVOW10s0502090514

385037LV00002B/3/P